Modern European cinema and love

Manchester University Press

Modern European cinema and love

Richard Rushton

MANCHESTER UNIVERSITY PRESS

Copyright © Richard Rushton 2023

The right of Richard Rushton to be identified as the author of this work has been asserted in accordance with the Copyright, Designs and Patents Act 1988.

Published by Manchester University Press
Oxford Road, Manchester M13 9PL

www.manchesteruniversitypress.co.uk

British Library Cataloguing-in-Publication Data
A catalogue record for this book is available from the British Library

ISBN   978 1 5261 4943 5   hardback
ISBN   978 1 5261 9122 9   paperback

First published 2023
Paperback published 2025

The publisher has no responsibility for the persistence or accuracy of URLs for any external or third-party internet websites referred to in this book, and does not guarantee that any content on such websites is, or will remain, accurate or appropriate.

EU authorised representative for GPSR:
Easy Access System Europe – Mustamäe tee 50,
10621 Tallinn, Estonia
gpsr.requests@easproject.com

Typeset
by New Best-set Typesetters Ltd

What choice can we claim over the writing, or the voice – sometimes it is manifested in a phrase – that carries conviction for us? It is not much help to say: Conviction should not be taken seriously that is not justified by argument. That sounds more like a threat (in my hearing it has typically been more that) than like part of an argument. And then there lingers the feeling that those who recommend the look of argumentation often regard themselves as already knowing the conclusion for which they are inclined to argue. Where is the intellectual adventure, or advance, in that? (Stanley Cavell, *Little Did I Know: Excerpts from Memory*)

Whomsoever I trust, his certainty of himself is for me the certainty of myself; I recognize in him my own being-for-self, know that he acknowledges it and that it is for him purpose and essence. (G. W. F. Hegel, *The Phenomenology of Spirit*)

Contents

List of figures   *page* viii
Acknowledgments   ix

Introduction: acknowledgment and connectedness   1
1 Remarriage in Hollywood and Europe   15
2 The falsity of social worlds: *The Rules of the Game*   32
3 Ingmar Bergman's *Smiles of a Summer Night*: acknowledgment and deception   49
4 Ingmar Bergman: comedies and tragedies   67
5 Alain Resnais and the communication of love   91
6 Michelangelo Antonioni: learning how to love   116
7 Agnès Varda: the construction and destruction of the couple   136
8 François Truffaut and the impossible couple   158
9 Federico Fellini: love and forgiveness   176
10 Jean-Luc Godard: in praise of two   199
11 Éric Rohmer: the ordinary miracle of love   222

References   247
Index   254

Figures

1.1 Jerry and Lucy Warriner (Cary Grant and Irene Dunne) in *The Awful Truth* (Leo McCarey, 1937)   *page* 15
2.1 André Jurieu and Christine de la Chesnaye (Roland Toutain and Nora Grégor) alone together in *The Rules of the Game* (Jean Renoir, 1939)   32
3.1 'How can a woman ever love a man?' Desirée Armfeldt and Fredrik Egerman (Eva Dahlbeck and Gunnar Björnstand) in *Smiles of a Summer Night* (Ingmar Bergman, 1955)   49
4.1 The end of conversation: Anna Fromm and Andreas Winkelman (Liv Ullmann and Max von Sydow) in *The Passion of Anna* (Ingmar Bergman, 1969)   67
5.1 She and he (Delphine Seyrig and Giorgio Albertazzi) in *Last Year in Marienbad* (Alain Resnais, 1961)   91
5.2 The man visits the woman in *Last Year in Marienbad*   103
5.3 The woman greets the man in *Last Year in Marienbad*   104
6.1 Giovanni and Lidia Pontani (Marcello Mastroianni and Jeanne Moreau) in *La notte* (Michelangelo Antonioni, 1961)   116
7.1 Émilie and Francois (Marie-France Boyer and Jean-Claude Drouot) in *Le Bonheur* (Agnès Varda, 1964)   136
8.1 Antoine Doinel and Christine Darbon (Jean-Pierre Léaud and Claude Jade) in *Stolen Kisses* (François Truffaut, 1968)   158
9.1 Guido and Luisa Anselmi (Marcello Mastroianni and Anouk Aimée) in *8½* (Federico Fellini, 1963)   176
10.1 Robert and Charlotte (Bernard Noël and Macha Méril) in *A Married Woman* (Jean-Luc Godard, 1964)   199
11.1 Pauline and Sylvain (Amanda Langlet and Simon de la Brosse) in *Pauline at the Beach* (Éric Rohmer, 1983)   222

Acknowledgments

As I have been writing this book, many of its subjects have passed away, most notably Alain Resnais (in 2014), Agnès Varda (in 2017) and, more or less as the book was in its final phases, Jean-Luc Godard (in 2022). Éric Rohmer also died in 2010, a little before I set out on this project. I'm not entirely sure what I am acknowledging here, but I might be hinting that the filmmakers being dealt with in this book belong to an age that is now past. But that means we can set ourselves at a clear distance from them, and judge them with more authority. It also means, I think I want to say, that I am grateful that such people made such great films (and so too for the other auteurs examined in this book). The world is is a better place because of them.

Most of all I need to thank the many students from Lancaster University who have taken my course on European New Wave Cinema, which has run most years since 2014. I dare admit that many of my students have had far grander and deeper insights into the films examined here than I have managed. Special thanks to Annie Nissen for her teaching on the course, and for the many illuminating conversations I shared with her about the films. I have benefited, as ever, from many conversations around these films with Gary Bettinson (and he has – again, as ever – been generous with his loans of DVDs and Blu-ray discs over the years of writing this book). I am grateful for the advice and support of Lucy Bolton, especially during some of the darker days of this project when I began to believe I would never see the end of it.

Some of the material from the book has been presented publicly: at the University of Chicago in 2016 (thanks to Daniel Morgan, David Rodowick and Robert Pippin); at the University of Stirling in 2017 (many thanks to Sarah Neely); at the SAAANZ (Screen Studies Association of Australia and Aotearoa New Zealand) at Monash University in 2018; and at the Film-Philosophy Conference at the University of Brighton in 2019.

Many thanks to the tireless efforts of Espen Bale at the British Film Institute for endeavouring to secure production stills to illustrate the book, even if most of those efforts, in the final reckoning, did not work out. Warm thanks to Maryam Ghorbankarimi for helping out (with most things!), and to Kelli Fuery for her enthusiastic positivity and kind words. Final thanks to staff at Manchester University Press, especially to Matthew Frost and Alun Richards for their efforts and patience.

The book is dedicated (as is always the case) to Donna.

Introduction: acknowledgment and connectedness

The guiding argument of *Modern European Cinema and Love* is that some of the finest films made in Europe during the 1950s and 1960s (and beyond) took as their most important theme modern conceptions of romantic love. These films ask: under the conditions of modern life, what is it like for one person to love another? The filmmakers examined here – Ingmar Bergman, Michelangelo Antonioni, Alain Resnais, François Truffaut, Jean-Luc Godard, Agnès Varda, Federico Fellini and Éric Rohmer, as well as an early chapter on Jean Renoir – all make matters of love and romance central to (most of) their films. The stakes of this current book are to demonstrate that these films and filmmakers cannot be properly understood without paying attention to the ways in which they approach questions of romantic love. What are *Hiroshima, mon amour* (1959) and *Last Year in Marienbad* (1960) about if they are not about love?[1] And some of Bergman's finest films, such as *Summer Interlude* (1951), *A Lesson in Love* (1954), or *Smiles of a Summer Night* (1955): these are concerned with questions of romantic love. Or some of Godard's key films of the 1960s – *A Woman Is a Woman* (1961), *Vivre sa vie* (1962), *Contempt* (1963) or *A Married Woman* (1964) – these are concerned with matters of love too. Antonioni's key films of the era: *Story of a Love Affair* (1950), *Le amiche* (1955), *La notte* (1961), *L'eclisse* (1962), *Red Desert* (1964); these again make romantic love central. And there are many other examples considered in this book. That is what this book aims to do: to explore the kinds of discourses, arguments and problems these films raise around issues of romantic love.

These films do not posit just any kind of love. The majority of the films I examine here approach the question of love from within the institution of marriage. This means that these films end up being about the nature of modern love, but they also make the question of marriage central, the question of whether modern marriage can bear the pressures of whatever the nature of modern love might be. The question these films ask might therefore be: can love exist under the conditions of modern marriage? Or, can love and marriage exist together?

One book I take as something of reference point for these arguments is Geneviève Sellier's exceptional work on the French New Wave, *Masculine Singular* (2008). Sellier sets out to explore the relations between the genders as they are depicted in French New Wave films during the period from 1957 to 1963. She investigates the multifaceted nature of relations between men and women in the films of this period, arguing that on the one hand it was a period of great moral and sexual emancipation, especially for women, while on the other hand a new range of constraints and restrictions also came into being. In her analysis, males come across as dominant, creative and the carriers of artistic spirit and ambition, while women are constantly afforded a second place. Women are associated with a negatively connoted consumer culture in ways that either support, inspire or thwart the central, masculine ambitions of the films and filmmakers. Sellier's book is meticulously researched and for the most part convincing. It sets the ground for a concerted discussion of issues surrounding the relations between cinematic men and women during this period, even if her research is restricted to the specificity of the French scene.

Sellier sets out to discover a relation between the genders that sees them as singular, as the title of her book suggests. I am going to set out rather differently to try to discover what the genders might discover *in common*. What does love allow the couples – or, very occasionally, more than couples – in these films to discover *together*? It will come to pass that, very often, these couples discover they cannot be together, so that modern love and marriage deliver little other than despair or tragedy. All the same, some of these films will show the significant ways in which a romance will allow one, two or more people to find ways of being together.

Sellier herself hints at the possibilities that getting away from a too-narrow view of singularity could promise. Writing of Agnès Varda's *Cléo from 5 to 7* (1962), she argues that 'Instead of the claim, inherited from romanticism, of a tragic solitude that alone permits the construction of a self, Varda maintains that each person is constructed through the encounter with another' (Sellier 2008, 219). Sellier's claim here, that 'each person is constructed through the encounter with another', will be visited many times throughout this book. In many ways it can be taken as this book's guiding thread: there can be no self unless there is also an other; that no self is whole or self-contained, but that any self will always be constructed and conjoined with other selves. What is at stake in such a claim is a move away from an understanding of subjectivity informed by a romantic or existentialist search for a true or authentic self to instead conceive of subjectivity in terms of one's relations with others. If *Modern European Cinema and Love* advances a theory of subjectivity, then it is a notion of subjectivity based on inter-subjectivity, on relationships, on coupling. And these are, I will claim, points central to the European films examined here. Again and again the themes to be explored in Bergman, Antonioni, Fellini, Truffaut and others are ones that involve an intense conflict between a character's inner struggle and the problems and compromises that occur when that inner struggle comes into contact with other people. All of the films on offer here explore such problems.

Against identity

This project has taken a long time. Original notes for it date back to 2011. It took me a long time to work out precisely why I was writing this book. And what is the main reason for writing this book? The main reason has to do with what I have already mentioned above. That is, I want to propose a theory of subjectivity that positions human subjects as (at least) two rather than one. In other words, 'each person is constructed through the encounter with another', as Sellier puts it. My overall point is to claim that we are not human subjects unless we are in contact with and are close to other human beings. Perhaps what I want to say is that we are not human subjects if we are not in love with other humans and also reciprocally loved by other humans. But I fear such a statement is too extreme: to state that without love we are not human would be rather overstepping the mark. I instead want to claim, more modestly, that all human subjects are divided or split to the extent that all subjects are constructed by encounters with others, and I have already called upon Sellier's claim in this respect. In short, human subjects cannot exist as humans without being exposed to and composed out of their encounters with other humans. Love begins here.

Statements like these are important for the philosophical tradition. Of particular note in that respect are G. W. F. Hegel's so-called 'ethics of recognition', wherein one human being gains their sense of self only by way of that self's mediation in relation to other selves – what Hegel termed *Aufhebung* (usually translated into English as 'sublation'). Most specifically, Hegel highlighted the importance of a two-way notion of subjectivity in his famous dialectic of the master and slave (Hegel 1977, 111–19). I take this as a conception which sees the human subject as fundamentally two rather than one. But I would also like to stress along these lines the importance of the theory of psychoanalysis and the contention that there is a fundamental otherness at the heart of human subjectivity, an otherness designated by psychoanalysis as 'The Unconscious'. Freud's theories will emerge at various points throughout this book even as I admit that, when I first embarked on this project, Freud and psychoanalysis had not initially been central to its concerns.

Nor had I predicted the importance of two theorists of love whose work has managed to grab my attention in working on this book. The first of these is Alain Badiou, whose book *In Praise of Love* can be counted as a minor masterpiece. At one point in that book Badiou makes the following claims: 'What is universal is that all love suggests a new experience of truth about what it is to be two and not one. That we can encounter and experience the world other than through a solitary consciousness: any love whatsoever gives us evidence of this' (Badiou 2012, 39). Badiou's contention that love indicates an extra dimension of human subjectivity, a subjectivity conceived as *two* rather than *one*, will turn out to be of great importance for the films and filmmakers examined in this book. I believe that Badiou's claims here may have been inspired by the work of fellow French philosopher Luce Irigaray. Across a range of works Irigaray has called for a revolution in relations between men and women, a revolution which she argues must occur 'first and foremost in the couple' (Irigaray 1996, 26). I return to Irigaray's conceptions at some points in this book. I will need to add here, and it will become obvious soon enough, that American philosopher Stanley Cavell can also be added to the list of significant philosophical influences on this book. Cavell proposes a philosophy of *acknowledgment* in ways that resemble Hegel's ethics of recognition, but which also resembles the kinds of claims Badiou and Irigaray make on the importance of two rather than one in accounting for human subjectivity. Insofar as Cavell has written extensively on film as well, it will come as no surprise in the following pages that he becomes a key figure in the arguments of this book.

Ultimately in trying to figure out some of these issues, I have had to admit that what these formulations are arguing against – or at least what I take these formulations to be arguing against – are conceptions of human subjectivity that prioritise identity. To conceive of human subjectivity as two rather than one is to smash conceptions of subjectivity that are based on identity. For many readers such a claim might feel somewhat old fashioned, at least as old as Michel Foucault's arguments in *Les mots et les choses* or Althusser's arguments against the Ideological State Apparatus (Foucault 1970; Althusser 1971). That is to say, wasn't the critique of the subject over and done with a long time ago? Surely no scholar working in the humanities today believes in anything like a 'unified subject', a subject whose aim is to discover its identity in ways that will free it from all difference and otherness, and thus make it pure, whole and universal. No one, it seems to me, would today advocate such a view of human subjectivity, one that would champion the self-sameness of a transparent and complete 'identity'. So what am I arguing against in declaring my advocacy of a conception of human subjectivity as two rather than one? Well, to some extent it is clear that today we live in an era defined by 'identity politics'. I do not quite know what to make of this except to say that to fully confront it would require me to write a different book altogether. But I do, at the very least, want to suggest that what I will affirm as 'love' throughout this book, and what I will affirm as a conception of human subjectivity as two rather than one, is at odds with anything that might be called 'identity politics'.[2] If Sellier positioned her book *Masculine Singular* as a response to arguments on subjective isolation in the 1950s and 1960s, then it is also not entirely clear that we have gone beyond those discourses of subjective self-centredness, narcissism and genius which defined that era. Perhaps today, in an era of identity politics, the quest for an isolated and impregnable subjective identity is stronger than ever. All of the discourses that once went by the name of the 'critique of the subject' or the 'death of the subject' may well have amounted to naught. If nothing else, the arguments in this book set out to offer a critique of the isolated subject and to argue for a conception of the subject that is, at least, *two* rather than *one*.

A new figure of woman

In *Masculine Singular* Sellier also observes the central role that women and the image of woman played in the French New Wave. 'After 1956 and the success of *Et Dieu créa la femme*' – Roger Vadim's film that made Brigitte Bardot an international star – writes Sellier, 'the New Wave became associated with the emergence of a new figure of the woman' (Sellier 2008, 145). Sellier claims that the new figure of woman realised in New Wave films was not entirely positive. Nevertheless, she also argues that the new woman was a lot better than the older view of woman (Sellier 2008, 178). But here I take her point as something of a touchstone, for Stanley Cavell, writing on a cycle of Hollywood romantic comedies of the 1930s and 1940s, made a remarkably similar claim. He argued that these films were to some extent about 'the creation of a new woman, or the new creation of a woman' (Cavell 1981, 16). Could it be that the European films of the 1950s and 1960s which I aim to examine here were in some sense engaged in a conversation with some of the romantic themes that emerged in Hollywood in the 1930s and 1940s, themes associated with what Cavell refers to as 'comedies of remarriage'? My simple answer to this question is 'yes'. Another guiding thread of the arguments throughout this book is that many of the major European films and filmmakers examined here were engaged in a conversation with a series of themes that had been established by Hollywood cinema. One of the modes of cinematic storytelling that gave rise to the classical narrative cinema in Hollywood sees itself repeated in these European films, as though one of the issues at stake for the emergence of a new cinema in

Europe was to in some way respond to the set of problems initiated in America both by its invention of popular narrative cinema and also by its portrayal of a new set of conditions of love and marriage. In short: the classical Hollywood romantic comedies form themselves around the central question, what is love? My argument here is that, to a great extent, many of the European films here ask precisely the same question. These are themes that *Modern European Cinema and Love* aims to investigate.

Readers may initially be alarmed by my attempts to link the domains of modern European cinema and classical Hollywood. For a start, surely the innovative European cinema represented by the *auteurs* examined here is completely different from classical Hollywood. Indeed, the whole point of the innovations of these European filmmakers – and many others that might be considered part of a European New Wave – was to offer something different from Hollywood in ways that were openly and directly opposed to Hollywood. Such an opposition forms the basis of Geoffrey Nowell-Smith's analyses, for example (Nowell-Smith 2008, 3), while Richard Neupert, in his excellent history of the French New Wave, begins by declaring that many of these filmmakers operated 'in direct defiance of commercial and narrative norms' (Neupert 2007, xvii). To mount an argument which declares that these European filmmakers are exploring domains somewhat similar to those of classical Hollywood might therefore present formidable conceptual difficulties.[3] And yet, the argument of this book does pursue this guiding thread, a thread which contends that the themes of these European films may be in many ways similar to those that had emerged in Hollywood.

A further point of criticism might be: classical Hollywood cinema advocates love and marriage in ways that are conservative, even imprisoning, whereas these innovative European filmmakers utterly oppose that advocacy with a biting critique of the conservative norms of modern love and marriage. And this point might well be granted – I can only urge the reader to read the remainder of this book in order to find out. I can initially suggest that the distinctions are not as simple as an either/or division. The fact that these European films are engaged with questions pertaining to love and marriage: is this not a point worthy of investigation? (Certainly it is for me.) Readers may well have to give up their convenient oppositional categories so as to accept that Hollywood's views of love and marriage are somewhat more complex and intricate than might ordinarily be accepted. In this respect, the current book is at odds with the propositions advanced in Reidar Due's *Love in Motion* (2013) and, to some extent, David Shumway's *Modern Love* (2003), as well as Mark Garrett Cooper's *Love Rules* (2003). Readers may also have to accept that a caricature of the existential bleakness, of the horrors and eviscerations of romantic love associated with European filmmakers like Bergman or Antonioni will be complicated somewhat: both

Antonioni and Bergman offer far more positive views of romantic love than might be suspected from a distance, as do many of the others filmmakers examined here (Godard, Truffaut, Rohmer, Fellini ...).

Another key reference point on these issues is provided by Kristin Ross's 1995 book, *Fast Cars, Clean Bodies*. Ross offers a strong critique of the influences of American culture on France during the 1950s and 1960s. The results of this American cultural invasion were manifold, but the production of the ideal couple as central to the transformation of everyday life in France during this period – and to some extent for other nations in Europe, especially Italy – is utterly integral to the narrative she tells. The production of the French couple and the sanctification of marriage, imported from the United States, were central components in the transformation of France into a consumer commodity society following the Second World War. Ross's arguments are compelling. But I do try to balance the effects of the importation of American love and coupling as ones that are potentially liberating, as well as imprisoning, for French culture and European ways of life more generally. I certainly assume that a social arrangement that aspires to equal relations between men and women is something worth striving for, but I am very far from being convinced that an institution such as modern marriage would be the ideal vehicle for that arrangement. I can accept, to the contrary, that the institution of marriage might well be one that excludes conditions of equality.[4]

I am not arguing that the films discussed in this book are in one way or another remakes of the earlier genres of romantic comedies from Hollywood. There are some specific cases where remakes are notable: Godard's *A Woman Is a Woman* is something of a remake of Ernst Lubitsch's *Design for Living* (1931). But this case is a very specific one that is not at all germane to these European filmmakers in general: the Europeans were to a large extent inspired by literature as much as any particular filmic tradition or genre. Rather, my contention is that the aspects of Hollywood conceptions of love and marriage as well as a new conception of the relations between the genders and couples were 'in the air'. My claim is therefore that these European filmmakers were responding to a social phenomenon that could not be ignored. In short, the simple facts of modern romance and marriage were ones that these films and filmmakers could not shy away from.

Broad concerns

Many of the films and filmmakers approached here, as I have already hinted, are associated with the themes of modern and modernist alienation. Bergman and Antonioni are paramount in this respect, for their films feature themes commonly associated with the complete and unbridgeable isolation of human beings. The problematics of Claudia (Monica Vitti) in Antonioni's *L'avventura* (1960), or Lidia (Jeanne Moreau) in *La notte* (1961), or Aldo (Steve Cochran) in *Il grido* (1957) as much as that of Elisabet (Liv Ullmann) in Bergman's *Persona* (1966), Monika (Harriet Andersson) in *Summer with Monika* (1952), or Andreas (Max Von Sydow) in *The Passion of Anna* (1969), are ones that focus on the dilemma of communication with other human beings, which is to say they are concerned with the ways in which the attempts to forge genuine bonds with other human beings can be extremely difficult to accomplish. What these films seem to say is that isolation reigns supreme and is a fundamental human state, perhaps an ontological condition (see, for example, the comments in Brunette 1998, 1; Kovács 2007, 89–98).

What *Modern European Cinema and Love* aims to make clear is that the films at issue here often concern themselves with issues of subjective isolation. That is to say, they foreground the dilemma of a human subject who is consigned to the situation of *being one rather than two*. More importantly, however, these films are concerned with the question of *how one finds one's way out of subjective isolation*. They investigate the conditions whereby *one can become two* (or where it can fail to become two, or take the conscious decision to avoid becoming two). If the characters and themes of these films foreground states of subjective isolation and human 'oneness', then that is only because they also open up the possibility whereby one might become two, that is, states of human existence in which isolation might be overcome.[5]

Sellier's claim that 'each person is constructed through the encounter with another' might be taken in various philosophical directions. What I aim to do for the remainder of this Introduction is to map out some of the directions in which Sellier's statement can be taken, and also to see how some of those directions are related to the broad concerns of the European films I will then go on to examine in the chapters that follow. As I have already stated, those directions are ones that pertain to the topics of love and romance. And as I have also suggested, it will emerge that a great many of my reflections on issues of love and romance are guided by the philosophical and film writings of Stanley Cavell. A major reason for this is that I believe Cavell's theories are worth defending. It is not so much that I believe Cavell is right, but that he opens up various possibilities for discussing love and romance in these films. That 'love stories' have been central for cinema is surely beyond contestation (as much as it is surely beyond contestation that issues of love have been central for the other arts, for literature, painting, music …). Taking such concerns seriously in relation to a body of European films, I contend, is something worth pursuing.[6] A second reason for taking up Cavell's discussions of these issues is that they provide a way of bringing modern European cinema into a closer relation with the tenets of classical Hollywood filmmaking (see Elsaesser 2005). I have rather wearied over many years of studying film to find that any non-Hollywood cinema tends to be defined by way of its apparently stark opposition to the conventions of Hollywood. This has then typically provided ways of denigrating Hollywood in the name of whatever other tradition is being defended, so that the greatness of European modernism, for example, has been best understood by declaring that it does everything that Hollywood was unable to do. As such, the greatness of many European films has hinged precisely on their ability to eclipse or destroy the methods of Hollywood. I am, contrary to such arguments, convinced that Hollywood achieved many great things, so the version I give here of modern European cinema is one that is not opposed to Hollywood, but is instead one which embraced what Hollywood had invented so as to expand on that invention. To some extent, this will strike readers as being rather incongruous and uncomfortable, perhaps no more so than in Chapter 5, where I discuss Alain Resnais's *Last Year in Marienbad* (1961) as a sort of distant remake of Preston Sturges's *The Lady Eve* (1941). In the next chapter I also place Godard's *Contempt* (1963) side by side with Leo McCarey's *The Awful Truth* (1937), and other such combinations tend to find their way into the pages of this book.

Cavell and acknowledgment

What are Cavell's arguments and why are they important for this book? I take Cavell's arguments as one way of addressing Sellier's contention that 'each person is constructed through the encounter with another'. For Cavell, encounters with others are pretty much a way of defining what the world is, for if we do not have encounters with others, then, he argues, it is impossible for us to construct such a thing as 'the world'. The world as we know it is a consequence of our encounters with others – such are Cavell's arguments.

Essentially, for Cavell, this amounts to claiming that the world we inhabit is a shared world. It is not simply a world that exists *for me*, and thus there is not a set of rules for that world which I could learn so as to then understand and master it. This is a way of saying that the world does not exist outside of the kinds of relations I have with it.[7] And this is also a way, therefore, of saying that there is no world *in itself* – that is, there is no world that conforms to objective, universal laws which – again – if I had knowledge of such laws, would allow me to come to know the world as it truly is, 'in itself'. Rather, Cavell argues that the world we can have knowledge of is not like that – or that it is certainly not like that for human beings. What it is possible for human beings to know is, and can only be, a product of each human being's ability to share their understanding of the world with other human beings. By sharing our understanding of the world we can begin to know the world. And for Cavell this is the only way we can come to know the world.

In essence this is a somewhat simple point. It amounts to proposing, for example, that there is no such thing as 'red' in nature. There is only something human beings call 'red'. If I see this pencil in front of me and call it a 'red' pencil, then calling it red only makes sense if another person both understands and recognises it as red. When I see this red pencil and refer to it as red, and then when you agree with me that it is red, a result of all this is that we have agreed upon and shared a world: we have agreed that such a thing as a 'red pencil' is a part of the world we share. What matters here for human beings is that they have the ability to construct how and what the world is, and they do this by agreeing and sharing their conceptions of that world. Cavell's point is therefore one of trying to define how we, as human beings, come to have knowledge of the world.[8]

Cavell's notion of sharing the world is something he calls *acknowledgment*. With this term he is declaring that the knowledge we have of the world is not so much *known* as it is *acknowledged*. I take this, therefore, as one way of conceiving that 'each person is constructed through the encounter with another', for Cavell's conception of acknowledgment amounts to declaring that the only knowledge I can have of the world is by way of other people. Acknowledgment can then stretch a good deal further than this. At its limit, acknowledgment is precisely what is at stake in human conceptions of love. To love another person is to share a world with that other person. And to be in love with another person is an expression of sharing the world with that other person. Cavell, although he never precisely defines what love is, comes close by calling love a 'best case of acknowledgment' (see Cavell 1979b, 477).

Acknowledgment, therefore, does not only matter for objects of knowledge, such as my contention that such and such a pencil is 'red'. It also matters for the people I know, for 'subjects' of knowledge. Acknowledgment is, to this extent, a response to another person. If someone comes to me and says 'Help me!' then I can acknowledge this other person, I can help him or her, and by doing so I can also say that I now know that this person needs help. But I can also refuse to help this person, which is to say I can refuse to acknowledge them. To this degree, acknowledgment is always a response of some sort: it does not happen automatically. As Cavell admits, 'the concept of acknowledgment is evidenced equally by its failure as by its success' (Cavell 2002, 243). The linkages made by Cavell between the conception of acknowledgment, the types of love that he will designate as 'best cases of acknowledgment', and then the marriages and remarriages that he discovers in a cycle of Hollywood movies in the 1930s and 1940s, are all ones that are explored in some detail in the chapters of this book that follow.

A counter-argument: connectedness

A point of contention that is central to the concerns of this book hinges on questions of romantic love and 'couples'. If, as Cavell argues, Hollywood films developed visions of romantic love and marriage when the talkies emerged in the 1930s (and no doubt well before that too), then can we be at all certain that this was a good thing? Mightn't we rather believe that Hollywood's versions of love have mostly been pernicious, escapist, damnably unrealistic, ideologically manipulative, politically conservative – in short, that Hollywood's romances have been bad in every imaginable way? (I can point to works by Shumway (2003), Due (2013), Cooper (2003) and Lapsley and Westlake (1993) as places to begin in such a direction.) Perhaps such arguments are warranted. To some degree they are confronted at various points throughout this book. I realise that many readers will hold such views and that no degree of argument on my part will change that.

The most extreme version of the critique of romantic love I have come across, both in Hollywood films and beyond, is that put forward by Leo Bersani, often while writing in conjunction with Ulysse Dutoit. Bersani's position may well be extreme, but it is also very attractive and persuasive, emboldened as it is by years of studious research and reflection. Bersani conceives of romantic love as reductive. When one person loves another person, then this is a result of their desire to reduce the other person to being something that can be controlled and possessed. To love another person is to imprison them within my own sphere, to reduce them to the context of my own self-hood. For Bersani, a positive future for humankind is one lived without love: a world in which love is done away with.[9]

Why would Bersani think such a thing? For a start, Bersani argues that notions of romantic love emerged out of systems of control so that the logic of romantic love is an outcome of one human being's power over another human being. He thus argues that there is another way for human beings to relate to each other, a mode of relation that is not based on love. This mode of relation is, for Bersani, not a mode that has its basis in language – and we have seen that Cavell bases his conception of acknowledgment on shared language (a 'red pencil', for example). Instead, Bersani conceives of a mode of connection based more directly on relations between bodies. Overall, he claims that human beings have been mistaken to put their trust in language and in regimes of love. Rather, what human beings ought to put their faith in is an intrinsic *connectedness* that all human beings have with the world and with other human beings.

Human beings do not need to discover ways of connecting with other human beings. They are always already connected with other humans: such is Bersani's claim. This claim might offer a quite remarkable way of understanding Sellier's contention that 'each person is constructed through the encounter with another', for Bersani proposes that humans are always intrinsically connected to one another. (He will call this a 'homo-ness of being'; Bersani and Dutoit 2004, 120.) Bersani's arguments thus take us well beyond Romantic and existentialist notions of an 'isolated self' who stands alone so as to confront the world. To get beyond notions of individual selves, Bersani argues, what we most need to do is to shake off the encrustations of civilisation, its rules and discourses and languages, so as to return to a state more in tune with nature and the cosmos. If we do this we will find that we are connected intrinsically to the world and to other people.

Bersani's conception is therefore two-fold: first, conceptions of human isolation have been misguided, for humans are always-already connected both to other humans as well as to the world and its objects. Second, a sense of human connectedness based on romantic love is also misguided, for it is based on a reduction of human relations to relations of power. At their limit, Bersani will argue that romantic love and coupling merely reproduce the structures of isolating subjectivity – that is, they reduce all otherness to conceptions of sameness – and thus contribute to modern, romantic modes of human isolation. On this account, love is a form of isolation (see Bersani and Dutoit 2004, 19–73 and Bersani and Phillips 2008, 57–87).

Some notes for coming chapters

Here, then, we have the two extremes of an argument. For Cavell, structures or states of love are a good thing and something to aspire to, while for Bersani notions of love are negative and best gotten away from. Key arguments from Cavell and Bersani having been introduced, what is the point of following these arguments through the remainder of this book? One reason for structuring the arguments in this book on the basis of claims made by Cavell and Bersani is that each has written on some of the films and auteurs central to this study. Cavell has written on Godard (Cavell 2005b; 1979a, 96–101), Bergman (Cavell 2005c) and Rohmer (Cavell 2004, 421–43; 2005d). He has also written on Renoir's *The Rules of the Game*, which is the topic of Chapter 2 of this book (see Cavell 1979a, 219–30).

Bersani (often writing with Dutoit) has written on Resnais (Bersani and Dutoit, 1994), extensively on Godard (Bersani and Dutoit 2004, 2010; Bersani 2015) and Rohmer (Bersani and Dutoit, 2009). For Bersani it is evident what the films of these filmmakers are not about: they are *not* about romantic love. And, even if on the surface they might purport to be dealing with romantic love or couples, then beneath that surface – especially in Godard's *Contempt*, *Passion* (1981) and various of Rohmer's films – these films are offering accounts of the restrictions and negativities of romantic love. These are films that offer support for Bersani's overall argument against romantic love and in favour of the notion of connectedness. They are ways of answering the question Bersani raises at one point: 'What would a relational mode beyond sex, beyond love, beyond relationship itself be like?' (Bersani 2018, 25).

Cavell's writings on Renoir, Bergman and Rohmer bring these auteurs into contact with the Hollywood cycle he calls 'comedies of remarriage'. In basic terms Cavell proposes that these auteurs, at least in the films he discusses, offer perspectives on love and marriage that put them in conversation with Hollywood's remarriage comedies. In short, these filmmakers are investigating notions of romantic love and marriage, notions that will, as this current book unfolds, place the logics of these films close to Cavell's conception of acknowledgment.

Where, therefore, might these filmmakers – Resnais, Godard, Rohmer, Bergman and others – be placed in relation to romantic love? On the side of connectedness or on the side of acknowledgment? I will admit right here that my sympathies lean towards Cavell's arguments, but I will also make it clear that I value Bersani's (and Dutoit's) writings immensely: the concepts and arguments found there have greatly assisted my own thought processes. Cavell's arguments occupy much of the book, however, and Bersani's claims make their way into my arguments only in rather specific instances. We shall see how valuable Bersani's arguments are in relation to the films of Varda, Truffaut, Godard and Rohmer, especially.

In the next chapter I examine Cavell's and Bersani's arguments in much more detail. I do so in relation to specific films: *The Awful Truth* (1937) one of the Hollywood films Cavell refers to as 'comedies of remarriage'; and *Contempt* (1963), one of Godard's films that Bersani and Dutoit examine in great detail.

Notes

1 A note on titles: I have tried to be as uncomplicated as I can be for an English-reading audience. Therefore, I have tried to use titles as they are commonly known

in the English-speaking world. So, *Hiroshima, mon amour* retains its French title because, for one reason or another, it is generally known by this title in English. This also goes for Antonioni's *L'avventura* and *La notte*, for example. By contrast, Resnais's *L'annee derniere à Marienbad* is most commonly known in Britain as *Last Year in Marienbad* (though, to complicate issues still further, in the US it goes by the name of *Last Year at Marienbad*). Needless to say, I have done my best to remain uncomplicated so far as film titles go throughout this book.

2 To some degree, the book might be seen as an extension of arguments I make in *The Politics of Hollywood Cinema* (Rushton 2013).
3 In his excellent survey of modern European cinema, Kovács (2007) does well to include a remarkable range of stylistic and thematic influences that go well beyond an anti-Hollywood rhetoric.
4 I am also quite conscious of the criticisms of equality rhetoric advanced by Luce Irigaray, whose theories and concepts are engaged with at certain points throughout this book.
5 Kovács makes these points too; see the chapter on Genres (Kovács 2007, 82–119).
6 I will not be the first scholar to have done so. See Passerini et al. (2012).
7 I am aware that an aspiration to a non-human definition of the world and knowledge is currently fashionable. I do not have the space to address such issues here other than to point to them. They have emerged under various guises of 'Speculative Realism' and 'Object Oriented Ontology' with thinkers such as Quentin Meillassoux and Graham Harmon (see Sparrow 2014). My bets stay firmly with those thinkers, such as Cavell, who cling to the Cartesian–Kantian tradition of 'Mind and World' (on the latter see McDowell 1996, and Pippin 2019).
8 I am trying to condense an enormous range of Cavell's works here. Perhaps the most concise explication of such issues occurs in an essay Cavell wrote on Ralph Waldo Emerson where he advanced the notion that humans come to have knowledge of the world only if this knowledge is shared with other human beings. As I note later in this book, this knowledge is primarily shared by way of language, for 'the condition of the possibility of there being a world of objects for us is the condition of our speaking together', wrote Cavell. He continued by declaring, contra Immanuel Kant, that this 'is not a matter of our sharing twelve categories of the understanding but of our sharing a language' (Cavell 2010, 207).
9 Bersani asks, for example, 'What would a relational mode beyond sex, beyond love, beyond relationship itself be like?' (Bersani 2018, 25). While writing with Ulysse Dutoit, Bersani also explores the possibility a world '[n]o longer darkened by the demand for love' (Bersani and Dutoit 2004, 70). I examine some aspects of this in what follows.

Chapter 1

Remarriage in Hollywood and Europe

1.1 Jerry and Lucy Warriner (Cary Grant and Irene Dunne) in *The Awful Truth* (Leo McCarey, 1937)

In Federico Fellini's *8½* (1963), filmmaker Guido Anselmi (Marcello Mastroianni) reflects on various aspects of his present and past life, while also worrying for his future. The focus of many of his memories hinges on various aspects of his relationships with women: with his wife, Luisa (Anouk Aimée), with his mistress, Carla (Sandra Milo), with his vision of an ideal woman, Claudia (Claudia Cardinale), as well as his childhood fascination for La Saraghina (Eddra Gale), among others. By the end of the film – noting that the ending is somewhat ambiguous – Guido comes to the realisation has he has been uncaring and unfaithful to his wife. He vows to change his ways and to affirm his love for her. Fellini's next film, *Juliet of the Spirits* (1965), examines some similar issues. This time, it does so from the perspective of the wife, Juliet (Giulietta Masina,). Her husband, Giorgio (Mario Pisu), is having an affair, and Juliet cannot quite work out what to do about this. She is tempted to be unfaithful herself, and is befriended by her libidinal neighbour, Suzy (Sandra Milo), while also being dazzled by various spirits and memories. In the end, her husband departs so as to reflect on his future and marriage. Juliet, having been overwhelmed by doubts, fears and visions, decides to continue her life with confidence: she will face whatever it is that she must face. Will her marriage survive? Perhaps. But, if nothing else, Juliet has developed the freedom and self-confidence – the independence – to pursue life separated from her husband, if that is what she must do. Lidia Pontani (Jeanne Moreau), the central character in Michelangelo Antonioni's *La notte* (1962), like Juliet in Fellini's film, is concerned that her marriage may be at an end. She believes her husband no longer cares for her and that she no longer has any feelings for him. At various points during the film's long night Lidia reflects on her plight, tries to establish some sort of connection with her husband, Giovanni (Marcelo Mastroianni), and is even tempted by another man, Roberto (Giorgio Negro). At the film's conclusion, Lidia makes a final attempt to rekindle her and Giovanni's love, and he seems to be awakened to the importance of that love, though the ending, like that of Fellini's *8½*, is indeed inconclusive.

Here, then, we have three Italian films from the 1960s that deal with issues relating to love and marriage. And these films were released in an atmosphere in which two other prominent Italian films, both starring Mastroianni (as had Fellini's *La dolce vita* in 1960), gained substantial international audiences: *Divorce Italian Style* (Pietro Germi, 1961) and *Marriage Italian Style* (Vittorio De Sica 1965, also starring Sophia Loren). To say that issues of love, especially as they relate to issues of marriage and divorce – the latter not being legalised in Italy until 1970 – are prominent in Italian cinema during this period seems a rather obvious point to make. I might also add that a distant remake of *Divorce Italian Style* emerged in Hollywood in 1965 in the form of *How to Murder Your Wife* (directed by Richard Quine), starring Jack Lemmon and Italian actress Virna Lisi. Lemmon's character wakes up one morning after a night of heavy drinking to discover he has married an Italian woman, played by Lisi. Lisi then also starred opposite Tony Curtis the following year in another sex comedy, *Not with My Wife, You Don't!* (directed by Norman Panama).

At the same time in France, Jean-Luc Godard's films were often concerned with issues of love and marriage. In *A Married Woman*, for example, Charlotte

(Macha Méril) is married to Pierre (Philippe Leroy), but is also having an affair with Robert (Bernard Noël). Her husband has already been through one marriage, so the couple cares for a child from that first marriage. Charlotte is not merely unfaithful to Pierre in the present, but has also engaged in various extra-marital affairs in the past. Godard's very complex film returns again and again to questions of love, faith and marriage. These are questions his films will constantly visit throughout his career, in early films like *Contempt* (1963), as well as in later films like *Hail Mary* (1984) or *In Praise of Love* (2000). For Alain Resnais, *Hiroshima, mon amour* (1959) concerns, among other things, a French woman's (Emmanuel Riva) attempts to deal with feelings of love in the present in relation to a doomed love she had suffered in the past. Her love in the present is for a Japanese man (Eiji Okada), while her love in the past was with a German soldier (Bernard Fresson) during the Second World War. Much later, in 1980's *Mon Oncle d'Amérique*, Resnais contrasts a cynical upper-class marriage between Jean (Roger Pierre) and Arlette (Nicole Borgeaud) with a marriage from lower down the social scale between René (Gérard Depardieu) and Thérèse (Marie Dubois). The former marriage ends the film as one based on class alliances and duplicity, while the latter emerges from various life struggles in ways that are underpinned by genuine care. A range of Resnais's other films – *Je t'aime, je t'aime* (1967), *Mélo* (1986), *On connaît la chanson* (1997) and others – also focus on themes relating to love, marriage and fidelity.

Bergman's *Scenes from a Marriage* (1973) begins with a happily married couple, Johan and Marianne (Erland Josephson and Liv Ullmann), being interviewed for a magazine. They have been married for ten years, have two daughters and live a good and happy life. Marianne states that she was previously married, at the age of eighteen, but that this marriage did not work out. A child from this first marriage died shortly after being born. When alone with the interviewer – a friend from her youth – Marianne states that she is happy and she presents her views on love and faithfulness. In the next scene, Johan and Marianne are hosting friends for dinner, a married couple named Katarina and Peter (Bibi Andersson, Jan Malmsjö). This couple declares that their marriage is hell, Katarina admits to having affairs, but the couple also claims that, for business reasons, they must remain together. I could go on describing what happens in *Scenes from a Marriage*, but, as should be clear from its opening salvos and its title, Bergman's film and television series focuses on questions of marriage, love and faithfulness. These themes, as I will argue throughout this book, are crucial for understanding what was at stake in modern European cinema. I modestly claim, at any rate, that these themes are crucial for a small group of filmmakers in France, Italy and Sweden.

Thus, *Modern European Cinema and Love* examines discourses of love and marriage in a range of European filmmakers who were active from the 1950s onwards. I suggested in the Introduction that, theoretically, my discussions are guided on the one hand by the defence of romantic discourses advanced by Stanley Cavell, and on the other hand by the critique of romantic love provided by Leo Bersani. My aim in this chapter is to delve further into these arguments, especially insofar as they pertain to cinema. I examine Cavell's conception of 'comedies of remarriage' first of all, and engage closely with Leo McCarey's 1937 film *The Awful Truth*, a key example of a remarriage comedy for Cavell. I then also engage in some detailed assessment of the approach Bersani, writing with Dutoit, takes to Jean-Luc Godard's 1963 film, *Contempt*. By taking a close look at each of these films, we will be able to see more clearly what is both similar and different about them, and we shall also see more clearly some of the differences between Cavell's and Bersani's approaches to conceptions of romantic love.

Love and marriage

What, first of all, does Cavell mean by a 'comedy of remarriage'? In relation to cinema, conceptions of love and acknowledgment find expression in what Cavell calls the comedies of remarriage in a book called *Pursuits of Happiness* (1981). The interpretation of Cavell's argument from *Pursuits of Happiness* that I want to pursue is one that goes in the direction of declaring that a cycle of Hollywood films in the 1930s and 1940s gave expression to a new kind of romantic love that had not been encountered before in the course of human history. That unique version of romantic love involved the articulation of a loving relationship between a man and a woman based on mutual understanding and equality. This new kind of love was different from the kinds of love that had come before. Prior to this, love had been based on any number of other foundations. More than anything, it had been based on the maintenance of social hierarchies, so that a marriage alliance was one made for the purposes of power, money or both. As one commentator suggests, 'Marriage in most cultures has been understood as a social institution and property relation rather than a personal commitment and an emotional relation. The traditional meaning of love is not romance but social solidarity' (Shumway 2003, 12). By the early twentieth century, it became possible – though this possibility was by no means easy or commonplace – for people of all classes (in the US and some other Western societies) to enter into a marriage on the basis of a love that required mutual understanding and equality between the two parties. The possibility of marriage was nowhere more championed than in the United States of America (see, for example, comments by de Tocqueville 2003, 684–700). It was the Hollywood cinema in its classical phase that celebrated this notion of romantic marriage, a vision of marriage based on a love between equal partners.[1]

One (American) historian claims the following, remarking along the way that modern marriage is an invention of very recent date:

> In the eighteenth century, people began to adopt the radical new idea that love should be the most fundamental reason for marriage and that young people should be free to choose their marriage partners on the basis of love. The sentimentalization of the love-based marriage in the nineteenth century and its sexualization in the twentieth each represented a logical step in the evolution of this new approach to marriage. (Coontz 2005, 5)

This writer goes on to add that 'basing marriage on love and companionship represented a break with thousands of years of tradition' (Coontz 2005, 149). The history of this process of discovering a new kind of marriage was a complicated one. During the nineteenth century, even as notions of love and equality gained ground, they also foundered on the back of the Industrial Revolution as the rise of capitalist industry brought about new work and family relations. This meant that a work divide between men and women came into force: men went out to work, while women stayed at home to do 'housework', thus establishing a strong sense of financial dependency of wives upon their husbands' abilities to bring home wages. It is fair to say that this kind of arrangement became idealised to some degree in nineteenth-century America. It is also during this period that marriage took on a defining role in a person's life in a way that it had not done previously.

Late nineteenth- and early twentieth-century women's suffrage movements placed even more emphasis on the desire for gender equality in ways that filtered through to conceptions of marriage. Problems remained: the increasing reduction and isolation of women to the home sphere often curtailed a wife's possible alliances and friendships with other women. On balance, however, modern marriage, as it developed in the early twentieth century, was substantially better in many ways – for women, men and for societies as a whole – than any conception of marriage that had preceded it. Shumway summarises all this in the following way: as the capitalist corporation replaced the family as the repository of social wealth during the nineteenth century, so too did marriage adjust to those capitalist conditions and become freed from the constraints of 'financial alliance' (Shumway 2003, 22).

If marriage moved from being conceived as a social, political or business alliance prior to the eighteenth century, to one based primarily on love by the twentieth century, then the Hollywood comedies of remarriage foregrounded that love as based on the couple's equality and mutual acknowledgment. The Hollywood comedies central to Cavell's conceptualisation of remarriage take love, equality and mutual acknowledgment as key tenets. It might be argued that it was in Hollywood cinema that the equation between love and marriage was codified most resoundingly and emphatically, for this seems to be at the heart of Cavell's claims in *Pursuits of Happiness*. Working out what love, equality and mutual understanding can or should be are the central questions posed by these films. If these can be accepted as key tenets for Cavell's theorisation of marriage in these Hollywood films, then what remains of this book is attempts to test out these concepts in relation to a set of European films that came a generation or so after the Hollywood popularisation of remarriage. Exactly what Cavell means by 'remarriage' is explained below.

These conceptions are fraught with difficulties. For a start, the institution of marriage might be seen as unnecessary at best and crippling at worst. Many good arguments could be made which would declare that marriage is the kind of social institution that should simply be gotten rid of. And even if we get rid of marriage, another problem arises via the whole conception of mutual acknowledgment insofar as it is based on the notion of a couple. Why a *couple*? And even then, if we do accept the couple as a conception, why would this couple need to be composed of a *man and a woman*, for that is certainly the case in the comedies of remarriage. And a spirit of mutual understanding and equality might strike many as mere rhetoric for a practice that delivers little but misery and subjection, especially for the women in these couples. Numerous books on feminism, as well as countless works on feminism and film, have declared as much.

Cavell has been to some extent aware of these potential shortcomings. The critiques of those conceptions found in Glitre (2006) and Shumway (2003) are compelling in various ways. To my knowledge Cavell did not confront these criticisms. He did, however, go so far as to invent a companion genre to the remarriage comedies in a book called *Contesting Tears* (1996). There, the grounds of mutual understanding and equality are nothing but a sham, especially insofar as the men who feature in the films Cavell discusses in the book utterly fail to know or understand the women they marry, to the extent that relations between them become entirely unequal. Cavell calls this cycle 'melodramas of the unknown woman'. One way to see such issues is to come to the conclusion that remarriage comedies and the American invention of romantic love did not automatically lead to happy endings. Or, another way of putting it might be to say that if Hollywood cinema embraced this version of romantic love, then that conception might not have lasted very long (on these points see Glitre 2006, especially Parts III and IV). Indeed, if the notion of remarriage brings with it a series of affirmations, then it also contains a series of questions, inadequacies and shortcomings. I think it is fair to say that those shortcomings are still topics of debate today, in cinema and elsewhere. The wider consequences of marriage, remarriage and the stakes of mutual understanding and equality might well be conceived in terms of asking what new kinds of social forms, what new kinds of human understanding, what kinds of coupling – and beyond – are conceivable in terms of romantic love.

The thesis of the present book is to take these Cavellian themes – the notion of remarriage as well as the quest to form love relationships on the basis of mutual understanding and equality – so as to see to what degree such themes are played out in certain European films and the 1950s, 1960s and beyond. As I have already suggested, a key theme of many of the breakthrough films of the European filmmakers examined here, especially in France and Italy, was that of romantic love. Granted, the work of a few filmmakers from France and Italy, along with another from Sweden (and another from Switzerland if we are to place Godard there), might seem like a small portion of European films of the era to consider, but there is no question that these films and filmmakers are dealing with these issues and also that they are doing so in ways that are innovative, challenging and, in many ways, remarkable. These filmmakers are certainly not the only ones dealing with such issues – love stories are a staple theme of cinema (and literature, poetry, popular songs and so on) – but the quandaries and interventions posed by these filmmakers are, for me, ones worth examining, even if I can make no claim to being comprehensive or all-encompassing.

Love and remarriage, Hollywood and Europe

What, then, to ask once again, is a 'comedy of remarriage', as Cavell calls it? In the cycle as he defines it a key film that marks an overt relationship between American marriage and European love is *The Awful Truth*. It is the group of issues that comes out of that film in particular that opens up the space for the arguments which will be developed throughout this book, though the themes Cavell discovers in *The Awful Truth* are ones that relate to the cycle of remarriage comedies more generally. A first point to consider: remarriage comedies do not conclude with weddings, as one might expect of a classical comedy of the Cinderella or Jane Austen variety. A reason for this, aside from the fact that the couples are already married, is that the couples who are united in these films do not need a public or ceremonial display of their coming together, because their coming together is something that is worked out between themselves. Their union is not something that needs to be decreed by an authority external to themselves. Rather, their union is something they have agreed upon and constructed 'by themselves together', as it were. Cavell writes, 'this comedy expects the pair to find happiness alone, unsponsored, in one another, out of their capacities for improvising a world, beyond ceremony' (Cavell 1981, 239). What is at stake here is less a marriage – that is mere ceremony; rather, what is at stake is a *re*marriage: a coming into being of mutual acknowledgment and equality between the members of the romantic couple.

A second point: if there are obstacles to the expression of love between the man and the woman in these films, then they are obstacles the couple have themselves constructed. The obstacles are not, therefore, placed there by society, by class differences, legal authorities, by family conflicts, political restrictions, aliens landing from outer space, or forces of nature, or whatever. If there are problems of love here, then they are problems this couple has to work out for themselves and by themselves. Of course they must also work out these problems by themselves *together*. 'The obstacles [this genre] poses to happiness are not complications unknown to the characters that a conclusion can sort out,' Cavell argues. 'They have something to learn', he continues, 'but it cannot come as news from others' (Cavell 1981, 240).

A third point: these are *re*marriage comedies. As a consequence, divorce and the threat of divorce become essential concerns. Films like *The Awful Truth* offer cinematic versions of a test of the conditions of marriage, but they also offer tests of the conditions of divorce. Cavell will declare that the stakes of marriage in these films cannot exist without the possibility of divorce (he gets the idea from John Milton's various divorce tracts; see Cavell 1981, 150–1). Indeed, the free and open availability of divorce becomes a defining characteristic of marriage in these films.

The Awful Truth

These are three key points toward a definition of comedies of remarriage: remarriage comedies do not conclude with a wedding; the couples have to work out their problems themselves; and marriage and divorce 'define' one another. To explain the stakes of these issues, it will be necessary to detail some aspects of the plot of *The Awful Truth*.

At the beginning of *The Awful Truth*, the couple at the film's centre, Jerry and Lucy Warriner (Cary Grant, Irene Dunne), decide on a divorce. Once it is legally agreed, there is a ninety-day cooling off period before the divorce can be finalised. Over these ninety days, the pair finds a way to get back together again so that by the end of the film they are remarried, as it were. Presumably, then, they might find a way to live happily ever after.

And yet, why is it that they decide on a divorce in the first place? Right at the beginning of the film, Jerry is at a New York sports club, eager to spend some time getting a sunlamp treatment. His plan is to then return home to Lucy – they live in New York – with the sun-tanned proof that he has been in Florida for the last two weeks. In short, he is deceiving his wife.

When he returns home, Jerry discovers that his wife, Lucy, is not there. When she gets home soon after, she is accompanied by her singing teacher, a man of French origin, Armand Duvalle (Alexander D'Arcy).[2] Lucy and Armand tell Jerry a story of having had their car break down as Armand was returning Lucy home the previous night, meaning they had to spend the night 'at an inn somewhere'. Jerry pretends to believe the story, and Armand duly compliments him on having 'a Continental mind'. And so it transpires that Jerry has been deceiving his wife, but so too does it appear that his wife might be deceiving him. Shortly afterwards, when Jerry and Lucy are alone, Jerry makes it clear that he does not believe his wife's story. The latter then declares their marriage bust. 'Marriage is based on faith,' she says. 'When that's gone, everything's gone'. It is then that they decide on a divorce.

Is there a simple moral fable here? Is *The Awful Truth* merely showing us that extra-marital activities have no place in a marriage, and that if such things do occur in a marriage, then that marriage must go sour? Or is there something more sinister happening here? From Jerry's perspective, all is fine so long as *he* gets to 'play the field' and deceive his wife, but as soon as his wife does anything of the sort, it's all over. In short, it is acceptable for the male of the couple to do as he pleases, but the wife must stay at home and keep to herself. Of course, the consequences of these acts may well be the other way round: Lucy rejects Jerry on the basis that he no longer believes her, that he regards her professions of innocence as fraudulent. Glitre is rightly critical of Cavell's arguments here: Cavell is so busy defending Jerry's reputation that he appears quite unable to see things from Lucy's point of view. I think Glitre is certainly correct to suggest that the film's sympathies lie with Lucy and its fault lines are caused by Jerry. 'It is Jerry', she writes, 'who must change his attitudes' (Glitre 2006, 50). What that changed attitude pertains to is Jerry's recognition at the end of *The Awful Truth* of Lucy's independence and strength, attributes which he denied her at the film's beginning. At the film's outset it is Jerry's inability to acknowledge Lucy as his equal that is the cause of their divorce: he does not believe her; he loses faith in her. It is only after his re-education at the hands of Lucy that he then recognises her equality with and independence from him (see Glitre 2006, 50–1).

Who is to blame for the divorce? This is an issue *The Awful Truth* fails to resolve. Indeed, the film revels in this issue's unanswerability. We never find out what Jerry was up to or why he was so keen to give the impression he was in Florida, nor do we discover precisely what Lucy had been doing with Armand. All the same, it clearly *was* Jerry's intention to deceive his wife, while there is no clear evidence that Lucy had designed to deceive Jerry. Cavell is generous to Jerry: the film makes it clear that Jerry has a reputation as a ladies' man, and that he very much wants to keep up this impression. So Cavell excuses Jerry's behaviour as something that is intended to *give the impression* that he is a 'free man' and a ladies' man when all the while he has no intentions to make true on that impression. Cavell calls it Jerry's 'wish for reputation' (Cavell 1981, 244). The film itself is remarkably sophisticated in forming a range of innuendoes and potential deceptions. In *Fast-Talking Dames*, Marina DiBattista spends four pages discussing the ins and outs of these opening few minutes of the film, and she finds that the philosophical intentions of the exchanges there cannot be denied (DiBattista 2001, 221–4). 'You've come home and caught me in a truth', declares Lucy, 'and it seems there's nothing less logical than the truth.' To these claims Jerry responds, 'Oh, a philosopher!'

That *The Awful Truth* is a film worthy of philosophy is beyond question for a writer like Cavell. He finds the stakes of the film's opening scenes and the couple's decision to file for divorce to fall in the following way. Each member of the couple wants the other to *think* they have been unfaithful, even if in truth they have not been. What this demonstrates is that each of them *could be unfaithful if they chose to be*. By the end of the film each convinces the other that neither wants to be unfaithful but, rather, that even though each knows the other *could* be unfaithful they *could* take other partners and lovers – as they indeed do throughout the film – that, in the end, they decide that they *really do* want and love each other. It is this desire for one to be with the other over and above being with anyone else that defines the love that also defines their (re)marriage. In simple terms: if a modern marriage is based on a choice to be together, then it goes without saying that the couple can also choose to *not* be together. In *The Awful Truth*, in the end, the members of the couple decide that they *do* want to be together.

Marriage is thus demonstrated in *The Awful Truth* to be a choice *freely* made, just as divorce is a choice freely made. And that becomes one of Cavell's key points: no one else, no other force is making this couple stay married or making them divorce. Rather, the members of the couple are deciding these things themselves, together. The point of all this is that *this* marriage – and along with it modern marriage, Hollywood remarriage – exists in the way it does only because divorce also exists. Divorce is marriage's difference, its constitutive absence, its defining other. Another way to put this is to declare that modern marriage cannot exist without the condition of divorce as a way to *get out* of that marriage: one can only freely choose to be *in* a marriage if one can also freely choose to *get out* of it; otherwise the choice to be in it is no choice at all. Cavell puts it in this way:

> I have noted that divorce is asked for by asking to be free. If what Jerry is trying to establish is what we might call the freedom of marriage, then his complex wish for reputation is logical. All that freedom requires is, so to speak, its own possibility. As long as he *can* choose he is free – free for example to choose faithfulness. This would be creating a logical space within marriage in which to choose to be married, a way in which not to feel trapped in it. (Cavell 1981, 244–5)

The films I discuss throughout this book will be, to a great extent, about precisely that: the problem or quest – or the impossibility – of 'creating a logical space within marriage in which to choose to be married, a way in which not to feel trapped in it'. Such are the arguments that these films and this book approach.

Contempt

A good sense of where that argument is heading can be provided by Jean-Luc Godard's *Contempt*. A contrast with *The Awful Truth* is immediately apparent: where the Hollywood film allows the couple to find their way back to marriage and thus to be remarried, the European film finds no reconciliation. It offers only the slow disintegration of a marriage. If that is a major difference, there are also significant points of similarity. Like *The Awful Truth*, Godard's film is one that charts the consequences of a disruption of faith in a couple's marriage. This begins at that moment early in *Contempt* when Paul Javal (Michel Piccoli) loses faith in his wife, Camille (Brigitte Bardot) ... or is it the other way around?[3]

Let us examine this scene a little more closely. American film producer Jeremiah – Jerry (like Jerry Warriner, that is) – Prokosch (Jack Palance) has just asked Paul to rewrite some scenes for the film he is in the middle of making, a version of Homer's *Odyssey*. Having briefly discussed terms at the studios of Cinecittà just outside Rome, Prokosch invites Paul and Camille back to his villa for drinks. And now comes the key point of action in the sequence: Prokosch offers Camille a seat in his small, red, two-seated convertible car while also suggesting that Paul take a taxi. Camille hesitates. 'Do you want me to go?' she asks Paul. The latter gestures, or seems to gesture that, yes, he does want her to go with Prokosch.

It transpires that this was a mistake for Paul to have made: at the moment when Camille wants him to declare his love by insisting that she *not* travel with Prokosch, Paul has not defended their love. By allowing her to go in

Prokosch's car, Paul has effectively declared that he does not care for her, or that he does not care for her as much as he should. Perhaps at some sort of limit we might declare that Camille is reduced to an object that is here bartered between men (in the manner Lévi-Strauss once wrote about) so that, at the end of the day, her love does not mean all that much to Paul.[4] In fact, it is far more important that he impresses Prokosch with the scriptwriting job, so the stakes of this exchange are ones in which he is minded to keep the American producer happy. In short, if landing this job means handing over Camille to Prokosch – and Prokosch clearly relishes the possibility of stealing Paul's wife away from him for this car journey – then that is a price Paul is willing to pay.

The scene is, of course, ambiguous. I nevertheless want to argue that issues relating to trust and faithfulness are central to this scene. What does it mean for Camille to abandon Paul here? Or, more to the point, what does it mean for Paul to have abandoned Camille to Prokosch? It is certainly here that the contempt of the film's title emerges most forcefully (and to this degree the film remains faithful to Moravia's novel from which it is adapted). It sets in train a series of insinuations, allegations and manoeuvres that continue for the remainder of the film, most notably in the extraordinary scene in Paul and Camille's Rome apartment. There is no lack of conversation here, and conversations like those between Camille and Paul will abound in the film analyses that follow in this book.

This early scene of Camille's abandonment is then repeated later in the film. Prokosch has invited Paul and Camille to the island of Capri, where filming of *The Odyssey* is taking place. They have been filming an ocean scene in a small bay when Prokosch's secretary and interpreter, Francesca Vanini (Giorgia Moll), tells him that a phone call from New York is expected at the villa where they are staying. Prokosch then suggests that Camille may want to accompany him back to the villa. Her immediate response is that she will stay with her husband. But Prokosch is insistent, and he asks Paul whether he minds if she comes along. Paul's response is immediate and unflustered: 'Not at all,' he says. 'Go on,' he urges Camille. And he simply states that he'll walk back to the villa with Fritz Lang – the director of the film within a film, played, of course, by Lang himself – so they can discuss *The Odyssey*. Strings in a minor key here well up on *Contempt*'s soundtrack, while the camera zooms in on Paul as he lights a cigarette, as though the camera is trying to find a way to get inside him, to know his thoughts. And so Camille goes. As she gets into the small boat that she will take back to the villa, she looks at Paul. She is wearing sunglasses, but she is responding to Paul's gaze. It is a shot/reverse-shot formation, complete with eyeline matches, a rare thing in a Godard film. And it is as though, through the lenses of those sunglasses, the full force of Camille's contempt is expressed.

In *The Awful Truth*, Jerry and Lucy lose faith in their marriage when each suspects the other of fooling around. In *Contempt*, it seems that Paul rather encourages his wife's fooling around, even if such a thing might be against her wishes (and against his own too). I merely want to suggest that *Contempt* is fully embroiled in the kinds of suspicions and innuendoes that emerge at the beginning of *The Awful Truth* and that assessing or examining *Contempt* on these terms is an important thing to do. Of course, we might also know that *Contempt* contains far less humour than *The Awful Truth*, but such distinctions should not disqualify either film from being capable of great profundity.

Love and contempt

One commentary on *Contempt*, put forward by Bersani and Dutoit, argues that the whole point of the film is to put to rest all of the associations of love and marriage that are promoted by the Hollywood-style institutions of romantic love. On that reading, *Contempt* shows us that the constraints of romantic love are too fixed and its professions of faith too restrictive, so that it is the institution of marriage based on love itself that causes this couple's decoupling. On this count, a key European film of the 1960s finds the American restrictions of marriage and romantic love too much to bear. Bersani and Dutoit go so far as to argue that it is nothing less than contempt which cements the relationship between Camille and Paul: contempt is nothing less than a fundamental requirement of traditional modes of love and coupling; love and contempt go hand in hand. For Bersani and Dutoit, this is pretty much what Godard's film is about: contempt is the basis for modern love and marriage. Modern love and marriage cannot exist without it.

I outlined some aspects of Bersani's notion of connectedness in my Introduction. Connectedness entails dropping many of the codes, practices and discourses of civilised society, and one of those sets of practices that needs to be dropped is that which is codified as romantic love. When one person loves another, then this is merely a matter of one person's attempts to control the other person. Love is, Bersani claims, merely a form of control and possession. Bersani, keeping in mind that he is writing with Dutoit in their commentary on *Contempt*, argues that this is what is at stake in the love between Paul and Camille: it is a matter of possession. This is not entirely straightforward, for the claim is that it is *by way of contempt* that

Camille manages to possess Paul. And eventually it will also transpire that Paul will have to develop contempt for Camille too, for this is the way to establish what love 'really' is. These claims sound somewhat counterintuitive at first, but Bersani and Dutoit's arguments are entirely logical. Thus we can ask: why is Camille upset that Paul abandons her, as though he is encouraging her to develop a relationship with Prokosch? Well, she is upset because this is a sign that Paul does not possess her. Rather, Paul seems to advance the notion that Camille can – or should – entertain relationships with other people, such as Prokosch. But Camille, it seems, *wants to be possessed* by Paul – to be possessed by someone: that is what love is.

Love therefore requires contempt: without contempt there would be no desire for possessiveness and therefore no need for love either. Love, contempt, possession: they all go hand in hand. And *that*, Bersani and Dutoit argue, is what *Contempt* is all about. Let's look at this from another angle. Isn't Camille in much the same position here as Lucy is in *The Awful Truth*? Lucy is upset that her husband, Jerry, has deceived her, but she is even more upset that Jerry thinks that she has deceived him (by spending a night alone with Armand Duvalle). To this degree she believes that Jerry no longer possesses her, that she is no longer possessed by him, and thus that Jerry believes she might be willing to sleep with other men. It is Jerry's lack of faith in her at which she takes offence. Thus, the remainder of *The Awful Truth* might be so many paths by which Jerry and Lucy find ways to once again possess each other. And from such a perspective, a marriage, a coupling, is merely a way of trapping another person, possessing them, of affirming an ongoing and underlying contempt for them.

How do Bersani and Dutoit conceive of a way out of the deadlock of contempt? What is their solution? They argue that, for *Contempt*, one way out would be to refuse the exclusivity of the Paul–Camille couple. The Paul–Camille couple would no longer be exclusive and possessive. Rather, another couple, the Prokosch–Camille couple, could exist alongside and in an equivalent way to it. And so could any other couple – a Paul–Francesca couple, for example. From such a perspective, the Prokosch–Camille couple 'is simply another variation, something tried out', they argue (Bersani and Dutoit 2004, 60). On this score, professions of love and faith in films like *Contempt* or *The Awful Truth* are merely strategies of monogamy and exclusivity, strategies of possession. The way out for Bersani and Dutoit is to abandon romantic love as such, to posit a world '[n]o longer darkened by the demand for love' (Bersani and Dutoit 2004, 70). For them, this is exactly what *Contempt* is about. One way to conceive of what Bersani and Dutoit are advocating here is to see it as a version of free love, a version of love that would place it very much at odds with the possessiveness of romantic love based on the exclusivity of the couple.

Arguments

It is not clear how a way can be found out of this tangle of opposed conceptions. Cavell is convinced that comedies of remarriage like *The Awful Truth* demonstrate the ways in which a couple can build a marriage in such a way that neither member of the couple will feel trapped in it. Bersani, perhaps working within much the same parameters, concludes the precise opposite: that what one claims is freedom in love and coupling is merely a way to be trapped, to possess another person in ways destined to deny their freedom. There is no way to win such arguments. We shall see later in this book some very convincing examples of Bersani's theories worked out via the films of Agnès Varda and François Truffaut. However, these examples remain tentative and it is uncertain what kind of world they foretell. Indeed it is difficult to conceive of the world Bersani is himself trying to conjure up. What kind of human relation can be beyond that of a human relationship? Or beyond love? Why would a connection between bodies be more authentic or ontologically pure than a connection based on language, conversation, discourse and argument? Bersani appeals to the ethical writings of Michel Foucault in order to define certain practices of the self, and those theories provide some sense of the world Bersani intends.[5] But those senses remain difficult to fathom, as difficult, perhaps, as trying to understand how contempt could form the basis of what we call love.

As I have already admitted, my sympathies in this book will fall to the Cavellian side of these arguments. This does not mean I discount Bersani's interventions. Rather, they act as a decisive brake on an all-too easy acceptance of Cavell's claims. And furthermore, I believe the films and filmmakers discussed here demand a response to the points Bersani makes.

Contempt does open up the possibility of discussing these issues, and Bersani and Dutoit's extraordinary interjection into debates on that film is a mark of the film's continuing pertinence. *Contempt* places issues of love, coupling and fidelity with America and Hollywood very much in the foreground (see Mulvey 2019). The film producer, played with such relish by Palance, might as well be positioned as the ultimate cause of the couple's break-up, as the harbinger of contempt, as though American movies and all their high expectations of love and marriage were themselves to blame for this couple's misdirected expectations. If Jerry Warriner is complimented in *The Awful Truth* for possessing something of a Continental mind, then what destroys the couple in *Contempt* is their possession of American minds as guided by the powerful lure of Prokosch and American movies.

Of these issues, I do not claim to offer any solutions. Is *The Awful Truth* right, or is it merely providing pernicious, ideological myths of marriage that favour entrapment, especially the entrapment of a woman by a man?

Or is *Contempt* right, that romantic love is by and large doomed to failure, to nullifying repetition and inhibition? And insofar as it admits this, does *Contempt* allow us (and its characters) to escape the imprisonment of marriage? (And yet, even then, no salvation is offered to the errant wife, Camille, or the Hollywood producer, Prokosch: both die in a very Hollywood-style car crash near the film's end.) The simple fact that these films are asking questions about love and marriage, about what constitutes – or destroys – a couple, is significant enough. That *Contempt* can be said to be responding to or conversing with conceptions of romantic love that are similar to those found in classical Hollywood films is significant too. That discourse constitutes a large part of what *Contempt* is 'about'. And it is that contention that is the guiding thread of this book: each of the films discussed in this book can be said to be 'about' a European cinematic envisaging of romantic love in ways that can be compared and contrasted with Hollywood's views of love.

It might appear that this chapter has provided little of assistance to guide the reader on what to expect for the remainder of this book. There could be significant reasons for this. It is entirely uncommon to approach the films and filmmakers here in terms of character traits, themes, plots and in terms of the psychological intentions of characters. Bergman might be the exception in this regard, but the others here – Godard, Resnais, Rohmer, Fellini, Antonioni, Truffaut – are all typically associated with formal innovations in film style and narrative – or anti-narrative – creativity. Varda's work is often discussed in terms of style too, but it is also thematically associated with feminism. Themes of romantic love certainly do not predominate in discussions of any of these filmmakers. All of the auteurs approached here are often discussed in biographical terms, so that their films are approached in terms of historical causality. It is a commonplace, for example, to find that, following the credits, the opening scene of *Contempt* was demanded by the film's producers, much to Godard's annoyance; and that Godard was constantly in conflict with Bardot and Palance throughout the production; that as a consequence Godard was determined to never again make a 'big' budget film; or – a favourite of commentators – that the scenes of Paul and Camille's break-up were modelled on Godard's own break-up with Anna Karina. For whatever reasons, these kinds of claims about *Contempt* have carried more weight than has any attempt to assess the motivations or psychological characteristics of Paul or Camille or to examine the film's themes of love and marriage. Bersani and Dutoit's concentration on these aspects is quite remarkable in this respect.

What this book tries to do, therefore, is to discuss and analyse the films of these filmmakers in terms of themes that relate to romantic love. I have to admit that this course of analysis lies well outside of the typically accepted avenues of analysis for these filmmakers. A key distinction I draw, as already described, is between what Stanley Cavell has theorised as *acknowledgment* and what Leo Bersani has called *connectedness*. I will go on to claim that, in my analysis, these films can be said to be, for the most part, dealing with issues pertaining to Cavellian acknowledgment rather than Bersanian connectedness. This is to say that these films approach questions of what it means for a couple to be in love, what it means for them to aspire to equality and mutual understanding. But these films and filmmakers also question these aspirations. They place them under intense scrutiny and pressure. I am convinced that the films studied here point to conceptions of acknowledgment that are worth pursuing, such that romantic love and its couplings are conceived as being inherently rewarding and aspirational for the characters who inhabit these films.

Notes

1 I use the word 'classical' rather loosely here to designate a time period – the 1930s–1940s – rather than a style. Glitre has very convincingly argued that screwball comedies of this period run counter to many tenets of classical Hollywood, especially as they offer radical assessments of marriage and coupling (Glitre 2006, 17).
2 Armand Duval is, of course, a key character in the Alexandre Dumas (*fils*) *Lady of the Camellias*, a sign that this American comedy is taking some of its cues from the European tradition. On this point see Cavell 1996, 17–20, 26.
3 The name Camille will once again draw attention to Dumas's *Lady of the Camellias*, a way of showing that both *Contempt* and *The Awful Truth* draw on similar traditions.
4 I mention Lévi-Strauss partly because his *Elementary Structures of Kinship* plays a key role on Cavell's discussion of *It Happened One Night* (Frank Capra, 1934). See Cavell 1981, 71–109.
5 Bersani's theories are especially indebted to Michel Foucault's late works, *The Use of Pleasure* and *The Care of the Self*. Also of note in this context are Foucault's Collège de France lectures on *The Hermeneutics of the Subject* and *The Government of Self and Others* – see Foucault 1985, 1986, 2005, 2010.

Chapter 2

The falsity of social worlds: *The Rules of the Game*

2.1 André Jurieu and Christine de la Chesnaye (Roland Toutain and Nora Grégor) alone together in *The Rules of the Game* (Jean Renoir, 1939)

Jean Renoir once declared that 'The most important thing in life, after all, is love' (Renoir 1974, 251). Stanley Cavell, following a brief discussion of Ingmar Bergman's *Smiles of a Summer Night* (1955), went on to claim a disappointment at the fact that his arguments relating to remarriage comedies in *Pursuits of Happiness* could not be expanded, for want of space, so as to consider European films. He points to Renoir's *The Rules of the Game* (1939) as one such European film 'obviously invoking the project of remarriage' (Cavell 1981, 166). Raymond Durgnat, in his book on Renoir, remarks in his discussion of *The Rules of the Game* that 'Beyond all question, it is by the destruction of Jurieu's and Christine's love that society, and the rules of its game, are found wanting' (Durgnat 1975, 209). These three brief quotations offer some ways into Renoir's 1939 film. First of all, that the question of love is a key theme. Second, that some sort of conception of remarriage, as Cavell calls it, is at play in this film. And third, that it is the failed or doomed romance between Christine and André Jurieu that takes us closest to what is signalled by the film's title, *The Rules of the Game*.

I here use Renoir's film as a way of opening up a series of points that will be repeated and revised throughout this book. I do so as a way to reckon that European cinema and European society had to some degree become preoccupied with the themes of American love and marriage during the 1930s. Renoir's film is all the more significant for having been an inspiration for many of those who would contribute to the cinema of the French New Wave – Truffaut famously claimed Renoir as 'the greatest filmmaker in the world' (Truffaut 2014, 45), and at another point stated that '*The Rules of the Game* can be considered the greatest film in the history of cinema' (quoted in De Baecque and Toubiana 1999, 35), while Resnais remarked that his first viewing of *The Rules of the Game* (in 1944) was 'the most overwhelming experience I have had in the cinema in my whole life' (Resnais 1970, 14). None of these statements will, of course, prove that *The Rules of the Game* has anything to do with the Hollywood comedies of remarriage (on Cavell's terms), nor does any of this prove that what I have to say here about *The Rules of the Game* could in any concrete way have impacted on the other European filmmakers I examine in this book. Why am I examining *The Rules of the Game* here? Because it introduces themes, characters and plot scenarios that will be repeated in many of the other films I approach in this book.

Love and marriage

The key themes being examined here involve love and marriage. Those themes are central to Renoir's film. The way they are approached there provides a number of ways into the other films and filmmakers in this book, as well as providing something of a historical context, on the eve of the Second World War, that will provide the background out of which many of the post-war filmmakers of this book will then build. I should warn readers that the themes invoked here are not straightforward, for Renoir's film is multilayered, somewhat ambiguous and in various ways rather difficult to interpret. *The Rules of the Game* will be revisited throughout this book in the light of subsequent films, for many of the themes, patterns and character relationships that emerge in *Rules* re-emerge in the films made by the European filmmakers who are examined in this book.

The two scenes with which *The Rules of the Game* opens deliver the key themes of love and marriage. The first shows us the arrival of André Jurieu (Roland Toutain) as he lands, in front of a large crowd of onlookers, journalists and radio reporters, at Paris's Le Bourget airport. He has just completed a record-equalling flight across the Atlantic – equal to that of Charles Lindbergh, so we are told. He lands there in the hope that the love of his life will be there to greet him. She is not there. André is remarkably disappointed. He even appears uninterested in the daring feat he has just accomplished, as though the feat in itself now means little, for it has failed to arouse the passions of the woman for whom the act was clearly intended. We will soon discover that this woman is Christine (Nora Grégor), and that she is married to a well-connected, aristocratic man, the Marquis Robert de la Chesnaye (Marcel Dalio). André's tremendous feat can therefore be taken as one associated with the chivalric tradition of 'courtly love'. André is, in many ways, a modern-day troubadour, in love with a noble woman who is out of his league.

In a second scene, immediately following our introduction to André, we are introduced to the woman he loves. Christine is seated in her bedroom in front of a mirror, accompanied by her housemaid, Lisette (Paulette Dubost). Christine has been listening to a radio broadcast of André's landing, so she is well aware of his accomplishment. During this scene, we come to realise that the housemaid, Lisette, is married to a man she rarely spends time with, and that this arrangement in some way contributes to her happiness. We also infer that she enjoys taking lovers, and that this arrangement may contribute to her happiness generally and to the happiness of her marriage more particularly. We will later discover that one of her lovers is André Jurieu's good friend, Octave (played by Jean Renoir himself).

The Rules of the Game here gives the impression that a marriage involves at least three people: a husband and wife, but then also a lover with whom the passions of love are truly shared: a 'couple + 1'. Love in marriage is not essential – indeed, love and marriage may even be incompatible. Such is Christine's question to Lisette: how can one be happy in a marriage? And Lisette's response is to suggest that one must keep one's husband at a distance while also keeping one's lovers close at hand. Of course, for Christine, as we shall discover, this creates somewhat of a conundrum. Should she keep her husband, Robert, at a distance and thereby bring André closer, in the manner of Lisette's arrangement? Or should she try to make good on her marriage and stay true to her husband?

Pretty soon into the film we discover that Robert himself has a lover, Geneviève (Mira Pirély), so this complicates matters even further. We also soon come to know that Robert wants to end this affair. He wants to stay true to his wife and he figures the only way to do this will be by ending the affair. Thus, if the film has introduced us to a conception of three people involved in a marriage – a 'couple + 1' – then Robert here demonstrates a determination to get rid of that third element. His explicit reason for wanting to end the affair is that he fears Christine will find out 'and not understand'. He is now married, and I suppose we must consider that he feels a true marriage must be one that exclusively involves a couple. At any rate, this seems to be what Robert himself wants to believe.

I think we can go so far as to declare that *The Rules of the Game* sets these two conceptions of marriage into conflict: one which contends that lovers and affairs are a satisfactory and pleasurable part of a marriage, and another which wants to believe that a loving couple should be what defines a marriage. The film's key turning point – one of the great scenes in the history of cinema – occurs when Christine discovers that Robert is having an affair. With the aid of a small spyglass, while a range of guests who have gathered at Robert's country estate, La Colinière, are enjoying a midday hunt, Christine quite by chance discovers Robert passionately kissing Geneviève. And so it becomes clear to her that her marriage is not restricted to a husband and wife couple but, rather, involves a third. And all of this happens after Christine had gone to substantial lengths to ensure that everyone at La Colinière knew that her friendship with André was and is just that: a friendship between a man and a woman that has gone no further than a good friendship should. Christine has forbidden herself from engaging with a third party, whereas she now discovers that Robert has granted himself no such restriction. And yet, even after Christine has tried to allay the potential scandal of a supposed affair with André – she admits to having spent a great deal of time with André while he was preparing for his Atlantic flight – the guests and staff at La Colinière are not entirely convinced. At dinner on the first night at which guests have gathered at the country estate, André finds himself seated next to Christine. To this, one of the female domestiques declares, 'I'm all for freedom, but that's not etiquette.' We might thus see yet another layer of complication here: yes, an affair is all well and good – for that is freedom – but do not make a show of it. If you must have a third in your marriage, keep it under wraps, keep it secret, for that is etiquette. Etiquette therefore trumps freedom, but also provides a space for – or a cover for – freedom.

There are more details to this plot. The affairs of the upper classes are mirrored by those of the domestiques, for we know that Lisette is married to Schumacher (Gaston Modot), head gamekeeper at La Colinière. Lisette is not, however, especially keen on her husband: when it was suggested early in the film that she would have to leave Paris to join her husband, she declared she'd rather get a divorce! When at La Colinière, she attracts the attention of Marceau (Julien Carette), a man who had been caught poaching on the estate, but to whom Robert had taken a liking with the result of taking him onto the estate's staff. Thus, for much of the film, Marceau is the third person – the lover – in the marriage between Lisette and Schumacher. And, of course, we have known since very early in the film that Lisette rather enjoys taking lovers, one of whom is André's good friend, Octave, whom we also discover was a childhood friend of Christine's.

All of this makes for a rather complicated set of relationships. I want to suggest a range of parameters by which some bearings can be set. The main point I want to bring out of *The Rules of the Game*, certainly for the arguments that will follow for the other chapters in this book, is that Renoir's film sets in place an *old version of marriage* against which it then shows us the possibility of what can be called *a new conception of marriage*. First of all, the old version of marriage is not primarily based on love. Rather, the old version of marriage is based on familial alliances or convenient arrangements. In short, the marriage between Robert and Christine is a class alliance, a marriage between members of the upper classes, with Robert claiming the French line and Christine hailing from Austria. What stands here as a marriage is therefore indebted to the traditions of grand houses and families, as much as to monarchies themselves – and surely the alliance between Louis XVI and Marie Antoinette is evoked by the marriage between Robert and Christine, with it also being likely that Hollywood's very successful 1938 biopic of Marie Antoinette was resonating in the public's imagination (*Marie Antoinette*, directed by W. S. Van Dyke, starring Norma Shearer). This marriage, therefore, is one of shoring up familial, class and property alliances. It is not a marriage made primarily for reasons of love. At its most stringent, such a marriage might be considered an 'arranged' one, that is, a marriage in which neither of the members of the couples has a say, but where the marriage is arranged by parents or other external agents.

The old conception of marriage is also here based on the notion of 'three': one is married to one's spouse, but one really loves another – a third party – who is outside the married couple. For *The Rules of the Game*, in this marriage, the third party for Robert is Geneviève, while for Christine it is André. (I realise that this all amounts to at least four parties, but for the sake of simplicity, I'll rely here on a logic of three, on a notion of the 'couple + 1'.)

The crucial point, and the key theme *The Rules of the Game* proposes, is that the old conception of marriage should give way to a new type of marriage. Old marriage based on property and class must give way to a new conception of marriage based on romantic love. Robert, for example, is determined to break off his affair with Geneviève in order that his marriage with Christine will become that of a loving couple and thus embody the new type of marriage. If this can transpire, then the wish is that the marriage will be based on love rather than on class and property. Much the same goes for Christine's interest in André: she emphasises that she and André are mere friends. There is no romantic love between them that could spoil the coupling of her modern marriage to Robert. That is the quest: to break away from old marriage so as to secure a new notion of marriage based on the notion of the loving couple. This is the principal theme of *The Rules of the Game*.

The stakes are somewhat less clear when it comes to the 'downstairs' marriage between Lisette and Schumacher. Lisette seems entirely content with a 'couple + 1' arrangement, as long as she does not have to spend too much time with her husband! She certainly does not seem to hold much love or affection for Schumacher. Perhaps we can take this as an indicator that the 'old' notion of marriage among the lower classes is one that does little for women – certainly that it is not designed to deliver pleasure or happiness for them – such that women need to search beyond the confines of the couple if they are to find happiness. Schumacher, for his part, wishes to leave La Colinière and go to Alsace, where he will be able to set up his own business. His dream here involves having Lisette by his side, which seems to me to be nothing but a way of possessing her.

The plot reaches its climax during the masquerade party that makes up much of the film's conclusion. It is during this party that Schumacher ends up chasing Lisette's lover, Marceau, through the halls of the château with the intention of shooting him. Following a series of gunshots which Schumacher has aimed at Marceau, Robert eventually calms him only in order to terminate his employment as the estate's gamekeeper. Schumacher's behaviour, Robert decides, has been unacceptable, and he must pack his bags. Robert also demands that Marceau leave. In response to this, Lisette states that she has no intention of leaving: she remains devoted to Christine. She seems to have no interest at all in spending her life with Schumacher. Can we simply say that, for this class, matters of making ends meet are simply more important than matters of love or marriage?

The consequences and fallout of the Robert–Christine marriage are substantially more complicated. During the film's famous hunting sequence, Christine is clearly upset to discover that Robert has been unfaithful. Later in the film Lisette will tell Christine that Robert's affair has been ongoing for at least three years, and thus since well before their marriage. Midway through the masquerade party, well after Christine has discovered Robert's affair with Geneviève, Christine and André find themselves alone. This is the only time they speak intimately during the film and their conversation is significant. André asks Christine why she was not there to greet his airplane after his Atlantic flight. And a conversation ensues.

Christine: Because I love you ... I never meant to admit it, but now I have the right to say I love you André.
André: That's marvellous ... I'd stopped believing it ... What now?
C: We'll go away
A: Where?
C: Anywhere ... This very moment.
A: I love you Christine. I think I can make you happy.
C: For months now I've planned what we would do together.

André then asks Christine if she is afraid, and she declares that she is not. Renoir shows us her response in a very close, full-face close-up, as though wanting to demonstrate to us – as viewers – that this is a moment of intense candour and openness: Christine is assuredly here being truthful and true to herself. She wants to escape with André and is not afraid to do so.

In response to all this André then makes the startling claim that he must let Robert know of their plans. Christine cannot understand why he feels the need to do such a thing. André simply states that it's the proper thing to do. Christine responds with the claim that 'if we're in love, what does it matter?' And André's fateful response here is telling: 'Christine,' he intones, 'there are rules.' 'André,' she states, 'I'll go away with you right now or never.' Even then, André resists. He does not want them to sneak away, but determines that their intentions must be squared with Robert. The rules and matters of etiquette are here deemed more important to André than his quest for love, and his sticking to the rules will lead to his downfall.

The action continues to unfold at a rapid pace. Robert confronts André and even strikes him when he senses that André is trying to steal his wife. At the same time, Christine has confessed to Octave. 'I've just told André that I love him,' she says. She adds that she had expected André to carry her off in his arms. She is taken aback that he has failed to do such a thing.

The consequences of all this fall in many directions. Geneviève, for example, now suggests that she might as well go off with Robert. In a confused state, Christine reckons she might be better off escaping with Octave, for they are old friends after all, and he is reliable and trustworthy. Previously she had even considered escaping with St Aubin (Pierre Nay), owner of an adjoining country estate. At the same time, André and Robert chat, and the latter declares that he loves Christine enough to set her free, and we may get the feeling that the romance between André and Christine will end happily after all.

A range of other machinations ensue up to the point where Schumacher, now seeking some kind of revenge on his dismissal from La Colinière, and believing he is firing at Octave, instead shoots André dead as the latter is attempting to flee with Christine. Schumacher had mistakenly believed that Octave was now trying to flee with Lisette, but in reality we see here that

André had, in the end, decided that this was the best time to leave with Christine. As André makes his way towards the greenhouse where he is to rendezvous with Christine, Schumacher opens fire, and André is shot dead. Robert immediately declares of these events, 'Gentlemen, it was merely an accident. Schumacher thought he saw a poacher and did his duty. Fate willed André Jurieu to be the victim of this error.'

There is a great deal to try to account for here. The perspective I want to bring to these events is this. Primarily it consists of claiming that *The Rules of the Game* is about the attempt to replace an old version of marriage, represented by Robert and Christine, with a new form of marriage, based on love, represented by André and Christine. (Durgnat had claimed as much when he reckoned, as we have already seen, that 'Beyond all question, it is by the destruction of Jurieu's and Christine's love that society, and the rules of its game, are found wanting'; Durgnat 1975, 209). This new type of marriage would break the old rules of marriage, based on familial alliances, property and class. Additionally, this new type of marriage would be based on love and something akin to a mutual equality between the members of the romantic couple. However, fate intervenes, by which I take it that the film means to declare that the old order – tradition, class, authority, the rules – intervenes so as to reassert itself: old marriage triumphs, and the rules of the old form of marriage stake their claim. André's death marks the victory of the old order over the new. I also take this to mean that the triumph of old marriage signals the victory of etiquette over freedom – that is, the victory of the rules of tradition over those things which might tend to break those rules – as well as ensuring the victory of the upper classes over the class of entrepreneur adventurers represented by André – call this class something akin to a modern bourgeoisie – and maintaining the subservience of the lower classes and their disillusionment, all represented by Schumacher, Lisette and Marceau.

None of this is neat or clean. We might begin by stating that André is himself an accomplice in his own demise, for it is his insistence on following etiquette, on bowing to the rules of tradition, on 'making it right' with Robert, that brings in the delay that results in his being shot dead. Therefore, the weight of tradition and its conception of old marriage is not simply carried by Robert, but also by those beneath him who ensure its continuance: André, but also Lisette and Schumacher. Lisette, for example, enjoys her subservience: her greatest wish is to remain as Christine's housemaid, and that may be taken as something like the condition of her freedom. But what freedom belongs to a member of a servant class? Schumacher, by contrast, represents the desire to be freed from servitude, to make a life of his own. It may be that fate also intervenes in Schumacher's quest for freedom: even as he is freed from being employed by Robert he nevertheless manages to do the latter's dirty work for him, as though the serving classes are destined by fate or history to perform the acts that keep them in servitude.

And, of course, the dark shadow of Nazism looms large over all these filmic events. Another way to interpret *The Rules of the Game* is to claim that the reinstatement of tradition, etiquette and old marriage based on class and property is Renoir's way of showing us that an old order of things in the style of National Socialism, with its brutality, repression and privilege, seems destined to win out over a spirit of freedom, love, democracy and equality, all of which could be embodied by a new understanding of marriage. Take two of the great works of New German Cinema, Fassbinder's *The Marriage of Maria Braun* (1978) and Helma Sanders-Brahms's *Germany, Pale Mother* (1979), as examples of the horrors of an old conception of marriage inspired by the National Socialist regime and as further evidence, perhaps, of the point I am trying to make here. To complicate issues still further, this is a way of saying that Robert – played by the Jewish Marcel Dalio (I suppose this to be an example of Renoir's irony, but also something of a personal snub to the spirit of Nazism) – is the representative of an aristocratic tradition that would be given new life under Nazism; that is, the resurrection of an order based on something like class lines (or, indeed, a new elite order altogether). We might take Renoir's *La Grande Illusion* (1937) as something of a commentary on such issues in the face of war. And yet, we also know that National Socialism needed its adherents from the entrepreneur classes who, history tells us, did far too little to resist Nazism, and André's appeals to etiquette or propriety offer ways in which *The Rules of the Game* provides its arguments on that front.

Cavell and *The Rules of the Game*

Needless to say, all of this is far too much to consider for my purposes here. A more pressing question for me relates to Cavell's reading of this film. Why does he consider it a film 'obviously involving the project of remarriage' (Cavell 1979a, 166)? To remind the reader of some of the ground covered in the opening chapters of this book, Cavell considers a cycle that he calls remarriage comedies to be films that involve a married couple who fall out of love and who, by way of conversation and reconciliation, find a way to get back together again. In other words, the couples in these films find ways to fall in love again and thus to be 'remarried'. If this is Cavell's claim, then how does such a claim play out in *The Rules of the Game*? Are we to presume that Robert and Christine are remarried, that they come to a greater understanding of each other by way of conversation and via some sort of project of building a world together? I cannot see how such an argument could possibly be made, especially given the fact that right up to the last moments of the film Christine is determined to flee from her marriage, and that it is only because André is shot dead that she returns to Robert. She returns to him because she has been forced to by fate, not because she has chosen to do so, and not because she has somehow, by way of conversation and reconciliation, come to the decision that she loves Robert above all others.

Where, then, is the project of remarriage in this film? If *The Rules of the Game* has anything to do with remarriage, then it can only be the case that it is about the *failure of remarriage*. This film is about the assertion and triumph of marriage over remarriage. Marriage, in this sense, therefore means old marriage, while, by contrast, the discourses of new marriage would be those which Cavell refers to as remarriage. One way to figure this distinction between (old) marriage and (new) remarriage would be to conceive of it in terms of what Cavell declares the remarriages are not. When embarking on one of his many summaries of the key aspects of remarriage comedies, he writes that 'what is normally called adultery is not to be expected in these structures, since normally it plays no role in remarriage comedies – something that distinguishes them from Restoration comedy and from French farce'. Cavell continues, 'In this genre it will not be the threat of social scandal that comes between a woman and a man' (Cavell 1996, 88). Therefore, issues of adultery and social scandal are not to be expected in remarriage comedies. And yet, I think we have to admit that what is normally called adultery is something significant for *The Rules of the Game*, certainly insofar as Robert has been committing such a thing, and that the repercussions of his adulterous behaviour are central to the marriage problems that then ensue in this film. And the same, of course, can be said for Lisette and her romantic adventures: it is her affairs that cause tensions in her marriage with Schumacher. Christine herself also invites 'social scandal' insofar as she has been spending a great deal of time with André, to the extent that she has to try to justify her actions to the guests at La Colinière. These are therefore all actions of *The Rules of the Game* that draw it towards adultery and social scandal and thus away from what Cavell defines as remarriage. For my purposes, this is a way of saying that a European tradition of morals and marriage, but also of filmmaking, finds itself in an atmosphere somewhat different from that of the American scene. Where the American scene, via Hollywood films, is endeavouring to found a new, modern version of (re)marriage on the basis of conversation and what will become known as 'companionate love', the European scene is still mired in traditional alliances and prejudices, with adultery hovering very near to the centre of a version of love that exists outside of marriage.[1] And if this is the situation in 1939, then one of the things at stake for post-war filmmaking in Europe – with Bergman, Fellini, Antonioni and others – will be to work through the inhibitions of the European structure of 'old' marriage in ways that bear upon the American formulations of 'new' remarriage specified by Cavell.

The importance of 'two'

Cavell, insofar as he advocates the notion of remarriage, calls upon a conception of *acknowledgment* in order to convey the philosophical stakes of this new conception of marriage. I examined the notion of acknowledgment at some length in the opening chapters of this book. A fine indication of that notion is offered by way of the statement that 'each person is constructed through the encounter with another', a statement made by Geneviève Sellier in a discussion of the films of Agnès Varda. In relation to *The Rules of the Game*, how can conceptions like acknowledgment or assertions that 'each person is constructed through the encounter with another' be made sense of? Certainly one of the factors at stake in Renoir's film is that little knowledge is gained via one person's encounters with others. Rather, encounters with others are marked by their failures, opened as they are by Christine's failure to greet André at his landing at Le Bourget airport at the beginning of the film, then closed by the 'accident' which kills André and which therefore cements the conditions of mistakenness and unknownness experienced by all those gathered at La Colinière. So, where Cavell sees the American comedies of remarriage as signalling the triumph of acknowledgment – where a loving couple genuinely come to know and understand each other by way of conversation and reconciliation – *The Rules of the Game* is marked by the failure to achieve any such state of acknowledgment.

Renoir's film nevertheless invokes the possibility of acknowledgment and mutual understanding. Christine engages in conversation with André – as we have already seen – but also with Octave near the end of the film. (Significantly, it is also worth pointing to her brief conversation with Geneviève after she has discovered that she is having an affair with Robert. Reflections on this episode will have to be taken up at a later point in this book.) It is the conversation between Christine and André that is most significant, for it is out of this conversation that the possibility of building a world together, of constructing a marriage that could be considered a genuine remarriage, begins to look like it might occur. As I have already noted, this is the only one-to-one conversation this couple has in *The Rules of the Game*. Prior to having this conversation, just when André has arrived at La Colinière, and in front of the guests gathered there, Christine had declared her relationship with André to have been one of friendship, not romance or love. She explains to those gathered that 'during his preparations [for his flight], André often came to see me. We spent many hours together – very pleasant hours – under the sign of that rare thing, friendship. He told me about his plans and I listened to him. It's something to know how to listen.'

One way to consider this take on friendship is by way of Ralph Waldo Emerson's essay on that topic, noting that Emerson's philosophy is central for Cavell's own conception of remarriage comedies. Emerson claims that 'Two may talk and one may hear, but three cannot take part in a conversation of the most sincere and searching sort' (Emerson 1898, 54). One does not need to agree with Emerson's claim to feel its appropriateness here. Christine's apology for her friendship with André are not words directed towards him. It is no conversation but, rather, a display for a gathered audience. It is one of several displays for audiences emphasised throughout *The Rules of the Game*, crowned by Robert's famous closing declaration to the audience gathered beneath him on the terrace of La Colinière that 'Gentlemen, it was merely an accident.' Emerson's argument runs that, when a conversation becomes a crowd, something like a 'social self' necessarily steps in to take the place of the individual. The implication of this is that the individual begins to form words in such a way as to please an audience rather than stay true to his or her own purpose. To speak among three is rather different from a conversation between two.

Christine changes her tune entirely when alone with André. The one and only time they are alone in the film, as we have seen, they declare their love for each other. We might believe they are being sincere and their love is true. But any declarations are short lived. André and Christine decide that they are going to run away together, only for André to get it into his head that he needs to square things with Robert. We can see a certain logic at work here: Christine wants to play down her intimacy with André when gathered before a social audience. And later in the film André senses that an assurance made between two people – call it a 'friendship' in Emerson's terms – needs the approval of an external authority (i.e., Robert). In other words, the potential of a love formed between two people is distorted or nullified when that coupling has to be presented to or verified by an external audience. As Emerson puts it, 'three cannot take part in a conversation of the most sincere and searching sort'. For a love and a marriage to add up to a new conception of remarriage, it does not need the approval of the social order, of a third person. It does not even need a marriage in the traditional sense of a contract externally ratified by a state or religion. Rather, all it needs are the members of the couple themselves, by themselves together. We shall see that the logic of 'two' plays a central role in many parts of this book.

Cavell plays out these issues in his reflections on *The Rules of the Game*. In the second edition of *The World Viewed*, published in 1979, some two years before his book on Hollywood comedies of remarriage, *Pursuits of Happiness*, Cavell added a long discussion of Renoir's film. Cavell's reflections here are on the ontology of film – not on the genre of remarriage comedy – and by way of *The Rules of the Game* he makes an argument that tries to summarise what *The World Viewed* has been about. He writes that, for *The Rules of the Game*, the truth of cinema triumphs over the falsity of theatre. He will eventually write, in a sort of summary of his thoughts on *The Rules of the Game*, that the film is about cinema's ability to lay bare *the falseness of our social worlds*. He writes, 'When society has become fully theatricalized (conscious of its rules but inaccessible to their backing, the fool of its own artifice, of its peculiar compacts), cinema reestablishes our sense of reality by asserting its own powers of drama' (Cavell 1979a, 225).

It is not easy to work out Cavell's theme here. Is he declaring that cinema has the ability to lay bare the illusions and deceptions of ideology; that is, that film's highest ability is to expose and critique the silent ideologies by which we unconsciously live? Hence, we could declare *The Rules of the Game* a precursor of Godardian techniques of foregrounding the apparatus (to the point where Cavell himself invokes Godard's *Two or Three Things I Know about Her*). I do not believe this is what Cavell is trying to say. Rather, what he is trying to say is that cinema gives to us the possibility of another way of seeing things, a perspective on the world that is not so much *in* that world as it is shielded or distanced from it. 'By my account,' he argues, 'film's presenting of the world by absenting us from it appears as confirmation of something already true of our stage of existence. Its displacement of the world confirms, even explains, our prior estrangement from it. The "sense of reality" provided on film is the sense of *that* reality, one from which we already sense a distance' (Cavell 1979a, 226).

These are a perplexing set of claims. At one and the same time cinema presents us with our distance from the world, our absence from it, while also providing a sense that this distanced view of the world is precisely how the world *is* for us ('us' being human beings living under the conditions of modernity). Is this, then, what *The Rules of the Game* is about: our distance from the world, our inability to connect with the world or even believe in it? There is certainly good evidence for such an argument, that *The Rules of the Game* presents us with characters who and actions which beggar belief, a world of preventative, stultified social codes and of withering, confused, unfulfillable human desires – a world drained of pleasure and hope. But surely such claims have little to do with the ontology of film or cinema. Rather, I would say they are claims specific to this particular film. What is especially striking is that Cavell will subsequently mark out a genre of supreme pleasure and hope – the comedies of remarriage – in ways that bear importance for an ontology of film. Perhaps here it is worth reiterating the possibility that *The Rules of the Game* shows us everything that would negate a remarriage comedy – call it a remarriage *tragedy*; that it negates or erases all of the pleasures and hopes that can be found in the genre of remarriage comedy. In so directly negating the pulse of those comedies – even as it tries to invoke a comedic élan – *The Rules of the Game* is, as it were, entering into a conversation with those very elements of pleasure and hope.

Ultimately what Cavell is claiming is that *The Rules of the Game* shows us a social order that has enforced rules, standards and codes of social etiquette without any longer knowing why those rules and standards are being enforced. In a simple sense, the rules of that game pertain to the rules of the marriage between Christine and Robert: they are married, but there is no underpinning reason or sense of mutual understanding that gives a backing to this marriage. Renoir is trying to depict all layers of society as so falsified that the members of that society are incapable of developing lives that could be meaningful or satisfying. Such a perspective climaxes, of course, with the 'accident' that kills André. No reasoning or explanation is offered for this accident other than to declare that fate intervened. And that appeal to fate is quite definitively an admission that things are the way they are because tradition, the gods, nature or destiny have made things that way – call this a matter of divine right – and the human society gathered here is powerless to prevent fate from stamping its authority. (Emerson famously wrote that 'Intellect annuls fate. So far as a man thinks, he is free'. He adds that ''Tis a weak and vicious people who cast the blame on fate'; Emerson 2001b, 269.) If nothing else, it can be declared that class wins the day, as though the classiness of the upper classes is determined by fate. Class and tradition emphatically reassert themselves with the death of André. It is needless to point out that the film's final words, spoken by another of the guests at La Colinière, the General (Richard Francoeur), offer an endorsement of Robert and his class. The General responds to St Aubin's retort that the death of André was surely not an accident, that if Robert believes it to have been an accident, then this surely is 'A new definition of the word accident', as St Aubin puts it. But the General refutes him: 'Not at all,' he says, 'La Chesnaye has a touch of class and that's a rare thing nowadays, a rare thing.' And these are the final words of *The Rules of the Game*: the virtues of class have won the day, order has been restored and social hierarchies have remained in force. There are rules of the game, and those rules must not be broken.

A recent reading of the film offered by Todd McGowan is especially illuminating in these respects. Of the romance between Christine and André, McGowan remarks that 'there can be no satisfying romantic union because the characters remain within the rules of the game. A satisfying romance exists, the film implies, only outside the domain of these rules' (McGowan 2015, 148). Such points are ones that I have, to a large degree, been trying to argue here. McGowan goes on to remark that 'André cares more for the rules of heroism than he does for Christine' (McGowan 2015, 149), again a claim with which I agree. But McGowan's keenest point, informed by the psychoanalytic theories of Jacques Lacan, emphasises the step that the plot of *The Rules of the Game* is unable to take: it cannot raise the *other*'s desire above the *Other*'s desire (McGowan 2015, 149). What McGowan means by this is that social pressure, social hierarchies, society's demand for rules that are not to be broken – what he here terms 'the Other's desire' – cannot be surpassed or transcended by the mutual understanding between one human being and another – 'the other's desire'. McGowan writes that 'The subject in a romance replaces the big Other with the little other, the social rules with the romantic partner. In doing so, this subject embraces the disruptiveness that accompanies the other's desire' (McGowan 2015, 149). The romance in romantic comedies is thus a way of disrupting the social.

Some commentators will claim that romances entail an avoidance of the social rather than its disruption, and such a claim, against the arguments of someone like Cavell, might be made of the comedies of remarriage (see Shumway 2003). And McGowan too hedges his bets. Yes, the romance counters the social world, but it does little to undermine or change that world. We might see that potential challenge to the social by way of an adulterous affair. As we have seen in *The Rules of the Game*, such an affair does not challenge the social order; it merely upholds the stability of the social law. The kind of couple envisaged by new marriage or remarriage, by contrast, very much aims to define its own social order. It aims to counter – or at the very least to ignore – the current rules of the social order so that the couple can make their own rules. Thus Cavell will often consider the behaviours and rules of such couples to be, in some sense, deranged: no one else will really be able to understand a couple's own rules. It is this kind of nascent social order – a set of shared beliefs and modes of conduct – that can have the ability to buck the mandates of the current social order. If the social order has become completely falsified such that its members go along with its rules even though they have no idea why they are conforming to those rules, then perhaps it is up to a couple of people – call them lovers – to figure a way out of those rules, to make their own rules and to build a world together. Of course, that is no guarantee that the social order will be overturned, though I would suggest that one has to start somewhere.

And it is the cinema – such is Cavell's argument – that has shown us how this can be done. The cinema can show us the falsity of the rules of our social worlds at the same time as it can show us how to overcome those rules, perhaps so as to enable us to make our own rules. At any rate, Cavell will claim as much of the cycle of films he calls remarriage comedies. As to 'the falsity of rules', that is how I take Cavell's argument on *The Rules of the Game*: 'When society has become fully theatricalized (conscious of its rules but inaccessible to their backing, the fool of its own artifice, of its peculiar compacts), cinema reestablishes our sense of reality by asserting its own powers of drama' (Cavell 1979a, 225). What *The Rules of the Game* shows us is a failure to assert one's own rules: Christine and André fail to find a way to begin to build a world together. Instead, *The Rules of the Game* shows us the ways in which the old rules have the ability to reassert themselves.

A final reflection on the notion of *two*, as distinct from *one* or *three*. My earlier chapters asked the question of how one escapes from isolation; that is, of how one defeats the condition of being *one*. Cavell's answer to this was by way of the notion of *acknowledgment*. I also noted that Leo Bersani's answer to this was by way of *connectedness*. I return to these conceptions throughout this book. I have tried to claim in this chapter, via a reading of *The Rules of the Game*, that deference to *three* – that is, deference to the social, to tradition, to the 'rules', or by deference to a notion of the 'couple + 1' – does not end in happiness. So what, then does it mean to invoke *two*: the couple, the pair? To some extent this is what all love stories aim for: the passionate desire to be so connected with another person that one's sense of self becomes blended with this other person: *one* becomes *two*. This is not my own formulation but, rather, is one proposed by Alain Badiou.

> We know how people get carried away by love stories! A philosopher must ask why that happens. Why are there so many films, novels, and songs that are entirely given over to love stories? There must be something universal about love for these stories to interest such an enormous audience. What is universal is that all love suggests a new experience of truth about what it is to be two and not one. That we can encounter and experience the world other than through a solitary consciousness: any love whatsoever gives us evidence of this. (Badiou 2012, 39)

Love for another human being gives us the ability to experience the world through them, with them, alongside them, *because* of them ... This is not the experience of a solitary consciousness, but the experience of something else. And yet, what on earth *is* this something else? This is one of the questions approached in the next chapter.

Note

1 Many of the films made by Ernst Lubitsch hover somewhere nearby in all of this, especially his very 'Continental' films of the 1920s and early 1930s, such as 1924's *The Marriage Circle* or 1934's *The Merry Widow*. To examine this element within the mix of my discussion here might well result in an entirely different book. Lubitsch's adventurousness was substantially toned down by the Production Code, such that one may see *The Shop Around the Corner* (1942) as a somewhat standard American drama, even though it is set in Hungary.

Chapter 3

Ingmar Bergman's *Smiles of a Summer Night*: acknowledgment and deception

3.1 'How can a woman ever love a man?' Desirée Armfeldt and Fredrik Egerman (Eva Dahlbeck and Gunnar Björnstand) in *Smiles of a Summer Night* (Ingmar Bergman, 1955)

The terrain charted by the previous chapter, on Jean Renoir's *The Rules of the Game*, placed love at the intersection between what I called 'old marriage' and 'new marriage'. Old marriage, as I argued, confines itself to the existing rules of society, whereas new marriage – or what Stanley Cavell calls *remarriage* – tries to find new and different rules for a potentially new kind of society. The characters in *The Rules of the Game* end up pinned down by the structures and rules of society. None of these characters discovers what might be called a true or genuine self (whatever such a thing might be), nor are there relationships which might be said to be free and equal between partners. We do not exit *The Rules of the Game* with the sense that any of the characters has discovered a love match or a happy ending in the manner expected of the Hollywood romantic comedies Cavell praises. I have tried to imply that *The Rules of the Game* offers themes that will be intensified when European cinema enters a post-war phase most notably identified with 'art cinema'. An initial feeling, suggested in the previous chapter, is that the European filmmakers I discuss in this book tend to favour a version of *tragedies* of remarriage rather than *comedies* of remarriage (as Cavell called a cycle of Hollywood films). The stark contrast there is that the Europeans find a lack of hope and pleasure in the prospect of love and marriage. Indeed, at their limit these films are doomed to end in death, as befits tragedy, and it is death which is offered as something of a climax in *The Rules of the Game*. The American comedies, by comparison, are grounded in the hopes and pleasures offered by the future of a couple who will live happily ever after (though there are no guarantees, of course, that they will do so). The guiding thread of an argument here is that European society and the European tradition are structured in such ways that they cannot accommodate a version of marriage – call it an American version – based on the ideals of mutual acknowledgment and equality. The class divisions of the European tradition instead make it imperative that marriage matches be ones dictated by social class, and to that extent Renoir's film offers a commentary on Marivaux's *The Game of Love and Chance* (Marivaux's play is one of the key sources for *The Rules of the Game*).

As if to make the contrast between a European and an American version of love and marriage crystal clear, when in Hollywood exile – the year is 1946 – Renoir made a distant remake of *The Rules of the Game*: *Diary of a Chambermaid*. Point-for-point, the irresolutions of the earlier French-made film are made into resolutions in Hollywood. Set in nineteenth-century France, a love match is made between a working-class domestique, Celestine (Paulette Godard), and the aristocratic Georges (Hurd Hatfield), who, significantly, has turned his back on the worldview upheld by his parents and his class. His overbearing mother (Judith Anderson) scorns everything the French Revolution aspired to – most especially the aspiration to be rid of the aristocratic class – and she is, at the end of the film, rendered powerless. The contrast with Robert's re-establishment of power at the end of *The Rules of the Game* (as I see it) is clear. The upper classes are painted as mildly decadent in *The Rules of the Game* but they are still capable of running the show. In *Diary of a Chambermaid* the upper classes are depicted as entirely decadent and without any saving graces – epitomised by the master of the house, Henry (Reginald Owen), and the master of the neighbouring estate, Captain Mauger (Burgess Meredith), both of whom are reduced to veritable childlike caricatures whose lack of any connection with social reality offers a demonstration of Renoir's clear disdain. Furthermore, it is no poacher (e.g., the Marceau of *Rules*) or romantic hero (André Jurieu) who is murdered in *Diary of a Chambermaid*. Rather, it is a member of the aristocracy – Captain Mauger – who is murdered by the valet, Joseph (Francis Lederer), as though Renoir is perhaps fantasising that some sort of justice would have been served up in *The Rules of the Game* if Schumacher had simply decided to do away with Robert instead of pursuing a member of his own class, Marceau. Finally, the setting of the climactic scene of conflict between lovers once again in a glass-walled greenhouse – where George and Joseph trade blows over Celestine – signals that *Diary of a Chambermaid* aspires to commentary on the earlier film. All I mean to say is that Renoir could find a comedy in Hollywood where he could find only tragedy while based in Europe. The promise or pact delivered by a film like *Diary of a Chambermaid* is one that declares that the building of a new society – a revolutionary society – will be one that allows or enables or is based on a version of love grounded on freedom, equality and mutual understanding. Granted, the stakes of any kind of mutual understanding are worn very lightly in *Diary of a Chambermaid* – its characterisations are hardly deep or complex – but it does make its American dream a direct opposite of the tragedy that befalls *The Rules of the Game*.

Smiles of a Summer Night

In a short essay written on Ingmar Bergman's *Smiles of a Summer Night* (1955), most explicitly on its connections with Shakespeare's *The Winter's Tale* and a theatrical production of that play directed by Bergman, Cavell speculates that he might have explored other aspects of Bergman's film, one of which would be 'to track the connection of *Smiles* with Renoir's *The Rules of the Game*' (Cavell 2005c, 197). In many ways, what I want to do here is to track the possible directions in which Cavell's thoughts might have gone, had he undertaken such a task. At the same time, however, I want to regard *Smiles* as an entry point into thinking about Bergman's films more generally, and it will be by way of those films that I'll more accurately begin to trace the themes that will be key for the other films and filmmakers examined in this book.

My reading of *The Rules of the Game* has tracked its plotting of relations between old marriage and new marriage, with the rules of society in the end reigning supreme. I have also claimed that *Diary of a Chambermaid* offers something of an antidote to the pessimism or tragedy of *The Rules of the Game*. Why, it is worth asking, does Cavell find so much of value in Bergman's *Smiles of a Summer Night*, and why does he mention it in the same breath as *The Rules of the Game* on at least two occasions?[1] First and foremost, I think it fair to assume that where Renoir's film ends in death, Bergman's film ends with a heartening affirmation of life. This is to say that the utter lack of understanding and conversation in *The Rules of the Game* are reversed, such that conversation and the steps taken towards inventing a world together are made into accomplishments in *Smiles of a Summer Night*. This is especially the case for the central pair of Desirée Armfeldt (Eva Dahlbeck) and Fredrik Egerman (Gunnar Björnstrand). If we are matching pairs across the films, then it is clear that these characters match the Christine and André pairing of the earlier film, right down to the fact that Desirée, early in *Smiles*, affirms her friendship with Fredrik in much the same way as Christine affirms her friendship with André. Only with a significant difference: Desirée's admission of friendship is made in private, just between herself and Fredrik; so here, in *Smiles*, the candour of intimate friendship is paramount. Suffice it to recall Emerson's claim, noted in the previous chapter, that 'Two may talk and one may hear, but three cannot take part in a conversation of the most sincere and searching sort' (Emerson 1898, 54). In *The Rules of the Game*, by contrast, Christine's declaration of friendship with André is made in front of a gathered audience. This is a social declaration made for the sake of that society rather than a confession made to an intimate other. And so the basic distinction between *The Rules of the Game* and *Smiles of a Summer Night* can be set: where the former grants priority to the social realm and the 'rules of society', the latter film rewards the intimacy and friendship – call it love – that is staked by the couple, 'by themselves together'.

The conversations between Fredrik and Desirée are central to their rediscovery of each other. They had engaged in an affair some years before, following the death of Fredrik's first wife (the film is set, so the script tells me, in 1901; see Bergman 1960, 5). It is only now, when Fredrik is two years into his second marriage with a young bride, Anne (Ulla Jacobsson), that he has met Desirée again. Fredrik admits to Desirée upon re-meeting her that she's been the only person to whom he has ever been able to reveal himself 'warts and all'. When reconciled at the film's end, Desirée reminds him of this: candour or sincerity or honesty have won the day, warts and all.

We can presume, if Cavell wishes to call *Smiles of a Summer Night* a remarriage comedy, that the stakes of remarriage are explicitly played out between Desirée and Fredrik. This couple achieves (or begins to achieve) what Cavell calls acknowledgment. Most simply this means that a self and another person can agree upon the things that make up a world. The achievement of acknowledgment, happening for Cavell so often as it does in literature or film between the members of a romantic couple (traditionally a man and a woman) can often only be an achievement built on an original failure – hence for Cavell the importance of *remarriage*. If a first marriage is a failure of acknowledgment, then a remarriage offers the possibility of success, a pursuit of happiness. This is what happens for Fredrik's relationship with Desirée. During their first affair he had denied or distorted his relationship with her. He had not recognised or valued her.[2] He admits, for example, that he had slept with other women during their time together, and we learn that Desirée had left him on the basis of feeling herself unloved and unknown. Fredrik in turn realises that his second marriage is utterly unsatisfactory. Anne is much too young for him and, as such, she aspires to creating a world for herself that is decidedly different from his. Furthermore, as though to emphasise the film's status as comedy, after two years of marriage they are yet to have sex!

There are other successful love matches in *Smiles of a Summer Night*. The housemaid, the sexually active and provocative Petra (Harriet Andersson), is promised in marriage at the end of the film to the coachman, Frid (Åke Fridell), who has presented to us the 'three smiles' of summer nights. (Suffice it to say here that the love matches made in this film do not jump across class lines, though it is notable that Desirée is a stage actress and a woman of 'easy virtue', as the clerks who work for Egerman put it in the film's opening scene.) Another match: Fredrik's wife, Anne, flees with none other than Fredrik's son from his first marriage, Henrik (Björn Bjelvenstam). Cavell makes an important point of this, that the flight into happiness is no guarantee of happiness but that it is nevertheless a flight towards the possibility of happiness. 'This marriage or elopement of young lovers', writes Cavell, 'shows true marriage to require the destruction of false marriage – a reckless dash into the unknown' (Cavell 2005c, 201).

These happy (re)marriages are contrasted with a false marriage between Count Malcolm (Jarl Kulle) and his wife, Charlotte (Margit Carlquist). Cavell calls this a traditional or conventional marriage, 'precisely the state that the women of these textures are seeking an alternative to' (2005c, 203). And this false marriage is played with grand amusement, especially via the count's insistence that a marriage involves both a wife and mistress, and it is not insignificant to note that his current mistress is none other than Desirée; she breaks off the affair partway through the film. Needless to point out that I spent some time in the previous chapter discussing the ways in which 'old marriage' encourages the formation of a 'couple +1', and Count Malcolm's affairs demonstrate this structure once again. The shadow of the Marquis Robert de la Chesnaye looms large here, for the count balances his romances and fills his life with numerous divertissements: skittle shooting, croquet, military service; all so many ways of avoiding love and acknowledgment in the same manner as Robert's automata and nick-nacks in *The Rules of the Game*. In such ways is a false marriage pitted against the possibilities of a true marriage. (I confess I might be overplaying the 'false marriage' between the count and Charlotte. By the end of *Smiles of the Summer Night*, we are supposed to believe that all of the couples lives happily ever after and we are supposed to accept that this couple, too, is as happy as can be. But I cannot avoid the sense that this is a marriage that avoids acknowledgment and merely concedes to fate.)

Smiles of a Summer Night as a comedy of remarriage

Cavell conveniently tracks the connections between *Smiles of a Summer Night* and the conventions of remarriage comedy. They can be listed, more or less, as (a) an 'estranged pair finding themselves again'; (b) a series of reflections on faithfulness; (c) the alternation of day and night; and (d) a move from town to country. For (a), Fredrik and Desirée are an estranged pair who find themselves again. For (b), *Smiles of a Summer Night* is full to the brim with conversations and discourses on faithfulness, whether this be via Fredrik and Desirée, Malcolm and Charlotte, or even by way of Henrik, Petra and Frid. Point (c) shows us that the troubles of the day are resolved by the magic of a summer night. For (d), in terms Cavell borrows from Northrop Frye's notion of a 'green world' in Shakespeare's plays (see Cavell 1981, 49–51), the move from town to country occurs when the action moves to Mme Armfeldt's country house, with this point being a clear note of similarity with *The Rules of the Game*: Mme Armfedlt's country house mirrors de la Chesnaye's country estate, La Colinière. Cavell will also note significant differences between *Smiles* and the remarriage conventions; for example, that the heroine's mother – here, Mme Armfeldt – plays a key role in advising Desirée and in manipulating events towards an outcome (she is the harbinger of the magic potion of seduction), whereas such a role of advisor is typically taken by the father in the Hollywood comedies.[3]

I do not wish to constrain *Smiles of a Summer Night* merely to the terms Cavell has set for it. Rather, alongside what Cavell has mapped out in the relations between *Smiles* and the remarriage comedies, I would also like to explore a number of other key issues relating to *Smiles* and to Bergman's films more generally that cannot entirely be accounted for by the remarriage framework. These will become central concerns for some other films made by Bergman which I examine in the next chapter, especially *The Passion of Anna* (1969). These points also provide some further themes that will be expanded upon in other, subsequent chapters of this book. The points are: (1) conversations between women; (2) reflections on loneliness; (3) sexuality; and, finally, (4) the origin of love. I shall deal with these one at a time.

Conversations between women

It is not only a conversation between Desirée and her mother that drives the narrative of *Smiles* toward its resolution; rather, two other conversations between women are of utmost significance. First of all, there is Anne's conversation with Charlotte in which they swap stories of their husbands' infidelities. Anne here discovers that Fredrik had spent much of the previous evening with Desirée, while Charlotte too confronts her knowledge of her husband's affair with the same woman. A streak of cruelty dominates Charlotte's reflections here, for she declares, 'I hate him, I hate him!' even as, at one and the same time, she also admits, 'I still love him.' Whatever the consequences of this – and we know by the end of the film that Anne will flee from her marriage to Fredrik while Charlotte will remain trapped in her marriage to Count Malcolm – we here have a conversation between women about the men they (think they) love in ways that are more or less absent from the Hollywood remarriage comedies. Amanda Bonner (Katharine Hepburn) shares one or two conversations with other women in *Adam's Rib* (1949), but these are of little consequence. Of major significance are the points of communication between Helen Morrison (Barbara O'Neill) and Stella (Barbara Stanwyck) in *Stella Dallas* (1937), one of the films Cavell calls a 'melodrama of the unknown woman'. There is no need to go into the details of those communications here, other than to point out that these women – Mrs Morrison and Stella Dallas – develop an understanding between themselves that defies or transcends the world of men. In many ways it is the exceptional understanding – or 'knowingness' – of these women that allows *Stella Dallas* to reach its emancipatory resolution, certainly as Cavell reads it. Conceived in this way, it is conversation between women that grants them something of an escape from the world of men as well as a resistance to the kinds of worlds men seem destined to trap women in. We need look no further than Fredrik's trapping of Anne, or Count Malcolm's trapping of Charlotte, to consider such entrapments at play in *Smiles of a Summer Night*.

The mode of 'conversation between women' in *Smiles* is later repeated between Charlotte and Desirée when they plan to teach the men in this film a lesson.[4] As they hatch their plan, Desirée states that 'Men seldom know what's best for them. We have to put them on the right track.' Her words here evoke the earlier image of Fredrik examining himself in a mirror while wearing a nightgown and nightcap, declaring to himself and Desirée, 'How can a woman ever love a man?' In short, if one of the key traits of Cavell's remarriage comedies is that it is most typically the woman who will require education from the man, then these gender roles are reversed in *Smiles* and we shall discover that this is true more generally for Bergman's films: it is the men who are for the most part clueless and who need a woman or women to educate them. Against Cavell, Glitre contends that such instances generally apply to the comedies of remarriage. For the most part it is the men who are dunces – the cases of Jerry in *The Awful Truth* and Charles Pike (Henry Fonda) in *The Lady Eve* (directed by Preston Sturges, 1941) being prime examples.

It is worth noting that there is a conversation between women of note in *The Rules of the Game*. Following the day of the hunt, Geneviève is resolved to leave, for she has made a spirited goodbye to Robert. (Readers will remember that Robert has been having an affair with Geneviève, but he is determined to break it off so that he can pursue an honest and faithful marriage with Christine.) As Geneviève is packing her bags, none other than Christine pays her a visit. Christine insists on frankness and asks Geneviève, 'Have I tried to thwart your relations with my husband?' Geneviève is surprised to hear that Christine knows of the affair and they converse in a light-hearted way, joking about Robert's various habits. This trait of conversations between women will be prevalent in some of the auteurs investigated in the remainder of this book (in Antonioni, Varda, Rohmer …).

Finally, in *Smiles of a Summer Night* there is also a short conversation between Anne and Petra early in the film. Here Petra advises Anne on the pleasures and virtues of sexuality and wickedness: 'I'll give three cheers for all things wicked!' she says. As with the other conversations between women in *Smiles of a Summer Night*, this scene demonstrates the ways in which women can articulate their own destinies away from the follies and vanities of men.

Loneliness

Near the beginning of *Smiles of a Summer Night*, as they speak of friendship, Desirée declares to Fredrik that he has never had any friends other than himself. He responds by saying that much the same goes for her. These are people who therefore remain unknown to others: they have kept themselves contained within themselves, within their narcissism, their loneliness. These declarations of egotism or narcissism come on the back of a claim made just moments before by Desirée in which she has said to Fredrik, 'I guess you know what loneliness is too.' The relationship between loneliness, narcissism and the bonds between one person and another will become major features of Bergman's works. It is signalled in *Smiles* somewhat lightly, but in many of Bergman's other films it will become a central theme – indeed, it is central for the film examined in the following chapter, *The Passion of Anna*. Readers will also note that arguments relating to aloneness and isolation emerged in the opening chapters of this book, where it was claimed that two possible ways out of 'aloneness' were by virtue of what Cavell calls *acknowledgment* or by way of what Leo Bersani calls *connectedness*. These themes will be returned to throughout this book. Needless to say that for *Smiles of a Summer Night* it is acknowledgment that emerges as a solution to aloneness, whether this be for Desirée or Fredrik, Henrik or Anne, or Petra and Frid. Certainly the film's central pair, Fredrik and Desirée, construct their 'getting back together again' on the basis of long conversations, arguments and reflections.

Sexuality

The theme or concept of virginity is crucial for the Hollywood remarriage comedies. As Cavell manages it, the women in these comedies are sexually knowledgeable: not one of them is to any degree chaste. 'In comedies of remarriage the *fact* of virginity is evidently not what is at stake,' he writes. 'Yet', he continues, 'is the *concept* of virginity still at stake' (Cavell 1981, 53). Cavell figures that this is the case for the reinvention or recreation of the women in these films, that they must be, as it were, 'cleansed' and rendered anew. Cavell will be astute enough to call these 'parodies' of chastity and its loss (Cavell 1981, 54), and he sees parody as a necessary element for the rebirths of the women in these films and the subsequent establishment of a union figured as a remarriage.

Pretty much nothing in this realm pertains to Bergman's films. If anything, it is the wanton gratuitousness of sexuality that throws everything related to the virtues of chastity and 'intactness' into the dark ages (the horrors of *The Virgin Spring* (1960) can attest to this). More or less all of Bergman's characters are sexually active in ways that require no parody or metaphor, and typically these characters are also entirely unconcerned with the kind of social morality that seemed relevant for the earlier Hollywood comedies. Of course, to some extent the American comedies knew all about this anyway – note the quips between Jerry and Armand in *The Awful Truth* about the 'Continental mind', not to mention that I find films like *The Lady Eve*, *It Happened One Night* (1934) and *The Awful Truth* to be brimming with a sexual vibrancy that playfully avoids explicitness.

And yet, Anne, of course, *really is* a virgin in *Smiles of a Summer Night*. She is, as it were, the exception that proves the rule. She is the sign of utter unknownness, the fact of her virginity mirroring the fact that her husband, Fredrik, essentially has no knowledge of her because there is likewise no acknowledgment of her either. Anne's 'reckless dash into the unknown' with Henrik is therefore a first step along the road to knowledge and acknowledgment, upon which road, no doubt, Anne's fact of virginity will be undone.

It is somewhere here that the Scandinavian Protestantism of Bergman, parodied in *Smiles* by Henrik's constant reprisals of Luther, delivers a marked contrast with American Puritanism – or its parody – in the Hollywood comedies. I do not know what to make of this other than to say it is there. Suffice it to point out that while Bergman pursued the earthy sexuality of *Summer with Monika* (1952), the Hollywood scene was still parodying virginity by way of Doris Day in the late 1950s and 1960s (in *Pillow Talk* (1959) or *Lover Come Back* (1961) for example),[5] and those films are post-war descendants of the remarriage genre, this time with the fact of virginity writ large, no matter how ironic that writing may be. Glitre is again brilliant on these films. She argues that in these films – which she calls 'sex comedies' – the stakes of speaking together and mutual understanding, central to the 1930s comedies, have been replaced by irreconcilable differences and an inability to communicate. And yet, even amid all this, these films remain comedies, with happy endings that fail any tests of mutual recognition or acknowledgment. 'In these cases', Glitre writes, 'the only diegetic explanation for the couple's union is the magic of "true love" – despite the fact that their relationship has been based on deceit and false impressions' (Glitre 2006, 157).

Nothing can signal the lack of 'intactness' in *Smiles* more than the brute fact that Desirée has a child, a fact that is never a possibility for the American comedies (the couples in those films are destined themselves to become children, so Cavell reckons). The son is named Fredrik so as to leave us in no doubt as to who the child's father is. But, of course, Desirée's sexual knowledge – as well as Petra's – is contrasted with the naive virginity of Anne. Ultimately, sexuality is foregrounded in Bergman's films in ways that it is not (or could not be) in the Hollywood films. Of course, much of this has to do with the imposition of the Production Code in 1933, and one has only to go back to the great pre-Code chamber comedies of Ernst Lubitsch – say, *The Love Parade* (1929) or *One Hour with You* (1932) – to discover a world not distant from that of *Smiles of a Summer Night*.

Where does love come from?

The origin of love

A direct question Cavell never asks of the remarriage comedies (or of Shakespeare's comedies) is: *what is love?* He gives something of a reflection on what love 'is' in *The Claim of Reason* by calling it 'a best case of acknowledgment' (Cavell 1979b, 477) – a point I have already noted – but he refrains entirely from positing an 'origin' of love or from defining any 'thing' that sparks love into being. He nevertheless offers some hints at what love is in his reflections on *Smiles of a Summer Night*. The first is his claim of a connection between this film and the Hollywood comedies in relation to what he calls the 'economy of love'. '[T]he economy of love', he writes, 'in those American comedies [is] measured in a pair's discovery of a mutual language and in their claiming to have known one another forever, or to have grown up together' (Cavell 2005c, 202–3). Cavell rather fortuitously links this in *Smiles of a Summer Night* with the admissions made by both Anne and Henrik to each other that 'I loved you all along'.

This is a point worth pursuing. In the comedies of remarriage, the admissions that 'I have loved you all along' or that 'we have known each other forever' are most elaborately figured in *It Happened One Night* and *The Lady Eve*. In the former it is evoked by Peter Warne's (Clark Gable) dream of a south sea island which comes as a response to Ellie's (Claudette Colbert) question, 'Have you ever been in love Peter?' Peter gets to his response:

> I saw an island in the Pacific once. Never been able to forget it. That's where I'd like to take her. But she'd have to be the sort of girl that'd jump in the surf with me and love it as much as I did. You know, those nights when you and the moon and the water all become one and you feel that you're part of something big and marvelous ... Boy, if I could ever find a girl who's hungry for those things. (See Cavell 1981, 97)

And so this fantasy evocation of love is indeed the fantasy that seals Ellie's love for him: she is a girl who's hungry for those things.

The situation in *The Lady Eve* presents a hinge on which that entire film might fall. If the stakes of acknowledgment are supposed to be seriousness and sincerity – Peter's words to Ellie in *It Happened One Night* are nothing if not passionate and heartfelt; and I have already noted that Desirée and Fredrik refind one another in *Smiles of a Summer Night* on the basis of honesty – then the insincerity of Preston Sturges's mockingness in *The Lady Eve* would seem to threaten the whole enterprise. Nowhere is this made more manifest than in the character of Charles. In this film, Charles first declares his love to Jean (Barbara Stanwyck), but their relationship founders. Later he finds another woman who looks remarkably like Jean, but this woman tells him that she is none other than the Lady Eve Sidwich (played again by Barbara Stanwyck). How can Charles fail to realise that Jean and Eve are 'one and the same dame', which is to say that if we are to believe that he does not realise this, then all claims to seriousness in this film must be thrown out of the window? This threat of insincerity reaches its crescendo in the fantasy reminiscence Charles recounts not only to Jean, but also subsequently to Eve. The speech itself is corny, to say the least, but a few select phrases stand out. He states rhapsodically that 'every time I've looked at you ... it wasn't only here I saw you; you seemed to go way back'. He continues, 'I know that isn't clear, but I saw you here and at the same time further away' – and he explains that this vision takes him back to childhood. And all of this allows Charles to build to his climax, 'that I've always loved you ... I mean I've never loved anyone but you'. And so, in *Smiles of a Summer Night*, Anne and Henrik's declaration that they have 'loved each other all along' will be Bergman's version of what the remarriage comedies had set out. Charles adds another point. He tells Jean/Eve that 'what I see inside I'll never be able to put into words ...'. He means here, I reckon, that he sees something inside Jean/Eve that captivates him so much that it is beyond what it is possible to express. The declarations we find here, that 'I have always loved you', seem to be ways of trying to capture this unsayable aspect of what love is.

What is at stake in these exchanges? Cavell tries to add it all up in rather complex ways, especially as they pertain to *The Lady Eve*. He argues that, if we believe that Charles cannot tell that Jean and Eve are one and the same, then we have been as gullible as we have presumed Charles to be. A sense of this whole charade, then, is that Charles decides *to play along with it*. In other words, he knows Jean and Eve are one and same dame, but he wants to play along with this game of deception. Why does Charles do this? Because playing along with Jean/Eve's game of deception is his one way of getting back in touch with and winning the love of this woman, whatever her name is (see Cavell 2004, 309). Additionally, the point Cavell makes is that we know films and their characters are not 'real', that they are deceiving us, but we can play along with this deception in ways that can be stimulating and rewarding.

I don't know quite how to phrase what I want to say except to state that Charles here *must be willing to be deceived*, he must be *willing to be duped* – and it is only this deception or duplicity that will lead him towards love. The added point to consider here is that such deception has also been said to pertain to the cinema: that it delivers nothing but illusions by which we are said to be seduced, deluded and led astray. Needless to say that I find such formulations unhelpful (is it *us*? or is it *they* who are deceived? – 'they' typically being the masses of gullible audiences who enjoy popular films ...?). All I mean to infer here is that something like the conditions of love mirrors the conditions of cinema (see Cavell 1981, 62). Charles's willingness to be deceived does *not* thereby lead him to deception or illusion or falsity. On the contrary, it leads him in the end to love, to 'true love', however such a thing might be defined.

Fantasy, love, psychoanalysis

The most obvious term for all of this is *fantasy*. Charles's fantasy is that he's never loved anyone else but Jean or Eve (or whoever she is), every bit as much as Peter's fantasy in *It Happened One Night* is of life on a Pacific island that he would wish to share with a girl who's hungry for those things. I realise this is a tremendously roundabout way of declaring that *fantasy is the origin of love*. It is a claim Cavell never makes, but it will return at various points throughout this book. I can offer the reader some general guidance at this point, guidance that comes by way of the writings of Jacques Lacan. Lacan more or less defines love in terms of deception. 'But one has to admit', writes Lacan, 'that if there is one domain in which, in discourse, deception has some chance of success, it is certainly love that provides its model' (Lacan 1977a, 133). For Lacan, love emerges when I fantasise something that is 'inside' the other person which attracts me to him or her. In his seminar on Transference, Lacan calls this something 'inside' the other the *ágalma* (he gets the word from Plato's *Symposium*; see Lacan 2015, 135–48), though the logic of the *ágalma* is related to the more famous formulation of the *objet a*. Where the *objet a* presents a general formula of desire, the *ágalma* is more closely related to the desire one has for another person. In its simplest form, for Lacan, love is the product of a fantasy one person projects onto or into another. If the other person then makes this fantasy into some sort of reality – if the fantasy is fulfilled – we have love.

Why does Lacan call this a deception? He merely assures us that love is something that has no existence outside the human discourses and schemas that human beings have created for it: if love exists, then it exists only as a product of human discourse; it has been invented and 'made up'. To that degree it is a deception – it is not 'natural'. To square the circle, if the fantasy of love is fulfilled – Peter's fantasy of finding 'a girl who's hungry for those things' or Charles's fantasy that he has loved Jean forever – if this fantasy becomes a reality, then a state of what Cavell calls acknowledgment will have been achieved. On all these points I do not see Cavell and psychoanalysis or Lacan as being at odds. Rather, Cavell's defence of acknowledgment sits side by side with Lacan's sense that love is a matter of deception. The resolutions of the comedies of remarriage are to a large degree founded in deception. If the couples in these films find their ways to the truth by means of lying or deceiving, then this is one way of saying that the best grounds we have for the truth are those that begin as deceptions.

From one perspective we might wish to declare that love can never be real or true. Certainly we might say that love can never be proven. But to say that there is no such thing as a pure and perfect love is akin to declaring that there is no pure or perfect knowledge. Cavell makes these kinds of claims central to his accounts of scepticism. For Cavell, the way to overcome the limitations imposed upon knowledge by scepticism is by way of acknowledgment. Does the world exist? Do other minds exist? Well, I cannot definitively prove that such things exist, but if I can agree with another person that they exist – *this* person, *this* world we can share – then I might as well accept that something like another mind – *this* person – and this world exist. What is the alternative? To declare that they do not exist?

I have tried to argue that truth and honesty win the day in *Smiles of a Summer Night*. Desirée and Fredrik manage to reconcile themselves, warts and all. Doesn't this suggest a love based on some kind of true discovery, that Desirée and Fredrik find true love? Surely such a love cannot be based on deception? Let us backtrack. Let us begin by asking why Fredrik has married his young wife, Anne, in the first place. Cavell notes the importance of the photographic portraits Fredrik has of Anne that he collects from a professional photographer at the very beginning of the film (some of these depict him and Anne together). On the back of this Cavell makes remarks about the ontology of film reminiscent of arguments from *The World Viewed* – that is, that the photographic ontology of film offers us projections of the world. The connection he fails to make, a more important one as far as I'm concerned, is that Fredrik is much more satisfied with the *image* of Anne than with her flesh and blood. He is in love with a *fantasy image* of her. These photographs are indeed deceptions inasmuch as they give rise to Fredrik's desire (such would be a Lacanian perspective on the issue – the fantasy image is the *ágalma*). What these photographs put at stake, therefore, and certainly one of the reasons Fredrik is drawn to them – he examines them, in private, on two other occasions during the film – is that they give a clear expression of his isolation, his aloneness. These are very much aspects of what Cavell has called modern privacy or anonymity, the sense in which modern human beings are doomed to look *out at* the world as if from behind a barrier or through a screen, like a movie screen, as Cavell so evocatively argues (see Cavell 1979a, 24). This barrier is called subjectivity. In short, these photographs offer a demonstration of the ways in which we – modern humans – are now convinced that we cannot have access to 'things-in-themselves' but instead are fated only to own subjective views of things: those imperfect organs of sense and intellect are all we have. And we additionally know how deceptive our minds, eyes, ears and the rest can be.... Fredrik looks upon those photographs as though searching for proof of his love, as though he might discover there what is hidden inside Anne that attracts him to her.

The lesson to be learned here is that *deceptions really can be deceptions*: they will not always – and perhaps rarely – give rise to any kind of truth. If Fredrik is deluding himself into believing his love for Anne is genuine, then it is as though he cannot discover any confirmation of this love apart from the photographs he has of her. Much of the film will thus transpire as Fredrik's coming to an understanding that he is kidding himself in this regard, that his attraction to Anne resides solely at the level of a fantasy that will not find any confirmation in reality – it is a fantasy that will not be acknowledged, as it were. Thus, if the origin of love is deception, then that origin can also lead merely to further deception, to isolation and unknownness and, certainly in the fictional works Cavell examines, to melodrama and tragedy.

Let me be clear on this point. If I have claimed that the origin of love is fantasy – the fantasy I have of another person or of what is inside the other person – then either that fantasy can be affirmed by the other person or the quest for confirmation can fail. It can lead to avoidance (as Cavell finds in *King Lear*) or denial (as he finds in *Othello*), rather than affirmation. These are deceptions, but calling them deceptions is to some degree unhelpful. Some deceptions can be tremendously worthwhile, whereas others will be insufferably painful. I think the way to characterise positive deception is to say that they are the kinds of deceptions that can be agreed upon. If I can agree with you that this flower is coloured red, then for all intents and purposes it *is* red. And there is no true red in nature: rather, humans have invented a colour they have agreed to call red. Call that a deception. But with such deceptions, a world can be constructed. And yet, if I call that flower red, and you call it pink, then our agreeing upon a world becomes stuck. I don't want to dwell on this example other than by noting an analogy with the state or condition of experience of love. If I can agree with you that we love each other, then that is enough for us to begin with. Out of our fantasising what that state or condition is, by deceiving ourselves into occupying that experience, perhaps we will be successful in creating a world that contains this love as part of it. There is no other way to make love than to make it.

Such deceptions may well lead to love, and *Smiles of a Summer Night* is optimistic enough to offer a 'positive' series of deceptions. If Fredrik with his photographs of Anne gives us one series, then that is not the only route deception takes. Desirée and Charlotte contrive a deception or series of deceptions that bring *Smiles of a Summer Night* to its conclusion. At the heart of all this is the question, posed as something of a game as the gathered party have dinner, of whether it is men who seduce women, or whether it might indeed be possible for a woman to seduce a man. The count is convinced of the former, that is, that it is men who are active in such matters, while Fredrik immediately concedes that this is not the case at all; rather, he says, 'I think that we men are always seduced'. And so Charlotte bets that she can seduce Fredrik 'in less than a quarter of an hour'. The mix of all this – and it is nothing less than a game, again in ways that recall the masquerade shenanigans of *The Rules of the Game* – is aided and abetted by the magic potion that has been infused into the dinner wine that gives it powers of seduction: a drop of milk from the breasts of a woman who has just given birth to her first child and a drop of 'seed' from a young stallion. When it does transpire that Fredrik and Charlotte exchange a kiss (well, at any rate, they disappear together into a garden pavilion – again recalling the glasshouse of *The Rules of the Game*), the count demands satisfaction. An innocent duel is played out between the count and Fredrik, with the result that Desirée and Fredrik are reconciled, while the count and Charlotte decide to remain together, even if the terms of that togetherness are strained to the last.

But what has been proven or demonstrated by this game or bet or deception or seduction? Does the active side win here, or the passive? The male or the female? The Cavellian lesson, as I take it, is that one cannot force love, which is another way of saying that love is something that cannot be possessed, not something that can be won, as in a military manoeuvre (the film mocks the count on this score). As Frid, the coachman, eloquently states near the end of the film, there are myriad things one can *do* with love, but one can never *have* it. In other words, if the count treats love like an object he can possess, then by contrast Fredrik's final position is one that is utterly passive, reduced as he is to an almost childlike status under the generous protection and motherly reassurance. 'You had a great fall, Fredrik Egerman,' Desirée says to him, and his response is, 'Don't leave me.'

Conclusions

There are parallels here in the distinction between the active and the passive with what Cavell will eventually articulate as a distinction between tragedy and comedy. Tragedy occurs when *one tries to possess a love object*. Comedy ensues, by contrast, when one assumes *a passive role towards the beloved*. Acknowledgment, by definition, cannot be forced upon another: I cannot force another person to acknowledge me (or love me). Rather, in cases of acknowledgment I must be passive, though I must also remain open to the other's advance, I must open myself up to them, be prepared to make myself known to them, as Cavell puts it. Many of the folds and creases of these concepts emerge in the key Shakespearian plays for Cavell, in *King Lear* and *Othello* on the tragic side, and in *The Winter's Tale* in the direction of comedy. The jealousies of Othello and Leontes are mirrored: each suspects his wife of infidelity. Othello finds no way out of this jealousy until it is too late, while Leontes is stopped short and is thereby remorseful, with the result that the acceptance of acknowledgment in *The Winter's Tale* is won only via a miracle of extraordinary theatrical proportions. Hermione, the wife whom Leontes has shunned to such a degree that she has turned to stone, is miraculously brought back to life at the play's end – call this 'deception'. Cavell, as we have already seen, tries to define love as 'a best case of acknowledgment', and we can reckon that the outcomes of such best cases are comedic, whether this is in *The Winter's Tale* or in the comedies of remarriage, in *Smiles of a Summer Night* or indeed in life itself. Tragedy shows us the opposite: it is the *failure* of a best case of acknowledgment. Such a claim will take much of the remainder of this book to be worked through.

For now, the best way to proceed is to say that tragedy ensues when one refuses any curtailing of one's own narcissism. What this means is that, in such cases, one's relationship to the other person – say, Othello's relationship with Desdemona, Leontes' with Hermione, Lear's with Cordelia, or Count Malcolm's with Charlotte – refuses to take the other's point of view into account. One way to put this might be to say that, in such situations, the other is reduced to the confines of the self, and Cavell goes close to writing such things. He writes, 'the failure to acknowledge a best case of the other is a denial of that other, presaging the death of that other' (Cavell 1979b, 493). The gist of what Cavell is aiming for in his reading of *Othello* is that Othello feels that if he gives too much of himself to Desdemona – that is, if he allows himself to 'make himself known' to her, if he 'opens up' to her, as it were – then she will in some way come to possess him, or at least she will take away some part of him. This will to some extent destroy his narcissism, his sense of self. It is a defence mechanism, on Othello's part, a refusal to be acknowledged and thus a denial of the other person as such (a similar thing occurs with Lear's avoidance of Cordelia). On the back of the fear that he will in some way be possessed by Desdemona, that he will thus be passive, that his sense of self will be destroyed or that his sense of independence will be shattered so as to reduce him to a state of dependency – for all of this, Othello pleases himself to accept Iago's promptings and to convince himself of Desdemona's infidelity. Cavell states (again evocatively), 'The violence in masculine knowing, explicitly associated with jealousy, seems to interpret the ambition of knowledge as that of exclusive possession, call it private property' (Cavell 2003, 10).

In *Smiles of a Summer Night* I think we can believe that Fredrik begins the film in a similar state of mind – which is not to say that he is in any way jealous. Rather, it is to say that he has created a series of relationships for himself that will uphold his narcissism and independence. He has entered into a marriage with Anne that makes of her a possession – and here we can posit a long history of the 'circulation of women' as central to traditional conceptions of marriage, conceptions that a modern understanding of marriage is determined to transcend – so that Fredrik will never have to make himself known to her, as it were, and the unknownness between this couple is foregrounded here by their lack of sexual intimacy. And we can also reckon that his relationship with Anne is something like a continuation of his past relationship with Desirée (though with Desirée there had been sexual intimacy, of course): that Desirée too was something like a possession who would not dent Fredrik's narcissistic carapace. He tells her, for example, that even though he had other lovers, Desirée was the 'headquarters'. When, at the end of the film, he is reduced to passivity, to a kind of dependency, then it is only here that something approaching a 'best case of acknowledgment' becomes a possibility, 'warts and all'. Cavell puts this kind of thing evocatively as a summation of his thoughts on Shakespeare's *Antony and Cleopatra*: all of this is 'a conclusion that must be conferred, given, not one that I can cause or determine on the basis of my senses. My senses go out; satisfaction happens in my absence; only in it, by it.' It requires absence, Cavell states, 'absolute passiveness' (Cavell 2003, 35).

We might also see Count Malcolm as a character who refuses this passiveness, for he has a collection of women in much the same way as he has a collection of hobbies and games, all of which are so many ways to ensure he will never have to make himself known to another. His narcissism does not lead to tragedy in *Smiles of a Summer Night* – unless one makes the continuation of his marriage to Charlotte a tragedy, and such a case might be well warranted – but the themes of narcissism, jealousy, possession and eventually of isolation, unknownness and tragedy arise throughout Bergman's works. These will be topics for the following chapter.

Notes

1 In Cavell 1981, 166 and Cavell 2005c, 197.
2 Cavell puts such issues in this way in 1979b, 428.
3 This is a bone of contention for Glitre: yes, the father is important for *It Happened One Night* and *The Lady Eve*, but not for the other comedies; and in *The Awful Truth* it is the aunt of the woman who advises her. See Glitre 2006, 52–3.
4 Cavell charts the connections between *Smiles* and Shakespeare's *The Winter's Tale*, but the scheming of the women here seems to echo that of Rosalind and Celia in *As You Like It* much more forcefully, while the use of a magic potion seems a clear reference to *A Midsummer Night's Dream*.
5 On these points see Jeffers McDonald 2013, 24–5.

Chapter 4

Ingmar Bergman: comedies and tragedies

4.1 The end of conversation: Anna Fromm and Andreas Winkelman (Liv Ullmann and Max von Sydow) in *The Passion of Anna* (Ingmar Bergman, 1969)

Smiles of a Summer Night stands out among Bergman's films as a light, farcical chamber comedy. It stands out because to a large degree it avoids the agonies and depths of despair that mark so many of his films – *Winter Light* (1962), *Persona* (1966), *Cries and Whispers* (1972), *Autumn Sonata* (1978) and so on. And even within the orbit of Bergman films with optimistic conclusions – say, *To Joy* (1950), *Summer Interlude* (1951) or *Scenes from a Marriage* (1973) – those optimistic conclusions typically come only at the cost of extraordinary moments of sadness or anger or loss or disappointment. And *Smiles of a Summer Night,* made at a time when Bergman was still finding his cinematic voice so that *Smiles* can be grouped with other works of historical romantic comedy such as *Waiting Women* (1952) and *A Lesson in Love* (1954), has very little of the harsh negatives that might be described as Bergmanesque: its battles are won with minimal upset and its tone and characters are hardly introspective in the complex ways Bergman explores elsewhere. This is probably a way of saying that *Smiles of a Summer Night* meets up with the American comedies of remarriage every bit as much as it provides an antidote to the conclusions explored in Renoir's *The Rules of the Game*.

If *Smiles* is optimistic, then Bergman had no difficulty in pushing his films to the opposite extreme. I think *The Passion of Anna* (1969) probably offers the best foil for *Smiles* in this respect. If the relationship between Desirée and Fredrik offers something approaching a 'best case of acknowledgment', as Cavell would put it, then *The Passion of Anna* provides, in the pairing of Andreas (Max von Sydow) and Anna (Liv Ullmann), a cutting example of the *failure* of a best case of acknowledgment. It will take a good deal of time to peel back the layers of analysis across these films of Bergman's, so that the following will demand some particular patience on the part of the reader.

What I mean to trace is the shape of something that will amount to a distinction between comedies of remarriage, on the one hand, and tragedies of remarriage, on the other. The rough contours of that distinction are provided by Cavell: a best case of acknowledgment versus the failure of a best case of acknowledgment. As argued in previous chapters, much of my approach here has been determined by distinctions between 'old marriage' and 'new marriage'. In Renoir's *The Rules of the Game*, this distinction is found via the old marriage between the aristocratic Christine and Robert, as well as that between the servant pairing of Lisette and Schumacher. The attempt to then construct a new marriage between Christine and André is shown to be an impossibility in the European context Renoir is portraying. André is shot dead, the aristocratic order is restored and the rules of the old game remain unchanged. We find a similar distinction between old and new marriage in Bergman's *Smiles of a Summer Night*. There, the old marriages emerge via the Fredrik–Anne and Count Malcolm–Charlotte pairings. By the end of the film, some sort of promise of new marriage has been found via the match made between Fredrik and Desirée, as well as between Anne and Henrik (then additionally by way of Frid and Petra). The coupling between Anne and Henrik is described by Cavell as 'a reckless dash into the unknown', a dash which is itself based on the repudiation of what he calls a 'false marriage'. The false marriage that is repudiated is that between Anne and Fredrik, and thus we might declare that a new marriage requires the destruction of an old marriage for the reason that old marriages are built on false premises. New marriage destroys the falseness of old marriage. To continue: a false or old marriage is one typically constructed on the basis of tradition, class alliances, financial concerns or otherwise by external agencies, such as marriages arranged by one's parents or wider family. A new marriage or remarriage, by contrast, is constructed on the basis of the mutual and equal consent of the members of the couple: they agree to be together on their own terms, 'by themselves together'.

An initial way to configure the distinction between comedies of remarriage and tragedies of remarriage might therefore be to state that comedies of remarriage discover the conditions of new marriage, whereas tragedies remain trapped in the old structures of marriage. Thus, Count Malcolm and Charlotte, in *Smiles of a Summer Night*, remain in an old marriage in much the same way as Christine and Robert do in *The Rules of the Game*. On the side of comedies and new marriage, in *Smiles* we have Fredrik and Desirée, Anne and Henrik, along with Frid and Petra. By contrast, as we have seen, in *The Rules of the Game* the potential for new marriage ends with the death of André.

All the same, such distinctions are in no way clear cut. How does one know if one is trapped in an old or false marriage? One can certainly believe one has entered into a marriage in ways that are felt to be freely chosen, but then one might eventually come to discover that it wasn't really a free choice after all, or simply that one was mistaken to have thought it free. Such is the discovery made in two of the key films that Cavell calls 'melodramas of the unknown woman'. In *Stella Dallas* (King Vidor, 1937), Stella believes all of her dreams have come true when she marries Stephen Dallas (John Boles), only to subsequently discover that her dreams have not materialised. (Here, Stella echoes the great European heroines, Nora in *A Doll's House* and Emma from *Madame Bovary*, as well as the American *Portrait of a Lady*'s Isabelle Archer, among others.) So too in George Cukor's *Gaslight* (1944), another of Cavell's unknown woman films, does Paula Anton (Ingrid Bergman) find that she has very much fallen out of love with her husband, the malevolent Gregory (Charles Boyer), who demonstrates the full force of the ways that old marriages are often configured by the manner in which a husband intentionally traps a wife (and so there are shades of *Portrait of a Lady* here too). But surely all of this raises the question of how one comes to know one is trapped in a false marriage. We saw in earlier chapters that a key issue for the female characters there – Lucy Warriner in *The Awful Truth* and Camille Javal in *Contempt* – was the question of whether they still love their husbands, and vice versa (their husbands being Jerry in the former and Paul in the latter). And we can certainly see the same sorts of questions being asked by Christine and Lisette in *The Rules of the Game*, and in different ways by Desirée, Charlotte and Anne in *Smiles of a Summer Night*. In other words, how does one determine a false marriage, and thus, also, a true marriage?

I tried to claim in the previous chapter that the origins of love lay in fantasy. I additionally argued that fantasy can only ever mean deception, so that love will invariably be based on a deception of some sort. Such designations must certainly appear on the surface to be unhelpful. Part of the reason for insisting on this point is to argue that one can never *know* definitively that one is in love, or one can never know what love 'is'. Rather, love can only ever be a matter of *acknowledgment*, as Cavell calls it. Love can only ever be something agreed between two people. I cannot force my love upon another person if that other person is not open to receiving or reciprocating it. One cannot *know* love. It can only ever be a matter of *acknowledgment*.

Another way to configure all of this is to declare that love involves a series of negotiations between a *self*, an *other* and a *social realm* (or group or community). As I stated earlier, some guidance on this point is provided by Emerson's statement that 'Two may talk and one may hear, but three cannot take part in a conversation of the most sincere and searching sort' (Emerson 1898, 54), or from Geneviève Sellier's claim that 'each person is constructed through the encounter with another'. Love is very much something that is worked out between two people, and what a couple works out will also often be something that is at odds with the social realm in which those people are placed. That much becomes clear in *The Rules of the Game*, where, as McGowan has argued, the forces of the social win out over the couple, where tradition and class outweigh the aspirations of a pair, Christine and André, who think they might be made for each other. These relationships – that is, those involving the negotiation of distinctions between the self, the couple and the social – are certainly not easy ones to negotiate. Much of this book is concerned with exploring such issues.

Some theory

I have tried to say that the discoveries of love and marriage dramatise the intersections between the self, the couple and the social fabric. Julia Kristeva's reflections in *Tales of Love* (first published in 1983) offer food for thought in this respect. She writes early in that book that when younger she believed strongly in the feeling or sensation or emotion of love – it was *something* – but she could never be certain that when others spoke of love they were indeed talking about the same thing she felt. This leads her to then ponder the possibility that love can only ever be solitary, solitary because incommunicable, a feeling or emotion that thoroughly eclipses all language. To expand on this, Kristeva writes,

> As if, at the very moment when the individual discovered himself to be intensely true, powerfully subjective, but violently ethical because he would be generously

ready to do anything for the other, he also discovered the confines of his condition and the powerlessness of his language. Are not two loves essentially individual, hence incommensurable, and thus don't they condemn the partners to meet at a point infinitely remote? (Kristeva 1987, 3)

Kristeva's reflections indicate some of the dilemmas central to any conception of love. Is love something in me? Or is it something in the one I love? Or is it something between self and other? In any case, how can love be communicated in such a way that I will know I am in love? Or rather, beyond such knowledge, if I feel my love too well or too intensely, might it then simply cease to be – it can only exist at a point infinitely remote, as Kristeva suggests? And might that be a reason to refrain from knowing or communicating that love? To communicate it will be to not quite put one's finger on it, and thus to expunge it, to kill its magic.

Kristeva reckons here that the moment or feeling of love is one in which the subject discovers him or herself to be *intensely true*. I think what Kristeva means is that this feeling of love or being-in-love makes one most true to oneself. To put this another way, if our everyday existence is in one way or another one of alienation[1] – of feeling out of touch with the world and with those around us; a general feeling of loneliness or angst or of 'not fitting in' – then the feeling of love or of being-in-love allows that alienation to melt away in such a fashion that I can feel like *myself* to as great a degree as is possible, as though finally intimately connected to the world. But Kristeva mixes this with another observation: this feeling of love, which is also a feeling of supreme selfhood, can be achieved only in conjunction with another person. Kristeva calls this 'ethical'. This feeling where I am *most of all myself* is also a feeling where I *give myself to another* ('ready to do anything for the other'). Call this a paradox of love: I am most myself when I give myself to another. This is another way of affirming Sellier's claim that 'each person is constructed through the encounter with another'.

And yet, Kristeva simultaneously withdraws: this feeling of love is somehow *just a feeling*. It is 'powerfully subjective'. It is not something I can grasp or point to or keep or even articulate. It is a love I have for another, but at the end of the day it remains *my* love and I cannot prove or make that love into a thing that is shared, say, in the way one shares a joke or a meal, or even in the way one shares a kiss or sex. 'Are not two loves essentially individual?' Kristeva finally asks, as though rhetorically affirming that this must be the case. And she reckons that this must be the case because, inarticulable, love is destined to exist only at 'a point infinitely remote'. Loves remain individual because there is no way to reach that point at which love would *exist*, as it were, for love can exist only in an imaginary realm, in fantasy, at an infinitely remote point.

I cannot help linking Kristeva's statement here with those rhapsodic musings of Peter Warne (in *It Happened One Night*) and Charles Pike (in *The Lady Eve*) which place the origin of love far, far way: for Peter it exists somewhere on a Pacific island, while for Charles it is something that goes 'way back', as we saw in the previous chapter. Needless to say that we can posit each of these characters as placing their love or their being-in-love at a point 'infinitely remote', every bit as much as Cavell makes the young couple, Anne and Henrik, in *Smiles of a Summer Night* engage in a 'reckless dash into the unknown', as though they are running away at full tilt in order to reach infinity. Charles's speech in *The Lady Eve* ends curiously: he says, 'what I see inside I'll never be able to put into words'. In saying so he is echoing or prophesying Kristeva's statement on the powerlessness of language. In many ways, therefore, Charles hits the nail on the head: 'what I see inside ...'. Inside what? Inside himself? Or inside Jean? Perhaps it is both or neither, but I would like to believe he is trying to express what he sees or feels inside Jean, inside this woman he believes he loves. And I think this is about as close as one can get to a description of what love might be, and that would be *the capacity to know what is inside another person*. What this would ultimately mean is that love would be a matter of coming to understand the way that another person sees the world, of being able to see their world 'from the inside', as it were, to see the world in *the way they see it*, rather than just in the way I see it.

These arguments link up with the discourses of Cavell in various ways. For Cavell, the question of love thus becomes a question of scepticism in ways negatively elucidated by his readings of Shakespeare's *King Lear* and *Othello*, and positively spelled out in his readings of *The Winter's Tale*, the comedies of remarriage, *Smiles of a Summer Night* and elsewhere. He engages in a specifically philosophical linking up of these themes in a reading of Emerson's essay, 'Fate' (Emerson's essay is dated 1860). There, Cavell twins Emerson both with and against Kant by arguing that, for Emerson, the conditions of possibility of there being a world are not conditions given in nature via the categories of the understanding, as Kant claimed. Rather, argues Cavell, what is at stake for Emerson is his contention that 'the condition of the possibility of there being a world of objects for us is the condition of our speaking together; and that', he continues, 'is not a matter of our sharing twelve categories of the understanding but of our sharing a language' (Cavell 2010a, 207).

These are, I admit, perplexing claims. What I want to emphasise, on the back of what Cavell and Kristeva have claimed here, is this: love is something that lies beyond language, so that it is something that cannot be spoken. And yet, the only way to discover and express love is by way of language, by speaking together, by way of conversation. Love is subject to this double bind: it cannot be spoken, and yet it can only be spoken. It is perhaps little wonder that the opening chapter of Cavell's *Pursuits of Happiness* is titled 'Words for a Conversation'. Love is something that exists beyond language: it is a *something* one cannot quite put one's finger on. But it is nevertheless the case that language – discussion, conversation, argument – is essential to what love is and how it comes into being, how it becomes an expression of what or who one is.

All of this is made into a central issue for Bergman's films (and for many of the other films approached in this book: those by Antonioni, Fellini, Rohmer …). Bergman offers characters whose loves go well beyond what it is possible to articulate, yet these characters must, in the end, defer to language so as to find ways of speaking together. Reconciliation – call it comedy – ensues when such a language is found, and we find such conversations between Fredrik and Desirée in *Smiles of a Summer Night*. Tragedy (of sorts) is the result when language escapes. We will see an example of such a breakdown of language in *The Passion of Anna*.

The proximity of these discourses to the theory of psychoanalysis should not be underplayed. As a theory and therapy based on a notion of the 'talking cure', the connections should be obvious. Cavell certainly thinks so. In *Contesting Tears* he very effectively characterises the psychoanalytic cure as a matter of, by way of talking with another person, discovering how one comes to understand the specific conditions that have produced one's life. The talking cure is thus a way of articulating one's understanding of one's place in the world (see Cavell 1996, 97). This achievement takes place in psychoanalysis by way of talking with another person, that is, by way of the talking cure. Cavell also writes of the talking cure while discussing the romantic scenarios produced by Max Ophuls's *Letter from an Unknown Woman* (1948): discourses of love go hand in hand with those of the talking cure. And any brand of psychoanalysis will certainly think so, for the talking cure is typically sparked by what is known as transference love, a fabricated love, a consequence of the analytic situation in which the analysand falls in love with the analyst. There are fine passages on this in Freud's 'Observations on Love in Transference' (Freud 2002), in which he at first contends that the kind of love that emerges in transference is merely an invocation of pre-existing psychical patterns derived from childhood repressions. Therefore, surely, Freud suggests, we cannot designate such emanations of transference love as 'true love', tied closely as they are to the analytic setting. Transference love is 'fake' love, a love made up of tropes that any particular psyche may happen to be attracted to. But Freud objects. He declares that *all love is like this anyway*: all love arises from personality structures and unconscious wishes derived from infantile experiences. That's what love *is* (see Freud 2002, 75–6). Transference love is one of the ways of enabling the analysand to begin to articulate what is deepest 'inside' him or her, that is, what is unconscious. The analysand must trust or have faith in the analyst in order to freely open up and discuss with uninhibited clarity his or her thoughts. In achieving this, the situation of transference mimics what love 'really is'.

Again, here we come upon the issue of deception. Love – transference love – is a matter of deception. In a very real sense the analyst deceives the analysand into a situation of being-in-love. Which is as much to say that *pretending* to be in love is pretty much what *really* being in love is. Precisely the same kinds of emotions, articulations and expressions will occur in the transference as also occur in 'true love'. It is all of this, after all, that enables the analysand to truly come to terms with the depths of her/his psyche, to come into contact with the truth of the psyche, to get in touch with what is genuinely 'inside'. What the transference and the hoped-for cure that results from the transference can produce is, precisely, a new sense of selfhood, a new understanding of one's place in the world.

This necessarily brings us to a point that will be revisited at various points throughout this book: that which I believe is *inside* the other person whom I love is none other than *something that is inside me*; what I imagine is inside the other person is actually the projection of my own desire. Once again, more than anything, these designations are taken from psychoanalysis, most specifically by way of what Lacan calls the *objet a*. The *objet a* is that which causes desire. In this context, I think it can be designated as an object 'inside' the other person that attracts me to that person. And yet, as Lacan will claim, this *objet a* that is inside the other person is nothing less than my own projection – most specifically, a fantasy I project onto the other person. We saw in the previous chapter that Lacan refers to this object of desire as the *ágalma* in his seminar on Transference – the *ágalma* is a treasure hidden 'inside' the person I am attracted to. And yet, it is in reality a something inside *myself* that I am trying to find, an object that will give me satisfaction, and which I believe I might have found in this other person to whom I am attracted, and with whom I may well be 'in love'. What I am trying to find inside the other person is a lost part of myself. In short, as I have already stated: that which I believe is inside the other person I love is none other than something that is inside me. (This is another way of putting Lacan's Hegelian dictum that 'Man's desire is the desire of the other'. Indeed, Lacan puts it nicely in his seminar on *Hamlet*: 'The object [of desire] takes the place, I would say, of what the subject is – symbolically – deprived of'; Lacan 1977b, 15.)[2]

For the analytic situation, the cruelty of transference love is that the analyst cannot return it. I find Kristeva more articulate than Lacan in this respect, for the engagement with transference love by the analysand opens up the possibility of bringing into discourse, into language, any or all of the things, feelings and thoughts that have been hidden away from the analysand, thus setting in train the key articulations of analysis. In short, the inducement to transference love is an important step along the road to the analysand's discovery and working through of her/his own desires and sense of self. Kristeva goes so far as to call this 'a true process of self-organization' (Kristeva 1987, 14). What is achieved by analysis, by the talking cure, Kristeva tells us, is a *reciprocal identification and detachment*, that is, a new-found ability for a person to self-identify their thoughts and desires, along with an ability to detach themselves from the madness of those thoughts and desires – not to repudiate those thoughts but, rather, to see them, to bring them into the open, to language. The analytic setting might be none other than a love relationship, and it is by way of love that the mind or psyche will most effectively, Kristeva claims, be itself; that is, self-reliant and self-organised. Kristeva writes, 'The psyche is the open system connected to another, and only under those conditions is it renewable. If it lives, your psyche is in love. If it is not in love, it is dead' (Kristeva 1987, 15).

Love or being-in-love is a feeling that is rather difficult to define. Its best designations seem to state that it is something that occurs between two people, but its contours are inexact. It is something worked out, articulated or constructed between two people primarily by way of conversation. The feeling of being-in-love seems to be one of extreme satisfaction, or hoped-for satisfaction – that is, the desire to achieve a 'point infinitely remote'. It is also a feeling of being most one's self. Paradoxically, that feeling of supreme selfhood can be achieved only in combination with another person. Love shows us that the truth of the self may be something that resides inside the other person, even as it also seems that what is inside the other person is a matter of the fantasies I project onto that other person.

If it is not in love, it is dead

Kristeva's claim is a stark one: 'If it is not in love, it is dead.' Of Bergman's films, *Smiles of a Summer Night* wears death very lightly, especially in relation to most (almost all) of Bergman's other films. I specifically have in mind (for a start) the pair of films *To Joy* and *Summer Interlude*, each of which is based on a flashback structure consequent upon the death of one of the lovers featured in these films. We are well away from the typically diurnal structure of the Hollywood comedies of remarriage here, as each of these films unfolds over periods of several years. *Summer Interlude* provides something like a vision of ideal love, for the summer of love depicted there might as well have been precisely that fantasised by Peter Warne in *It Happened One Night* as a south sea island (though Bergman's film is set in Sweden, of course). Needless to say that this setting is something like a 'green world'. The summer interlude of the film's title – and these are young lovers, Maria (Maj Britt-Nilsson) and Henrik (Birger Malmsten) – is an evocation of ideal love, as though this couple has ventured into an ideal, hence unreal world. Henrik asks Maria at the height of their passion, 'Everything is so unreal tonight, isn't it?' Her response: 'It's beautiful. We're in the same soap-bubble. So beautiful I wish I could burst into bits, vanish, become nothing.' Note the similarity to Peter's 'those nights when you and the moon and the water all become one …' in *It Happened One Night*. But Bergman's plot steers a course well away from comedy: Henrik plunges to his death in an accidental fall from a cliff, in full view of Maria, as they are swimming and sunning themselves towards the end of summer. This makes the film every bit as much a reflection on death as it is a reflection on the idealism of love.

One way to interpret the idealisation of this love is to place it as a flashback, as a memory, in the same way Lacan reminds us that Hamlet's love for Ophelia is rekindled only as a consequence of her death. Lacan writes, 'only insofar as the object of Hamlet's desire has become an impossible object can it become once more an object of his desire' (Lacan 1977b, 36).[3] And this is a powerful way to figure the object of love: that it is beyond words, beyond knowledge, to the point where it is an impossible object. Hamlet is driven to his death – which might be a way of saying that he cannot overcome the impossibility of his love (though many other factors are brought to bear in *Hamlet*). Maria in *Summer Interlude*, on the other hand, is not driven towards death. Rather, hers is a story of resurrection: at the end of the film she has just about completed the work of mourning and rediscovered the possibility of a new love in the character of David (Alf Kjellin). Life goes on.

It is certainly worth noting *Summer with Monika* here as well. This film provides a vision of ideal love in a manner quite similar to *Summer Interlude*. Monika (Harriet Andersson) and Harry (Lars Ekborg) are young lovers who escape from the social world to a Swedish isle so as to create a paradise of love for themselves. This escape shows us the stakes of a 'reckless dash into the unknown' – that such a dash might *not* be destined to end happily ever after. And that might be Bergman's point: this love is an impossible love, a 'secret love', for when reality impedes upon the couple's paradise – they run short of food, Monika falls pregnant, Harry is beaten up by an old foe who has sought him out, the long days of summer begin to shorten – their ideal love cannot be sustained. The couple returns to the social world, they leave their paradise, Monika starts an affair and cannot cope with motherhood. In the end, Harry and Monika go their separate ways:

Harry decides to bring up the baby himself, a decision Monika seems content with. Ideal love here is shattered, deemed untenable and, ultimately, destructive. But life goes on.

The ideal love of *Summer Interlude* – or even that of *Summer with Monika* – is complicated by *To Joy*, even as this film precedes the others (*To Joy* is from 1950, *Summer Interlude* 1951, *Summer with Monika* 1953). This film charts the contours of a difficult love, a love that is won via marriage, argument, triumph and despair. Conversation is key here, for the couple in this film, Stig (Stig Olin) and Martha (Maj Britt-Nilsson), musicians in a provincial orchestra, do talk often and at length. Sex is up front too (call this a form of conversation) insofar as Martha is willing to sleep with Stig before marriage if it will strengthen their bond. Their marriage is a remarriage (I suppose) because Martha has been married before, a marriage, she tells us, that was 'all lies and cheating'. On the back of this she also says to Stig, 'we can promise each other honesty: that's absolutely necessary.' In time they have a child (twins, in fact), but this leads to all manner of monetary woes, especially when Stig's ambitions of becoming a star violinist are dashed (he lacks the necessary brilliance). The ins and outs of their relationship are filled with joy, but also with bitterness and betrayal: Stig retreats into himself by way of his failure to become a soloist; he has an affair and often comes to treat Martha with desperate and horrible cruelty.

Some of these factors show an implicit debt to the remarriage genre: a love that aspires to honesty as well as a foregrounding of the importance of conversation. But there is no magic potion or playful charade to save this marriage. This is a way of saying that in *To Joy* the deceptions *are* deceptions, though this doesn't quite sound like enough to say. What seems to be genuinely at stake here is a sense of wanting *too much truth*, *too much honesty*, a sense in which the quest for love here is based on ideals which are impossible. What this means is that something in the love between Stig and Martha aspires to *knowledge* rather than *acknowledgment*. They desire a proof of their love beyond the bounds of what is exchanged between them, beyond what is said between them.

What I mean to emphasise here is another definition of tragedy given by Cavell. If we have already seen Cavell try to define tragedy as inspired by 'a failure of the best case of acknowledgment', then that failure can take the form of a belief that one possesses knowledge of something 'once and for all' (see Cavell 1979b, 451). Here, knowledge tries to eclipse acknowledgment. Cavell's prime example is that of Desdemona's handkerchief. For Othello, the handkerchief provides a 'proof' of Desdemona's betrayal. This proof exceeds any gesture of acknowledgment Othello can receive from her. Conversation leads to nullity, a failure of 'reciprocal listening'. We know that this leads to death in *Othello*.

This might be too many jumps to make, but the point I want to make here, which I believe is central to Bergman's films, is that love fails when it tries to *break the bounds of what it is possible for love to be*. In the worst cases it leads to tragedy. In other words, things begin to fall apart when love becomes idealised and impossible – it becomes 'unconditioned' in the same way that metaphysical dogma had become impossible for Kant. (The links with arguments relating to scepticism should by now be apparent: at its limit, scepticism requires a proof of things 'beyond all doubt', without conditions. But such proofs are impossible.) Indeed, isn't the principal lesson of the American remarriage comedies that love is always compromised, that it is never ideal, that it is riven by all manner of suspicions, betrayals, arguments, appeals for forgiveness and, hopefully for those films, reconciliation? Perhaps, therefore, what Bergman's films show us more than anything is how a modern version of love – based on argument, compromise, forgiveness – can square itself with a Romantic version of love which conceives of love in ideal terms. In other words, Bergman's question is: how do we cope with love when it is no longer considered ideal? Is love still love when no longer ideal?

These are Lacanian concerns – indeed, the entire seminar on Transference (coming, as it does, to a large degree, from the analysis of Courtly Love in the seminar on *The Ethics of Psychoanalysis* from the previous year, 1959–60 (Lacan 1992)) is designed to reposition the great myth of love proposed by Aristophanes and then exemplified by Alcibiades in Plato's *Symposium*. Lacan wants to destroy this model as a viable one for love. Aristophanes' myth, as is well known, posits that humans were originally doubled: they were a combination of either man–man, woman–woman or man–woman. Each of these beings, Aristophanes tells us, was globular in shape, with rounded back and sides, four arms and four legs.[4] Zeus, at one point, decided to cut these beings in half, thus allowing them to walk upright on two legs. Then, as Aristophanes puts it, 'when the work of bisection was complete it left each half with a desperate yearning for the other', and this yearning is the origin of love, especially a love conceived in terms of desire and sexual satisfaction. Here, then, love is a matter of 'trying to reintegrate our former nature, to make two into one', and to 'bridge the gulf between one human being and another' (Plato, *Symposium*, paragraphs 189–91).

If this is a version of love, then psychoanalysis, via Lacan, can see such a love only as an idealisation, a version of impossible or hyperbolic love that is destined to end in disappointment and psychical illness (Cavell uses the term 'hyperbolic love' in Cavell 2003, 18). Such hyperbolic love may also be tragic, as Lacan tries to show in his reading of *Hamlet*. Lacan emphasises there that the love for Ophelia which Hamlet rediscovers after her death is an impossible love, a love that is a consequence of its impossibility.

But I would claim that it is this version of love that Bergman is also willing to interrogate in his films – call it a transition from Romantic love to modern love. If Romantic love is impossible insofar as it is unconditioned and hyperbolic, then modern love has to move beyond or through this in ways that mirror the psychoanalytic cure. Beyond this idealised, unconditional love, it is hoped one will discover some sort of reconciliation.

To Joy finds its way back to reconciliation and in this way again meets up with the Hollywood comedies and a sense of the invention of 'new' marriage. The resolution is not found by way of a magic potion, a masquerade, a series of lies that yield the truth, or by whatever machinations the American comedies manage. Stig and Martha, having separated for some months, maintain contact via an exchange of letters, and it is a remarriage which seems to be based on Martha's capacity for forgiveness. Bergman does not quite allow issues to end happily ever after: we have known since the beginning of the film that Martha has died and that the bulk of the film is a flashback from Stig's perspective. And thus, for Bergman, love cannot shake the shadow of death. While the orchestra in which Stig plays pounds out a version of the finale of Beethoven's Ninth Symphony, the 'Ode to Joy', at the end of the film, one senses that this is a joy hard won and enveloped in crises of bitterness and stultifying levels of hatred, however temporary.

Tragedies of remarriage

These levels of hatred, negativity, of something like tragedy, as well as the spectre of death, weigh heavily upon a great many of Bergman's films. For films like *A Lesson in Love* (1954) or *Dreams* (1955), these depths are worn with a relative lightness (never, it seems to me, as lightly as in *Smiles of a Summer Night*), but in *Through a Glass Darkly* (1961), *The Silence* (1963), *Persona* (1966), *Cries and Whispers* (1972) and up to *Autumn Sonata* (1978) these depths are scraped to the limit of what it is possible to depict (I point to the examples that stand out definitively for me). *Winter Light*, like *To Joy* and *Summer Interlude*, provides something of a flashback structure – at any rate, a memory structure – of a lost love. However, unlike those earlier films, *Winter Light* barely escapes the bleakness, the utter lack of light provided by this winter, until its miraculous reconciliation right at the end. Bergman has remarked on this reconciliation in extraordinary ways. At the end of *Winter Light*, Märta (Ingrid Thulin) saves Jonas (Gunnar Björnstrand) by virtue of her love.

> Only at the end when they're in the empty church for the three o'clock service that has become perfectly meaningless for him, her prayer in a sense is answered:

he responds to her love by going on with the service in that empty country church. It's his own first step toward feeling, toward learning how to love. We're not saved by God, but by love. That's the most we can hope for. (Bergman 2007, 45)

He continues: 'What matters most in life is being able to make contact with another human. Otherwise you are dead, like so many people today are dead ...' (Bergman 2007, 46). Note how close Bergman seems to be to the formulation we saw from Kristeva: 'If it is not in love, it is dead' (Kristeva 1987, 3). This potential for death, this lack of light and the depiction of the depths of despair and madness caused by love distinguishes Bergman's films starkly from the Hollywood comedies of remarriage. But this still means that Bergman's films can be said to be in conversation with those films, or the themes of those films, that couples in these films are involved in disquisitions on faith, with arguments, with appeals for forgiveness, with conversation. And *The Passion of Anna* is the great example of this, a negation of the Hollywood comedies (and of *Smiles of a Summer Night*), but also substantially different from the social critique provided by Renoir's *The Rules of the Game*. Where the Hollywood comedies feature successful examples of couples creating a world together, Bergman's negative examples – call them tragedies – show us some of the ways in which the attempted creation of a world can crumble into dust. (It is worth noting that Bergman does not place himself at a distance from American comedies: he declared an aversion to Renoir and Godard, for example, but, as he put it, 'to go on about directors who have influenced me ... technically, Cukor, very much': Bergman 2007, 81).

The Passion of Anna features two couples, Andreas Winkelman and Anna Fromm on the one hand (played by Max von Sydow and Liv Ullmann), and Elis and Eva Vergérus on the other (Erland Josephsen, Bibi Andersson). The action of the film takes place in somewhere akin to a 'green world' on the small island of Fårö where Bergman lived for much of the year.[5] At the start of the film Anna meets Andreas when she stops at his house to ask if she can use his telephone. She makes a call and then leaves, but she forgets to take her handbag and Andreas cannot resist rummaging through it. There he finds a letter from Anna's former husband, also named Andreas, and it charts a marriage in the course of its disintegration, and states that if this couple were to stay together things will only get worse in ways that will lead to violence and mental breakdown. All of this is evocatively represented by way of the typewritten script which Andreas reads. Bits of this script will return at other points during the film, often highlighting the foreboding of 'physical and psychical violence' the letter points to.

Andreas Winkelman is a loner. 'He has tried to hide from the world around him,' he tells us in voiceover – at least, Max von Sydow tells us this, reflecting on his character in one of the four Brecht-style interruptions in this film whereby each of the main actors delivers a summation of the characters they play. It turns out that Anna is staying with close neighbours, a married couple, Elis and Eva, and soon afterwards Andreas is invited over for dinner. At this dinner the characters air what will become the major themes of the film. Elis is a successful bureaucrat whose latest venture involves setting up a cultural centre in Milan. He suggests that this will be a futile task, one of trying to bring culture to a thoroughly uncultured people. He scoffs at the bourgeois aim of 'bringing culture to the masses'. Anna immediately questions and criticises his attitude, declaring that he should pursue something he really believes in, something from deep inside himself. But Elis simply dismisses this possibility to the effect that he really doesn't have anything inside him – at any rate, nothing he believes in. And so this is one limit of the universe Bergman paints here: the person who has developed complete contempt for the world, a person who has given up on himself, who has nothing inside him.

Anna reveals herself to be from the opposite end of the spectrum. She dedicates herself, as she puts it, to living 'in line with some form of the truth' and strives for 'spiritual perfection'. Anna's proclamations of the desires for truth and perfection go hand in hand with her account of the ideal love shared between her and her former husband. 'We lived in harmony,' she says, 'we were truthful and honest.' Later in the film, the high point of Anna's idealistic reminiscence of ideal love between herself and her former husband comes in the form of a six-minute single-take monologue, shot in extreme close-up, in which she recounts the depth and perfection of her love. (For me, this is one of the great cinematic achievements of Bergman's career as a director – and of Ullmann's as an actor). Her words might not be too far distant from those of Charles in *The Lady Eve*, for Anna admits that her words sound a little corny. 'We were together in everything.' They were examples of 'how two people become part of each other'. She also states that the words she's using cannot come close to describing what it felt like (and we are close to Charles's declaration in *The Lady Eve* that 'What I see inside I'll never be able to put into words ...').

Here, then, are the two limit cases *The Passion of Anna* provides: complete resignation in the form of Elis, and absolute devotion as described by Anna. Of Elis perhaps all that can be said is that he has given up on himself and so has given up on the world too. He knows that the world he lives in, and the public world of cities and buildings and culture and work, is a world he despises, a world he does not consent to. He has withdrawn from any kind of engagement with or commitment to that world. Externally he is content to participate in the making of a world, but this is not a result of his own striving or desire.[6] Rather, it is a mere concession to what society expects of him, a wry contentment to play 'the rules of the game' even as he hates that game. The deceptions in his livelihood abound. His wife, Eva, has had, and continues to embark on, affairs with other men – she will sleep with Andreas later in the film – to the point where Elis no longer seems to care one way or another. The marriage between Elis and Eva is a more tragic version of the flawed marriage between Count Malcolm and Charlotte in *Smiles of a Summer Night*.

Elis has given up on the attainment of perfection, of love or fulfilment, and has thus kept well away from the idealisations that can cause so much trouble for Bergman's characters (we will discover this with Anna and Andreas). In simple terms, Elis is a realist, a pragmatist: he sees the world for what it is, and he is willing to go along with it because he fails to imagine any possible alternative. He has given up on the quest for satisfaction; he has abandoned the pursuit of happiness. He has withdrawn his investment from the world – no fantasy, no desire, no *ágalma*, and certainly nothing in the realm of what might be called love. To point to psychoanalytic discourses here seems appropriate. Yes, the love object is something external – the *objet a* – but it is simultaneously something inside oneself. If one loses that object, or if this object in the external world no longer satisfies or stimulates desire, then it is also as though something inside oneself has ceased to exist, that it has died.[7] Such is Elis's predicament: Eva has abandoned him, more or less; there is no longer any spark in their love. As a consequence, Elis withdraws from the world. He sees the world as composed of emptiness and meaninglessness. Life becomes something merely to be tolerated. Elis tolerates his wife, as much as he merely tolerates his work. But he has given up on his desire – at any rate, this is what he would have us believe.

Is this deception? Well, if it is a deception, then it is a deception Elis has chosen and determined by himself. If I have tried to emphasise the notion that 'each person is constructed through the encounter with another', then, if one no longer has encounters with others, one renounces some sense of selfhood. And this is what has happened with Elis: he has repudiated the world, and no longer wants to build a world in conjunction with others. Instead, he withdraws into himself and tries to salvage what he can there. All that is left is isolation. If that is deception, then it is a deception he has constructed by himself, without others.

Anna goes in a direction that is opposite to that chosen by Elis. Anna is bound to the impossible reminiscence of a supposedly ideal love. She has aimed for that 'point infinitely remote' that we find so often located in the past for Bergman's characters – as with Stig's memories in *To Joy* or Maria's in *Summer Interlude*. And precisely like those earlier films, we know, by the time Anna delivers her monologue, that her former husband has died, that he as well as their child were killed in a car crash while Anna was driving.

Anna too now suffers from a long-term injury to her leg. As if this weren't already enough, we have also known from nearly the beginning of the film that the marriage between Anna and Andreas was far from ideal, that the letter in her handbag detailed the miseries, quarrels and threats of violence that are so often part of any marriage. And yet, Anna very much places the memory of her love beyond words. It is here, once again, that the specific meaning of deception makes its mark. It is words that are deceptive for Anna, the quest for articulations or expressions or conversations are all things that tarnish the sanctity of experience and feeling and memory for her.

Words are deceptive for Anna, and so it is by idealising her memories of her husband that she can escape the deception of words. The quest to go beyond language is something we have seen theorised in several ways. First of all, it is the stimulus of love – the *ágalma* – impossible to put into words, but nevertheless at the origin of love and desire. Second, the beyond of language is a 'point infinitely remote', as Kristeva puts it. As she goes on to suggest, a belief in this infinite, impossible love and a consequent retreat from language can only condemn the subject to isolation and an individuality separated from others. Finally, we have seen this 'beyond language' equated with unconditioned knowledge, pure knowledge, what Cavell calls knowledge 'once and for all' or a knowledge beyond acknowledgment. This quest for the pure and the impossible that is depicted as idealised or hyperbolic love is central to Bergman's films and it is predicated on the breakdown of language and conversation. This is a way to conceive of love: love is something that cannot be put into words, and yet, in order to experience love we must nevertheless speak it, converse about it, put it into words. This might also be a way of drawing a distinction between Romantic love – a 'love beyond words' associated with nineteenth-century Romanticism – and a modern form of love that emerges in the twentieth century based on conversation and mutual recognition and the promise of a 'new' kind of marriage.

In Bergman's films the distinction between Romantic and modern love is given clear expression: in *To Joy*, Stig and Martha find their way back to conversation and reconciliation by way of an exchange of letters; Maria in *Summer Interlude* slowly climbs out of her isolation – a consequence of the idealisation of her love for Henrik – by way of her conversations with David; and of course Fredrik and Desirée in *Smiles of a Summer Night* discover a way of speaking together that gets them back together again in the manner of the American remarriage comedies. Monika and Harry, by contrast, in *Summer with Monika*, fail to find words to transcend their idealised escape from the social world. In these ways, Bergman's films, even the bleakest of them, share the themes and consequences with the American comedies of remarriage: primarily that it is a matter of conversation that ensures a pursuit of happiness in matters of love and romance. What is needed for the endurance of love is the Miltonian formula of a 'meet and happy conversation', an exchange of words, a language of love (on Milton's claims, see Cavell 1981, 87).

It is precisely this language, a language of love, that is absent in *The Passion of Anna*. First of all, this absence of conversation emerges via the way in which the letter from Anna's former husband has failed to reach its destination. On the one hand, Anna has failed to accept its consequences: their love was not ideal. On the other hand, the letter also reaches its wrong destination in the hands of Andreas Winkelman, who fails to speak to Anna about this letter until the very end of the film. The letter shows us nothing less than a failure of communication and conversation. This, and many other things besides, condemns the potential love between Anna and Andreas to tragedy. The fact that so much remains unspoken between these characters, that each, to varying degrees, keeps themself hidden from the other, is expressed in two scenes late in the film. A first scene features a conversation which occurs just after Anna has accidentally dropped a bowl of milk while she was taking it out of the refrigerator. She had been unnerved by Andreas. Her dropping of the bowl signifies something akin to fear or anxiety, a lack of understanding about what is happening in their relationship. And it is certainly worth pointing out that this occurs immediately after Andreas, feeling somewhat off-colour, has been fantasising about his first wife, and viewers will surely sense that Anna felt all of this in Andreas's behaviour. It goes some way towards accounting for her dropping the bowl. Anna suggests that she and Andreas take a trip away from the tensions and sorrows of where they live. We know by this stage of the film that one of their friends on the island, Johan Andersson (Erik Hell), has committed suicide – he has hanged himself – after being beaten up by a group of locals as retribution for a number of animals on the island he was accused of killing. We also know by the end of the film that Johan was not responsible for killing these animals, so that his persecution by others living on the island was entirely without reason.

The conversation that follows is remarkably staged. Both Anna and Andreas are reduced to faces floating in a sea of darkness. Their faces are shot individually: we never have both faces in the one shot. The atmosphere is therefore dreamlike, as though unfolding at one or several removes from reality. Andreas takes most of the dialogue. He claims that he is a failure and that he lives a life of humiliation, that he lacks self-respect and almost feels that he is dead. Amid all this, Anna devotedly signals her understanding. She does her best to comfort him. But Andreas cannot get beyond his conviction that he has built a wall around himself; that he is walled in and no one, not even Anna, will be able to understand the humiliation and sadness he knows. The scene ends with Andreas declaring that they will never leave the island: it is too late for all that, he states.

If this extraordinary scene begins to show us that any reconciliation between this couple will be tremendously difficult to achieve, then it is not long after this that all hopes for reconciliation are dashed. Any sense of even being able to hold a conversation disappear. Anna and Andreas share breakfast at a small table, and Anna asks, 'What are you doing today?' But Andreas gives no response. After a pause he then asks, 'What are you doing?' Anna responds, 'I don't know.' But she also then interjects that 'I asked you.' Even now Andreas fails to respond. He gets up and walks outside. What then occurs is a vicious and desperate argument in which Anna accuses Andreas of living in lies. His only response to these accusations is to attack her physically and one genuinely gets the sense here that he might go so far as to kill her – he goes at her with an axe, for instance. What has occurred here is an absolute failure of language. Instead of building a world together it is as though this couple has destroyed a world together.

There are no equivalents of this kind of violence and abandonment of the world in the Hollywood comedies Cavell writes about. The darkest moment in those comedies occurs when Adam Bonner (Spencer Tracy) slaps his wife, Amanda (Katharine Hepburn) with cruelty and malice in *Adam's Rib* (1949). Cavell notes that this casts a dark shadow over the remainder of the film and over the remarriage genre more generally. This darkness will reach the depths of cruelty in the companion genre of 'unknown woman melodramas' Cavell writes about, especially in Cukor's *Gaslight*. Darkness pervades most of Bergman's films, but the conditions of cruelty one finds there seem to me to be more akin to the Shakespearian madness of Lear and Othello, and perhaps even more significantly, of the cruelty of Leontes in *The Winter's Tale*.[8] Cavell has, of course, written on each of these dramas. The venomous rage of Leontes, directed towards his wife, Hermione, is enough to turn her to stone, as it were. The circumstances of Shakespeare's play are brought about by a failure of language, a breakdown of mutual understanding, but also by a quest for knowledge beyond acknowledgment, beyond conversation, beyond the speaking together that can constitute the creation of a world. Leontes' suspicion of Hermione and his fierce abuse of her signal his desperation and unwillingness to open himself to another person. In the first half of *The Winter's Tale*, Leontes is, as it were, walled in, in ways that are akin to the experience of Andreas in Bergman's film.

I am confident enough to say that a fairly clear distinction structures much of Bergman's oeuvre. On the one hand, there is the possibility of finding a way to language as a way of discovering love, and thus of finding a way to comedy and happiness. Such happiness can be found in *Smiles of a Summer Night*, as much as it can be found in the remarriage comedies discussed by Cavell. On the other hand, resides the possibility of the failure of language and conversation and, thus, a consignment of individuals to isolation which often leads to tragedy. Such happens in *The Passion of Anna*. In the end, Andreas says to Anna, 'I want my freedom. I want my solitude back.'

Hyperbolic love

What does Andreas's plea for freedom and solitude – freedom via solitude – mean? It means that his quest for conversation, for togetherness, for experiencing the world in conjunction with another person, has failed. His quest for acknowledgment has failed – it is a failure of a best case of acknowledgment.

My suggestion as to why Andreas decides to withdraw into himself and thus abandons all attempts to find love is that he has placed too high a set of expectations on love. When, as we saw above, Kristeva asks 'Are two loves essentially individual?', then the answer Andreas would deliver to such a question is 'yes'. And these loves – expressions of the love between Andreas and Anna – are individual to the extent that they will be destined never to meet. My suggestion is to refer to such a notion of love as 'hyperbolic' love (see Cavell 2003, 18; and Bersani 2015, 85). Hyperbolic love is idealised love that goes beyond the bounds of what it is possible for love to be. It is the kind of love envisaged by Alcibiades in Plato's *Symposium*. Hyperbolic love thus operates on the model whereby two becomes one, where two people in love are joined together so as to form a unity. Furthermore, if we follow Lacanian dicta, this kind of love is an impossible love, the kind of love Hamlet has for Ophelia after her death, so that it is a love that can be idealised and made 'pure', only insofar as it cannot possibly exist in reality. It is, in other words, idealised, and hyperbolic to boot. Much the same can be said for the love between Romeo and Juliet in Shakespeare's play of that name. The love there is hyperbolic because impossible. For *Romeo and Juliet* that love is also a hidden love.[9] *The Passion of Anna* shows us that Andreas believes that this is what love is: when two people become one. But his quest to become one with Anna comes undone, as it always will, for such a love is, by definition, impossible. Andreas clings to it as an impossibility – he thus makes it impossible. He remains walled in. He remains individual, separate, isolated.

As briefly explained in earlier chapters, I argue for much of this book that the versions of love and marriage encountered here, instead of proposing that *two becomes one*, rather, claim that the love that defines new marriage or remarriage requires a conception whereby *one becomes two*. The formulation is from Alain Badiou, but we shall see that Luce Irigaray makes similar and more substantial claims. Being in love requires seeing and experiencing the world as two. And this is, quite precisely, what Andreas is incapable of doing in *The Passion of Anna*. He cannot escape isolation and loneliness – he cannot escape the condition of being *one* – so as to experience and understand the world in conjunction with Anna. He withdraws into his own narcissism and loneliness. He prefers to experience the world as one rather than from the perspective of being two.

These elements of *The Passion of Anna* therefore show us the connection between narcissism and loneliness. We have seen, for example, at the beginning of Bergman's *Smiles of a Summer Night*, that Desirée had stated to Fredrik that he had never had any friends apart from himself. Fredrik responds by claiming much the same of Desirée. These are people who have remained trapped within themselves, trapped in subjectivity (as Cavell would say). It is by way of conversation – mutual understanding, acknowledgment and a little magic – that, by the end of the film, Desirée and Fredrik find their ways out of isolation. By contrast, in *The Passion of Anna*, Andreas cannot find his way out of isolation. We can add that isolation affects all the characters here: Elis, Anna, Eva. Andreas remains trapped in subjectivity, loneliness, narcissism. His narcissism is most pertinently signalled by his continued devotion to his first wife – still his wife, in fact, for they are not yet divorced. Andreas has even hoped that they might even be reconciled. The sexual fantasies he engages in near the end of the film, which to some extent precipitate his violent break-up with Anna, demonstrate that he has maintained a connection to this 'lost object' – his wife – within himself. This withdrawal of the lost object of his love within himself, into the possessiveness of the self, is a sure sign of narcissistic withdrawal. It is this withdrawal – and he states it himself: he has walled himself in – that is the reason he cannot form a lasting tie with Anna.[10]

What Andreas's behaviour demonstrates is a withdrawal into himself that is also a withdrawal from language. He ends up at a point where he seems incapable of speaking with Anna. We might say that by the end of the film he knows only how to speak *at* her, not *with* her. In doing so he cancels any possibility of a relationship with her. But correlatively, this withdrawal into himself also allows him to maintain a connection with the lost object – his first wife. I do not think we need to look very far in *The Passion of Anna* to call this withdrawal tragic.[11]

The final moments of *The Passion of Anna* are extraordinary. Immediately after Andreas and Anna have fought, when he comes at her with an axe, sirens indicate that a fire has broken out on a nearby property. The fire, it transpires, has been lit with the intention of harming and killing a number of horses kept in stables on this property. This act shows us that the now dead Johan Andersson was not responsible for the attacks of cruelty toward animals that have been committed on the island. Andreas runs to the property in order to help. After this, Anna drives there to join him. Andreas gets into the car and they drive. It is here that he finally tells her of the letter he had read just after they had first met, the letter from her husband that was in Anna's handbag. Andreas thus accuses her of always living in lies even as she proclaims a devotion to the truth. It is also here that Andreas states that he wants his solitude back. We get the feeling Anna might be about to lose control and crash the car, perhaps in the same manner as had occurred with her husband and child. But this does not happen. She brings the car to a halt on an empty road. Andreas continues angrily until, calming somewhat, he asks Anna why she came to fetch him from the fire. Her answer is astonishing. 'I came to ask your forgiveness,' she says. As she does so she looks at him longingly, with care. It is the first time she has dared to look at him during the entire scene. Forgiveness. Andreas gets out of the car. Anna drives off. And the film famously ends with Andreas broken, distraught, collapsed in on himself upon this road – he punches the road with his fists – while a distant camera slowly zooms in on him until, in the scene's final moments, we are presented with only a blurred image of Andreas's figure. A closing voiceover states, 'This time he was called Andreas Winkelman.'

Cavellian themes are writ large here. Anna asks Andreas for forgiveness, and we know that acts of forgiveness are central to Cavell's conception of remarriage. And yet, Anna's forgiveness, her attempts to reach out to Andreas, to understand him and care for him, are not returned. As much as Anna is determined to acknowledge Andreas, to accept his faults and learn to love him, Andreas cannot do the same for her. He remains walled in. I ought to mention that the theme of remarriage must also be considered central to *The Passion of Anna* in overt ways. Both Anna and Andreas have been married before – indeed, Andreas remains married, but separated from his wife. Their quest to build a world together, their failed quest, is one that occurs entirely within the realm of 'remarriage'.

To conclude

If the relationship between Anna and Andreas in *The Passion of Anna* ends in an almighty conflagration of sorts, then the film seems merely to abandon the marriage between Elis and Eva. At a reasonable distance from the film's conclusion, Erland Josephson delivers his view of Elis in one of the film's Brechtian interruptions. His character, says Josephson, is contemptuous of the kinds of virtuous souls who demand truth and justice in the world. Furthermore, this man couldn't care less about the sufferings of other people. And yet, we have known since very early in the film that Elis does in fact have a secret passion. Hidden away in a renovated mill building on his property is a small retreat where he has stored a vast number of photographs over many years. He will, as the film unfolds, take a series of photographs of Andreas. There are boxes and boxes of photographs of people in various poses: asleep, angry and so on; faces of people suffering from violent emotions. Elis has even made the effort of trying to catalogue the photos according to behaviour. What is the meaning of all this? On the one hand, this passion gives a lie to Elis's resignation and condemnation of aspirations to 'culture'. If he externally declares contempt for the world and has taken up a position which effectively abandons that world, then this extraordinary passion shows us that he does in fact care deeply for something. On the other hand, this passion appears completely isolated and withdrawn from the world. We have come full circle, for Elis's photographs here function in much the same way as Fredrik's portrait photographs of his young wife, Anne, functioned in *Smiles of a Summer Night*. These photographs are expressions of isolation. They are indicators of the ways that Elis is trapped in his own subjectivity, that he is screened from the world. As Cavell would put it, such photographs show a world present to Elis but from which he is absent (see Cavell 1979a, 18–23). This passion also demonstrates a tendency towards narcissism that Elis shares with Andreas: he has withdrawn from the objects of the external world, only so as to more tightly embrace the objects that he keeps in his own internal, secret world. Like Andreas, Elis also dissolves his relationship to the external world in order to wall himself in, to keep himself enclosed within an isolated world he has created in order to contain himself.

And perhaps this is as far as we can go with Bergman. Isolation from the world and from others will lead to despair and tragedy, while a speaking together and sharing the world with another person, with other people, will open the way to a pursuit of happiness. Across his works, Bergman shows us both possibilities. In doing so, he shows us a universe that is very much in contact with the world framed by the American comedies of remarriage.

Notes

1 Cavell simply calls this 'modern subjectivity'. As he puts it in *The World Viewed*, 'At some point the unhinging of our consciousness from the world interposed our subjectivity between us and our presentness to the world' (Cavell 1979a, 22). I discuss these issues in Rushton 2011 (114–15).
2 The later translation of Lacan's seminar on *Desire and Its Interpretation* is somewhat more extended: 'The subject is present in fantasy, and the object – which is the object of desire solely insofar as it is one of the terms in fantasy – takes the place, I would say, of what the subject is deprived of symbolically' (Lacan 2019, 312).

3 A more recent translation puts it a little differently: '[T]here is always a note of impossibility in the object of desire, which has to do with the very structure and foundations of desire. The fact that the object of desire is impossible is just one of the especially manifest forms of an aspect of human desire' (Lacan 2019, 335).
4 I am relying on a 1935 English translation by Michael Joyce (Plato 1938).
5 A green world, perhaps, but certainly not a dreamworld. Of the conclusions of literary romantic comedies, Northrop Frye writes that 'Normally, we can forget in this way only when we wake up from a dream, when we pass from one world to another, and we often have to think of the main action of a comedy as "the mistakes of a night", as taking place in a dream or a nightmare world that the final scene suddenly removes us from and thereby makes illusory' (quoted in Cavell 1981, 51).
6 These are Cavellian issues, more or less, arising from his readings of Thoreau (2008) and Emerson (2001b, 261–78), especially of the former's essay on 'Civil Disobedience' and the latter's essay on 'Fate'. Cavell asks what happens when you find yourself taking a place in a society, but you also discover that you don't like that place; you discover that the society you are in is not one you consent to. 'Let's put this demand' – the demand to give consent to the society in which you live – 'as the expectation of your "taking your place" in society.' Cavell continues, 'And let's suppose that you do not see the place, or do not like the places you see' (Cavell 2004, 23). Elis, in *The Passion of Anna*, does not like the places he sees, and this causes him to withdraw from the world, from society.
7 All of this more or less from Freud's 'Mourning and Melancholia' (Freud 1984b).
8 Jumping to Shakespeare is to overlook Bergman's indebtedness to August Strindberg, of course. To take up a discussion of those connections would, I fear, require another book entirely.
9 See Kristeva's discussion of *Romeo and Juliet* in Kristeva 1987, 209–33.
10 Kristeva writes brilliantly about these states in her book *Black Sun*. She describes it as a mode of 'learned helplessness': 'When all escape routes are blocked, animals as well as men learn to withdraw rather than flee or fight' (Kristeva 1989, 34).
11 On the psychoanalytic aspects of these processes see Kristeva 1989, 48ff.

Chapter 5

Alain Resnais and the communication of love

5.1 She and he (Delphine Seyrig and Giorgio Albertazzi) in *Last Year in Marienbad* (Alain Resnais, 1961)

I have argued in the preceding chapters that one way to approach the films under discussion in this book is to conceive of them in terms of a distinction between comedies and tragedies of remarriage. That may not amount to much more than saying that in the comedies a romantic couple will live happily ever after, while in the tragedies they will not. That much is certainly true, more or less. And yet, much of what is at stake here comes down to questions of how a couple might achieve happiness and, on the other hand, why they might fail to find it. Or, correlatively – as we have found with couples like Christine and Robert in *The Rules of the Game* or with Count Malcolm and Charlotte in *Smiles of a Summer Night* – we might ask whether a union at the end of a plot is a worthwhile union, whether it is one founded on principles of happiness, or whether some other fortune has encouraged a couple to stay together. Issues like these will become more complicated as this book progresses.

I have additionally tried to make a distinction between old marriage – based on tradition, class alliances and economic principles, rather than being based on love matches – and new marriage or remarriage, these latter being conceptions of marriage based on notions of mutual understanding and what Stanley Cavell calls acknowledgment. One of the aims, it seems to me, of Bergman's films, is to demonstrate just how difficult the conditions of acknowledgment are. The rewards of mutual acknowledgment may be realised in a form of happiness we call 'love' – a 'best case of acknowledgment', as Cavell puts it. A version of this is presented in Bergman's *Smiles of a Summer Night*. But the risks associated with acknowledgment, that is, of opening oneself up to the possibility of rejection, as well as taking on the burden of seeing the world from the perspective of two people rather than one person, and thus of accepting the claim that 'each person is constructed through the encounter with another', are risks that can result in losses that come at a terrible price. *The Passion of Anna* shows us a version of this, as do many other of Bergman's films.

In this chapter I trace a number of these concerns in films directed by Alain Resnais, especially in his 1961 film, *Last Year in Marienbad*. As will become clear, I examine this film in terms of a distinction between old and new marriage. Some of its connections with *The Rules of the Game* are therefore highlighted too. First of all, however, some preliminary comments.

Les Amants

Louis Malle's *Les Amants* (1958) pays particular homage to *The Rules of the Game*. *Les Amants* upturns the ending of Renoir's film: instead of a tragic accident in which the (potential) romantic couple's pursuit of happiness is rendered impossible, in Malle's film the newly formed couple thunders away from the past in an extraordinary escape into the future. *Les Amants* is not subtle or ambiguous (and nor is it formally adventurous). Rather, it is uncompromising and brazen in advancing the couple's spur-of-the-moment getaway. The escape of these young lovers, Jeanne (Jeanne Moreau) and Bernard (Jean-Marc Bory) – a 'reckless dash into the unknown' if ever there was one – occurs right in front of the eyes of what might be termed 'old marriage': both Jeanne's husband, Henri (Alain Cuny), and her lover, Raoul (José Villalonga), can only gawk in astonishment as Jeanne leaves them behind as though dispensing with them entirely. Notably, there is one other character here: the gamekeeper, played by Gaston Modot, the same actor who played Schumacher in *The Rules of the Game*. I can offer this as some sort of proof that *Les Amants* is a remake of Renoir's film. Jeanne does this, flee in full view, with a man she has met only some twelve or fourteen hours before. This couple has spent the night engaging in dreamy conversation and passionate sex right in the same house as Jeanne's husband (granted, it is a comfortably large château: we are dealing here with the moneyed classes verging on high aristocracy). Surely this is as scandalous as any film of this period can afford to be (it is 1958). Indeed, so scandalous that it sparked an obscenity trial when screened in Cleveland Heights in the US. *Les Amants* turns its back, with flagrant disdain, on centuries of tradition, propriety and conventional romance.

Les Amants provides something like a total condemnation of marriage. Indeed, this film not only condemns marriage inasmuch as a marriage contains a married couple; it also condemns the extensions often appended to the structures of marriage – what I have been calling the 'couple + 1' formation: the lover, Raoul, is here also ridiculed as an old-fashioned and empty caricature. Surely, then, we are about as far as we can be from the affirmations of marriage and romance conceived by Stanley Cavell as comedies of remarriage. *Les Amants* calls not for an affirmation of marriage but its destruction. This film is a comedy and its ending is happy (if also somewhat circumspect), but its pursuit of happiness is a matter of escaping from and destroying marriage.

And still ... if examined more closely there are correspondences between *Les Amants* and the comedies of remarriage, for this film certainly contains the destruction of a false marriage, a central theme for Cavell's genre, and the destruction of what I have been calling 'old marriage'. That it then fails to go so far as to seal the replacement of this false marriage with a potentially true one – that it instead focuses its concerns on a 'reckless dash into the unknown', the kind of reckless dash Nora takes in Ibsen's *A Doll's House* towards freedom and education and away from her marriage, but also the kind of reckless dash engaged in by Anne and Henrik in Bergman's *Smiles of a Summer Night* – is worth noting. Malle's film makes no bones about it: it presents us with no form of true marriage, for what this world needs first and foremost, *Les Amants* seems to say, is the destruction of false marriage and the eradication of old marriage, if not the obliteration of all forms of marriage per se.

If a film such as *Les Amants* embraces the destruction of a false marriage, might it also be the case for the filmmakers I approach in this book that *all marriages are false*? Might this be a European response to the American notion of a modern version of marriage based on mutual acknowledgment and equality, which is to say that the conventions of any marriage cannot support those stakes? Such might be a conclusion drawn from some of Bergman's films, as discussed in Chapters 3 and 4. Bergman's most complex reflection on marriage is, of course, *Scenes from a Marriage*. The struggles of the main couple in this series (its long version is a nearly six-hour series for television) are ones that go to extreme lengths to identify the falseness of marriage, and one way to interpret its closure – whereby the now-divorced couple, Johan (Erland Josephson) and Marianne (Liv Ullmann), reunite against the backdrop of the failures of their current remarriages – is simply to declare that marriage doesn't work, that *all marriages are false*. This is another way of declaring that true love can exist only outside a marriage.

As though to drive home this point, early in *Scenes from a Marriage*, Marianne, a divorce lawyer, is visited by a woman who has been married for twenty years but now claims that she has never loved her husband. She married young and had children and figured that it was best to stay married for the sake of the children. Now that her children have left home, she is ready to be divorced. This woman states to Marianne that her life and all of her senses have been deadened due to a lack of love. Needless to say, this series was extremely popular in Sweden and one sure consequence, it seems, was that the divorce rate jumped. Bergman's response was, 'That's got to be good!' (quoted in Cowie 1982, 291) A rise in the number of divorces is interpreted by Bergman as a positive thing: it indicates that many had given up on their false marriages and were determined to escape from them. All the same, this woman from *Scenes from a Marriage* had remained in a marriage for twenty years in ways that had robbed her of much of her life. Surely it is this potential for the conventions of marriage to snub out a life that these films – I mean Bergman's films, Malle's *Les Amants* and, as we shall see, to some degree, those of Alain Resnais – are determined to smash. And yet, in smashing such conventions these films are explicitly replaying the themes central to Cavell's imagining of the genre of remarriage. They are destroying false marriage in the hope that something better will take its place. Such will be my argument with respect to several of Alain Resnais's films in this chapter.

Last year ...

I want to begin my reflections on Resnais with the suggestion that *Last Year in Marienbad* might be considered a distant remake, with variations, of *The Rules of the Game*. But I also want to suggest that one thread of *Marienbad*'s interwoven layers could be considered as advancing concerns very similar to those of Malle's *Les Amants*. Finally, most provocatively, I want to suggest that, in some respects, *Marienbad* might be considered in the light of Preston Sturges's *The Lady Eve* (1937), a film that has come up in earlier chapters and which is one of the examples of a remarriage comedy that Cavell theorises. My suggestion emerges by virtue of a small moment in Sturges's film, shortly after the Lady Eve Sidwich (Barbara Stanwyck) has introduced herself to various persons at the Pike mansion on the occasion of a party there. Only then is Charles Pike (Henry Fonda) introduced to her, and his immediate response is quite simply to be dumbfounded upon coming face to face with the Lady Eve. He knows (surely!), as much as we know, that he has met this woman before, except that when he met her previously, she was another woman, a woman named Jean. This woman instantly asks him whether something is the matter, and Charles's response is to ask, still in a state of astonishment, 'I mean ... haven't we met?' Eve knowingly replies, 'Well, of course, your father just introduced us!' She then corrects herself and states, 'Oh, I'm sorry. You meant hadn't you met me *before* some place.' This is indeed what Charles had intended, so that Eve then ponders the possibility: 'Oh very probably, let me see, where could it have been?' And so the action goes on. My point here is to emphasise that this film dramatises a moment in which the two central protagonists ask the question, 'didn't we meet somewhere before?' Neither of these characters ponders the possibility that they might have met last year in Marienbad, but I take the conversation as, at the very least, a starting point for thinking of the relationships between these two films. The stage of this relationship is set by the question, 'Haven't we met somewhere before?' Ultimately, my point here is to suggest that *Last Year in Marienbad* may well be a remarriage comedy.

Reading *Last Year in Marienbad* in this way requires putting a straightjacket on it. Many of the film's rightly famous ambiguities will need to be dispensed with so that a clear narrative trajectory can be discerned. I wouldn't dare claim my reading as definitive. I would, however, regard it as plausible and compelling. I would certainly not declare it the only possible reading of the film, for *Marienbad* is a film that invites multiple interpretations (some would say the film demands it).

I think it is safe to infer this much: designated as 'X' in the script, the man (Giorgio Albertazzi) introduces us to the film's setting and to its main dilemma. Early in the film he addresses his statements to the woman, called 'A' in the script (Delphine Seyrig). He guides her through the rooms and gardens of the hotel where the action of the film takes place. 'You're familiar with the setting,' he tells her, 'but you hardly seem to remember.' He states that the hotel hides many secrets. For a second time he isolates the issue of memory by stating to her, 'You hardly seem to remember me....' At this point, they are dancing arm-in-arm. Then we get something more definitive. The man states, 'I first saw you in the gardens at Frederiksbad. You were alone, apart from the others. Standing by a balustrade, resting your hand on it, your arm half outstretched....' He continues to recount the details of this scene, and in many ways his recollection here seems concrete.

And yet the woman responds, 'It was not me. You must be mistaken.' As is well-known, and irrefutable it would seem to me, it is this conflict that is woven throughout the remainder of the film. Did this couple meet last year in Marienbad? Or was it in Frederiksbad? And if they did meet, what was the nature of their meeting? If the woman cannot remember, why is it she cannot? Or does she simply not want to remember? And then, finally, at the end of *Last Year in Marienbad*, do we presume the woman has been shot dead, or does she escape with the man? Or what, exactly, happens?

Strange as it may seem at first, *Last Year in Marienbad* yields some startling answers if it is presumed to be a descendant of the comedies of remarriage. My reading of the film will insist that the man and the woman do escape at the end of the film. They engage in a 'reckless dash into the unknown'. In doing so, the woman is achieving an escape from a false marriage, for she is married – my reading must assume it. She is married to the man designated as 'M' in the script (Sacha Pitoëff), and this marriage is by no means a good one. The couple, X and A, plan their getaway to coincide with a play that will take place at the hotel, a play called *Rosmer*. The woman excuses herself from attending the play on account of her having fainted shortly before it was to begin. Her husband attends the play. This therefore gives the couple the chance to escape: and so they do. To me, the closing scenes of the film confirm all this. The closing words, again uttered by the man (X) in voiceover, offer a description of the garden and the hotel as arranged in strict symmetrical order so as to make it impossible to lose one's way. At any rate, this is how it seems, he tells us, at first sight. And yet, 'Along those stone paths,' he says to the woman, 'and amidst the statues, you were already losing your way forever, in the still night, alone with me.' The man is trying to tell us – and the woman – that the hotel, as much as her marriage, is arranged in accordance with a strict order – call this tradition, convention, conformity – so much so that escaping from such an order might appear impossible. But escape they do, both from the hotel and from the woman's false marriage. And they do so in words that might well be taken directly from Cavell: 'alone with you'. Cavell might put it as 'by themselves together', but the inference I want to make should be clear: this couple is escaping into the future, and the man here has led the woman away from a false marriage and into the promise of a different future, a 'reckless dash into the unknown'.

Some details

If one accepts the precepts of this reading – that *Marienbad* is a descendant of remarriage comedy – then it shows us a reversal of the terms set by *The Rules of the Game*. In *Marienbad* the couple manages an escape in a way that Christine and André were unable to in Renoir's film. The murder – the 'accident' – that brings *Rules* to its climax is invoked by *Marienbad*'s dreamed or imagined scene of the woman's being shot dead by her husband. (If my reading insists on the couple's escape, then it will also need to place this murder in the virtual realm, in that realm of events that are imagined by the film but which do not actually occur in the reality of the diegesis.) The placing of the action of *Marienbad* in a traditional château (the film calls it a hotel) also positions such action somewhere akin to a 'green world' and in a setting not at all dissimilar to the château of La Colinière in *The Rules of the Game*. And, given Resnais's admitted admiration for Renoir's film – 'the most overwhelming experience I have had in the cinema in my whole life' (Resnais 1970, 14) – the inferences of homage in *Marienbad* might well be authorially intended. Of course, the key difference for my own reading of these films is that where *The Rules of the Game* ends in tragedy, *Last Year in Marienbad* ends with the prospect of a future that might be just enough to call it a comedy.

I began this chapter with some words on Louis Malle's *Les Amants*, as much as to call attention to the relationship between that film and *The Rules of the Game* as to also hint that it offered a spirit of escaping from a false marriage that would be repeated in *Last Year in Marienbad*. Perhaps all I want to say here is that Malle's film, audacious and scandalous, made it not *merely* audacious and scandalous that such an event as a woman's escaping from a false marriage in so brazen a fashion might be possible. Rather, *Les Amants* also made such an event exhilarating, liberating and joyous. Even with its vastly different imagery, its ambiguity, its anti-realism and cinematic adventurousness – all things *Les Amants* is not – I would still like to believe that the ending of *Last Year in Marienbad* also contains something of that joyousness of the couple's escape that pervades the ending of Malle's film. The world of *Marienbad* is stultified, traditional, conformist, a society of rules, just as restrictive and claustrophobic as that of *The Rules of the Game* and *Les Amants*. Escape from that world is the only reasonable option.

Is there any evidence that this couple, A and X, might fulfil the requirements of mutual understanding and equality which I have said, following Cavell, are integral to the comedies of remarriage? *Last Year in Marienbad* is a film of conversations. To that degree it is a film in which a man and a woman come to agree upon a world. This couple creates a world which they might be able to share and agree upon, and to that extent they achieve something like mutual understanding. To call this love might be a difficult claim to make, but by the end of the film there are certainly grounds for claiming a *case* of acknowledgment between the members of this couple, if not quite a *best case* of acknowledgment.

The couple's conversations in *Last Year in Marienbad* are many and varied. They are explicitly contrasted with the meaningless conversations of the other people who surround them. 'I've never heard a voice raised at this hotel,' the man says at one point. 'Conversations took place in a vacuum, as if the words meant nothing, as though they could have no meaning.' And he will go so far as to contrast this lack of meaning in other people's conversations with the ability for himself and the woman to engage in acts of meaningful conversation. He reminisces about their meeting (last year, we presume) and that she was chatting with friends. And yet these friends were unable to understand what she was trying to say. 'I alone understood,' the man declares. 'I felt these people didn't know who you were,' he continues. 'I alone did.' He then goes on to suggest that they continued to speak to each other and that they seemed to be the only ones who really understood what they were saying. This is a way of affirming their conversation as meaningful, but meaningful in a way that is singular for them, in the way that Emerson, for example, describes the conversation of friendship as one in which 'Two may talk and one may hear'. Emerson adds, and we have already seen, that 'three cannot take part in a conversation of the most sincere and searching sort' (Emerson 1898, 54). The talent this man and woman have for conversation singles them out as a couple so that it is indeed only they who understand the stakes of their conversations. Cavell will note this of the couples of remarriage comedies: to outsiders their union will appear as one that cannot be understood. 'To outsiders', he writes, 'as remarriage comedy repeatedly demonstrates, such a couple will seem incomprehensible' (Cavell 2004, 299).

And the union of this couple in *Last Year in Marienbad* goes deeper than this. 'What do you hope to get from me?' the woman asks midway through the film. 'What other life would you have me live?' she adds. The man responds: 'I don't mean another life. I mean your life.' There is an edit between the man's two sentences, as though we are switching from one life to another, or from past to present, or vice versa. Whatever the visual rhetoric, to me the meaning is clear: he is aspiring to deliver this woman from a life in which she has merely haunted the world into one in which she could become who she is, where she would truly exist. Cavell would call such a trajectory one that offers 'a journey, or path, or step, from haunting the world to existing in it', that it would provide ways of acquiring 'one's own experience of the world', he adds (Cavell 1996, 220). Cavell makes these claims in a context considerably different from that of *Last Year in Marienbad* – he is writing on King Vidor's *Stella Dallas* (1937) – but the implication is that a false marriage entails a haunting of the world and that an escape from such a marriage will open a path towards a future in which one might genuinely experience the world. This brings us close, I believe, to what is at stake for *Last Year in Marienbad*.

False marriage

What is false about the marriage here? In an influential reading of the film, Lynne A. Higgins argues that *Last Year in Marienbad* is concerned with the covering up of a rape. On these terms, it is X (the man) who has raped A (the woman), and *that* is what happened last year in Marienbad. Therefore, when this man once again comes face to face with this woman, he is determined that she in no way reveal what happened last year. All of his speech, argues Higgins, is designed to cover up the fact of his rape of the woman. Indeed, his conversations are designed so as to badger the woman into believing that no such rape occurred, that she merely imagined it and that she is in some way deluded or traumatised. Convincing evidence for this reading comes from the film itself, but also from Alain Robbe-Grillet's script, in which there is indeed a rape scenario (not at all surprising to those familiar with Robbe-Grillet; see Higgins 1991, 307–8). Significantly, however, Higgins tells us that this scene was 'removed by Resnais during filming' (Higgins 1991, 308).

I find Higgins's analysis both plausible and valid, but it does rather make the film one dimensional and it leaves a good deal about the film unaccounted for. I am prepared to accept that the woman (A) has been violated and traumatised in some way. I think the film insists on this point: here we are presented with a deeply unhappy woman who wants and needs to change her life. But I do not believe the film makes her a victim of the man (X). Rather, my claim is that she is the victim of her husband (M). He is the cause of her suffering. The reason for this is that she does not love him anymore. Because of this she wishes to flee, something she achieves in concert with the man (X).

I want to defend this reading because I am convinced it is valid. There is one key scene and two related scenes which make it valid. The key scene occurs halfway through the film. It occurs as an extension of the scene, discussed above, which features the woman's questioning of the man. She asks, 'What other life would you have me live?' The man tries to conjure up an answer to this question. In doing so he first of all tries to relate to her the kind of life she has been living. And that life is one in which she is restricted and persecuted in various ways by her husband. He therefore describes a scene – a scene we would have to figure must have happened 'last year' – in which the husband (M) approaches the woman (A), only for her to shrink back in fear. The point of the scene is to describe the ways in which the woman is afraid of her husband. They are in one of the rooms of the hotel – this year? Or is it last year? My sense is that it is the latter, for the man is once again trying to tell the woman about one of the things that happened last year. And yet, the man is also speaking these memories as though we are here witnessing the past and the present at the same time.[1]

The man continues his recollections. 'Remember. One evening, the last, I think' – that is, the last night they spent together last year. He goes on at some length:

> It was almost dark. A shadowy figure slowly advanced through the dusk. I could distinguish your features, I knew it was you. When you recognized me, you stopped. We stood there, a few yards apart, without saying a word. You were standing before me. Waiting, perhaps. Unable to move either forward or back. You stood there, motionless. Your arms at your sides. Looking at me. (*The camera has been focused on the man in close-up. The camera now pans so that the woman is brought into the shot. They look at each other.*) Your eyes open even wider. Your lips parted as though to speak, or groan, or cry out. (*The camera has tracked towards the woman so that she is now centre screen.*) You are afraid. You open your mouth a little more. Your eyes get wider. You hold your hand forward, uncertainly, as if waiting, appealing, or perhaps in defence. Your fingers tremble. (*Now the film cuts to reveal the husband (M) as he walks towards the camera. He is about to enter the room occupied by the man and the woman. The man continues his monologue.*) You are afraid.

The husband walks closer in to join them, but they each have their backs to him. I see no reason to avoid what seems to me is a fairly direct interpretation of this scene: if the woman is afraid, then it is her husband she is afraid of. It is not the man, X, she is afraid of, and it is certainly not X who might have raped her. Rather, it is her husband, M, she is afraid of. We may even infer that it is her husband who has raped her. As soon as the husband comes near to them, the man describes, 'Your fingers tremble. You are afraid.' The scene moves on. The husband stops momentarily, turns, and walks away in the direction he has come from. 'Who is it?' the man asks. 'Your husband?' he speculates.

> Perhaps. He was looking for you or maybe passing by. He was already nearing you. But you remained rigid as if you were not there. He didn't quite seem to recognize you. So he stepped forward. Something about you escaped him. One step further. You looked through him. He chose to go. And now, you stare into the void. You still see him, his grey eyes. His grey shape. And his smile. And you're afraid.

There is nothing simple about this scene, and my reductions here mainly to the scene's dialogue – and even then, it is entirely monologic talk from the man – can hardly do it justice. But we can discern some key elements: the woman's husband comes near and this causes the woman to tremble. And when he comes close to her he also seems to miss her; he sees through her, or she sees through him (or both). It is as though they are unable to connect. I think we can take this as a marker of their inability to understand or recognise each other. Cavell might call such a scene an exhibition of the ways in which the members of this marriage remain unknown to each other.

Granted, we hear the woman neither affirm nor deny the man's reminiscences, and we surely don't have to believe him, nor does she have to believe him. But I think there are good reasons to believe the man is genuine. Shortly after this, the man says to the woman, 'You don't want to remember because you're afraid.' Why does he accuse her of not wanting to remember? And why is she afraid? Afraid of what? Afraid of her husband? Well, surely one may speculate that she is afraid that her husband might find out about the affair she has had (is having) with this man last year in Marienbad (or Frederiksbad). That is certainly what I want to infer from just about everything we see in *Last Year in Marienbad*: the woman (A) and the man (X) had an affair 'last year in Marienbad'. They enjoyed it. And the woman has been living with the guilt of having betrayed her husband (M) ever since. She is afraid that if he does find out he might harm her, perhaps going so far as to shoot her dead – and indeed she has a premonition of such a thing near the end of the film. She thought she would never again see this man with whom she had an affair last year, but here he is again. He has seen her again, and he realises that a 'reckless dash into the unknown' might deliver to them a chance of happiness. But this is a tremendous risk to take: for the woman to leave her husband, a husband she has become afraid of. This is the reason why the man spends so much time trying to convince her of what happened last year in Marienbad; that is, that they had an affair, and they both enjoyed it. And now it is time to act on it, to take a risk on the future.

An affair?

The scene I have described above is the one I regard as the key scene that demonstrates the 'false marriage' at the heart of *Last Year in Marienbad*. It shows us that the woman is afraid of her husband. In what follows I will concentrate on the other two scenes that enable us to understand the overall shape of Resnais's film in terms that pertain to remarriage comedy. A first thing to note is that much of the conversation between the man (X) and the woman (A) in the second half of the film turns on the question of whether the man visited the woman in her room – and I presume the film is exploring the question of whether the man visited this woman 'last year'. I don't think we have to read too deeply here to see this as being a question of whether or not this couple had sex last year in Marienbad; that they had an affair. But it is this visit to her room and the nature of this visit that the woman is most reluctant to remember. 'Again I come to your room,' insists the man. But the woman retorts, 'I've never been in any bedroom with you.' Again the man challenges her: 'You don't want to remember because you're afraid,' while also adding statements like 'You dreaded his return,' or 'You had just had a row of some sort.' Again the man gives us the impression that she is afraid of her husband, afraid that the husband might discover this woman's affair, and afraid that she enjoys the company of the man more than she enjoys that of her husband, and that to follow through on that enjoyment will mean breaking the codes of traditional, civilised society as well as the codes of 'old marriage'. I take the man's statements here as some sort of proof that he is genuine, that he is telling the truth, first and foremost because he wants her to remember. The psychoanalytic analogy will not be too far wrong here: the man is trying to allow the woman to remember something that has been repressed, and it is none other than their affair that has been repressed. It is not, as Higgins would have us believe, that the man has raped the woman, a fact which the man, according to Higgins's commentary, is now trying to deny or cover up. And yet, why is the woman so reluctant to remember? I think she resists the man's suggestions – suggestions that some might say border on torment or badgering – because remembering what happened last year in Marienbad – that she was in a bedroom with this man and that she had an affair with him – will be enough to convince her that her marriage is doomed, that it is a false marriage, and that she might well love this man a good deal more than she loves her husband. This would be enough under the conditions of old marriage – the action of the film is set in the 1930s (this brings it closer to *The Rules of the Game* as well as to the remarriage comedies) – to make her very afraid of her husband (much more afraid, for example, than Christine is in *The Rules of the Game*, and more afraid too than Jeanne in *Les Amants*).

There are two moments when the man and the woman paint a memory of his having entered her room. The first occurs immediately following the discussion above in which the man declares to the woman, 'You are afraid.' In this scene the woman sits alone in her room. She is wearing a dark-coloured dress (the film is, of course, filmed in high-contrast black and white). The man – as usual – offers his commentary: 'You dread his return' – meaning she dreads her husband's return. And the man goes on to claim that he (X) came to her room. He adds that this was an easy thing to do, for all the doors had been left open. As he is explaining this, the camera slowly tracks toward the woman. She is seated at a dressing table and has her back to the camera. As the camera draws closer, she slowly turns around so as almost to face it. She looks upwards, as though greeting the man who, it appears, has now entered the room (we do not see him) (Figure 5.2). The

Alain Resnais

5.2 The man visits the woman in *Last Year in Marienbad* (Alain Resnais, 1961)

man continues his voiceover: 'You know the rest,' he says. Immediately after this the woman screams, and it is quite clear that she screams in fear. The scene continues. She does not quite get to complete her scream before there is a cut to a shooting gallery where a number of men, including the husband (M), stand in line with pistols at their sides awaiting the next round of firing at targets. We have seen this activity once or twice before. Needless to say, there are no gunshots this time, as the film immediately cuts back to the man (X) and woman (A) in conversation. In response to the man's claim that 'You know what happens next,' she states, 'No I don't.... I don't know you,' she adds.

As with most scenes in this film – and this is an extremely brief moment in the film; perhaps no more than ten seconds – there is nothing simple or straightforward here. Higgins takes this as one of the scenes denoting the man's rape of the woman (Higgins 1991, 308–9). I do not believe this is the case. I simply want to reiterate that this is a scene which demonstrates that this couple had an affair: the man prefaces his reminiscence of the scene by declaring that the husband was not there, that he was playing cards (though we must infer that he was in fact at the shooting gallery). In his absence, this couple could secretly fulfil their desires. And so they did – they did, if we are to trust the man's reminiscences. If that is the case, then why is the woman so insistent that it did not happen? She goes so far as to declare to the man, 'I don't know you.' My answer: she insists it did not happen because she does not want to destroy her marriage. If she admits her affair and its sexual consummation, not to mention its enjoyment, then it is as much as declaring that her marriage is a sham, that she is afraid of her husband and that she does not love him. These are not easy admissions to make, but the man convinces her that they are, by the end of the film,

5.3 The woman greets the man in *Last Year in Marienbad* (Alain Resnais, 1961)

admissions worth making. And the woman gains the courage to escape from her marriage.

The second moment when the man seems to enter the woman's room is one of the more extraordinary sequences of the film: a tracking shot storms along one of the corridors of the hotel leading to the woman's bedroom before exploding into a series of rapidly edited moments. The movement of the camera is jagged, urgent, as if tormented or nervous. It seems to me that the camera's movement is supposed to be a subjective shot from the man's point of view. The camera finally enters the woman's room, where this time she is dressed in white and what follows is a series of embraces (Figure 5.3). That is, the woman embraces the man, and this is repeated several times by way of a series of rapid jump-cuts. It is worth noting that the soundtrack here is quite deliriously loud: we are here witnesses either to a traumatic event or to an event of wondrous pleasure. My sense is that the latter is the case and that this scene offers substantial proof that this couple had an affair last year in Marienbad, and that it was a passionate, fulfilling and joyous affair (every bit as joyous and passionate as the affair in *Les Amants*, for example). It is this memory that is 'true', so that the earlier memory in which the woman screamed is erroneous. She does not scream at this man. Rather, she embraces him with joy.

There is (at least) one more scene in which the notion of an escape from a false marriage seems to me to be foregrounded. This occurs about one-third of the way through the film (it may be the most famous scene of the film). There is a long drinks bar and a dance floor at which many couples from the hotel are dancing. The woman is leaning against the bar, holding a glass of wine. The man stands two or three feet away from her. He narrates, 'One night I went up to your room …'. Visually, this scene, ostensibly a series of long takes, is intercut with flashes, images of the woman in her white room, dressed all in white, so that the cuts to these images act as white flashes into the predominantly dark lighting and *mise en scène* of the bar. (All of this helps to create one of the most visually stunning scenes in the history of cinema.) The intensity of the flashes increases and the duration of the white shots lengthens; one shot, for example, shows the woman in the white room surrounded by various shoes, one or two of which she casually tries on her feet. She then begins to laugh. Her laugh is followed by a series of rapid edits between the white and the black, between the past and the present, and of various angles of the bar, until another woman at the bar eventually stumbles backwards and into the woman causing her to drop her glass. As the glass of wine shatters, the image cuts back to her white room and the man is there walking towards where she is seated. She moves back and away from him, as if in dreaded fear. We then cut back to the broken glass on the floor of the bar: the symbolism of sexual violation is laid on rather thickly here, to say the least.

Enigmatic? For many commentators I imagine this scene would seem to offer proof that the man raped the woman last year in Marienbad, or at any rate, that he forced himself on her. However, I think we need to be careful, and to link this scene with others in the film. This scene occurs relatively early on. It is therefore showing us that the woman has not yet clarified to herself quite what happened last year. Is this man to be trusted, or is he to be feared? Such are the sorts of questions she is asking herself, and at this point she does not know how to answer. From one perspective he has quite unequivocally violated her: by making love to her he has violated her marriage; together they have broken apart the ties of old marriage. This is no mere affair of the 'couple + 1' variety. Rather, it is an affair that threatens to demolish a false marriage. For my own interpretation of *Last Year in Marienbad*, if anything has been violated here, then it is nothing other than the traditional institution of marriage. If this scene is linked with later scenes in the film, then ultimately this reminiscence of the man visiting the woman in her white room is a reminiscence of their affair and of the fact that this affair has caused a crisis in the woman's marriage. That ought to be enough to cause her to drop her glass.

There is another factor in this scene too: it is replayed later in the film as the prelude to the couple's escape. Multiple time frames are certainly being played with here – this scene is occurring both now and later, in the past and the present, and yet also in the future. But these multiple dimensions of time do not therefore cancel all meaning. Rather, if we take the entire film into account, what happens is this. Having remembered and accepted her affair with the man, and now having made the decision to leave her husband and escape with this man, she does so. The scene, as I have stated, is replayed later in the film. Near the film's end, the man and the woman are once again conversing. The time periods jump from one layer to another. She asks if he can wait a year before they escape (or is she asking him to wait *another* year?). He protests that he has already waited too long. 'It's as though you couldn't decide to leave him,' he says, but then she interrupts him: 'Be quiet. Someone's coming!' And indeed this someone is her husband. He does not approach her until we have flashed back (or forward?) to see the couple in the garden, in the same place we have seen them meet before, near the statue. It is here that her husband approaches, causing the woman to scream. It is also here that we see the balustrade collapse (we have seen this happen before). If this is not all proof that it is the husband who is to be feared and that he has sexually violated this woman, then I have difficulty finding another way to interpret this scene. To amplify the issue still further, her scream leads to a cut (a 'sound bridge') directly back to the bar scene where we have seen the woman exclaim before, that is, when she dropped her wine glass. It is as though it is only now that she is coming to terms with the cruelty of her husband and her shame or guilt over her affair. But at the same time it is here that she definitively realises that her marriage is over: it is time to leave her husband. And so she does at the end of the film.

Marienbad and *Rosmersholm*

My reading of the film insists not only that the husband and the woman are married, but also that they are unhappily married – in Cavell's terms, that the woman remains unknown to her husband: it is a loveless marriage. It is a loveless marriage, but it is a traditional marriage – let's call it an old marriage or a European marriage – which means it is a marriage that should not be broken. And thus my main claim for the film is this: that yes, the woman (A) did meet the man (X) last year in Marienbad (or Frederiksbad or wherever it was), and yes, not only did they meet, but they had an affair; and yes, going still further, they had an affair which was very pleasurable, so pleasurable in fact that the woman began to harbour severe doubts over her marriage.

The task of the film, as I see it, can be seen very much from within the framework of Cavellian comedies of remarriage: the woman wants to be educated, and, as is the case in remarriage comedies, the woman finds in the man someone who might just have the potential to educate her. Together they might just come to some sort of knowledge of the world and thus together discover something that can be called acknowledgment. Thus, much of the film is composed of conversations between the man and the woman, so that by way of these conversations they come to discover a world together. It is entirely appropriate that the woman rebukes the man by declaring that he must be mistaken, that it must have been someone else he saw last year in Marienbad, that it wasn't her. It is appropriate because this is a sign that she won't merely accept what the man says, that she will question it, argue against it, demand justification for it.

What the film is about therefore is the discovery of communication for this couple. By the time we reach the end of the film, they have found faith in language, they have managed to create a world together. They have defined a relationship that can be characterised by what Cavell calls acknowledgment. They have discovered or invented some degree of faith in language. *Last Year in Marienbad* shows us, at its end, that this couple makes an escape while the husband attends a performance of a play called *Rosmer*. It would appear that this play alludes to Henrik Ibsen's *Rosmersholm* (1886). If I am arguing that *Marienbad* is a film that thematises a *gaining* of faith in language, then Ibsen's *Rosmersholm* is very much a play concerned with *losing* faith in language. Indeed, 'Losing Faith in Language' is the title given to a chapter written on *Rosmersholm* by a scholar, Toril Moi, whose work is very much influenced by the philosophies of Cavell (Moi 2006, 269–93). I want to argue here that *Last Year in Marienbad* is about gaining faith in language, so ultimately the relationship between *Marienbad* and *Rosmersholm* is one of inversion: *Marienbad* is the inverse or reverse of *Rosmersholm*.

It is not mere whim that draws me to Ibsen's *Rosmersholm*: it is explicitly evoked in *Last Year in Marienbad* by way of the play performed both near the beginning and the end of the film, a play titled *Rosmer*. I also figure that the play functions in a crucial way in the plot, for its performance near the end of the film provides the context in which the man and the woman make their 'reckless dash into the unknown' while the woman's husband attends the play. Furthermore, *Rosmersholm* has provided fuel for interpreting the film. The most provocative and extensive interpretation that goes in this direction is provided by T. Jefferson Kline in his book *Screening the Text*. Kline's interpretation is one that sees *Marienbad* as a film that tries to repeat or replay the themes of *Rosmersholm*. Thus, there is a clear point of difference between what I want to do here and what Kline does: Kline wants to more or less say that what happens in *Last Year in Marienbad* can be taken in much the same way as what occurs in *Rosmersholm* (Kline 1992). My argument takes the opposite stance: I claim that *Marienbad* reverses the stakes of *Rosmersholm*. Furthermore, the key interpretation of *Rosmersholm* that Kline relies on is Freud's interpretation from his essay on 'Character types Met with in Psychoanalytic Work' (Freud 1990). The interpretation of *Rosmersholm* on which I rely is, by contrast, that given by Toril Moi, with Moi's reading offering a completely different interpretation from that of Freud.

I cannot go into great detail on these interpretations, but a few points are necessary. Kline's interpretation of *Marienbad* is essentially a symptomatic one, and so too is Freud's reading of *Rosmersholm*. I can summarise each of these interpretations by virtue of the question they seem to be guided by, and that question is: What's wrong with the woman? Freud, in his reading of *Rosmersholm*, comes to the conclusion that what is wrong with Rebecca, the central female character in Ibsen's play, is the product of a dark secret from her past. This secret is that not only is she the daughter of Dr West, but she is also his mistress. Essentially we have a reversal of the Oedipus myth: Oedipus inadvertently married his mother, as we all know. In *Rosmersholm*, Rebecca inadvertently becomes the lover of a person she didn't know was her father, Dr West. As a result, she suffers from a mental illness, all a result of this dark secret.

Kline, on the back of Freud's reading of *Rosmersholm*, therefore looks for the 'dark secret' in *Last Year in Marienbad*. That secret has something to do with sexual violation, and Kline exposes several characteristics of an 'incest victim' in the character of the woman (A). During the film, therefore, the man (X), by way of his conversations, reignites the woman's incest trauma. The man's sexual advances or intimations have brought about something of a return of the repressed. Interestingly, Kline's reading of the film appeared at about the same time as Lynne Higgins's reading of the film in which she argued, as we saw earlier, that the film is something of a mirage that is constructed in such a way so as 'to deny the existence of rape' (Higgins 1991, 305). Higgins claims that '*Last Year in Marienbad* can be seen as a rape story narrated by a rapist' (Higgins 1991, 307).

Ultimately I think Kline's reading of *Marienbad* is very much overdriven by Lacanian psychoanalytic theory and Higgins's is very much over-influenced by a certain kind of feminism. I can only say that my own reading of the film is very different from these two. There are a couple of reasons why this is the case. First of all, I take both Kline's and Higgins's readings to more or less be what used to be called 'symptomatic readings'. These readings are looking for some kind of illness or symptom in *Last Year in Marienbad*. In short, they are looking for what is 'wrong' in this film. For Kline, the illness relates to the supposed incestuous background of the woman, while for Higgins it is a matter of the woman's rape. Such readings of film and media texts have often been very attractive: for a reading to point to what a film hides or erases – in the classic Althusserian schema, it is a matter of pointing to what is 'only visible insofar as it is invisible' – is to highlight both the deceptiveness of film and media texts and also the brilliance of the master reader who has the ability to uncover the hiddenness within the text.[2] Designating such a thing a 'constitutive absence' is one way of putting it. My point is simply that what Kline or Higgins think is hidden in the text is, as far as I'm concerned, simply not there. X does not rape A, nor is A suffering from some kind of incest-related return of the repressed. Rather, I contend that *Marienbad* points to issues that reside on its surface and which are discussed at length by the protagonists. Those issues pertain to love and acknowledgment; that is, of one person's (X) attempts to know another person (A).

Where does this leave Ibsen's play? There are a number of intertwined themes and plots in *Rosmersholm*, but for my purposes here I want to concentrate on the central romantic plot between Rebecca West and Johannes Rosmer. Each of these characters carries a traumatic past event or secret with them. As I have already mentioned, Rebecca's past relationship with Dr West carried a suggested measure of incest with it, while Rosmer's past is blighted by the recent suicide of his first wife, and he very much begins to believe, as the play progresses, that he had driven her to her death. Rebecca had been living at Rosmersholm (the name of the Rosmer house) as a housekeeper and maid up until the death of Rosmer's first wife. Rebecca continues to live there now, and it turns out that she and Rosmer have fallen in love. This love is doomed, however, by the lengthy shadows of the past, as well as by the peculiarities of Rosmer's character. Rosmer is a classic Ibsen idealist, a man whose ideals are ill equipped for the messy realities of the everyday world, to the point where these ideals become utterly destructive. For the romance between himself and Rebecca, the poisonous nature of Rosmer's idealism takes the form of the aspiration towards ideal love. We have already seen this kind of excessive romantic ideal of love wreak its destruction in Bergman's *The Passion of Anna* in the previous chapter, and *Rosmersholm* indeed follows a not dissimilar course.

Rosmer desires a love that will transcend language and, in so doing, he believes it will heal or render insignificant the wounds of the past. He is very clear about this love as he proposes marriage to Rebecca midway through the play. 'We two will be one,' he declares (Ibsen 1958, 78). Rosmer's view of love thus presents us with a classic Romantic vision rooted in fusion, the fusion of two into one and a consequent denial of difference. It is an example of what I called in the previous chapter 'hyperbolic' love. This marriage and this love are supposed to take place on a mystical or religious level: they are supposed to transcend both language and the deficiencies of the everyday. But Rebecca refuses him: she refuses Rosmer's proposal of marriage.

One question to answer here is: Why does Rebecca refuse the marriage? I accept Moi's reading of the play here. She claims that when Rebecca first moved to Rosmersholm she had been a free spirit, full of life force, sexual desire and self-determination. But Rosmer's idealism has crushed her spirit. 'Living at Rosmersholm', Moi writes, 'Rebecca has been transformed from an amoral Nietzschean to a guilt-ridden, post-Christian idealist' (Moi 2006, 278). There is a primary reason why this has occurred: Rosmer is deaf to language and to Rebecca's own statements and conversations. In Cavellian parlance, Rebecca is very much an 'unknown woman' here: Rosmer fails to acknowledge her. Moi by and large attributes this failure to Rosmer's idealism, for he believes the love between him and Rebecca should transcend language. He cannot abide by the proofs of mere language, but desires some ultimate proof, a transcendental, spiritual truth. 'I shall never be able to free myself from the doubt,' he states. 'Never know for certain I have your love' (Ibsen 1958, 111). Rebecca tries to reassure him by speaking with him. But this is not enough. 'Proof! I want proof!' Rosmer demands, in ways that relate him to the kind of sceptic who demands unconditional proof in matters of knowledge. In the play's tragic and supremely melodramatic ending, the couple is driven to the same fate as Rosmer's first wife: they commit suicide together by drowning.

What, then, is the relationship between *Rosmersholm* and *Last Year in Marienbad*? In terms of plot and theme, the connections are quite direct (if also somewhat tenuous, I must confess). Rosmer's idealism is reflected by the order and symmetry of the hotel and gardens of Resnais's film. The woman (A) in *Marienbad*, like Rebecca, feels that her life is stifled here and that any sense of freedom has been quashed in her. To this degree, then, her husband (M) takes on the Rosmer role, that is, of the man who stifles the woman's spirit. In attending the play-within-the-film that is called *Rosmer*, the husband is signalling some sort of companionship with the philosophy and ideals of Rosmer. This seems to me to be an entirely legitimate, if not altogether convincing, way to posit a relationship between *Rosmersholm* and *Last Year in Marienbad*.

But there is a far more compelling connection. In both Ibsen's play and Resnais's film there are a great many conversations. In *Rosmersholm* the bulk of these are between Rosmer and Rebecca, while in *Marienbad* they are primarily between the man and the woman. It is the differences in the courses of these conversations that are significant: where *Rosmersholm* charts the continued failure of understanding between Rosmer and Rebecca, the conversations in *Marienbad* depend upon an increase in understanding and recognition between the members of the couple, to the point where they can be said to have created a world, a past and a future together. They have gained faith in language and invented a new world for themselves – at any rate, their 'reckless dash into the unknown' at the film's end provides the possibility for the creation of a new world, and the creation of a new woman. By contrast, *Rosmersholm* shows us the destruction of a world as a result of losing faith in language. (As I have already pointed out, the title of Moi's chapter on *Rosmersholm* is 'Losing Faith in Language'.)

The key to Moi's reading of *Rosmersholm* is this: that Rosmer, by way of his idealism, desires to negate all difference between himself and Rebecca. In effect, even though they are two people, he wants them to become one – this is part of his quest for 'ennoblement'. What this means is that he desires a form of communication between himself and Rebecca that will not be sullied by words or communication or conversation: to transcend language will be an expression of the truest, deepest kind of love – such is Moi's interpretation of Rosmer's actions. Of course, Moi contends that this is no way to live, and she believes that this is the central theme of Ibsen's play: to deny the necessity of communication and conversation is to deny the human. Communication and conversation are ways in which we, as human beings, can relate to each other, but they also signal the ways in which we will always be separated from each other, the ways in which we will always be different from each other. There can be no guarantees that we will mean what we say, but if we reach a point where we believe true communication is beyond words, then we have reached a point where our humanness has been left behind. Such is Rosmer's problem: he abandons what it is to be human. The failure of the relationship between Rosmer and Rebecca – and a failure it is: Rebecca refuses to marry him, and in the end they commit suicide together (needless to say I see this ending as the direct opposite of the escape A and X manage at the end of *Last Year in Marienbad*) – the failure of Rebecca and Rosmer's relationship is a consequence of Rosmer's inability to acknowledge Rebecca.

As I have said, my reading of *Last Year in Marienbad* is one that declares it to be something of the reverse or inverse of *Rosmersholm*. Therefore, where the couple fails in *Rosmersholm*, they succeed in *Marienbad*: the man and the woman do accept conversation and communication, they discuss, contend with each other, challenge each other. There are many examples of them doing this throughout the film – their discussion over the statue is the most obvious example. I see the entire film and this pairing's attempts to reconstruct a past and a memory and in so doing to construct a world and a future together as markers of their ability to find a way towards language. I see all of these episodes and understandings and misunderstandings as so many steps towards acknowledgment. The consequence is that by the end of the film they have learned acknowledgment: and they escape into a new world, by themselves together.

Resnais's other films

If the above offers a reading of *Last Year in Marienbad*, then what of Resnais's other films? I do not have the space to offer anything comprehensive here, but I can point to the importance of the relation between communication and love across his films. Often the deficiencies of love and marriage will be ones associated with inadequate language or the inability to communicate. Such inadequacy is foregrounded, for example, in *Hiroshima, mon amour* (1959), which might easily be said to be a film that is about the inability for language and representational systems more generally, including memory, to capture the past and to register the intensity of existence and experience. The crucial question for *Hiroshima* and for many other of Resnais's films is the question of how one manages the inadequacies of language. Does one give up? Or does one persevere? Or does one try to transcend language in the manner of Rosmer and Rebecca in Ibsen's play? For Resnais, the inadequacies of language can be worked through only by way of conversation, that is, by communication.

Like *Marienbad*, *Hiroshima* is a film of conversations. And many of Resnais's films can be said to be conversation films: *Providence* (1977), *Mon Oncle d'Amérique* (1980), *Mélo* (1986), even *On connaît la chanson* (1997) with its lip-synched pop music conversations. And yet, with so many of these conversations what becomes crucial is that language and communication *miss their mark*. *Muriel* (1963), *Providence*, *Mélo*, all the way up to *Coeurs* (*Private Fears in Public Places*, 2006), are all films of missed communication and missed encounters, of words that do not fit, or of actions that have been delivered without communication. For example, the video tapes that Charlotte (Sabine Azéma) sends to Thierry (André Dussollier) in *Coeurs*, or the missed encounter between the young couple, Dan and Nicole (Lambert Wilson, Laura Morante) in that same film; Claude's (Pierre Arditi) attempts to extricate himself from his marriage to Odile (Sabin Azéma) in *On connaît*;[3] the mystery surrounding Muriel for the son, Bernard (Jean-Baptiste Thierrée), in *Muriel* as well as the missed meeting many years ago for the mother, Hélène (Delphine Seyrig), and Alphonse (Jean-Pierre Kérien); or Marcel's (André Dussollier) affair with Romaine (Sabine Azéma) in *Mélo* that he refuses to confess during that film's extended final act. All of these are examples of how communication fails and, as a consequence, how love or marriage falters as a consequence. If anything, this makes *Marienbad* something of an exception for Resnais (though *Mon oncle d'Amérique* performs its own exceptionality, which I discuss below). If my own reading can be considered valid, *Marienbad* features a successful communicative exchange, a communication that amounts to something approaching love or acknowledgment (on Cavell's terms).

The key paradox of love for Resnais's films is, therefore, that love cannot be spoken, but nevertheless must be spoken (I say a little more on this below). And typically these attempts to speak of love and to discover its truth occur outside marriage – this is as true for *Marienbad* as it is for *Mélo* or *Je t'aime, je t'aime* (1968) as well as *Love unto Death* (1984). Marriages in Resnais's films never seem to fare well, with the prime example being the utterly toxic marriage in *Providence*, but in many of the later films – *Mon oncle d'Amérique*, *Mélo*, *On connait* ... – marriages are filled with compromises and disappointments. Of course, *Marienbad* fits well within this pattern too: it features a false marriage, as I have tried to argue.

The major exception is *Mon oncle d'Amérique*, a film that deals with several different versions of marriage. The key distinction in this film is between the aristocratic marriage between Jean (Roger Pierre) and his wife, Arlette (Nelly Bourgeaud), on the one hand, and the 'peasant' marriage between René and his wife, Thérèse (Gérard Depardieu, Marie Dubois). The aristocratic marriage is a classic traditional alliance that preserves familial privileges: it is a prime example of what I have been calling an 'old marriage'. It follows the course of old marriage all the way to the clear convenience of having an affair – a 'couple + 1'. Jean has an affair with the film's other key character, the once-working-class Janine (Nicole Garcia). When convenient, that affair can be easily disposed of. Jean acts in accordance with the biological-behavioural determinism of Henri Laborit (the film's professor in the so-called documentary sequences of the film), so that he comes to the realisation that his great love for Janine will jeopardise both his marriage and his social standing. He returns to the safety of old marriage, security and success. And even as his return is engineered by his wife, he later admits that it was the right thing to do.

By contrast, the film's other marriage is stretched to breaking point by the competitive spirit of the age (and countless commentators have noted the film's critique of French society's drift to the Right in the late 1970s; on this see Wilson 2006, 151–5). René's career stalls and grinds to a halt. He has been unable to keep pace with the economic demands and management modernisations of his job, to the point where he is reassigned to a town well away from Lille, where his wife and two children remain, leaving him to see them only at weekends. Ultimately, he attempts suicide. However, with his wife by his side, he realises the foolishness of his act and is reconciled both to his family and to life itself. He will be 'remarried' to her, as it were, and he will reinvent his life (at any rate, this is the promise the film holds). For René, *Mon Oncle d'Amérique* ends with the communication of love and the restoration of a new marriage. By contrast, the aristocratic Jean is left to spar with Janine, whom he has abandoned, so that film's final scene – Jean is hunting – immediately evokes *The Rules of the Game* and its upholding of aristocratic rules of marriage at the expense of love.

Conclusions

We saw in the previous chapter that, when reflecting on the nature of love, Julia Kristeva argued that humans consider love a feeling that cannot be communicated. Love cannot be communicated because it also cannot be clearly defined. It is a feeling, and I can never be certain that my feeling of love is the same as yours. What this means is that any love must be defined only by a process of constant negotiation and change. Primarily this negotiation occurs by way of conversation. By speaking together, two people work towards discovering a way of defining a world together. Cavell, in ways that are commensurate with Kristeva's arguments, calls this acknowledgment – or a 'best case of acknowledgment' where love is concerned. Thus, the problem with Rosmer in *Rosmersholm* is that he wants to define his love for Rebecca in ways that are beyond what can be spoken. I have referred to this conception of love as 'hyperbolic' and we saw some evidence of this in Bergman's *The Passion of Anna*.

Last Year in Marienbad, by contrast, puts its faith in language. This is a game of language won, in this film, with great difficulty. Indeed, the lop-sidedness of the conversations in *Marienbad*, for they are very heavily weighted in the man's favour, may push these dialogues away from being classed as conversations: in many ways they are far more akin to monologues. I can defend my reading only by deferring to Cavell's contention that the Hollywood remarriage comedies, as well as the unknown woman melodramas, are marked by a woman's desire to be educated and that some of this education can come from a man. I admit that Cavell's arguments on this score are not entirely convincing, though they are persuasive in some instances. In *It Happened One Night*, it can be argued that Peter Warne educates Ellie in ways that King Westley (Jameson Thomas) was very much unable to, with Peter being a clear figure of 'new marriage' while Westley reeks of 'old marriage'. Of the companion set of films Cavell calls 'melodramas of the unknown woman', *Now, Voyager* (1942) provides some evidence in this direction – Jerry (Paul Henreid) and Dr Jacquith (Claude Rains) provide Charlotte Vale (Bette Davis) with an education of sorts – while *Gaslight* (1944) provides the clearest example of a man's educating a woman. In *Gaslight*, Paula Anton (Ingrid Bergman) is mercilessly persecuted by her husband (Charles Boyer), a husband who is intentionally miseducating her to the point where she is driven to the verge of madness. To some degree she is saved by the detective, Brian (Joseph Cotten). He teaches her to believe in herself and trust her own convictions. At the film's conclusion, Paula leaves her marriage, and while she does not quite embark on a reckless dash into the unknown with Brian, it is hinted that such a dash may occur in the near future. *Gaslight*'s concerns are close to those of *Marienbad*: a woman comes to believe that an escape from a false marriage and a persecuting husband of whom she is afraid is the best thing for her. I am convinced that this is precisely what happens in *Last Year in Marienbad*: a woman takes the decision to escape from a false marriage and to embark on a new life with a man who has convinced her that such a new life is worth the risk.

Notes

1 For Gilles Deleuze, *Last Year in Marienbad* provides a key example of what he calls 'the time-image'. See Deleuze 1989, 116–25.
2 I criticise this kind of approach to film studies at length in Rushton 2013, 33–56.
3 Nevertheless, key aspects of remarriage emerge in this film: Claude and Odile get back together again, and so too do Nicola and his wife, Jane (Jean-Pierre Bacri, Jane Birkin), at the film's end.

Chapter 6

Michelangelo Antonioni: learning how to love

6.1 Giovanni and Lidia Pontani (Marcello Mastroianni and Jeanne Moreau) in *La notte* (Michelangelo Antonioni, 1961)

I am conscious that my interpretation of *Last Year in Marienbad* in the preceding chapter will strike many readers as somewhat fanciful. To call it a comedy (almost, at any rate) is to surely miss what is central to it. To ascribe a reasonably clear story to it, full of characters who have motivations and desires, also seems somewhat inappropriate. I have already claimed that this book does not offer anything like a history of modern European cinema. It is instead a work of interpretation. I offer a series of interpretations of film and groups of films. I suppose many will call it a work of theory (and I have no problem calling myself a 'film theorist'). What is required in all this is a quest to discover what something means. Along with that, certainly for the cinematic examples I examine here, an attitude of interpretation requires a belief that those meanings are significant. Therefore, it is important – for me – to claim that *Last Year in Marienbad* finds its significance in a woman's attempt to escape from a marriage in which she feels she is trapped. Such an interpretation is guided by Cavell's theses on acknowledgment and remarriage comedies, but my interpretation is in no way determined by those theories. It is not, in other words, a 'top down' theory, as such things have been called, as though a 'bottom up' theory could somehow avoid theory all together.[1] I would argue that my interpretations of *Last Year in Marienbad* and other films in this book are very specific. I am not trying to prove one theory or another, but trying to understand what is at stake in these films. My interpretations of these films therefore resist any claims to generality. That is a way of saying that these readings are ways of resisting any desire for generality – for a 'Theory' (with a capital T). Such an appeal is made by Toril Moi in a recent book in ways that I am sympathetic to (Moi's work on Ibsen was touched on in the previous chapter). She writes:

> Instead of giving in to such cravings for generality, we should consider when (under what circumstances) an occurrence or phenomenon requires an explanation, and how far those explanations need to go. If we pay attention to the specific reasons why doubts and questions arise, then the questions of meaning that arise are no longer general and abstract, but concrete and specific. (Moi 2017, 81)

Moi's claims, I think, reflect those proposed by Cavell in the epigraph to this book. One of the things he is saying there is 'I know I am making arguments I cannot prove, but if I make a proof that cannot be disproven or refuted, then I am no longer making an argument. Rather, I would merely be stating a fact.' And, Cavell therefore asks, 'Where is the intellectual adventure in that?' (Cavell 2010b, 344).

What irks me about my reading of *Marienbad* in the previous chapter is that I have to put so much faith in the man, X, for it is his words that guide pretty much everything in the film. The woman, A, is subservient, reduced to murmurs of agreement or disagreement with the man's constant bombardment of 'this happened', and then 'that happened'. So here, with Antonioni, we have a chance to focus more closely on the plight of women. Antonioni's films, up until *Red Desert* (1964) – with the one exception of *Il Grido* (1957) – all focus on women who are in various states of love. To a great extent they emphasise the ways that men mistreat women. I cannot clearly identify in any of these films something that can be definitively called a happy ending, so these films are not comedies in any straightforward sense of the term. Elements of tragedy are everywhere in these films – death, suicide and fractured lives abound – but even then, none of these films can easily be called a tragedy. In what I think are his finest films – what Seymour Chatman (1985) dubbed the tetralogy: *L'avventura* (1960), *La notte* (1961), *L'eclisse* (1962) and *Il deserto rosso* (*Red Desert*) – optimism wins the day.

Life goes on, characters make discoveries and look towards futures of positive possibility, however hesitantly.

Antonioni never shows us a successful love, that is, one in which a couple ends happily ever after (perhaps with the one exception of Nene and Lorenzo in *Le amiche* (1955)). Does this therefore condemn these films to conditions in which love is declared impossible? Antonioni shows us love's *difficulties* rather than its impossibilities. Love is everywhere a lure and an aspiration in these films even if many (in fact, pretty much all) of these loves end unfulfilled. One of the key dilemmas faced by Antonioni's characters involves a certain fear of connecting with another person, as though getting too close to another person will in some way lead to the self's erasure. His characters ask, 'If I give myself to another, will I therefore lose part of myself?' Antonioni explores the two poles of this question, one in which the self rejects all otherness and retreats to isolation and narcissism, and the other where one tries to erase all aspects of the self so that one can give oneself entirely to the other – that is, where the self disappears to a degree that it is almost wholly externally determined, determined by others. The conflict between isolation, on the one hand, and the quest to be with another person (or other people) is the central dilemma of all Antonioni's Italian films, noting that I do not deal here with the films after *Red Desert*.[2] His characters confront the difficulty of wanting to open themselves to other people – to someone they might come to love – while at the same time sensing that, in giving oneself to another, the nature of one's self will invariably be altered. Perhaps that is why much of the critical focus on Antonioni's films has been on conditions of alienation; that is, on modern conditions of isolation and aloneness. Such alienation cannot be separated from the dialectic of self and other, acknowledgment and equality, central to modern conceptions of love and marriage which I have tried to stress so far in this book. These are also points I will emphasise in this chapter. Any singular 'I' in Antonioni's films is alienated because they are searching for human contact, for love and acknowledgment. That these characters so often fail to find any confirmation of love or acknowledgment does not mean such things do not exist or no longer exist. Rather, it shows us that such things as love and acknowledgment are hard to come by, that they require attitudes of openness, understanding and forgiveness that are sorely lacking in the 1950s and 1960s Italy where Antonioni made his films.

The tension between the singular I, and the I's quest to be acknowledged by others, is evident in *Red Desert*. Near the end of that film, Giuliana (Monica Vitti) tells Corrado Zeller (Richard Harris), 'When I'm alone, I'm ill.' Without other people, Giuliana feels ill. All of this unfolds amid the context of her affair with Corrado, the difficulties of her marriage with Ugo (Carlo Chionetti) and the complexities of her relationship with her son

(Valerio Bartoleschi). But it is here, as she is about to sleep with Corrado and thus cement her conjugal infidelity, that she elaborates her condition. 'You don't love me, do you?' she asks Corrado. He replies by asking her why she feels the need to ask such a question. She in turn replies, 'I don't know why. I never get enough affection. Why should I always need others?' And this will be the film's most definitive claim for Giuliana's neurosis, precisely that no one knows or acknowledges her. In other words, she feels utterly alone and that is why she is ill. Her response is to then issue the wish that everyone who's ever cared for her would surround her, like a wall. This would offer a complete cocoon of protection: a wall of others.

This is one fantasy, that of the dissolution of the self into a cocoon of protective others, where the 'I' would cease to exist. The second and opposite fantasy Giuliana pursues in *Red Desert* is that of complete isolation, a repudiation of all otherness, a celebration of aloneness – an affirmation of the 'I' above all else. She articulates this fantasy by way of a fairy tale she recites to her son. She does so in order to soothe him during his period of feigned illness, an illness in which he is clearly seeking to imitate his mother's sense of illness: he is identifying with her. In short, he wants her attention. In response to this need for attention she tells him a tale of the glories of aloneness, of a young girl who discovers happiness while all alone, away from all 'grown-ups', in a small, idyllic beach paradise. Thus, *Red Desert* articulates these two poles, one fantasy of complete aloneness and self-sufficiency that is entirely away from other people, and another in which all traces of the 'I' would fade to such an extent that any sense of self will be deferred onto others. In the latter case, the 'I' is merely there as a support for others.

These are constants in Antonioni's films. For example, in *Le amiche*, the distinction is played out via the contrast between Rosetta (Madeleine Fischer), who needs others and cannot survive without them, and Clelia (Eleanora Rossi Drago), who ends the film utterly self-sufficient, confidently alone and isolated. This is repeated in *L'avventura* via the contrast between Anna (Lea Massari), who wants to be alone, and Claudia (Monica Vitti), who cannot separate herself from Sandro (Gabriele Ferzetti), even after he has betrayed her. These are problems faced by women (with the exception of Aldo [Steve Cochran] in *Il Grido*) and it is on the plights of women that Antonioni's discourses on modern love and marriage turn.

Marriage and acknowledgment

Female characters in Antonioni's films most often desire to be acknowledged by others, whereas to a great extent the male characters are narcissistic and uncaring in ways that make the call to acknowledgment difficult, to say the least. The state of marriage – in *Story of a Love Affair* (1950), *The Lady without Camellias* (1953), *Le amiche*, *La notte*, *Red Desert* – is an impediment to acknowledgment and it is typically only outside marriage that glimpses of acknowledgment are discovered. Suffice it to say that something like a crisis of modern marriage is placed at the heart of Antonioni's cinema. *Red Desert* is again exemplary. At one point, Giuliana tells Corrado that he understands her in ways that her husband has been utterly incapable of. (We can note that this repeats the man's declaration to the woman in *Last Year in Marienbad*: that he understands her in ways that her husband cannot.) Giuliana also tells Corrado that she had tried to commit suicide, a fact which she concealed from her husband, but which she has now been able to confess to Corrado. Even further, she confesses to Corrado that her doctor had advised her that the best thing for her was *to learn how to love*. She has been unable to love – certainly, unable to find love via her husband – and the best way to cure her illness will be for her to learn how to love. This is a theme in all of Antonioni's Italian films; that his characters must learn how to love. The implication here, as I take it, is that the traditional modes of love can no longer be accepted and that a new kind of love must take its place. I have in some places in this book already tried to imagine this as a distinction between old marriage and new marriage, with the latter being conditioned by a new kind of love. And I believe this is what Antonioni is exploring across this range of films. Of course, any new kind of love or marriage will not automatically be an improvement on any traditional conceptions of love or marriage, but of one thing Antonioni seems certain: the traditions of old marriage are no longer acceptable.

These condemnations of traditional love and marriage take myriad forms. In *The Lady without Camellias* (1953), the reference to Dumas's *La Dame aux Camélias* (1848) is clear: where Dumas's novel introduces the potential of modern romance, a romance not bound by traditions of old marriage and morality – that is, the scandal of a courtesan who becomes the most desirable woman in Paris – Antonioni's film demonstrates the ways that the shackles of those outmoded conceptions of love and marriage, by contrast, maintain their strength, 100 years after Dumas's novel. Clara (Lucia Bosé) begins the film full of ambition for her acting career and life. Her hasty marriage to Gianni (Andrea Checchi) at first seems to intensify that ambition. Marriage soon forces Clara, however, into myriad compromises, compromises that serve only to make her into a traditional wife whose ambitions and morality are now closed off by her husband. He urges her to cease her acting career and turn her thoughts to having children.

Clara thus seeks romantic potential elsewhere. She begins an affair with the suave diplomat, Nardo (Ivan Desny). And yet, even though her love for him is sincere and heartfelt, there is no sense of mutual acknowledgment between them. Rather, Nardo's affair with her is one of convenience – call this an affair of the 'couple + 1' variety that I have alluded to at certain points of this book: certainly the affair takes such a form from Nardo's perspective. At the end of the film Clara is left without any hope of fulfilling her ambitions. She had wanted to succeed in a career as a great cinematic actress, but is now condemned to accepting exploitative roles. At the same time she is also condemned to accepting the emptiness of her marriage to Gianni as well as the superficial convenience of an adulterous romance with Nardo. In short, Clara's is a traditional marriage in which love is found beyond the marriage bed, but even then there is no satisfaction, fulfilment or happiness. For Clara, all ambitions are dashed. She forgoes any chance of self-fulfilment and all ambitions to what Emerson called 'self-reliance' (I will say more on this point below). But Antonioni also seems to be telling us that the traditional modes of love and marriage are also unacceptable. What they give rise to is *conformity*: they render impossible the quest for self-reliance. Such is Clara's dilemma in *Camellias*. At the end of the film Clara capitulates to a world in which she builds a wall of others around herself, in which the only things she does are those that are designed to please others: to please Nardo, to please her husband and to please the film producer who entices her to perform in the exploitative *Slave of the Pyramids* movie near the end of *Camellias*. She even curtails her ambitions in order to please her actor-friend, Lodi (Alain Cuny), who advises her to lower her expectations late in the film. All aspirations to selfhood or self-reliance have vanished. Clara has lost her sense of self and exists as an empty form who is surrounded by others and guided by their expectations.

In *Le amiche*, Antonioni explores the same themes – that is, the distinction between isolation and being surrounded by others. This time, instead of focusing on a single character as is done in *Camellias*, Antonioni explores the self–other distinction across a range of characters. In *Le amiche*, Clelia is a young and successful career woman of working-class origins, while Rosetta, by contrast, is a young, rich woman of wealthy origins. Near the beginning of the film, Rosetta had attempted suicide. Clelia's declaration to her shortly after this is that 'love and affection are the most important things in life'. 'People can rarely be self-sufficient,' she continues, 'we can't do without other people.' Clelia believes Rosetta is too closed in upon herself, too isolated, and that is what has driven her to attempt suicide. In other words, she has not made connections with other people. She therefore offers Rosetta a job as a sales assistant at a new fashion salon she is about to open, not because Rosetta needs the money, but, rather, because Clelia thinks it will enable Rosetta to look 'outside herself'.

All of this becomes rather complicated as the film progresses, for Rosetta does look outside herself, but only as far as Lorenzo (Gabriele Ferzetti), an artist she fell in love with while he was painting her portrait. The first problem is that Lorenzo is already married, and, although he is attracted to Rosetta, he realises by the end of the film that he does not love her, for he loves his wife, Nene (Valentina Cortese). Rosetta's infatuation with Lorenzo intensifies as the film progresses, and she pursues him at the expense of all other concerns, including her job at the fashion salon – she is late, for example, for the big opening night of the salon. When Lorenzo finally rejects her, she commits suicide.

Clelia, by contrast, is both self-made and self-sufficient, even as she preaches the virtues of love and affection. Throughout the film she cultivates a romance with Carlo (Ettore Manni), a man who has been leading the fitting out of the new fashion salon. At the end of the film, Clelia, jaded by the self-centredness and superficiality of the fashion world that surrounds her, asserts her freedom and independence. She does not want to stay with Carlo, less still to marry him. Her work takes priority. 'Working is my way of being a woman, of loving, of taking part in the world,' she declares.

The contrast between Rosetta and Clelia is clear: Rosetta's desire for love is based on a possessiveness that is utterly narcissistic. She wants Lorenzo to conform to the fantasy she has of their life together, and thus reduces their joint concerns to her own sphere. This is a way of seeing the world from the perspective of one rather than two: it is a failure of acknowledgment. In Chapter 3 I discussed the impossibility of forcing acknowledgment upon another person, that there is no way that one person can make another person acknowledge them. Rather, for another to acknowledge me requires my absolute passivity. I must open myself to another person for acknowledgment to be possible, but there is no guarantee that such a thing as acknowledgment or mutual understanding will therefore transpire. It cannot be forced: one must remain passive and open. It is this passivity of which Rosetta is entirely incapable. Contained in this incapability is a class critique, a contention that the wealthy (Rosetta) and privileged are used to forcing themselves upon others in matters of love, as in many other ways. The only consequences of such moves are hollow at best, as we saw with Clara in *The Lady without Camellias*, but also tragic at worst, as occurs in *Le amiche* via Rosetta's suicide.

Clelia rejects the person she loves, Carlo, in an extraordinary affirmation of her independence – significantly, perhaps, she is the only woman in Antonioni's films who manages such a thing. The implication here is that women do not need to be defined by their relationships with men. Clelia celebrates the moments in the film where women speak among themselves, away from men, as a unique form of camaraderie. She goes so far as to state that it is right for women to collectively confide in themselves. (I noted in Chapter 3, on Bergman's *Smiles of a Summer Night*, that women speaking together constitutes an important trope for the films I examine in this book.) Of course, this camaraderie will be shattered as the film progresses, leading to Rosetta's suicide. Clelia, unlike Rosetta, does not need the affirmation or acknowledgment of a man's love. Rather, she can affirm her existence away from the lies, loves and marriages of men. Clelia ends *Le amiche* as self-sufficient and independent, but this does not mean she is narcissistic or isolated. It is, on the contrary, Rosetta who exhibits all the traits of narcissism. Narcissism here means that one's relations with others can be comprehended only in terms of the self. In short, for Rosetta there is no otherness except an otherness that is reducible to the self. What I mean to point to here is that self-sufficiency or self-reliance is not the same thing as narcissism. This, as we shall see, becomes the central conflict for Antonioni's Italian films.

Self-reliance

Some words on 'self-reliance' are necessary. Emerson's essay on self-reliance is of critical importance for Cavell's philosophy and for his cinematic writings, so much so that a recent commentary on Cavell's cinema writing is subtitled 'self-reliance at the cinema' (Wheatley 2019). Emerson, in his essay on 'Self-Reliance' written in 1841, makes a distinction between self-reliance and conformity (Emerson 2001a, 120–37). To live a self-reliant life is to live a life that can be said to be self-determined so that the decisions and actions you make are ones that have been determined by yourself. By contrast, a life of conformity is one lived by rules that are external to the self; that is, a life in which one does not make one's own rules, but instead performs the rules that have been determined by others, by regulations and traditions external to the self. (I will leave it readers to think back to *The Rules of the Game* and the triumph of conformity over self-reliance in that film.) Cavell convincingly argues that a sense of how to live one's life – to live it well; to live it with a tone of happiness in view – is often at odds with what society wants or with what society expects from us. Society expects us to conform. We are expected to find a place within that society where we will contribute to that society and make its successes part of our own personal successes. But Cavell balks. 'And let's suppose that you do not see the place, or do not like the places you see,' he suggests. He then continues:

> You may of course take on the appearance of accepting the choices, and this may present itself to you as your having adopted a state of fraudulence, a perpetual sense of some false position you have assumed, without anyone's exactly having placed you there. A mark of this stage is a sense of obscurity, to yourself as well as to others, one expression of which is a sense of compromise, of being asked to settle too soon for the world as it is, a perplexity in relating yourself to what you find unacceptable in your world, without knowing what you can be held responsible for. (Cavell 2004, 23)

Cavell is here trying to characterise what Emerson means by conformity, a 'state of fraudulence', a 'false position', as Cavell puts it. This will further be qualified as a state whereby one has conformed to the demands of one's society, but in doing so one now realises that one's principles have been betrayed, that what society wants from me is not at all what I want from myself. Hence the contention that one gains a sense of falseness.

Marriage may well be taken as one of the demands our society places upon us: that to be married is to conform to what society demands of us. And so often one will then discover that marriage is a state of conformity that fosters only a sense of fraudulence and falseness. Such falsity has been evident in the films so far discussed in this book: in *Rules of the Game*, *Last Year in Marienbad*, *The Passion of Anna* and others. Perhaps it is nowhere clearer than in the case of Fredrik Egerman from *Smiles of a Summer Night*. By the conclusion of that film he has realised that his marriage to the much younger Anne is a false marriage. Correlatively, he comes to realise that his friendship with Desirée delivers something more truthful than does his relationship with Anne. And these might be said to be common tropes of romantic fiction dating back at least to Austen's *Pride and Prejudice* (published in 1813): that one tries to dispel false companionship in the quest for a love that is freed from pride and prejudice. Such fictions of escape from false marriages continue at pace in the nineteenth century, with Emma Bovary, Dorothea Brooke, Nora Helmer and many others. Thus it is worth noting that Anne also comes to recognise the falseness of her marriage to Fredrik and elopes with his son, Henrik. As I have said, many of these moves are standard romantic ones.

The breakthrough Cavell makes is to establish the 'truth' of a marriage on the basis of acknowledgment. If a false marriage – a marriage of 'conformity' – leads one to a sense of fraudulence, then a true marriage, by way of acknowledgment, amounts to an achievement of 'self-reliance'. What this initially means is that the genuine acknowledgment of another person is simultaneously an acknowledgment of one's self. Therefore, what Emerson means by self-reliance is not an individualism that refuses the world or escapes from it. Self-reliance is not individualism. It is an achievement that comes from discovering ways of sharing the world with another person.[3] We see as much in Fredrik's transformation in *Smiles of a Summer Night*: Desirée, in teaching Fredrik to know and acknowledge her also teaches him how to acknowledge and understand himself. This is something he is unable to do with Anne, and he is also unable to realise this when alone reflecting on the photographs of Anne. Acknowledgment entails the discovery or creation of a world in conjunction with another person. It cannot be achieved alone. And nor can self-reliance: one learns to rely on oneself only in conjunction with another.

And we can surely affirm that Clelia, in *Le amiche*, means all of these things when she states that 'People can rarely be self-sufficient; we can't do without other people.' Self-reliance and acknowledgment are states achieved in conjunction with others. Readers will know by now that the guiding thread of this entire book is Sellier's claim that 'each person is constructed through the encounter with another' (Sellier 2008, 219). And yet, these issues are somewhat complicated in Antonioni's film: these achievements are not successfully realised in *Le amiche*. Roberta's relationship with Lorenzo fails, and so too does Clelia decide that a life away from Carlo is the best course of action for her. Antonioni gives us another marriage, that between Cesare (Franco Fabrizi) and Momina (Yvonne Furneaux), an old marriage in the clearest sense: Cesare maintains his marriage by buying lots of gifts for Momina, while she satisfies her desires by engaging in extra-marital affairs. Such are the stakes of traditional, old marriage. Antonioni's films seek to destroy these stakes.

Why does Rosetta's relationship fail? I have already suggested that it fails because Rosetta's love is possessive and narcissistic. It is not a matter of building a world together or even of constituting a sense of mutual understanding. Rosetta's expectations in love are hyperbolic as I have called it in earlier chapters in relation to *The Passion of Anna* and Ibsen's *Rosmersholm*. Hyperbolic love entails a quest for love beyond acknowledgment, and thus a model of love built on the notion of *two becomes one*, rather than on the notion whereby *one becomes two*. Rosetta, entitled and narcissistic, cannot escape the position of seeing the world as one.

But does not Clelia also end as one, not two? She decides that a relationship with Carlo is not what she wants. Rather, she marries herself to her work. She declares to Carlo that 'Working is my way of being a woman, of taking part in the world.' She goes on to speculate that she may very well meet a man in the future with whom she will be able to live without giving up on her own self, with the implication being that to stay with Carlo would mean giving up on her self, her ambitions for herself. This is a way of saying that she cannot attain self-reliance with Carlo, and that she can achieve such a state without him. We could say that she has been able to achieve a state of acknowledgment with Carlo, but that she has also transcended that state. She has perhaps decided that, while she is able to acknowledge Carlo, it is not a 'best case' of acknowledgment. In short, she does not love him. But this is nevertheless still a case whereby self-reliance has been achieved by way of acknowledgment: Clelia has gone through a case of acknowledgment and 'come out the other side', as it were. She has developed a maturity and knowledge of the world that enables her to judge the stakes of her decision to part with Carlo, and that is an achievement she could not have made without Carlo. Clelia's rejection of Carlo is not a rejection of the world, nor of Clelia's intention to participate in that world – to 'take part' in the world, as she puts it. Rather, it is a way of advancing her capacity for knowing the world. The analogy, via Cavell, is with Stella's walk towards the camera at the end of *Stella Dallas*. Cavell calls this Stella's way of 'ratifying her insistence on her own taste, ... the announcing of her *cogito ergo sum*' (Cavell 2004, 281), her assertion that she exists and that she can do so without a man.

I do not feel that I have quite done justice to *Le amiche*, but we shall see such characterisations as Clelia and Rosetta repeated in other of Antonioni's films. Clelia's later companion in Antonioni's films is Anna in *L'avventura*. The immediate context of Anna's disappearance in that film is an argument with her lover, Sandro. Anna has made it clear that she wants to marry him, even as her rich father tells her at the beginning of the film that Sandro will never marry her. When the group of friends get to the island that is central for the first half of the film, Anna tells Sandro that she wants to be alone, that she feels cut off from him. 'I don't feel you anymore,' she says to him. And that – famously – presages her disappearance: we do not see Anna again. What then transpires in *L'avventura* is well known: Sandro, after Anna's disappearance, falls in love with Claudia. Claudia, who had been Anna's close friend, is attracted to Sandro, but she feels ashamed to have fallen for him even as they are still searching for the missing Anna. This love triangle gives rise to the first and most superficial of the film's romantic themes: that men treat women as interchangeable. From such a perspective, no individual woman contains uniqueness or speciality. Rather, for men, women can come and go; one can be replaced with another. This theme is exacerbated near the end of the film when Sandro sleeps with a seductive Gloria Perkins (Dorothy de Poliolo), even as he has declared his love for Claudia.

And yet, it is not enough to call *L'avventura* an extended critique on the meanness of men towards women. To do so would be to place rather too much emphasis on the man and not enough on the woman, Claudia. In this respect, Chatman provides an excellent place to start by declaring that the films of Antonioni's tetralogy typically feature 'a woman who has been disillusioned by a lover but who continues to muster the courage to seek and speak the truth' (Chatman 1985, 83). Claudia's disillusionment with Sandro centres on the fact that he has been able to transfer his affections so swiftly from Anna to herself. Claudia's question is therefore a classic lover's query: *how can I know that he loves me?* If acknowledgment is key to love, then it is acknowledgment that Claudia seeks.

Claudia's hesitation and reticence towards Sandro are never far away, and she seeks reassurance in the form of words. Halfway through the film, in a hotel room as they continue their search for Anna, Claudia asks Sandro to tell her that he loves her. His reply is to declare, 'You know I do, so why should I say it?' This doesn't entirely satisfy Claudia, so that when Sandro then tries to force himself sexually on her, she repudiates him by saying, 'I feel as though I don't know you.' Her words here are, of course, the classic words that signal a failure of acknowledgment, that is, for one member of a couple to declare that they do not, or that they no longer, know the other.

The dilemma of acknowledgment and its failure is repeated at the end of *L'avventura*. Once again in a hotel room, Claudia again asks Sandro to tell her he loves her, and he does so, only for her to insist that he say it again. This time he replies, 'I don't love you,' and Claudia admits that she had deserved this response. She smiles in a manner that assures both of them that their love is real and that it doesn't need the reinforcement of words. Immediately, as he leaves the room, he turns to her and says, 'It's not true. I love you.'

Sandro leaves their hotel room, for he is heading to the hotel's bar to meet friends and enjoy the evening. Claudia does not feel like doing such things and has decided to catch up on some sleep. The next morning, melodramatically, Claudia discovers Sandro has betrayed her and slept with Gloria Perkins during the night. Claudia is appalled, and she walks out of the hotel. Utterly ashamed and crestfallen, Sandro follows her, and *L'avventura* delivers its famous ending. Sandro sits on a bench, weeping. Claudia gently, nervously, caresses his back, before her hand moves to the top of his head and affectionately ruffles his hair. There is hope for this love.

Can it really be declared that there is hope for this love? Antonioni himself claims as much (see Brunette 1998, 49), and it brings *L'avventura* into harmony with the other films of the tetralogy. These are all films dedicated to ambiguity, but ambiguity does not mean resignation or defeat. Antonioni calls it pity. 'They come,' he says of Sandro and Claudia, 'to a kind of shared pity. This, you may say, is nothing new,' he continues. 'But without that, what is left to us?' (quoted in Brunette 1998, 49).

Such is forgiveness, one of the central traits of the remarriage comedies theorised by Cavell. From a Cavellian perspective, Sandro's final betrayal with Gloria Perkins opens the way to (the possibility of) acknowledgment. This is not at all to excuse his behaviour. Rather, it is to admit that humans have failings and, additionally, to note that the men in Antonioni's films do. The film does not seek Sandro's outright condemnation or vilification, but instead seeks compassion and understanding. This seems to be the flavour of Antonioni's hope here. The ending of the film thus opens onto the future, a future in which the faults of the past will need to be acknowledged and not hidden. In this way the film gestures towards the turning of a false marriage into a true one, or turning a false relationship in the direction of truth (see Cavell 2005c, 201). This same problematic is repeated in *La notte*, as we shall see.

L'eclisse

Before approaching *La notte*, some words on *L'eclisse*. Doesn't *L'eclisse* demonstrate the impossibility of love, the impossibility of acknowledgment, the triumph of isolation and the estrangement of all humans from one another, especially under the conditions of advanced capitalism and economic miracles? And furthermore, isn't this Antonioni's point across the tetralogy, to demonstrate that the conditions of love in modern times are mired in futility, impossibility, betrayal and misunderstanding (see, for example, Kovács 2007, 96–9)? As Antonioni himself said, following the release of *L'avventura*, the point is that 'Eros is sick'.[4] (And one could possibly note continuities on this point across the entirety of Antonioni's output.) Such interpretations might well be valid, but I would rather suggest that, at the end of *L'eclisse*, Vittoria (Monica Vitti) has simply realised that Piero (Alain Delon) is not the right man for her. Indeed, we have surely known it all along, that Piero is superficial, materialistic, self-centred and uncaring. He is the one male figure, certainly when compared with Sandro in *L'avventura* or Giovanni in *La notte*, who demonstrates no inclination to or possibility of change. The most meaningful thing he says in the entire film is 'I just bought a car. A BMW!'

What is most significant in *L'eclisse*, in the relationship between Piero and Vittoria, is the complete lack of meaningful conversation, the fact that no matter what it is that one says to the other, what is said never leads to any kind of insight into or knowledge of the other person. Needless to say that this is the very opposite of what ought to be achieved by acknowledgment in Cavellian terms. Vittoria's attraction to Piero is merely one of conformity: she is attracted to a successful, flamboyant, modern man, because 'that's what a modern woman is supposed to be attracted to'. Their inability to communicate is a mark of this conformity.

There are enough examples of missed communications for me to conclude that this is what *L'eclisse* is about. Thus, for example, when Piero suggests that Vittoria come to see his home, she is surprised that he takes her to his parents' house rather than to his own small flat. (Sam Rohdie claims that 'Piero is a stranger in his own house'; Rohdie 1990, 144.) While there, they ask each other questions that go nowhere, to the point where Vittoria eventually says, 'To love, I think one shouldn't know the other.' This is enigmatic enough, but then she follows it by declaring, 'But, then, maybe one shouldn't love at all.' Once again the conversation goes nowhere, with the consequence that Piero tries to kiss and make love to her, a staple response for Antonioni's men. To call these men uncommunicative is something of an understatement (it recurs in Nardo, Lorenzo, Sandro, Giovanni, Ugo ...), and this lack of communication in men is foregrounded right at the beginning of *L'eclisse* in the extraordinary sequence of Vittoria's break-up with Riccardo (Francisco Rabal), whom she had intended to marry.

Later in *L'eclisse* the conversation between Piero and Vittoria becomes even more blocked.

> *Piero*: I feel like I'm in a foreign country.
> *Vittoria*: Strange. That's how you make me feel.
> P: Then you won't marry me?
> V: I don't miss marriage.
> P: How can you miss marriage when you've never been married?
> V: That's not what I meant.
> P: Then I really don't understand you. I wonder if your ex-fiancé understood you.
> V: As long as we were in love, we understood ... There was nothing to understand.

A few moments later we come to the end of this conversation and Vittoria simply declares to Piero, 'I wish I didn't love you, or that I loved you more.' Their conversation is a mere catalogue of missed remarks and questions without answers, attempts at communication gone wrong. It is as though they are strangers who speak different languages (each of them is in a 'foreign country'). Vittoria clearly gives a hint of what she would like to feel: that to be in love there should be nothing to understand. What she means is that, if two people are in love, what they say to each other should transcend the 'mere' nature of words; or, to put this another way, one should easily be able to find the right words, one should have developed a language of 'speaking together', a shared language, and language of 'acknowledgment', an availability for conversation of 'the most sincere and searching sort', as Emerson puts it in his essay on Friendship (Emerson 1898, 54).

Vittoria's attitude here and throughout *L'eclisse* exhibits the frustration of wanting love to be beyond words. And yet, as I have declared at various points, one lesson we learn from many of the films I examine in this book is that love exists only as spoken, as a matter of conversation. This is the lesson of the remarriage comedies examined by Cavell, as much as it is true for the films of Bergman and Resnais so far approached in this book. And so Antonioni's films can be added to that list: love is doomed when it cannot be spoken, and this is none other than the lesson of *L'eclisse*.

All of this is confirmed by the tension of the final scenes. 'We will see each other tomorrow,' says Piero. Vittoria nods. 'And the day after tomorrow,' he adds. 'And tonight,' she says. 'Eight o'clock,' he confirms. And yet, everywhere apparent in this exchange is the sense that these words are meaningless, that these characters do not mean them, that they have no intention of meeting. It is as if they know it's all over, and this scene, as well as the film's conclusion, offers a magnificent poem to the failure of acknowledgment.

Acknowledgment can fail and very often does (cases of acknowledgment's success are remarkably rare, and not just in the movies ...). But that is no bad thing. The optimism of *L'eclisse*'s ending provides a celebration of the failure of acknowledgment, a celebration of the fact that these two people who do not belong together have realised that they do not belong together. And so the film's famous final scenes show us a world that remains to be discovered, that is full of potential, that is open to the future. Antonioni has produced a film in which a happy ending is composed of a couple that fails to end happily ever after, but nevertheless casts its glance with some positivity towards what the future may hold. Later in this book I will discuss how this scene relates to Bersani's notion of connectedness.

La notte

Seymour Chatman claims (as I have already noted) that Antonioni's plots often feature 'a woman who has been disillusioned by a lover but who continues to muster the courage to seek and speak the truth' (Chatman 1985, 83). *La notte* provides the most extensive proof of this claim, for it is in this film that Lidia (Jeanne Moreau) harbours doubts over her husband, Giovanni Pontano (Marcello Mastroianni). Lidia spends most of the film in a state of utter despondency. The 'story' of *La notte* is very much the story of her despondency and her attempts to rescue herself from it.

The film begins when Lidia and Giovanni visit a friend in hospital. This friend, Tomasso (Bernhard Wicki), is at death's door, and by the end of the film it is made clear that Lidia had a relationship with him before marrying Giovanni. The most jarring event at the hospital occurs when Giovanni is seduced by a young female patient as he is about to leave. In a manner which suggests he 'cannot help himself' (and in this he joins a host of other Antonioni males), Giovanni begins to make love to her. They are interrupted by nurses, and Giovanni leaves. When he is reunited with Lidia – she had left the hospital before him – he tries to describe the incident to her, half-apologising for what transpired. Her response is one of mere disdain, as though this is the kind of behaviour she expects of him to the extent that she has pretty much given up on their love. She suggests that perhaps the woman who seduced him will be happy now, for she has embraced an ethos of irresponsibility. As the film progresses, Lidia will be tempted towards irresponsibility too.

Lidia does not hate or even castigate Giovanni. Rather, she has removed all of her passion from him. Lidia's withdrawal of affection from Giovanni therefore leads to her own emptiness, as though all passion has been drained from her. (Lidia therefore approaches the same sort of condition we find in the character of Andreas in Bergman's *The Passion of Anna*, though for different reasons: Andreas cannot quite get over the loss of his marriage; Lidia is still trying to save her marriage.) Lidia's despondency can very surely be described as melancholic in Freud's sense. Freud described melancholia in dynamic terms as a matter of the withdrawal of libido from an object one loves. And yet, as Freud explains, one will also have identified intensely with the loved object, so withdrawing libido from this object is akin to withdrawing it from part of oneself. As a result, the loss of the object is also felt to be a loss of the self, or a loss of some substantial part of the self (see Freud 1984a, 1984b).

Much of the film is a series of attempts by Lidia to rediscover her lost passion, to refind the 'lost object' of her love for Giovanni. The series of her wanderings that makes up much of the first half of the film – wandering around the streets and alleyways of Milan; a journey to a suburban neighbourhood where she lived with Giovanni when they were first married; an encounter with some male youths engaged in a brawl (the symbolism of this scene is clear: men are naturally aggressive and cruel); and the spectacle of kids playing with rockets that shoot high into the air with great excitement, just as they had, Lidia mentions, when she and Giovanni had lived there – are wanderings in the hope of discovering something that will return her to life. When Giovanni arrives there to drive her home, he is surprised to see how little the area has changed. It is clear that Lidia is trying to rekindle the spirit of what life had been like for them when, in the past, they had been in love. But there is no indication at this point that their love will be rediscovered.

There is an abrupt cut from this exterior scene in an open field to a shot of Lidia soaking herself in a bath. She asks Giovanni to hand her a sponge. He does so, but he nonchalantly throws it towards her in a disinterested manner. Lidia had clearly been asking not merely for a sponge, but for some attention, some care, some affection. It seems that such things are too much to ask, and the disappointment is writ large on Lidia's expression. Immediately after getting out of the bath, she then models a new dress for Giovanni, once again seeking a response, some approval from him. His response is not entirely understated, but Mastroianni plays the scene as though he is ogling the dress, which impresses him greatly, while the woman wearing the dress seems somewhat inconsequential (one could note the proximity here to Laura Mulvey's contention that, in the cinema, many women are merely made into objects that are to-be-looked-at; Mulvey 1989). Once again Lidia has more or less ceased to exist in Giovanni's eyes, so that all signs of affection, of interest, of love, have faded. Again this is registered brilliantly on Jeanne Moreau's visage, the limit of disappointment.

Eventually the couple go to a party being held by a wealthy industrialist, Gherardini (Vincenzo Corbella) – who, it will turn out, is trying to hire Giovanni – and the action of the second half of the film occurs here. Giovanni spends much of his time at the party flirting with Gherardini's daughter, Valentina (Monica Vitti). This flirtation culminates in one of the great moments of Antonioni's cinema. Lidia has just made a telephone call to the hospital to check on Tommaso's condition and she is devastated to hear that he has died. It is immediately after this that she spies, through a window, Giovanni and Valentina sharing an affectionate kiss. (It is worth noting that we have not once seen Giovanni kiss his wife.) Antonioni shoots this moment masterfully. The scene is focused on the flirtatious conversation that transpires between Valentina and Giovanni, until they finally kiss. As they kiss, we cut to a wider shot which shows us that Lidia has been watching these events unfold, unseen, from a distance. The effect is somewhat similar to the effect of Christine's spying on her husband, Robert, from afar, as he kisses his lover, Geneviève, in *The Rules of the Game*. Indeed, the party in *La notte* gestures in obvious ways, even if unintended, to the events staged at La Colinière in Renoir's film. To this degree, *La notte* is something of a remake of *The Rules of the Game*.

Lidia now feels entirely betrayed and she is determined to experiment, however briefly, with being irresponsible. In this spirit, she is whisked away from the party in the car of Roberto (Giorgio Negro), a man who has shown an interest in her. In another series of magisterial shots (*La notte* is full of them), Lidia and Roberto chat while heavy rain pounds down upon the car that encloses them. We do not hear what they say: we merely see them. The car stops. They both get out and stand in the rain. Roberto moves as though to kiss Lidia. She pulls back. 'I'm sorry,' she says. 'I can't.' She cannot kiss him. Why does Lidia refuse to betray Giovanni even as she has seen his own ability to so easily betray her? Is it simply because she loves him, so that as much as she tries to make herself believe she wants to leave him and does not love him, the truth of the matter is that she *does* love him? (Of course, far more simply we could declare that she's not interested in Roberto.)

Self and Other

Lidia conceives and perceives the world from the perspective of *two* rather than *one*, as Badiou would say. Throughout *La notte*, she tries to determine the ways in which her own subjectivity functions in tandem with Giovanni's, so that if he were to exit her life then a substantial part of her own subjectivity would be erased. Again this can be viewed in terms of Freudian melancholia, which is to say that the withdrawal of Lidia's love for Giovanni is also a withdrawal of love from someone who has become part of herself – a withdrawal of love from herself, one might say. Thus, Giovanni's failure to acknowledge and care for her is as though fatal for her own subjectivity, and she remarks on one or two occasions that she feels like dying. So, if much of this book has tried to describe the conditions of falling in love or being in love, *La notte* shows us a markedly different perspective: what happens to the subject when he or she falls *out of love*?[5] One of the markers of Antonioni's films is that they try to show that the love one human being can have for another human being is a special thing. As Badiou would claim, it is a matter of seeing the world as two rather than one (Badiou 2012, 39). And to lose that perspective of two entails a great loss to any subject's structuring coordinates. For Lidia, it might be said to amount to a loss of self-reliance. To lose the love one has for another human being is not simply to lose that other, it is also to lose a substantial part of one's self.

From Cavell's perspective, these are matters of acknowledgment. To acknowledge another and be acknowledged by them, to engage in a relation of mutual recognition to the degree that one might discover a *best case* of acknowledgment: these are the things that Lidia is here on the verge of losing. And might she believe that she has never had them from Giovanni? That he has never recognised her and that he has never shared her perspective on the world as that of two rather than one? If he acknowledges Lidia, then why does he betray her with the woman at the hospital, or with Valentina?

Lidia (and Valentina too, as we shall see) refuses to affirm Giovanni's subjectivity in any simple way. She insists on *difference*. As Badiou puts it, that is what love *is*, to 'experience the world from the point of view of difference' (Badiou 2012, 56). It is the point of view of difference that Lidia is determined to present to Giovanni, to foreground his difference from her, but also from himself, from the self that he once was, as much as from the self that he is now.

How does Lidia aim to achieve this point of view of difference? By way of language. *La notte* is the one film of the tetralogy that features significant attempts at conversation, and the contrast with *L'eclisse* here is especially stark. It is also true that Lidia's attempts to talk with Giovanni are most often stalled or unsuccessful – witness the episodes of her asking for a sponge in the bath or asking him to admire her in a new dress. Nevertheless, she is determined to the end to try to communicate with him, and it is the couple's final dialogue that provides one of the few great communicative moments of Antonioni's cinema. At any rate, it provides a forthright attempt at communication.

Before we get to that closing conversation, however, some other issues are worth pursuing. Valentina rejects Giovanni when she discovers he is married. 'I'm clever enough not to break up a marriage,' she says to him. She goes on to complicate her statement when she declares, 'I think love restricts a person. It creates misunderstanding all around.' Valentina's claim does not clarify much, and what follows is very much an aphoristic exchange of non sequiturs that are standard fare in the tetralogy: Giovanni claims to be suffering from writer's block; Valentina plays some audio recordings of poetry she has written, only to then suggest that Giovanni indeed needs a new girl, which he then takes as an invitation to kiss her.

Immediately following this exchange, Lidia returns to the party with Roberto. She is soaking wet from the rain shower that has occurred, and Valentina offers to help her dry herself. She and Lidia chat, and what follows is an extraordinary exchange of affections that immediately echoes Christine's conversation with Geneviève in *The Rules of the Game*. As with Renoir's film, the exchange here contains no bitterness. Instead, the women demonstrate great understanding and compassion. Their conversation contrasts starkly with that of the men in a nearby room chatting on Hemingway, money, politics. Giovanni interrupts Lidia and Valentina's conversation, and manages to overhear Lidia declaring that she is fed up with everything, that she cannot even feel jealousy for what Giovanni has done to her, effectively saying that all feeling has been evacuated from her. Where Lidia finds comfort and companionship with Valentina, with Giovanni she can feel only estrangement.

Learning how to love

Lidia and Giovanni leave the party and accompany the film to its conclusion on a golf course adjoining the Gherardini mansion (it is now early morning). Lidia makes something like a final appeal to her husband. She tells him that Tommaso has died, and that she had once thought she loved him. She had chosen Giovanni, however, on the basis that, back then, she did love him dearly. Nowadays she is certain she no longer loves him. Giovanni tries to assure her that if she feels this way and tells him so, then that must mean she still loves him. 'No,' is Lidia's response. 'It's only pity.' The ending of *La notte* thus echoes that of *L'avventura*, of which Antonioni said, as we have already seen, that without pity, 'what is left to us?'

Giovanni's response seems genuine. At the very least, he admits his failure, which is a good deal more than any other male character in Antonioni's films manages. 'I never gave you anything,' he says. 'I was completely unaware. I go on wasting my life, like a fool, taking without giving, or giving too little.' He goes on to say, 'I've been selfish. Now I realise that what we give to others comes back to us....' He assures Lidia that he loves her and wants them to stay together. Her response is to take a letter from her handbag and read it in full. It seems as though Giovanni believes it is an old letter from Tommaso that Lidia has kept as a kind of memento, so when she tells him, after having read the letter, that it was written by Giovanni himself, he is surprised at how distant from himself he has become. It is a long letter – and in fact it is a less a letter than a poetic description of Lidia as she lay peacefully sleeping one morning – the key phrase of which might be the moment when he writes of Lidia, 'That was the most miraculous thing, to feel, for the first time, that you had always been mine.' Giovanni's words are an evocation of one of the key traits of the comedies of remarriage theorised by Cavell, the admission or sensation that 'I have loved you all along'. We found instances of this in *Smiles of a Summer Night* in Chapter 3. And so this appeal might be one way that Giovanni and Lidia find their way back to love.

The ending maintains ambiguity. We do not know if this couple will survive. But what is central to Antonioni's films is an optimism and hope that something like love will be possible in this world. If these films are critical of this world, of its materialism, cynicism and jaded morality, then this film brings forth the hope that love between two people will still be possible, and that it is a love that will open the way to a new morality. This is true of all the films in the tetralogy, but its most impassioned expression occurs in the final sequence of *La notte*. Lidia and Giovanni have tried to begin to talk, however frustrated and curtailed that conversation might be. Giovanni has begun to speak of the errors of his ways in ways that no other male character in Antonioni's films does. Even then, we cannot be sure we believe him. Life goes on, and these characters will continue to try to learn how to love.

Notes

1 See, for example, David Bordwell's criticisms in Bordwell 1989.
2 Why do I fail to deal with films after *Red Desert*? I feel Antonioni's films go in a different direction after *Red Desert*, away from a close focus on human relationships and onto wider issues of film genre and representation, not to mention his move to filmmaking in England and then the US.
3 Cavell emphasises such things in his chapter on Emerson in *Cities of Words* (Cavell 2004, 19–34).
4 These words were spoken by Antonioni at a press conference following the premiere of *L'avventura* at the Cannes Film Festival in 1960.
5 We have of course seen an instance of this via Andreas in *The Passion of Anna*.

Chapter 7

Agnès Varda: the construction and destruction of the couple

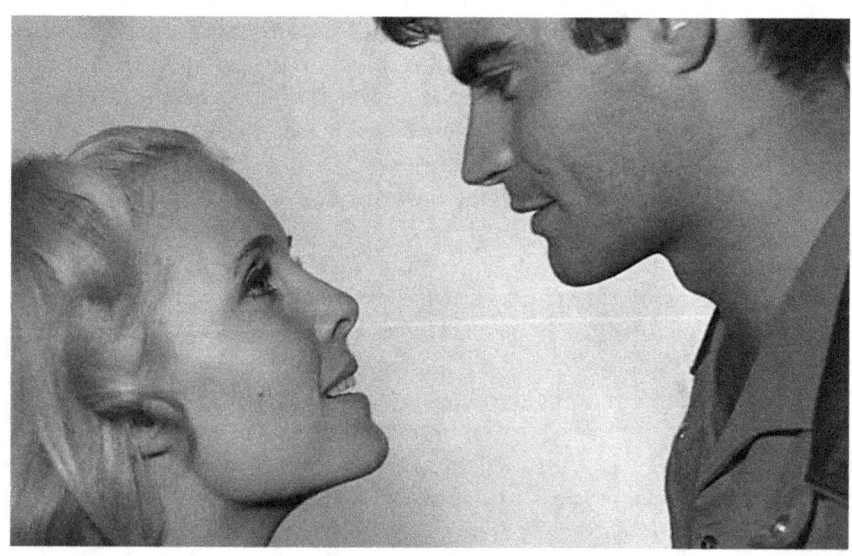

7.1 Émilie and Francois (Marie-France Boyer and Jean-Claude Drouot) in *Le Bonheur* (Agnès Varda, 1964)

I argued in the previous chapter than many of the films directed by Michelangelo Antonioni, up to 1964's *Red Desert*, can be said to be organised via the notion of 'learning how to love'. At the end of *La notte*, for example, we are left with a couple, Giovanni and Lidia, who are uncertain whether their love will survive, or perhaps both are convinced that their love has already expired. And yet, Antonioni leaves us with the hope – with a portion of optimism – that this love might find a way to reinvent itself, that this couple might be able to find a way of speaking together, that they might come to form something that could be called a 'remarriage'. Ultimately, one might conclude from Antonioni's films that one never quite learns how to love. Love is an ever-changing, ever-evolving thing.

One aspect of Antonioni's films that I praised pertained to their defence of the notion that love is a matter of seeing and experiencing the world from the perspective of two rather than one. Much of the conflict in these films, I claimed, is a matter of how one person breaks out of their private isolation or narcissism – that is, from the perspective of one – so as to be able to see and experience the world in conjunction with another: to experience the world as two rather than one. As I also tried to explain, seeing the world as two requires an embrace of difference: to see the world as two I need to curtail my own mastery of the world so as to accept and advocate another person's way of seeing the world. And, as I have also argued so far, Badiou's conception of love as two – he defines it in terms of 'what it is to be two and not one' (Badiou 2012, 39) – offers another way of considering what Cavell calls acknowledgment. In relation to acknowledgment I have emphasised the 'sharing of a world', specifically exemplified by a loving couple who create a world together – a 'best case of acknowledgment' as Cavell calls it (Cavell 1979b, 477). And what is this other than a way of seeing the world as two rather than one?

To be two rather than one, and thus to prioritise the experience of difference over identity or singularity, might entail notions of sexual difference. In the films examined here, the difference put in place by love is very much a difference between male and female. An emphasis on sexual difference – perhaps nowadays better expressed as gender difference – as a form of difference central to human life has been emphasised in various ways by French philosopher Luce Irigaray over many years. I rely to some extent on ideas put forward by Irigaray in what follows when discussing some films directed by Agnès Varda. Irigaray will remain of importance for the remainder of this book. Varda will also remain important – indeed, we know she has already been important, for it was by way of Varda's *Cléo from 5 to 7* that Geneviève Sellier came up with the formulation that 'each person is constructed through the encounter with another' (Sellier 2008, 219) that has been integral for my reflections so far in this book.

Before I approach Irigaray's concepts, however, I want to propose a counter-argument to the notions of love, acknowledgment and 'the experience of two'. These arguments are advanced by Leo Bersani. Instead of emphasising difference, Bersani argues for what he calls 'the homo-ness of being' or the 'cosmic oneness of being' (see Bersani 2015, 81ff; Bersani and Dutoit 2004, 120). Bersani stresses less our difference from other humans and objects in the world than our connectedness and similarity with other humans and objects. The world 'replicates' us, he argues. By this he means that the world and its objects respond to us and we respond to them. When I throw a ball, for example, something of me goes 'into' that ball, and conversely, something of the ball goes into me, into my 'being'. 'The viability of our being-in-the-world', states Bersani, 'depends on a certain continuity in our exchanges with an otherness never wholly differentiated from ourselves' (Bersani 2018, 48).

I find such an approach, first of all, to foster a way of thinking about the ending of Antonioni's *L'eclisse*. In the previous chapter I referred to this closing scene as 'a magnificent poem to the failure of acknowledgment'. But I also went on to argue that this is not at all a bad thing. Rather, the failure of acknowledgment between the two main characters in *L'eclisse*, Piero and Vittoria, opens them to the possibility of rediscovering the world. At the conclusion, the film's protagonists fail to meet for their evening rendezvous. The film's closing scenes show us various points in the neighbourhood where they were supposed to meet but from which both protagonists are absent. And yet, rather than being conceived as an absence or failure, the near-magical nature of the scenes and objects presented in this final sequence are typically interpreted as optimistic, life affirming and in some sense pleasurable. It is not a happy ending in the traditional sense, but it is in no way an unhappy ending. Pascal Bonitzer famously called it 'a final point freed from the negativity of intentions, of passion, of human existence' (Bonitzer, quoted in Brunette 1998, 89).

What does all this mean? I see a potential answer via Bersani's notion of connectedness. Our connectedness with the world need not be tied down by the messiness of trying to understand others – as occurs with Vittoria's and Piero's attempts to understand one another in *L'eclisse* – or of trying to prod those others to change themselves in various ways – as Lidia asks of Giovanni in *La notte*, for example. Rather, and to avoid the messiness of misunderstanding and of attempts to control or possess other people, we can instead accept and foster an openness to the world: to accept a oneness with the world rather than an opposition or antagonism towards it. That might be the lesson of the ending of *L'eclisse*: get beyond one's worrying about others and simply accept the world in all its majesty. We could find similar moral tales in the endings of *L'avventura* or Antonioni's *Blow-Up* (1966). The ending of *Red Desert* is perhaps more ambiguous, but a sense of optimism is maintained. Brunette states the following: 'By the end of the film, Giuliana seems to have a somewhat surer grasp on this "real life" that she seeks connection to' (Brunette 1998, 107). Significantly Brunette charts this ending in terms of 'connection': Giuliana has emerged from the entrapment of her accident and neurosis and re-established a connectedness to the world.

In this chapter I aim to chart some of the different dimensions of Varda's films. Primarily these dimensions are defined on the one hand by a quest for mutual acknowledgment. From this perspective, characters in Varda's films seek love, companionship and mutual understanding in ways that can be informed by the structure of what Cavell calls 'comedies of remarriage' and also via his conception of acknowledgment. On the other hand, however, and in ways that become more and more evident throughout Varda's career, the characters in these films seek less the understanding or acknowledgment of other human beings and much more a sense of being connected to other people and things in the world. If we consider, for example, Varda's late documentaries – *The Gleaners and I* (1999), *The Beaches of Agnès* (2007), *Faces / Places* (2017) and *Agnès by Varda* (2018) – then these focus primarily on the relationships or connections various human beings (including Varda herself) can have with objects in the world. They are much less concerned – if at all – with strictly human relationships of love, desire or romance. Many of the earlier films, by contrast – such as *La Pointe Courte* (1955), *Le Bonheur* (1964), *One Sings, the Other Doesn't* (1977) – are substantially concerned with human relationships of love, acknowledgment and mutual understanding. This chapter is primarily concerned with discussing this contrast.

Communication and acknowledgment

Varda once noted her distance from Resnais and Antonioni in an interview about *Cléo from 5 to 7*. She claimed that 'At that time, the fashion consisted in saying there wasn't any possible communication ... It's a notion Antonioni cultivated fervently, Resnais as well ... I don't agree ... I believe in "encounters"' (quoted in Sellier 2008, 219). Varda goes so far as to say that all people *need* such encounters, and that those who have such encounters are invariably happier than those who do not. It is on the back of these claims that Sellier argues for this perspective as one that is central for *Cléo*: that 'each person is constructed through the encounter with another' (Sellier 2008, 219). Although these statements are ones that aim to separate Varda's works from those of her male contemporaries, I would rather claim – as I have done throughout this book – that these issues are central to all of the European directors I examine here. Rather, what sets Varda apart from her male contemporaries is that she achieves perspectives on her topics that are freed from any moral judgment, and this will be one of Varda's distinctive marks. Is it good or bad that the couple (Silvia Monfort and Philippe Noiret) in *La Pointe Courte* stays together? Well, it is good *and* bad, either way. Is it good or bad that François (Jean-Claude Drouot) decides to continue his relationship with Émilie (Marie-France Boyer) after his first wife, Thérèse (Claire Drouot), has died in *Le Bonheur*? Well, it is good *and* bad, either way. In *One Sings, the Other Doesn't* is it right for Pomme (Valérie Mairesse) to break up her marriage with Darius (Ali Rafie) and so be separated from her son? And is it good or bad that Suzanne (Thérèse Liotard) marries Pierre (Jean-Pierre Pellegrin), or is it a betrayal of feminine independence? Well, these are both good *and* bad, either way. Varda's films offer wonderful moral tales, but those tales offer up no moral judgments. As she says, specifically of *Le Bonheur*, 'I wasn't interested in showing "this one is good, that one is bad." I tried to show everything that happened in such a way as to leave viewers free to make their own judgments' (Varda 2014c, 40). Varda's films can certainly be placed alongside those of Bergman, Resnais and Antonioni (along with others who will follow in this book) in that she often constructs plots in which the stakes are those of falling in or out of a couple. What she avoids, however, is any sense in which 'being a couple' is a right or wrong way to be.

If Varda's films refrain from moral judgments, then so too, for the most part, do the characters in those films. We can certainly say this of the husband and wife in *La Pointe Courte*, and of François and Émilie in *Le Bonheur*, though it will be more difficult to make such a claim for François's first wife, Thérèse. We can certainly declare it of Mona (Sandrine Bonnaire) in *Vagabond* (1985), a character who builds a life beyond judgment. But there is a significant exception in *Vagabond* that Varda herself points to: the shepherd (Stéphane Freiss). At first, the shepherd appears to be free from moralistic attitudes insofar as he accepts, houses and feeds the wanderer, Mona. But when Mona refuses to conform to the shepherd's way of life, that is, she refuses to help with the farm work and grow potatoes, he turns against her. In short, he passes judgment on her. Of this kind of moral judgment, Varda is critical: '[H]e's the worst kind of judge,' she states, 'because he wants to be marginal, but in *his* way' (Varda 2014f, 137).

It is here that we can begin to get a sense of Varda's project. This might be expressed as something like: *do not impose your views and judgments on others; leave others to make their own judgments in their own way*. Of course, at first, such claims are rather too simplistic, and it will be the aim of this chapter to complicate them. But I would like to point out some proximity to Cavell's statements on remarriage comedies here, for the couples in those films can become couples only on the basis that they choose to be. What I mean to emphasise here is that, for a remarriage, one must not force one's views onto the other person. Rather, the choice to remarry a person must be a choice that is freely made, not one that is forced. It cannot be forced by tradition, economics, one's parents, moral codes or whatever. The choice to be a couple is made on the basis of what it means to be free. As we saw in Chapter 1, when writing on *The Awful Truth* Cavell argues that Jerry (Cary Grant) can consider himself free so long as he has the ability to choose. As we know, by the end of that film he chooses to remain married to Lucy (Irene Dunne). He is not forced to stay with Lucy. He can divorce her and choose another woman, Dixie Belle (Joyce Compton) or Barbara Vance (Molly Lamont), if he so desires. And that is what is key: he chooses to be with Lucy, and insofar as this is a choice freely made, then it is a sign of Jerry's freedom as such. And one presumes the same freedom of choice also pertains to Lucy. As I have claimed a number of times already, Cavell contends that all of this is a matter of 'creating a logical space within marriage in which to choose to be married, [of creating] a way in which not to feel trapped in it' (Cavell 1981, 245). In short, no one is imposing their judgment on Jerry or Lucy. Nor is Jerry imposing his judgment on Lucy, and so too can we say that Lucy is not forcing her judgment on Jerry. All of this is crucial for Cavell's arguments: the decision to choose marriage is a decision to choose freedom as such.

Cléo from 5 to 7

Above all, in Varda's films, choosing involves practices of freedom, so that choosing is always a matter of choosing one's freedom. Sellier, as we have seen, places importance on the ways in which Varda's characters are formed by way of encounters with others. This claim is made specifically in relation to *Cléo from 5 to 7*. How, then, do encounters with others work in this film? It is commonly felt that the film can be divided into two parts, a first in which Cléo (Corinne Marchand) is narcissistic and self-centred, and a second in which she drops the mask of egotism and goes out into the world where she discovers the significance of that world and other people. Kelley Conway points out that the first half of the film is about *looking at Cléo* – that is, other people as well as Cléo herself, examine and look at Cléo – while the second half concerns *Cléo looking*. (Varda puts it this way: Cléo begins as a 'looked-at subject', then becomes a 'looking subject'; Varda 2014d, 73.) In the second half of the film Cléo looks beyond herself: she learns how to see (Conway 2015, 39).

The turning point comes when Cléo, a pop singer who has recorded some hit records, is rehearsing with other musicians (including a character played by Michel Legrand). She sings a song about love. As she sings the words, she suddenly realises their significance. Sellier claims that Cléo has begun to 'revolt against the image to which she has been reduced – that of a woman alienated in love' (Sellier 2008, 218). It is after this that she changes: she 'becomes a consciousness', Sellier argues (Sellier 2008, 218). Varda herself made a similar point, and she also points to the significance of the film's second half.

> Cléo belongs to that category of people who ordinarily don't really take in what's really happening around them. And suddenly she begins to look, to

really see the people she passes in the street, the state of things around her, the guy eating frogs, the art-students in the studio. The more she enters into the life of the people around her, the more she finds herself at a loss. She's looking for an answer. And the answer comes in the person of the young soldier she meets. (Varda 2014a, 19–20)

Thus, Cléo finds her way out of narcissism, out of her self-focus or solipsism, by coming to see the world anew, and especially by way of the 'answer' she finds in the soldier near the end of the film. The soldier is played by Antoine Bourseiller, a former lover of Varda's and father of her first child, Rosalie.

If we take this section of the film seriously, and I think we must if we are to believe that it provides the film's answer, then Cléo finds her way out of solipsism by way of conversation. It might be significant that this conversation is with a stranger, for it means she can be open and unconcerned about the consequences. They talk openly. She tells the soldier, Antoine, she is awaiting the results of a cancer test. He suggests to her that women love to be loved. He then adds that women are also scared to give too much of themselves because, if they do, they will lose a part of themselves. Cléo admits that she has felt that such has often been the case for her.

Soon after this, Cléo receives the results of her cancer test: she will need at least two months of chemotherapy. This is not really the news she was after, but it is also not as bad as it could have been. Her doctor is confident she will defeat the disease. Antoine is caring and wishes he could stay. He must, however, return to active duty in the Algerian War. He, like Cléo, is potentially staring death in the face. 'I'd like to be with you,' he says. Cléo gives her reply: 'You are.' The message here is clear. One gets beyond narcissism and isolation by connecting with other people. Cléo has discovered a new outlook on herself and the world. She is no longer fearful and has found consolation by way of her encounter with another person. For *Cléo from 5 to 7*, couples are good things, especially if a couple's relationship is based on conversation, expression, understanding.

Elements of *Cléo* fit within a Cavellian schema. We certainly do not have a remarriage, but we have the beginnings of sharing a world by way of 'meet and happy conversation' (as Milton would have it). Sandy Flitterman-Lewis stresses these sorts of points by declaring that Cléo moves from a position of woman-as-spectacle to one where she becomes a woman-as-social-being (Flitterman-Lewis 1990, 273). She refers to this latter position as 'a more social form of human relation' (Flitterman-Lewis 1990, 281). Additionally, Flitterman-Lewis claims that conversation is of major importance for this new form of social relation; that Cléo's transformation is a matter of 'shared communication' (Flitterman-Lewis 1990, 281). In short, Cléo moves towards a scenario that may well be defined in terms of Cavellian acknowledgment: she is acknowledged by the soldier and, in turn, she acknowledges him.

Another Cavellian way to figure these turns would be to see Cléo's transformation in terms of her desire to be educated. And we know that Cavell conceives of such things in Hollywood remarriage comedies to be configured in a particular way: it is the man who educates the woman. I have already noted the problems with such a conception in Cavell's theorisations, but for *Cléo from 5 to 7* the case might be all too clear. Indeed, Sellier aims a criticism at the film by virtue of the fact that it is the educated male soldier who is charged with educating the supposedly naive woman. The film therefore partakes of a social regime in which naive, uneducated women who thrive on popular culture – Cléo is a singer of popular songs – need to be educated by men who have the requisite schooling and knowledge that will lift them above the level of the popular. 'Cultivated' male culture can rescue women from cheap, mass culture (see Sellier 2008, 218–20).

These are valid observations, and Sellier's claims make interesting crossovers with Cavell's theses on acknowledgment and remarriage. These themes are even more intense in Varda's earlier feature film, *La Pointe Courte*, made in 1955 (*Cléo* appeared in 1962). Conway's comments on *La Pointe Courte* are exceptional (see Conway 2015, 14–18). She focuses to some degree on the conversations between the husband and wife, while pointing to the aesthetic and thematic role their conversations play. She also links this style to future European filmmakers – Godard, Antonioni, Bergman, Resnais (noting that Resnais was *La Pointe Courte*'s editor). Conway identifies 'conversations between couples' as a significant trope for some of the European filmmakers I examine in this book (and I take her comments as a sign that these are issues worth investigating).[1]

One point Conway downplays is the shape of the conversations between the couple in *La Pointe Courte*. That shape conforms to pretty much everything Cavell will consider as acknowledgment when it concerns relations between one human being and another. In *La Pointe Courte*, the central couple begins as estranged from each other. Then, by way of conversation, they agree to get back together again. Much of their conversation focuses on matters of acknowledgment: how do they know each other? What does it mean to know another person? What kinds of knowing are there? By the end of the film, the woman decides she wants to stay with the man, for it is she who had precipitated their separation in the first place. She considers, as she puts it, that their bonds as a couple are stronger than what they are as individuals. It is therefore clear that she is expressing that their love is now a matter of being two rather than one. She also considers that, as a result of their conversations, they now have a love based on knowledge (*connaissance*) rather than passion, and thus it is a love based on language rather than feeling or emotion. The neighbourhood of La Pointe Courte, where the husband had spent his youth, is akin to a green world, a place away from the city where this couple can work out their differences – they live in Paris. All of these aspects situate the couple of this film as an exemplary remarried couple in Cavell's terms.

The other major dimension of the film is represented by the fishing village and its residents, filmed with a documentary quality that evokes Visconti's *La terra trema* (1948). These depictions of the social aspects of existence are explicitly contrasted with aspects of coupling that are central for *La Pointe Courte*. It is the contrast between the couple and the social that Varda herself highlights as an important quality of the film (on this point see Conway 2015, 14–15). *La Pointe Courte* can thus be said to be split between *modes of acknowledgment* between the members of the couple, on the one hand, and *modes of connectedness* expressed by the fishing villagers. This is also to say that Varda's films can be mapped via the distinction between couples and social worlds, between acknowledgment as articulated by Cavell and connectedness as theorised by Bersani (I will say more on this below).

We see a similar split in *Cléo from 5 to 7*. Cléo finds her way out of isolation by conversing with the soldier. She therefore comes to a new relation to the world via acknowledgment: the sharing of the world with another human being. But she also finds her way out of loneliness by connecting with the world around her: the events, places and attractions of Paris, especially Parc Montsouris. As Varda puts it (as we have already seen), 'And suddenly she begins to look, to really see the people she passes in the street, the state of things around her, the guy eating frogs, the art-students in the studio' (Varda 2014a, 20). To some degree, therefore, for Cléo, acknowledgment and connectedness go hand in hand.

Le Bonheur

If we are concentrating on couples, then Varda's extraordinary 1964 film, *Le Bonheur*, cannot fail to spark discussion. I have already pointed to Varda's own claim that 'I wasn't interested in showing "this one is good, that one is bad." I tried to show everything that happened in such a way as to leave viewers free to make their own judgments' (Varda 2014c, 40). Such a claim is not at all an easy one to make. In *Le Bonheur*, François is happily married to Thérèse. He soon falls for another woman, Émilie, and begins an affair with her. We might ordinarily expect that a man will be torn by such a situation. He will feel as though he must choose between the two women, or he will live in the fear that his wife will discover his affair (as happens, for example, with Robert's affair in *The Rules of the Game*). Or even then, he will come to detest his wife in preference for his mistress or lover: he will be 'trapped' in his marriage. None of these occurs in *Le Bonheur*. Two-thirds of the way through the film, François confesses the affair to his wife. In fact, he is exceptionally positive about it. He explains to Thérèse that he still loves her very much and that he may even love her more now than he has ever done. He admits that he also loves the other woman, Émilie. He explains that loving both of these women has made him tremendously happy. François's happiness has grown and grown as a result of this arrangement. He is very happy, he claims, and he suggests to Thérèse, isn't this is a good thing? He is trying to maximise his happiness. The analogy Varda makes is with money. We have no difficulty in understanding and appreciating that someone can make lots of money, and more and more money. So why shouldn't someone strive to expand their happiness in precisely the way François does? More and more happiness: isn't that a good thing?

Current interpretations of *Le Bonheur* do not support a positive reading of happiness on these terms. Rather, for these analyses, the happiness depicted in *Le Bonheur* is pernicious and degrading. Varda's title is therefore ironic. If this is what happiness is, then it is a fake happiness at best, and a desperate and miserable one at worst. Death, such as occurs for Thérèse – she turns up dead in a stream shortly after François has admitted his affair – is a justifiable outcome of such a negative version of happiness. Varda has herself endorsed this kind of interpretation. '*Le Bonheur* is not a psychological portrayal of an egotistical man caught between two blondes. Rather, it's an extremely detailed almost maniacal exposé in images and clichés of a certain kind of happiness. It focuses on gestures and the function of gestures with such insistence as to provoke the very explosion of their meaning' (Varda 2014a, 75; cf Flitterman-Lewis 1990, 233). The film therefore offers a critique of the ways in which women are trapped in marriage and domesticity while also being subjected to patriarchal norms.

This mode of interpretation – broadly speaking it can be called feminist – has been bolstered in recent work on *Le Bonheur*, especially that of Rebecca DeRoo (2018). DeRoo focuses on what she calls the film's images of the housewife's 'serving hand' (DeRoo 2018, 53–63). *Le Bonheur* strives to debunk myths of domestic harmony, and it does so, DeRoo argues, by offering a 'critique of the popular representation of women', especially of the ways in which women are depicted in popular women's magazines such as *Elle* and *Marie Claire*. Varda uses some very specific images of women's domestic chores in *Le Bonheur*, for we are presented with Thérèse's hands as she irons clothes, does the washing up, prepares food, tucks the children into their beds at night and so on. DeRoo notes the ways that these images mirror the kinds of images found in French women's magazines of the period, so that *Le Bonheur* presents a commentary – and a negative one at that – on the menial roles which women are assigned by the patriarchal structures of society. Furthermore, images of the 'serving hand' are repeated when Émilie, towards the end of the film, takes Thérèse's place as the domestic servant and new wife–mother of the family. The implication here is that women are replaceable: it does not matter whether the wife–mother is Thérèse or Émilie or anyone else, so long as she can fulfil the domestic roles assigned to her.

These are strong arguments: *Le Bonheur* is a feminist film that offers a critique of the patriarchal norms of 1960s French society, especially as those norms are represented in popular women's magazines via their images of happiness. And yet ... Might we once again be entering the territory Sellier warned us against? That is, might not the strong feminist interpretations proposed by Flitterman-Lewis, DeRoo and others be bolstering the notion that the French New Wave built its identity to a great extent on the back of the denigration of popular images of women? In other words, as Sellier argues, the male filmmakers of the French New Wave wanted to denigrate images of women that associated them with consumer culture and popular media in order to position themselves as more elite, cultured and sophisticated. The point I want to make here is that these strong feminist critiques of *Le Bonheur* fall prey to the same problem: they denigrate popular images of women.

Might there be another way to approach the images of the serving hand in *Le Bonheur*? Might it be possible to see such images as potentially positive ones? Can it be possible that such images of women might be ones in which women can discover senses of fulfilment? In short, might Varda be focusing on images of the serving hand not so as to criticise them but, rather, to observe them? And further than that, to praise them? Might she be declaring that this is one of the realms women can occupy that is not the domain of men? That this is a space where women can take pride in themselves and what they do?

To many readers these will sound like awful claims: that a woman trapped in the domestic sphere might somehow discover fulfilment from such demeaning tasks. DeRoo especially makes the case that, in *Le Bonheur*, the world of men is public and social, while the world of women is enclosed and solitary. Thérèse works as a dressmaker, which means she works within her own home, away from the social world. François, by contrast, goes out of the home, and occasionally out of their home town, in order to work. The man is free to live a public life, whereas the woman is trapped in the home. And it is while François is undertaking some work in a nearby town that he meets Émilie. Émilie herself spends most of the film as an independent woman who, by contrast with Thérèse, works outside the home: she works at a post office. She thus represents a kind of new woman, a career woman with aspirations to make a life for herself that avoids the pitfalls of trapped domesticity. And yet, by the end of the film, she has given up all that: she has slipped seamlessly into the role of wife–mother. Her job is now to look after the children and François. The potentially independent woman has been tamed, captured and imprisoned in the wife–mother role.

All of this is to assume that the role of wife–mother is necessarily one in which the woman is trapped, repressed, oppressed and unfulfilled. That is the case in many instances: feminist scholars have assured us of this countless times.[2] I am not, however, wholly convinced that this is what Varda herself intends with the images of the 'serving hand' in *Le Bonheur*. We have seen already Varda's claim with reference to this film, 'I wasn't interested in showing "this one is good, that one is bad." I tried to show everything that happened in such a way as to leave viewers free to make their own judgments' (Varda 2014c, 40). Earlier in this chapter I also argued that a central imperative of Varda's films is *do not impose your views and judgments on others; leave others to make their own judgments in their own way*. In other words, do we automatically declaim 'women's work' as demeaning and unnecessary; that is, do we demean the unpaid labour of the home, or the paid labour of working from home as a dressmaker in ways that have been undertaken by women for many centuries (as weavers, knitters, seamstresses ...)? Or might we claim it as work that is worthwhile and potentially rewarding, while also noting that such labour has been underpaid and underappreciated. Additional questions concern whether such work is better off undertaken by an underclass of 'servants'. Or whether it is better undertaken by men.

Such questions go well beyond the bounds of *Le Bonheur*. There can be no definitive answers to them. However, it is worth examining one of Varda's later films for an interesting perspective on domestic labour. *Jacquot de Nantes* (1990), Varda's wonderful love letter to her husband, Jacques Demy, as he was on the verge of death, is based largely on Demy's memories of his childhood and later youth. One key factor in these reminiscences is the family kitchen. The kitchen was the centre of family activities, and often, as we see depicted in *Jacquot de Nantes*, the young Jacques would be doing his school homework in the kitchen while his mother prepared the evening meal. The evening meal was also an essential expression of the family's togetherness. These scenes are remembered with great kindness and tenderness, as though these were some of the happiest and most rewarding memories of Demy's childhood. Time spent in close proximity to his mother while she undertook those tasks of domestic labour: such tasks delivered some of the great memories of his life. And such memories are specific to the mother, for the father was often at work and thus distanced from these intimate family moments. I cannot see any other way to interpret these scenes other than to declare that Varda presents them as wonderful moments, as memories of the intimacy and delicacy of Demy's time spent with his mother. And some of these scenes of Demy's mother preparing food, mending clothes and so on mirror those scenes of domestic labour from *Le Bonheur* in ways that are not at all critical. Rather, if anything, they are reverential. They are some of the most cherished moments from a life. Of course, these are Demy's moments: they are seen from his perspective, and one could certainly counter that his mother was not quite so touched by the daily toil of her familial chores. My sense, however, is that Varda's film makes those moments precious for Demy's mother. Varda is trying to convey the special intimacy of these moments.

Couples in *Le Bonheur*

Where does this leave the question of couples in *Le Bonheur*? No commentaries today defend François's actions. Indeed, it is an unwritten and unsaid given that what François does in this film is wrong. That is where we start from. Varda's own claims are contradictory. On the one hand, especially in interviews conducted shortly after the film's release, she was keen to defend François's actions. As stated above, she was content to leave viewers to make their own judgments. She was aware that, from her perspective, there was an 'absence of moralism' in the film (Varda 2014b, 31–2). Along similar lines, Alison Smith writing in 1998 argued that '*Le Bonheur* is simply a set of images presented for the viewer, who observes their appearance, and, gradually the way in which their content fits together to reveal unexpected patterns … There is no authorial voice in this process' (Smith 1998, 44). Varda at one point went so far as to declare that 'there is nothing to prove that the woman has committed suicide', which means that perhaps Thérèse's death was accidental and not at all a reaction to François's affair. It might even be possible to believe that Thérèse may well have been able to live happily ever after with the *ménage à trois* arrangement. And even if Thérèse did commit suicide, its consequences are not ones of moral concern. 'If his wife committed suicide', Varda states, 'and [François] wants to feel good with another woman, he has the right! Do you think he should cry for twenty years?' (Varda 2014e, 89).

In later interviews, however, Varda changes her tune somewhat, especially in the period around the release of *One Sings, the Other Doesn't*, when Varda was keen to foreground her feminist credentials (and with good reason, it should be added). Varda becomes much more insistent that *Le*

Bonheur delivers a moral message. Therefore, at one point she declared that the film presents us with 'the very cruel idea that the woman/wife can be replaced by another woman/wife as long as she performs the same functions as her predecessor: cook the meals, take care of the kids, water the plants, kiss her husband, and let herself be fucked, etc.' (Varda 2014d, 75). It is also during this period that she is critical of Thérèse's actions, considering her too passive. 'That woman wants to be an angel,' Varda states. 'Nobody is an angel. She should have said to [François], "Go to hell! I want to be alone with you"' (Varda 2014e, 90).

What, then, can we conclude here about *Le Bonheur*? I think the only conclusion can be that it is difficult to come to any conclusions. What *Le Bonheur* dramatises, more than any other film I examine in this book, is the conflict involved in the distinction between 'coupling' and the sorts of arrangements that are *beyond the couple*. These are issues that are important for Varda's work, and in 1969 she will go to California and make a film called *Lion's Love*, a film that explores the consequences of a triple romance. In short, exploring the possibilities of human relations that lie beyond the couple is one of Varda's concerns in *Le Bonheur* and *Lion's Love*. And Varda will not be unique among French New Wave filmmakers to explore such territory: Godard, as we have already seen, opens up 'beyond the couple' possibilities in *Contempt*, and he does so even more adventurously in *A Woman Is a Woman*. Truffaut had received extraordinary international success in 1962 with *Jules and Jim*, in which two male characters are romantically involved with one woman. Significantly – perhaps – all of these examples depict one woman's experiments with two men, as also occurs in *Lion's Love*. *Le Bonheur* is perhaps more traditional in focusing on one man's relationships with two women, as is customary in what I have been calling, throughout this book, a 'couple + 1' arrangement.

So far I have avoided discussion of Stanley Cavell or acknowledgment in relation to *Le Bonheur*. I have argued that notions of acknowledgment can provide a helpful framework for thinking about *La Pointe Courte* and *Cléo from 5 to 7*, but issues relating to acknowledgment are somewhat more complicated for *Le Bonheur*. The central question here is whether something approaching a 'best case of acknowledgment' can occur *beyond the couple*. It seems to me that it would be difficult for such an arrangement to be satisfactory for what Cavell calls remarriage. For a couple to choose to be remarried, then that couple must be remarried to the exclusion of others – this is integral to Cavell's account of remarriage.

These points can bring us to a distinction between acknowledgment and connectedness that emerged in the opening chapters of this book. As I argued in relation to Jean-Luc Godard's *Contempt*, for the marriage between Paul and Camille Javal, issues of acknowledgment are at stake. Those issues concern reflections on faithfulness and the possibility of forgiveness, as well as the search for a way to speak together, to converse. But the quest for acknowledgment between the members of this couple fails, their marriage is bust, and Camille ends the film by embarking on a reckless dash into the unknown with the American film producer, Prokosch. The dash of this couple is as if to mock the spirit Cavell gives to such dashes elsewhere, in *Smiles of a Summer Night*, for example, where Anna and Henrik dash off into the new dawn with the hope of discovering happiness. In *Contempt*, by contrast, Camille and Prokosch find no such happiness. Rather, their dash concludes when both are killed in a car crash, as though Godard is delivering an entirely negative verdict on the possibilities of remarriage and reckless dashes. The key moment (or moments) of *Contempt* are those in which Camille's faithfulness is put to the test: will she or won't she go with Prokosch back to his villa? Such tests of faithfulness occur first in Rome, then later at Capri. I will simply say that questions of fidelity and adultery loom large in *Contempt*.

We have also seen Bersani's take on these kinds of issues (much of this occurring while he was writing in conjunction with Ulysse Dutoit). Bersani and Dutoit claim that it is contempt that guides the relationship between Paul and Camille. It is a possessiveness between them that is their way of trying to keep their relationship together: Paul wants to possess Camille, and vice versa; or Camille wants to be possessed by Paul, so that her dalliance with Prokosch is a kind of revenge, an expression of contempt. This is their way of 'forming couples' (the title of Bersani and Dutoit's chapter on *Contempt*; 2004, 19–73): *couples are formed by contempt*. For Bersani and Dutoit, this possessiveness and contempt are precisely what produces the coupling between Paul and Camille.

Immediately we can see the ways in which *Le Bonheur* presents a very different case from that of *Contempt*. François's relationships are based on non-possessiveness. He does not conceive of his relationship with Thérèse – or Émilie – in terms of possessing her. His discourse on the apple orchard can be taken as a description in miniature of what Bersani calls connectedness: not restriction, but openness. The 'apple orchard' analogy is François's way of confessing his affair to Thérèse. François compares his family to an apple orchard in a square field and then supposes that there might be an apple tree that grows outside the orchard. Wouldn't this simply mean more flowers and more apples? And what could be wrong with that? And so too for his happiness. If François discovers more happiness, what could be wrong with that? No possession, no contempt. In *Contempt*, Bersani and Dutoit consider that the Camille–Prokosch coupling is something worth trying out: the Prokosch–Camille couple, they argue, 'is simply another variation, something tried out' (Bersani and Dutoit 2004, 60). Such a coupling does not need to submit to the restrictions of possession and contempt. For *Le Bonheur*, therefore, from such a perspective, surely the François–Émilie coupling is one that can be advocated: it is 'something tried out'. It may be on such grounds that a new mode of relation between human beings can be advanced, a mode of relation beyond the confines of contempt, acknowledgment and romantic love.

I may well have written a book based on theories posed by Simone de Beauvoir. As will become evident in much of the remainder of this book, we find (male) filmmakers who more and more try to depict the ways in which men have treated women cruelly. These are themes that certainly emerge in de Beauvoir's *The Second Sex* and elsewhere ('feminine subordination remains useful to society in cases where the woman is married'; 'marriage chains her to a man and makes her mistress of a home'; and so on; see de Beauvoir 2009, 113, 456). What is at stake for de Beauvoir, above all, is an ethics of equality between the genders. The achievement of equality will be a consequence of reciprocal recognition – call it acknowledgment or mutual recognition. In this, as numerous commentators have pointed out, de Beauvoir radically distinguishes herself from Sartre. For Sartre, the freedom of the individual is paramount and recognition and acknowledgment are not at stake. By contrast, de Beauvoir claims – in ways that surely resonate with Cavell – that one's own freedom can be assured only by granting freedom to others. 'We can only be who we are', she writes, 'because of the others in our lives' (de Beauvoir 1976, 66). And I need to add that, by way of *Le Bonheur*, Varda is surely commenting on the most famous 'open' relationship of the twentieth century: that between de Beauvoir and Sartre. That the consequences of such an open relationship seem to have weighed more heavily upon the woman than the man is surely intended by Varda. And yet, even with all of this in mind, Varda is also exploring what new modes of love and new modes of relation might be like.[3]

One Sings, the Other Doesn't

If we take this as a place to start, then *One Sings, the Other Doesn't* (1977) pushes such claims even further. I have been arguing that Varda's films are guided by the precept that one should not impose one's views on another: leave others to make their own judgments in their own way. Additionally, as I have claimed throughout this book, Varda's films can be conceived in terms of Sellier's statement that 'each person is constructed through the encounter with another'. These precepts can be approached in various ways in *One Sings*. A significant point of difference emerges by way of the film's primary characters, Suzanne and Pomme. Suzanne ends the film happily married to Pierre. She has chosen marriage and appears happy with that choice. Pomme, by contrast, leaves her marriage and is content to do so. She discovers happiness as part of a group of singers, called Orchidée, who travel to various places performing songs and agit-prop pieces, many of which involve feminist and women's liberation themes. On the back of the difference between Suzanne and Pomme, I will claim that *One Sings, the Other Doesn't* shows us a clear distinction between acknowledgment and connectedness. Suzanne's marriage to Pierre shows us a triumph of remarriage and acknowledgment, while Pomme's decision to develop a set of relationships that are 'beyond the couple', and beyond romantic love (as Bersani would have it), shows us the conditions of connectedness.

Some other interpretations: DeRoo offers a reading of *One Sings* as an experiment in Brechtian strategies of contradiction. Flitterman-Lewis, by contrast, lambasts the film as a conventional retreat from the supposedly more adventurous, anti-mainstream experiments of *Cléo* and *Le Bonheur* (Flitterman-Lewis 1990, 216). I agree with DeRoo that Brechtian elements are definitely evident in the film, but the reader will sense that my aims and concerns are somewhat different from the kinds of arguments which advocate Brechtian distanciation and so on. Brechtian techniques are certainly in use, but for this film, story is central (DeRoo 2018, 71ff). The feminist storyline of *One Sings* is everywhere evident: this is not a film that needs to rely on Brechtian interruptions to make its politics felt. The film tells the story of two women who search for senses of selfhood. Insofar as Suzanne and Pomme do this, they are answering a call that demands the liberation of women. This does not mean that the aims of these women are to be equal with men. No. Because each of these women seeks to define who they are as women – singularly – then they are also trying to define the various possibilities of what a woman can be. In this sense, *One Sings* is a continuation of themes established in *Cléo*. Neither of these women is content to be defined according to traditional codes of what a woman must do or be. The film therefore presents a marked advance, it seems, on the roles given to women in *Le Bonheur*. Rather than being defined in terms of what others want them to be, Suzanne and Pomme forge their own unique identities.

Irigaray and *One Sings* ...

In making these points I am echoing Luce Irigaray's call for women to develop the capacity to define themselves on their own terms. Typically, Irigaray states, 'woman is deprived of the possibility of interiorizing her female identity. It is imposed on her as pure exteriority' (Irigaray 1996, 47). For a woman to find a way to interiorise and express her identity is no easy matter, according to Irigaray. In ways that I have tried to foreground throughout this book, Irigaray's conceptions rely on the notion of a 'we' that advocates human subjects as *two* rather than *one*. She writes that 'Being *we* means being at least *two*' (Irigaray 1996, 48). She additionally points out that being 'we' offers a way to get beyond individualism.

Irigaray characterises the importance of the 'we' in the following ways. First of all, she claims that, in contemporary Western societies, money and property are the dominant ways in which relations between people, as well as relations between people and the world, are conceived (Irigaray 2000, 9). Things, as well as people, are conceived as possessions that have a price or cost. Certainly Irigaray wants to propose human relationships that go beyond property relations and relations of exchange. If such relationships are considered in terms of the 'we', then one person cannot be conceived as the other's property (Irigaray 1996, 51). To this degree she echoes Hegel's dictum of 'The "I" that is "We" and the "We" that is "I"' (Hegel 1977, 110), while also criticising Hegel's demeaning of the role of the woman in marriage (in *The Philosophy of Right*; see Hegel 1991, 206–7). In ways that resemble Cavell, Irigaray argues that 'What has not yet been imagined in thought is: how to remain together while still being two, how to be and become subjectively two, how to discover a way of coexisting as two beings' (Irigaray 2000, 112).

Irigaray's advocacy of the 'we' is also a matter of recognition – again her debt here to Hegel is significant. It is not, however, a recognition that returns one to oneself. Rather, it is a recognition of one's limitations: it is a recognition of the negative in oneself. This limitation, at one level, is gender specific. As Irigaray puts it, 'I am sexed', and this means that 'I am not everything' (Irigaray 1996, 51). If I am a woman, then that means my 'self' cannot be representative of all human beings. It is representative of women only, and Irigaray sees this as being of great importance. The same goes for men, too: they are not universal; they do not speak for or represent all of humankind. The distinction between the sexes or genders is a limitation: to recognise oneself as a woman or a man is to recognise that limitation.

All of this brings Irigaray to questions of the differences between women and men. Men are guilty parties in two ways: they tend to conceive of themselves as universal. Men therefore crush the possibilities of the recognitive 'we'. Furthermore, they tend to prioritise property relations: men conceive of things, as well as people, in terms of their capacities to be possessed and exchanged. Women, Irigaray argues, by contrast with men, favour relationships with people rather than those defined by property and possession. What this means is that women crave communication with other people. Women prioritise their relations with other people and the conversations they can have with them. Men, by contrast, 'talk', as Irigaray puts it, but they do not communicate (Irigaray 1996, 101). Even though this is the case, the language which fosters communication is typically created by and for men. The result is that attempts by women to communicate tend to be blocked: language works against women.

All of this is a lot to take on board. I want to suggest that these are the kinds of issues that are at stake for *One Sings, the Other Doesn't* (and many other of Varda's films). From this perspective, what is at stake for women first of all is to find ways to claim their identities, their 'selves', in ways that are commensurate with an identity that is a 'we'. A second issue is that women find ways to speak for themselves, something along the lines of a feminine language, a female mode of expression. We shall see how important such conceptions are for the friendship between Suzanne and Pomme in *One Sings*.

Acknowledgment and connectedness

The perspective I want to propose here is that *One Sings, the Other Doesn't* hinges on the distinction between acknowledgment and connectedness. Suzanne's 'remarriage' to Pierre is a triumph of acknowledgment, while Pomme's departure from marriage and her embrace of a nomadic mode of existence are triumphs of connectedness. These are both triumphs of a conception of the self as a 'we', though the one is achieved by acknowledgment and the other by way of connectedness. I cannot extensively detail the many fascinating aspects of *One Sings*, but I will conclude this chapter with some further reflections on Bersani's notion of connectedness. I will also trace the ways in which some aspects of connectedness emerge in *One Sings* and some of Varda's other films.

There are three aspects of Bersani's conception of connectedness that I will highlight:

1 the desire to go beyond notions of individuality or the individual subject, and thereby to destroy the distinction between subject and object;
2 the desire to dismantle any sense in which there is a division between human subjects and the world; i.e., to foster the connections between humans and the world, rather than endorsing a disconnection between them;
3 the desire to advocate a principle of 'self-expansion'; i.e., that any 'self' is composed of its connections with the world (see, for example, Bersani's arguments in Bersani 2015, 58–76; 2018, 85–105). Thus, any self can be expanded by fostering more and more connections with other things and people in the world.

From Bersani's perspective, therefore, the kind of coupling and remarriage between Suzanne and Pierre in *One Sings* would negate the principle of self-expansion. Yes, it might be clear here that '*one* becomes *two*' – the 'I' becomes a 'we'. But, again to situate Bersani's argument, such a 'we' is no expansion of the self. Rather, it merely offers a new form of containment. It is a couple, yes, but such a 'we' will still exist as a 'we' that is cut off from the rest of the world. This 'we' merely reproduces the distinction between subject and object, or subject and world, which Bersani aims to counter. (I say more on this in the following chapters.) In short, Bersani discounts the possibility that the formation of a couple can be a matter of 'one becoming two'. Any couple is merely a reinforcement of the principle of one, of sameness, a coupling whereby 'two becomes one'.

Pomme, in ways that Bersani would surely endorse, manages to free herself from the restrictions of coupling. She comes to the realisation that the love she believed to exist between herself and Darius is a matter of his possession and domination of her. She finds a way to free herself from that entrapment in marriage and thus embarks on a voyage of discovery, a voyage that, broadly speaking, becomes her life project. We could call it a project of exploring her connectedness to the world. It is a matter of exploring her different possible connections with the world, precisely what Bersani would call a project of self-expansion.

Varda then makes these principles of connectedness and self-expansion central to her films. We have seen that elements of connectedness exist from the beginning of Varda's cinematic career – in the fishermen of *La Pointe Courte*, in Cléo's awakening in *Cléo from 5 to 7*, in the account of the life of the single mother (Sabine Mamou) in *Documenteur* (1981) and then in the extraordinary depiction of Mona in *Vagabond*. These are aspects of Varda's filmmaking that highlight moves away from the notion of the couple. The couple as a concept – as a 'we' – is central to *La Pointe Courte*, *Cléo*, *Le Bonheur* and *One Sings, the Other Doesn't*. After the latter film, the notion of the couple tends to disappear from Varda's films. (One could certainly argue that some sense of a couple returns in *Kung-Fu Master* (1988), but in that film we are presented with couplings that are far from traditional or exclusive.)[4] In the later documentaries – *Jacquot de Nantes*, *The Gleaners and I*, *Faces / Places* and the self-portrait films, *The Beaches of Agnès* and *Varda by Agnès* and others – a guiding thread is the theme of connectedness. A major theme that runs through all of these films concerns the ways in which people are connected with each other and with the world beyond the confines of the couple.

Ending with a couple

I am aware that I can offer no proof of these claims here (I do not have the space to do so). I continue some discussion of Varda's films in the next chapter, which examines the films of François Truffaut. To conclude this chapter I turn again to *One Sings, the Other Doesn't* in order to offer some final reflections on Varda and the 'couple'. It has been noted that Suzanne remarries, while Pomme leaves her marriage. At one point Suzanne tells of her need to find a way of life in which a coupling will be central, while Pomme, by contrast, tells of the ways in which being a couple has felt imprisoning to her. She even goes so far as to invoke Ibsen by declaring herself as though trapped in a doll's house.

A concentration on these heterosexual pairings leads one to overlook what is surely the film's central couple: Suzanne and Pomme. Over a period of fourteen years they correspond with and care for one another. The delicacy of this relationship emerges nowhere more effectively than in three key scenes in the middle of the film that follow one after another. They are long takes in which Suzanne and Pomme converse, and the camera typically follows their movements into and away from one another, with great delicacy and care. This is the film's way of saying: here is a couple, and aren't they wonderful! The scenes occur when Pomme stays with Suzanne upon returning to France from Iran in order to give birth to her first child. First of all, in an interior scene, they speak of Jérôme's suicide, for, at the beginning of the film, Suzanne had been in a relationship with a married man, Jérôme (Robert Dadiès). With French divorce laws being the way they were in 1962, Jérôme had been unable to secure a divorce from his wife, even though he had fathered two children with Suzanne. With tensions and debts mounting, Jérôme committed suicide. In this scene, Suzanne and Pomme talk of the effects of the suicide, on Suzanne herself – she admits that she has struggled to find a loving partner since the suicide – and on her children. It is a single take as we listen to the women talk. The camera focuses on them, occasionally racking focus to bring one or the other into focus, then from time to time gently moving from the face of one to the face of the other.

The camera then cuts to an exterior scene: seated at an outdoor table, Suzanne and Pomme shell peas together. Surely we might see here another invocation of the joys of 'women's work', the joy that can be found in women working together and speaking together. (With more space I could also highlight the exquisite uses of colour in this film, a use of colour that rhymes with those uses of it in *Le Bonheur*.) I can also point to the significance of such a scene in view of the trope that emerges in many of the European filmmakers examined in this book whereby women find ways of speaking together. Here the talk takes the shape of a shared intimacy away from the interests and concerns of the men that overshadow the lives of these women. They speak of Suzanne's new interest in Pierre. She states that he is married and that she would not dare to break up that marriage, still noting, as of this point in time, laws make divorce a difficult thing to achieve (we seem to be in 1974, immediately before the 1975 changes in divorce laws, a fact that this film will later celebrate when Pierre wins a divorce from his wife). The camera moves in close. There is no shot/reverse-shot here. Rather, it is a portrait of intimacy, a two shot of togetherness.

Another cut, and the women are again inside Suzanne's home. They speak of the money Pomme had given to Suzanne so that she could procure a safe abortion (in Switzerland – the year was 1962). Suzanne now confesses that she used the money to pay off debts, and that she therefore had a backstreet abortion which rendered her infertile. These confessions are moments of deep intimacy and friendship made all the more poignant by the impending birth of Pomme's first child. 'I wanted to talk to you, to cry with you,' says Suzanne. Pomme gently caresses Suzanne's hair. It is once again a two shot, a frame of togetherness. 'Sharing is good,' states Pomme. 'Never mind. We'll have it together,' she adds as she touches her pregnant belly. 'And have fun.' They both smile and the scene comes to a close.

Notes

1 Conway also makes a link between *La Pointe Courte* and Roberto Rossellini's 1954 film, *Voyage to Italy* (Conway 2015, 19). I had wanted to make Rossellini's film a significant precursor for the arguments of the present book, alongside Renoir's *The Rules of the Game*. Reasons of time and space have prevented this from being the case.
2 DeRoo takes up some arguments made by Simone de Beauvoir (DeRoo 2018, 62). Also see de Beauvoir's own arguments: for a woman, 'marriage chains her to a man and makes her mistress of a home' (de Beauvoir 2009, 456).
3 On the relationship between de Beauvoir and Sartre, see Kirkpatrick (2019) and Fullbrook and Fullbrook (2008). Also see Moi (2008). On Cavell and de Beauvoir see Moi (2010).
4 *Les Créatures* (1965) also features a couple, played by Michel Piccoli and Catherine Deneuve. I don't think I am alone in calling this film one that is unsuccessful, and very few scholars seem to have written on it. There is little question that *Les Créatures* is indebted, to some degree, to the visual innovations of Bergman's films of the period, an association sealed by the casting of Eva Dahlbeck in one of the film's main roles. This is a way of saying that Varda's films of the mid-1960s are concerned with couples and are in conversation with other European filmmakers of the period.

Chapter 8

François Truffaut and the impossible couple

8.1 Antoine Doinel and Christine Darbon (Jean-Pierre Léaud and Claude Jade) in *Stolen Kisses* (François Truffaut, 1968)

'Each person is constructed through the encounter with another': we have seen this statement time and time again in this book. A variation on this claim was introduced in the previous chapter on the films of Agnès Varda. There, I argued that a range of Varda's films explore the positives and negatives of the 'couple', while another trope in the films emphasises the ways in which human beings connect with other objects and people in the world. For this latter point, the chapter offered some reflection on Leo Bersani's theorisation of 'connectedness'. Bersani's conception will be further examined in this chapter in relation to François Truffaut's films, especially those of the Antoine Doinel cycle. I identify a series of reflections on the notion of connectedness in ways that are expressed in Truffaut's films. To some extent,

I am guided by Anne Gillain's magisterial study of Truffaut, *The Lost Secret* (2013), and it is to these arguments that I will initially turn.

Gillain's book on Truffaut is arranged in accordance with what she claims is the guiding thread of the films: the search for the ideal mother. Gillain summarises the underlying fantasy contained in Truffaut's films by calling it 'the projection of a personal lived experience in which the son tries to comprehend his relationship with his mother and to restore the possibility of having a relationship and communication with her' (Gillain 2013, 15). Gillain's ideas are derived from psychoanalysis, especially the writings of D. W. Winnicott. In this model, the situations conceived in Truffaut's films are primarily expressions of separation anxiety, that is, the infant's initial separation from the mother, often in ways commanded by the father in accordance with an Oedipal matrix. And all of this carries with it the desire to repair or overcome the separation so as to be reunited with the 'lost' mother. All of this is evoked very effectively in some of the early scenes of *The 400 Blows* (1959), especially during the scenes when Antoine (Jean-Pierre Léaud) has bunked off from school and, with his friend (Patrick Auffey), engages in a series of enjoyable activities: they go the cinema, play pinball and then, in a key moment, go to a fairground and ride on the 'rotor'. As the ride spins, Antoine climbs up the sides of the rotor, an experience of freedom and dizzying ecstasy. It is immediately following this that Antoine spots his mother kissing another man, a man who is not his father. The connection between the two incidents is clear for Gillain. 'We can', she writes, 'associate the famous scene involving the rotor with [a] desire for fusion with the maternal body' (Gillain 2013, 30). In short, Antoine's constant misbehaviour and disruptiveness, handled in very sympathetic ways by the film, can be traced to the infantile anxiety of separation from the mother. Activities like that of riding on the rotor express the ways in which Antoine tries to restore a lost relationship with the mother. And, Gillain argues, Truffaut's characters repeat this trajectory in various ways across most, if not all, of his films.

Of course, psychoanalysis posits separation, in one way or another, as fundamental to the social existence of humans. Lacanians, for example, refer to this facet of human sociality in terms of the 'lack' fundamental to desire, while Freud posits it as a factor central to 'civilisation' as such (and to the 'dissolution' of the Oedipus complex; see Freud 1991, 1977). All of this amounts, for psychoanalysis, to a fundamental split between human beings and the social – and natural – worlds they inhabit: human beings are alienated from the world, we might say. For psychoanalysis, therefore, there is no intrinsic connectedness between humans and world. If we look again to Lacanian psychoanalysis, language is a decisive factor. Once human beings enter the social realm of signification, that is, words and meanings, then they are irrevocably cut off from any natural or immediate relation to the world. All experience will now be mediated by way of language, and once the realm of language has been entered there is no way that a return to non-language or pre-language can be engineered. In short, language and signification are definitive (see Lacan 2006). Less dramatically, perhaps, the Kleinian tradition will instead conceive of this lack in terms of separation from the mother. If, as an infant, there is no differentiation between child and mother, then individuation – when the child develops a sense of oneness and selfhood – involves an irrevocable separation from a prior state that we might call one of 'connectedness' with the mother. Klein, as is well known, calls this phase the depressive position (Klein 1986).

For psychoanalysis, lack is all. Bersani rejects the psychoanalytic account of the ways in which human beings are supposedly disconnected from the world. The clearest expression of this occurs in his *Thoughts and Things* (2015). There he argues that Western thought has predominantly proceeded by way of erecting a division between humans and a world conceived as external to them. Such thinking begins at least with Descartes's *Meditations* and its invention of the *cogito*: 'I think, therefore I am'. For Descartes, thought (*res cogitans*) is separated from the world (*res extensa*). The only way to bridge that separation is to enlist the power of thought. For Bersani, such an imposition of thought – that is, a reduction or containment of the world to the forms of thought – amounts to a desire for mastery and domination of the world. Therefore, from a Cartesian perspective we do not *connect* with the world, we subdue and subordinate it. And psychoanalysis, by and large – also noting that Bersani is a brilliant reader of Freud – repeats this division, 'a prior structural assumption', Bersani calls it, 'between the subject and the world' (Bersani 2015, 3).

In response, Bersani asks what alternatives there might be to this philosophy of disconnection and mastery that characterises the dominant strains of modern Western thought. He argues that an alternative can be posited by way of 'an aesthetic ethic of correspondences between the self and the world' (Bersani 2015, 5). Rather than emphasising separation and difference, Bersani focuses on connectedness and similarity. He focuses not on our differences from others and the world, but on what he calls a '[r]ecognition of the oneness of being' (Bersani 2015, xii). Bersani regards this oneness as an ontological given, though it is a given that has been quashed by traditional power relations and by the Western penchant for individualism and subjective domination. If modes of connectedness were to be advocated in human life, what would such a life be like? In a sense, for Bersani, what is at stake is the injunction to connect. One might almost reduce his thesis in a Cartesian manner: 'I am, therefore I connect'. And one must never stop connecting. Rather, one ought to move from one connection to another, then another, and another ... Such connections are ones that should never be permanent or long lasting, argues Bersani, to the point that such connections should never 'insist long enough to become an identity that might exclude other positions and extensions' (Bersani 2015, 82).

I claimed in the previous chapter that many elements in Varda's films could be characterised in terms of a logic of connectedness. Even in the films which feature couples, such as *La Pointe Courte* or *One Sings, the Other Doesn't*, there are significant elements of connectedness: the fishermen in *La Pointe Courte*, the singing group in *One Sings*. It is in the later films that Varda abandons notions of coupling altogether and instead charts some of the many dimensions of connectedness. This can be seen in the murals of *Mur Murs* (1980), in Mona's wandering travels in *Vagabond*, or in the reminiscences and memory-connections of *Jacquot de Nantes* (and back to Varda's earliest documentaries too). In *The Gleaners and I* such connectedness multiplies in many ways – via hands connected to large trucks on the motorway, the connections between women's work (a woman's unpaid labour, once again), painting and landscape (Millet's *The Gleaners*) and, by way of Alain, the man who teaches French to new migrants (noting that he does so for free, perhaps an ideal act of connecting). The key connection in *The Gleaners* is probably that which Varda herself makes by way of her own gleaning of potatoes – with the heart-shaped potato being a key figure of 'correspondence', a shape that Varda feels corresponds to her – with all of this itself connected with the digital filmmaking process, a process Varda regards as a form of gleaning. Such gleaning processes then continue in *The Beaches of Agnès*, *Faces / Places* and *Varda by Agnès*, all of which seek out elements of connectedness (beaches, faces, artistic creation).

Ways into Truffaut

I have built this book out of the various ways that the filmmakers examined here have conceived of issues relating to love, marriage and the formation (and deformation) of romantic couples. In the films, some couplings – or remarriages – have been successful, such as that between Fredrik and Desirée in Bergman's *Smiles of a Summer Night*, or the husband and wife of Varda's *La Pointe Courte*. More often than not, however, questions of marriage and coupling have been mired in ambiguity, miscommunication and disappointment. Such would be the way to characterise the endings of Antonioni's great films – *L'avventura*, *La notte*, *L'eclisse* and *Red Desert*. Similar dilemmas also emerged in *The Rules of the Game* and a range of Resnais's and Bergman's films. The most destructive or negative example I have concentrated on has been that of Bergman's *The Passion of Anna*, a film in which the forgiveness essential to the construction of a new form of marriage based on equality and mutual acknowledgment could not be achieved.

It is with François Truffaut's films, beyond any other filmmaker I examine in this book, that the conception of the romantic couple finds its most sustained impediments. Shattered couples are everywhere in these films. Married couples especially seem destined to fail, and we see marriages destroyed in one way or another in *Jules and Jim* (1962), *The Soft Skin* (1964), *Fahrenheit 451* (1965), *The Bride Wore Black* (1968), *The Story of Adèle H.* (1975), *The Green Room* (1978), *The Last Metro* (1980), *The Woman Next Door* (1981), *Finally Sunday* (1983) ... I have already suggested that Anne Gillain discusses these films with psychoanalysis as a guiding theoretical framework or explanation for the failed relationships of these films. At one point in her discussion of *Stolen Kisses*, the third instalment of the Antoine Doinel cycle, Gillain suggests that the film's energy and the forces of its characters are organised by virtue of the 'circulation of desire'. Indeed, it is characteristic of most of Truffaut's films that they chart circuits of desire in one way or another. Gillain is adamant that, especially in *Stolen Kisses*, there is a clear way in which the circulation of desire can be brought to a halt: marriage (Gillain 2013, 114). Gillain then adds a caveat to the circulation of desire in this film. She writes, 'to sustain it with the other, one has to flee it' (Gillain 2013, 116). In short, for desire to be sustained, it has to keep moving. If its stops, as happens with marriage, it will cease.

I'll quite simply declare that Gillain is correct here. In Truffaut's films romantic attachments tend to remain mobile: they never settle down; they are never contained. And such will be a guiding principle for Truffaut's films: love exists, but it never exists in a permanent form. Rather, love is fleeting and constantly changing. Even the titles of his films tend to affirm this: kisses are stolen and fleeting (*Stolen Kisses*) and love is constantly on the run (*Love on the Run*).

Perhaps all of this is nowhere more evident than in *Day for Night* (1973). The playfulness of partner-swapping in this film is at once hilarious and joyous. We are worlds away from Varda's *Le Bonheur* here, and much closer to the frenzy of *The Rules of the Game* (notably referenced in *Day for Night* when a chef declares 'I cater for diets, never to fads!'). Where in Varda's film there is a burning sense of moralism and a fear of any love that extends beyond the couple – there is certainly a fear of such arrangements in recent commentaries on *Le Bonheur* – in *Day for Night* there is a constant stream of infidelities and escapades. Truffaut's film is suffused with a comedic charge that is not there in many of his other films (*Jules and Jim*, *The Soft Skin*, *The Woman Next Door* and others) and which is markedly different from the serious tone of Varda's exploration of happiness.

Day for Night is a film about filmmaking. In the film-within-a-film, called *Meet Pamela*, a young man marries a young English woman, only then for the man's father to fall in love with the young woman. Eventually the father and the young bride escape together to Paris. Infidelity reigns supreme. Meanwhile the actors gathered together for the making of *Meet Pamela* are in and out of one another's beds. Thus, the actor playing the deceived young man, Alphonse (Jean-Pierre Léaud), falls in love with the script-girl, Liliane (played by Dani) (the reference here is to Lillian Gish, and Truffaut's film is dedicated to Lillian and Dorothy Gish), and he even proposes marriage to her. For her part, Liliane has taken a liking to the prop-man, Bernard (Bernard Ménez). Liliane then eventually runs off with the British stunt man (Marc Boyle) who briefly works on the film. Bernard, for his part, ends up sleeping with a range of members of the film crew: with the young actress who is pregnant (Stacey, played by Alexandra Stewart); with Odile (Nike Arrighi), a young assistant helping with the production, as well as with the continuity girl, Joëlle (Nathalie Baye), this latter rendezvous occurring in an amusing scene when Bernard helps Joëlle change a flat tyre on her car.

One of the film-within-a-film's actors, Julie (Jacqueline Bisset), who plays Pamela, the young woman who falls in love with her husband's father, has recently had something akin to a nervous breakdown. She was helped through this breakdown by her doctor (David Markham), whom she subsequently fell in love with and married. Everyone involved in *Meet Pamela* is rather shocked to see how old the doctor is, so that the actress is in many ways mirroring the character she is playing by falling love with an older man, a father figure. And yet, at the same time, Julie ends up sleeping with Alphonse. Amid all of this there is the stage manager, Lajoie (Gaston Joly), whose wife (Zénaïde Rossi) constantly accompanies him as he works for fear that he will 'fool around' with one of the other members of the film crew – she is aghast at the moral depravity of cinema! She is the moralistic outsider of *Day for Night*, the character who insists on affirming an old morality in the face of the film's romantic excesses.

I could go on. But one thing is surely clear: there is very little sense of love relationships here being either exclusive or permanent. All is fluid, all is change. And that is precisely what gives the world of *Day for Night* its charm, its madcap movements in which desire is repeatedly on the move and multiplying. The one permanent relationship here – that between Lajoie and his wife – is mocked for its naivety and tyranny: a wife who refuses to let her husband out of her sight for fear that he will be unfaithful. Such is Truffaut's negative view of the utter stasis produced by traditional marriage and coupling.

A critique of marriage is in place from Truffaut's first film, *The 400 Blows*: the infidelity of Antoine's mother immediately paints marriage as a system that, in Truffaut's world, quite simply fails to work. (There is a subsequent reworking of Antoine's relationship with his father and mother in *Love on the Run*.) In *Jules and Jim*, then, we are offered an experiment: what happens when a romance extends beyond the couple? Yes, it is Jules (Oskar Werner) who marries Catherine (Jeanne Moreau), but it is not long before he suspects her of infidelity, and he is convinced she wants to leave him. Catherine eventually sleeps with Jim (Henri Serre) too, and he moves in with the married couple – call this a 'couple + 1' arrangement, though by this point it is also clear that Catherine is having an affair with another man, Albert (he is helping her to write songs, one of which is called 'She was a Femme Fatale').[1] *Jules and Jim* continues in this vein until its faux-tragic ending which delivers the deaths of Jim and Catherine. Various mottoes emerge in the film, such as when Jim tells us that 'Catherine's motto is that for a couple to be successful at least one of them has to be faithful,' while he also later admits that 'For love, I know a couple isn't ideal.' I think it is fair to say that notions of romantic couple come under intense pressure in this film.

Jules and Jim cannot be seen, therefore, as a film in which the aim is to find the perfect couple – or even to find *any* couple. If Leo Bersani and Ulysse Dutoit find in Godard's 1963 film, *Contempt*, a critique of the notion of the couple, then *Jules and Jim* predates that critique by over a year. And it does so in ways that are surely more overt. The characters in *Jules and Jim* tend to follow a logic of 'trying things out' (as Bersani and Dutoit put it; see Bersani and Dutoit 2004, 60). Here, no coupling arrangement will be 'for all time'. Rather, there will always be new couplings to try out, to experiment with. If Bersani and Dutoit follow this logic of trying things out – and *Jules and Jim* too follows such a logic – then this is not a matter of trying things out in the hope of finally, eventually, achieving an ideal. Trying things out is not a means to an end. Rather, trying things out *is* the end: it *is* the achievement.

All of this means that we do not need to characterise these relationships in terms of 'lack' or in terms of the son's desire to be reunited with the mother. On such a reading – and Gillain makes these points – Catherine is the ideal woman by means of whom Jules and Jim are trying to overcome their Oedipal desires (Gillain 2013, 87–8). But I do not think this is what is at stake for Truffaut's narratives and characters. Rather, what is at stake is much more along the lines of 'trying things out', as I have claimed above. Gillain's accompanying point is of far more value: that the circulation of desire in Truffaut's films comes to a halt when a couple is married, and his characters go to great lengths to ensure that such a halting of desire never occurs. That would certainly be one way to describe the machinations of *Jules and Jim*, for the marriage between Jules and Catherine is never stable. Rather, desire – Catherine's desire – is always looking for new connections, new outlets and possibilities.

The constant circulation of desire and the quest for new connections is thus not necessarily a matter of overcoming a lack and is surely more in concert with what Bersani calls a 'new mode of relation' (see Bersani 2018, 35). As we have seen at various points throughout this book, Bersani offers a strong critique of traditional modes of love and coupling. Traditional romantic pairings, Bersani claims, are based on possessiveness and exclusivity, a desire for one member of the couple to possess and control the other. A couple is thus defined in terms of mutual possession: each member of the couple possesses the other. Bersani, often while writing with Dutoit, argues that such a logic of romantic love depends upon a logic of mastery and domination that is part and parcel of modern, Western modes of thought originating more or less with Descartes. Bersani, in an attempt to break with this tradition of mastery, wants to establish a new mode of relation that is not based on love, possession and control, as he sees it. That new mode of relation is one I have called 'connectedness', a mode of relation that celebrates the connections between humans and the world, rather than positing a lack or gap between humans and world. *Jules and Jim* may well be considered an attempt to portray and express this new mode of relation.

For *Jules and Jim*, one aspiration is to find a mode of love that is beyond the couple. Nevertheless, the film offers a demonstration of the ways in which society – France of the twentieth century, but let us also add that perhaps little has changed since then – ensures that romances 'beyond the couple' will fail to work. Truffaut himself claimed that *Jules and Jim* was a 'hymn to life and death, a demonstration through joy and sadness that there is no possibility of any combination of love relationships outside of a couple' (quoted in Gillain 2013, 89). In other words, Truffaut can see the joy and intimacy at play in 'coupling', but he also laments the fact that it seems the couple is the only form of love relationship of which society approves. To this degree, Truffaut is channelling Bersani and Dutoit's arguments on 'forming couples' some forty years before the latter's arguments were made.

In *The Soft Skin*, by contrast – but also with a similar point at stake – we have a simple plot. A middle-aged man, Pierre Lacheney (Jean Desailly), is having an affair with a younger woman, Nicole (Françoise Dorléac). His wife, Franca (Nelly Benedetti), discovers his affair and proceeds, while he is dining out one evening, in plain view of a restaurant full of people, to shoot him dead with a shotgun. Thus is meted out the punishment for romantic love that extends 'beyond the couple'. We need to keep gender distinctions in view here. The sheer energy of Catherine's love affairs in *Jules and Jim* – characterised by freedom, openness, experimentation – is very different in atmosphere from Pierre Lachenay's affair in *The Soft Skin*. The latter is burdened by deception, fear, secrecy and a kind of misogynistic paranoia that is all angled in favour of the man. (Truffaut's capacity for misogyny, as well as his capacity for the idealisation of 'woman', can make for some uncomfortable viewing today, and I feel that such discomfort will only worsen as time passes by.) Wherever we look in Truffaut's films, it seems that a 'happy couple' is something of an impossibility.

A similar kind of plot to that of *The Soft Skin* returns some years later in *The Woman Next Door*. In this film a married man (Gérard Depardieu) has an affair with a married woman (Fanny Ardant), and we learn that this couple had engaged in an intense romance when they were younger. The plot goes through various machinations until, at its climax, the woman shoots the man dead, only to then turn the gun on herself. At a basic level, the message is clear: love beyond the couple, beyond the married couple, a 'couple + 1' arrangement, is impossible.

And there are other examples. In *The Bride Wore Black* we have a marriage that is successful, but it is successful only in death. A woman's husband is accidentally shot dead on the day of their wedding. For the remainder of the film (though much of the film is arranged in flashback form), the widow exacts revenge on the five men responsible for her husband's death. In *Mississippi Mermaid* Truffaut desperately tries to construct a marriage that might succeed. However, this marriage functions only on the basis that it never settles down. The kind of marriage on display here is exceedingly closed off. It is closed off from the external world; it is the world and its social rules – 'society' as such – that places immense pressure on this marriage and its love. Gillain makes such a point concerning the hero of *Mississippi Mermaid*, Louis Mahé (Jean-Paul Belmondo). 'In the face of the constraints of the external environment', she writes, 'he chooses to steal away and strip himself, little by little, of everything that constitutes the social being of an individual' (Gillain 2013, 191).

On connectedness

This much is clear: marriages do not work in Truffaut's films, and while couples do emerge briefly, they never last. If they do last, then it is only in the most hesitant and problematic ways, as with *Mississippi Mermaid*. I will argue that we see the most sustained account of the ups and downs of love and marriage in the Antoine Doinel cycle. I began this chapter with some reflections on Leo Bersani's notion of connectedness. Instead of positing a gap between humans and the world, Bersani instead argues that everything is connected. Humans are composed of their connections with the world rather than being defined by a disconnection which must then be overcome. We have seen that Anne Gillain approaches Truffaut's films primarily in terms of the gap opened up by the child's – the son's – separation from the mother, and the repeated attempts throughout life to close that gap – and we might see such things in the Doinel of *The 400 Blows*, or in Jules's and Jim's idealisations of Catherine, and elsewhere. And yet, I am going to claim that this is not what is at stake for Truffaut's films. I will follow Bersani's lead and declare that, instead of being defined by a disconnection or gap between humans and the world, as Gillain argues, Truffaut posits a mode of connectedness between humans and the world.

All of this will surely lead us to a key question: in Truffaut's films, why does the impossibility of the couple amount to a notion of connectedness? Modes of connectedness might be evident in *Jules and Jim*, *Day for Night*, *The 400 Blows*, *Small Change* (1976) and elsewhere. But it is difficult to see where connectedness might be a concern for *The Soft Skin*, *Mississippi Mermaid* or *The Woman Next Door* (or for some other films I have not yet mentioned in any detail, such as *The Story of Adèle H.* or *A Gorgeous Girl like Me*; 1972). What, therefore, is at stake? For Truffaut, yes, there are many couples. But couples are, at best, temporary arrangements that stall the possibility of other connections. At the limit, couples restrict the possibility of other connections. Beyond the couple, by contrast, the potential for connectedness is opened up.

Much of this becomes clear in the final three films of the Doinel cycle, *Stolen Kisses* (1968), *Bed and Board* (1970) and *Love on the Run* (1979). Antoine marries Christine Darbon (Claude Jade) – they become engaged at the end of *Stolen Kisses* and are married by the time *Bed and Board* begins – so it is the ups and downs of that marriage which these three films chart in interesting ways. Gillain, as I have already pointed out, provides a way into *Stolen Kisses* by declaring that desire circulates freely in this film until it comes to a halt in ... marriage. To some degree, what Gillain argues is that, in order to sustain desire for another human, one has to constantly be fleeing that other human being. We can perhaps see this at its clearest in *Mississippi Mermaid*: it is as though Louis and Marion (Catherine Deneuve) cannot stay together at the same time as they also cannot bear to be apart, and the film plays out the constant negotiation between their attempts to flee each other at the same time that they also feel that they love each other and cannot endure separation. In accordance with Truffaut's typical focus on the male, it is typically Marion who flees Louis, so that his desire is one of constantly trying to be reunited with her. Desire, in this way, plays a constant game of toing and froing, and it is by means of this toing and froing that desire is sustained. It can never settle down to a point in which a couple might assume an ongoing identity – certainly never a permanent one.

And yet, do we not see in *Mississippi Mermaid* the desire for a perfect marriage or an ideal coupling? When, late in the film, Louis returns to his homestead on the island of La Réunion, he discovers that the manager of his cigarette factory, Jardine (Marcel Berbet), has moved into the large house in which Louis used to live. Jardine is happily married with a faithful wife and children. Louis sees there the happy life he too wishes he could have. Or does he? Does he merely look at the 'impossible' image of conjugal life (as Gillain puts it)? Why is it impossible? For whatever reasons – I shall attempt to discover some potential reasons below – a permanent love relationship or marriage of the kind Jardine has is rendered impossible for the heroes of Truffaut's films. We do see some successful marriages in the Doinel films. Colette's parents in *Love at Twenty* seem contentedly married in ways that the young Antoine envies. He envies both their secure marriage and also their ability to care for their child, Colette (Marie-France Pisier), in ways that his own parents had failed to do for him. And in *Stolen Kisses* he will later assume the same place in relation to the parents of Christine Darbon: they welcome Antoine into their home, as though he were one of the family, and their marriage too seems a success. The father even helps Antoine to find a job when he is dismissed from military service. And in the same film Antoine will be welcomed to the luncheon table of Georges and Fabienne Tabard (Michael Lonsdale, Delphine Seyrig), again providing us with the image of a happy family in which seemingly contented parents spend enjoyable leisure time with a son figure. Of course, here all is not innocent, as eventually Antoine will engage in a romantic escapade with Fabienne.

What can be said of all this? Are these images of the possibility of conjugal life, or of its impossibility? Readers will remember that in the early chapters of this book I made a distinction between 'old marriage' and 'new marriage'. The former was typically based on family alliances, or on power and financial partnerships, rather than being based on love. So-called new marriage, by contrast, was based on love. It was a new version of marriage that emerged most prominently in the US in the early twentieth century, an emergence that had its most sustained expression and celebration in a cycle of films made in Hollywood in the 1930s and 1940s, a cycle which Stanley Cavell called 'remarriage comedies'. What was most characteristic of 'new' marriage was that it was based on the mutual understanding of the members of the married couple: a free and equal agreement to experience life and the world together, as two people rather than one. This agreement or acknowledgment was something agreed upon by the couple alone. It was not an agreement brought to them by external factors such as parents or money or power or history or even a legal decree defined as 'marriage' – hence Cavell's contention to call such couplings '*re*marriages'.

Thus, when Antoine sees these supposedly contented married couples in *Stolen Kisses* – the Darbons and the Tabards – are these examples of old marriage or new marriage? They are surely examples of old marriage, especially as they signify the being together of an older generation: such couples are old, and what Antoine and his generation aspire to is something in love and marriage that is new. Will the romances of the younger generations in Truffaut's films deliver forms of love and marriage that can be deemed new – that might be called remarriages? We shall see. But we should also expect by now that the answer will be 'no'. If old marriage has to give way to a new form of human relationship, then, for Truffaut's films, those new relationships will not be ones defined in terms of remarriage. As readers surely must suspect by now, these films will aspire to 'a new mode of relation' (as Bersani puts it); they will aspire to connectedness rather than acknowledgment or remarriage.

Marriage/remarriage?

To some degree *Stolen Kisses* follows the shape of a typical remarriage comedy. Early in the film Antoine is reunited with a former girlfriend, Christine. As the film progresses, Antoine and Christine grow estranged from each other. This estrangement is especially evident in Antoine's infatuation for Fabienne Tabard, and he pursues a fleeting affair with her. By the end of the film Antoine and Christine are reunited, mainly by virtue of the latter's machinations in wooing Antoine to her house while her parents are out of town. They here share intimate moments of reconciliation. Very near the end of the film the couple share breakfast, including a tender moment in which Christine shows Antoine how to properly butter a piece of biscotte (or Zweiback). I cannot help but see in this scene a reprise of the famous donut-dunking scene from *It Happened One Night*. In my mind, therefore, *Stolen Kisses* is here linked to one of the key films of the remarriage comedy genre, as Cavell calls it.

Even more than this, and as is typically the case for the comedies of remarriage, the love between Antoine and Christine is sealed by a mode of conversation. Rather than speaking directly, they exchange small notes with each other, culminating in Antoine's placing the ring-shaped end of a bottle opener on Christine's finger to seal their engagement. Members of the audience do not know the contents of these notes and therefore are not privy to the couple's conversation. Rather, it is the couple's conversation and theirs alone. By means of this conversation we might say they reach an agreement – a mutual acknowledgment – to experience the world together; to experience the world as two rather than one. Of course, it seems evident to me that such a mode of conversation is contrasted with the failed conversation between Andreas and Anna in Bergman's *The Passion of Anna*. Like Antoine and Christine, this couple also share a breakfast together, but their conversation is not a conversation at all. It is a series of missed bits of communication, unanswered questions and hidden resentments, which soon explodes in violence. The positivity of *Stolen Kisses*' denouement can thus be contrasted markedly with the dark conclusion of *The Passion of Anna*. (And it must also be noted that there are significant 'table' moments in *Mississippi Mermaid*, especially casual mornings spent at Louis's mansion on La Réunion, which can then be contrasted with the small mountain cottage in which the couple take refuge at the end of the film. In a replay of the early idealised scenes of domestic bliss, here we see Louis and Marion share some tea, only for Marion to lace Louis's with poison with the intention of killing him. She does not succeed, and comes to regret that she had tried to do such a thing.)

I am not going to declare that *Stolen Kisses* is, in some way, a distant member of the genre of comedies of remarriage. I am simply pointing out that some aspects of this film signal an indebtedness to the tropes of that genre and its aspiration to define the contours of a new kind of romantic partnership based on equality and mutual understanding. If the relationship between Antoine and Christine shows us the potential of a new kind of love, then what other loves or marriages are on display in this film? Of the Darbon parents I do not really know what to say other than that they seem to be devoted to looking after the well-being of their daughter. As for the marriage between Georges and Fabienne Tabard, it is difficult to come to any conclusions here too. On the one hand we know that Georges is a person nobody likes. He thus goes to the detective agency where Antoine is working to try to discover why nobody likes him. On this basis, I think we must presume that his wife does not really love or even like him. We also know that Fabienne shows little hesitation in sleeping with Antoine: it is she who makes the moves; she turns up at his apartment and initiates their sexual encounter. And all of this latter scenario is played out against a backdrop of references to Balzac's *The Lily of the Valley*, which indicates an intention for the film to demonstrate that, in the romance between Antoine and Fabienne, we have to some degree gotten beyond the repressions of the Victorian age: here the characters have the confidence to act on their passions, and no moral punishment is meted out to them. Their affair is not scandalous, in other words. And this is where the film's title comes from: it is in the moments of bliss that Antoine and Fabienne spend together that we must comprehend one of the central themes of the film. Moments of happiness are fleeting, and nothing is permanent, certainly not in matters of love. All of this is a very different kind of arrangement when compared with the affair between Robert and Geneviève in *The Rules of the Game*, for example, or even that between Lachenay and Nicole in *The Soft Skin*. We get little sense that Fabienne would ever consider leaving her husband, and it is also unlikely that Antoine would consider living happily ever after with her. The emphasis in *Stolen Kisses* is on encounters and their fleeting qualities.

Stolen Kisses evokes other marriages. When, near the beginning of the film, Antoine is working as a night watchman at a hotel, he inadvertently – stupidly and amusingly, the film wants us to think – allows a detective to break into a room in which a man is conducting an affair. With the man caught in the act, the man's wife will now have enough proof to file for divorce. As argued earlier in this book, a defining factor of new marriage is that it is in some sense based on divorce: the freedom to choose marriage must have as its correlate the freedom to choose divorce; without the freedom to get out of a marriage, one is necessarily trapped in marriage. Thus, in a marriage such as the one depicted here, divorce is not a choice easily made (in much the same way as Jérôme is trapped in his marriage in Varda's *One Sings, the Other Doesn't*), but instead requires an entanglement of proofs and drawn-out legal processes. In the last of the Doinel films, *Love on the Run*, we will see Antoine and Christine divorce under a new legal framework, based on a free and open process, under laws first introduced in France in 1976 (see Ecolivet-Herzog 1977). The significant change here is in the conception of divorce. Where formerly divorce had been based on a conception of fault – adultery, cruelty, criminal conviction – it was now to be based on mutual consent. *Love on the Run* celebrates this transition and spends a good deal of time on the legal processes of the divorce between Antoine and Christine, while also engaging in the fictional ruse that they are the first couple to be divorced under the terms of the new law. If there is propaganda in any of Truffaut's films, then it is here: a celebratory advertisement for the virtues of divorce.

Other marriages in *Stolen Kisses*? M. Albany (Albert Simono), by today's standards rather shockingly mocked as a cuckolded homosexual, discovers that his male lover, a magician, is in fact married (to a woman) and that they have a child. One might take this as a joke at the expense of M. Albany (and I fear that such was Truffaut's intention: his views on homosexuality during the 1950s and 1960s were problematic (see De Baecque and Toubiana 1999, 80–2)) though by 1973 a great deal of sympathy is accorded the homosexual Alexandre (Jean-Pierre Aumont) in *Day for Night*). But one may otherwise see a critique of the heterosexual trappings of marriage: the magician prefers to repress his true love so as to be in accord with dominant social standards. Here marriage is a way of hiding from oneself. The magician's marriage is one defined by external factors – by the pressures of social propriety and expectation – rather than being a choice freely made, a choice based on love or mutual acknowledgment.

Yet another marriage: in passing, Antoine happens upon Colette, the girl with whom he had been infatuated in *Love at Twenty*. She is married to Albert, the man with whom she had fallen in love in *Love at Twenty*, and they have a young child. To all appearances, they are happily married. By the time we reach *Love on the Run*, Colette's child has tragically been killed in a road accident, and her marriage has been unable to survive. *Love on the Run* then opens this character onto myriad other complications: Colette is training to become a lawyer; she is investigating the case of a child murderer; she also tells a story of having to work as a prostitute to make ends meet ... None of these is a simple point to square. All I can declare is that Colette's is a marriage that has not survived.

Finally, there is one other key account of love in *Stolen Kisses*: that of the 'madman' in a trench coat (Serge Rousseau) who, at various points, stalks and spies on Christine. He appears in the film's final scene to declare his undying love for her. He says to Christine as she sits with Antoine on a park bench, 'I know that everyone betrays everyone, but you and I will be different. We'll never leave each other, not for a single hour.' As he walks away, Christine simply declares that he must be mad. And surely it is here that we can discern Truffaut's clear judgment on what love is. This madman who believes love is permanent and that a proper measure of love is that the members of the loving couple will never leave each other, not even for a single hour – well, this really is madness! Call this an old version of love which would have a corresponding mode of marriage: a coupling in which each partner is possessed by the other, trapped in conditions of coupling that amount to a kind of imprisonment. By contrast, *Stolen Kisses* and the Doinel cycle more generally advocate modes of love based on impermanence, fleetingness and temporary structures; loves that are to some degree merely 'tried out', rather than consolidated or made permanent in any way.

Loneliness and connectedness

To push further in the direction of remarriage comedies, it is clear that *Bed and Board* conforms to the tropes of that genre more than any other Truffaut film. At the beginning of *Bed and Board*, Antoine and Christine are married. Then they quarrel; Antoine has an affair with a Japanese woman, but in the end he and Christine are reconciled and get back together again: they are 'remarried'. And yet, such a remarriage will not turn out to be a permanent one. Antoine and Christine will go on to choose divorce some years later, as we have already seen. For Truffaut, it appears that any kind of permanent love is impossible. Romances are destined to be temporary, fleeting.

It is important to note that this fleetingness is not a negative judgment for Truffaut. The temporary nature of love is not a condition to be mourned. Rather, it is to be celebrated. How is this so? Graham Petrie, in a very interesting and insightful book on Truffaut published in 1970 (immediately prior to the release of *Bed and Board*), makes the observation, primarily with reference to *Stolen Kisses*, that Truffaut's characters tend to be lonely. 'Perhaps the most characteristic single feature of the people Truffaut creates on screen', Petrie writes, 'is *loneliness*' (Petrie 1970, 171). They find it difficult to find the right kinds of relationships with other people, he adds (Petrie 1970, 171). So, even though Antoine endeavours to reach out and connect with other people, he also seems to be closed off to some extent. We fail to obtain deep insights into his character; and that lack of deep insight occurs across all of the Doinel films. Antoine lacks the kinds of motivation we might normally associate with a film hero. He does not aspire to success in his working life. In *Stolen Kisses* Antoine fails miserably at each of the jobs he attempts: in the army; as a hotel night watchman; as a detective; and finally as a TV repair man. Even his novel in *Love on the Run* is not especially successful. (He does seem quite competent at, though not at all interested in, his job in *Bed and Board*, a profession that is reprised in the tanker-pilot instructor of *The Woman Next Door* in one of those numerous amusing intertextual references Truffaut characteristically makes to his own films.) Fabienne and Christine are the ones who take the steps to consolidate their relationships with Antoine – Antoine is very much passive, while the women are active. Out of all this, Petrie offers an admirable interpretation: that *Stolen Kisses* delivers a hero who is completely out of step with the conventional markers of social success. Antoine is not locked into the quest for marriage or career success that can be said to be typical of the society of his age (and ours too, to a large degree). *Stolen Kisses* instead creates for us an atmosphere of openness to the variety of life, especially of those experiences not normally sanctioned by civilised society. Those small touches can be said to be special: a kiss stolen in the wine cellar, tender caresses while watching a magic show, chance encounters with friends (Colette, René), the curiosity of Antoine's enchantment with Fabienne's spoken English (and his attempts to learn some English phrases via long-playing records), the charm of a spilt cup of coffee, the wonder of *la pneumatique*, the coincidental surprise of a minor car accident, the delight of properly buttered *biscotti* ... The small moments of *Stolen Kisses* may well be the most important ones, and that may well give us the key to Truffaut's films more generally.

Petrie will therefore go on to claim that, yes, Truffaut's characters are lonely, but this loneliness is a choice positively made. (Readers should remember that Petrie's book was published in 1970.)

> [T]he films are by no means as sombre as this [loneliness] might imply, and Truffaut is far from presenting us with the standard *clichés* about alienation or lack of communication. His people *are* lonely, they *do* find it difficult to find the right kind of relationships with others, and yet Truffaut can communicate better than any other film director the quality of friendship and love, the moments of joy and fulfilment that all of the characters experience, even though they may lack or eventually be deprived of the possibilities of permanent association with others. (Petrie 1970, 171)

I want to claim that Truffaut's characters aspire to relations of connectedness rather than to those of love and coupling that signify remarriage and mutual acknowledgment. For Truffaut, being in a couple amounts to being cut off from the world, feelings that are evident in *The Soft Skin*, *Mississippi Mermaid* and *The Woman Next Door* (also a theme in *The Green Room*, in which the obsession with coupling amounts to an obsession with death). Against coupling, Truffaut's characters aspire to a connectedness with the world. This means that Truffaut's characters seek connections or relationships that are not based on exclusivity and possession, as Bersani would argue is necessary for traditional modes of romantic love, and those characters always ensure that desire is kept mobile; that it never becomes static or permanent.

Although there are many married couples in Truffaut's films, one thing is certain: in those films, marriage does not work out. This is probably nowhere clearer than in the Doinel cycle: we begin in *The 400 Blows* with the disappointments of the marriage between Antoine's parents, while in the final three films of the cycle, the romance, marriage and divorce between Antoine and Christine are traced. Marriage does not work out, certainly not in any permanent way, divorce is championed and love ends up on the run. This world is in no way a negative one for Truffaut, so we could say that Petrie is a little off the mark when he insists that Truffaut's characters are 'deprived' of permanent relationships. The lack of permanent relationships is not a negative state of being. Rather, it is a mode of connectedness that Truffaut's films celebrate.

We have seen some of the ways that the mode of connectedness functions in the Doinel films, especially in *Stolen Kisses*. In that film, Antoine's passivity is foregrounded. His passivity ensures that he does not impose himself on the world – he does not attempt to master the world. He is, by contrast, open to what the world presents to him: he connects with the world. As we saw earlier in this chapter, Anne Gillain argues that Truffaut's characters are always trying to overcome the 'gap' that exists between them and the world, including other people. And this gap, Gillain argues, is typically a product of the son's separation from his mother, so that Antoine's love affairs – and his lack of success in those affairs – are attempts to re-establish a link with the world, a search for an ideal woman who might fill the gap left by way of separation from the mother. But, against Gillain's claims, we do not need to see these relations in terms of a gap or lack that needs to be overcome. On the contrary, Antoine sails through life, from one encounter to another, and at no point does he get depressed or worried about his situation. We might declare that a state of sombreness pertains to *Love at Twenty*, where Colette has the status of an unobtainable, ideal woman that Antoine seeks, to the point where he rents an apartment across the road from Colette and her parents so he can be closer to her. Then we also know that he fell madly in love with Christine, so that his decision to join the army was very much a response to his obsession with her. At some point, however, it is clear that he gets over his desire to possess these ideal women, he transcends the desire to capture and possess the women with whom he falls in love. It is then that Antoine becomes passive (though we surely also see this passivity already there in *The 400 Blows*: what is the rotor other than a machine of passivity, but also a machine of connectivity: when he rides upon it, Antoine becomes connected to the rotor). His infatuation with Fabienne comes to fruition not because Antoine makes it happen but, rather, because she proposes a rendezvous. Antoine is passive. And so too with Christine: it is she who puts in place the events that will see her and Antoine united once more. Antoine does not make things happen; rather, things happen to him.

In *Stolen Kisses* Antoine is passive in ways that eschew all control. He is content to accept the modes of relation that pass through him. We can list them: via the various jobs Antoine falls into; with the various sets of relationships that are established between him and other human beings, especially Christine and Fabienne, but also with Christine's parents, and then with the detective he first meets while working as a night watchman at a hotel, then M. Tabard, the magician, the old friends Colette and René whom Antoine just happens to meet in passing, all the way up to the car accident – a 'connection' with the world – that leads to his being reunited with Christine. Antoine embodies a spirit of connectedness.

Might we see a sort of alter-ego of Antoine in the character of Bertrand Morane (Charles Denner) in *The Man Who Loved Women* (1978)? I begin the next chapter with some reflections on that film, and on Bersani's notion of connectedness, all as a way of entering into the films of Federico Fellini.

Note

1 Albert is played by Serge Rezvani, but credited as Boris Bassiak. See De Baecque and Toubiana 1999, 176.

Chapter 9

Federico Fellini: love and forgiveness

9.1 Guido and Luisa Anselmi (Marcello Mastroianni and Anouk Aimée) in *8½* (Federico Fellini, 1963)

The films of Federico Fellini are best known for their excess, flamboyance and a certain amount of chaos. I think it is true to say, however, that Fellini is out of favour. The editors of a 2002 collection of essays on Fellini begin by declaring that, 'Since the 1970s, there has been a decline in critical and theoretical attention to Fellini's work, accompanied by an assumption that his films are self-indulgent and lacking in political value.'[1] Still today it is difficult to gauge what Fellini's legacy will be. I will unashamedly defend *8½* in this chapter as one of the finest films ever made. I will also argue that Fellini is very much in conversation with the other filmmakers approached in this book, especially Bergman and Antonioni. In relation to the latter, it will become clear that Fellini's themes in the key films of the early 1960s – *La dolce vita* (1960), *8½* (1963) and *Juliet of the Spirits* (1965) – are in conversation with the kinds of themes being explored in Antonioni's films of the same period (Antonioni's films were discussed in Chapter 6). Those themes pertain to love, marriage and fidelity, while also gesturing towards remarriage (as Stanley Cavell calls it).

I begin here by stating that the title of François Truffaut's 1977 film, *The Man Who Loved Women*, might easily have been a title given to one of Fellini's films, especially those films upon which I will focus here, not to mention *Casanova* (1975), a film Truffaut praised highly (see Insdorf 1994, 213). To some degree, Truffaut's film is an uncomfortable watch for viewers today, for it features a man, Bertrand Morane (Charles Denner), who 'collects' women. The film shows us conquest after conquest achieved by this seemingly irresistible man, as he sleeps with one woman, then another, then another and so on. The women this man encounters are mostly objectified and fetishised in ways that are, we would want to declare nowadays, simply wrong and unacceptable. And yet, I want to claim here – first of all – that *The Man Who Loved Women* demonstrates one version of Sellier's claim that 'each person is created through the encounter with another', that Bertrand is a man who creates himself by way of his encounters with women and that he is a subject who is composed of those encounters. Further, I will also claim here that Bertrand exemplifies, to some degree, Bersani's claims of connectedness: here is a man who aims to maximise his connections with the world by way of his encounters with women. Each woman shows us Bertrand's ways of 'trying things out', of opening himself up to another variation, another encounter, another experience, what Bersani might call a project of self-expansion. And one could even argue that Bertrand's refusal to get too close to any of his women – he does not want to fall into a lasting relationship – would be a way of celebrating Bersani's hope that we might enter a world no longer darkened by the demand for love (see Bersani and Dutoit 2004, 60, 70). We can further add that Bersani advocates connections and modes of relation based on bodies and pleasure, rather than on 'thought', for the latter is a mode of subjective domination and control, while the former presents a set of open relations, where desire is not captured and tamed but instead remains mobile and in circulation. We saw in the previous chapter that this was one way in which Anne Gillain characterised Truffaut's approach to desire; that as soon as desire is captured or maintained, it ceases to exist.

Bersani is very explicit about what he sees as being the dominant modes of Western thought. 'The desire to know the other', he writes, 'is inseparable from the need to master the other. The desire for mastery motivates the desire to know, and knowledge is the precondition of mastery' (Bersani 2015, 3). We have seen such claims already in operation for Bersani: knowing the other means controlling the other. Against such control, Bersani advocates a new relational mode, derived from Michel Foucault's late ethics. Bersani calls this 'an aesthetic of correspondences between the self and the world, a community of being in which the recognition of various degrees of similitude is itself a sensually appealing deconstruction of the prestige of knowledge' (Bersani 2015, 5). When the other is different, I must control it by way of knowing it. By contrast, if I approach the other in terms of its similarity to me, I no longer need to master it: instead I can connect with it. Such are Bersani's claims.

From Bersani's perspective, one could argue that, in *The Man Who Loved Women*, Bertrand is trying to connect with the women he seduces, that he is developing an 'aesthetic of correspondences between himself and the world', as it were. Those correspondences and similarities could be found in Bertrand's particular penchant for women's legs, a 'correspondence' attributable to the moment in his youth when he saw his mother in stockings, which the film shows us in flashback. From a psychoanalytic perspective, of course, Bertrand thus shows us a classic case of fetishistic fixation, and certainly this is the typical way in which Bertrand's conduct is explained (see Gillain 2013, 258). His separation from his mother has brought about a lack that is definitive for his unconscious, and his repeated trysts with women are so many attempts to heal that lack. Bertrand thus replays the dominant conflict of the desire to be restored with the lost mother, and we have seen this as central to Gillain's arguments on Truffaut.

I admit that all of this is might be rather complicated. I therefore want to focus on what I see as being the key distinction here. As has been the case for much of this book, that distinction is between acknowledgment and connectedness, where acknowledgment is a matter of thought and knowledge, and connectedness, by contrast, is a matter of bodily encounters, correspondences and connections. In this respect, in relation to *The Man Who Loved Women*, Insdorf identifies some pertinent points in a detailed and very sympathetic account of the film. There are three points. First of all, Insdorf writes that 'it is neither sex nor the hope for a lasting relationship that spur him [Bertrand] on, but a need to escape from his solitude' (Insdorf 1994, 206). Second, Bertrand desires 'unknown' women: as soon as he begins to get to know any of these women, he loses interest. '[O]nce the unknown woman becomes known to him', Insdorf claims, 'he says *au revoir*' (Insdorf 1994, 201). Finally, Insdorf argues that 'the real unknown in Bertrand's case seems to be his own identity'. She goes on to say that 'His pursuit of women can be seen as a pursuit of self, a desire to prove his existence' (Insdorf 1994, 213).

As I argued near the beginning of this book, acknowledgment and connectedness represent two ways of responding to human isolation, with acknowledgment being a mode of mutual understanding achieved in concert with another person, while connectedness is a matter of exploring one's correspondences with the world and other people. And we see both possibilities in Bertrand: an intensive search within himself in the hope of discovering something like a 'true' self, a task undertaken primarily by way of his writing a book about his experiences.

Bersani would call such a search one of 'introspection', and he relates such attempts at introspection to Proust's writing, an introspective search for lost time (Bersani 2015, 44–5).[2] Bersani goes on to argue here that 'The world seen as differential otherness is a misrecognition of the subject's perception of a differential otherness within the subject's self' (Bersani 2015, 45). He is critical of these modes of self-searching and introspection, for they point to the ways in which humans are separated from themselves and the world. Such notions of the subject are ones that stress a 'split' subject, a subject who sees otherness in the external world as well as within the self (with the latter often being called an unconscious by psychoanalysis in ways that Bersani traces back to Descartes's dualism). Against all of this, Bersani wants to conceive of a sense of connectedness with the external world, along with a self that is not split or doubled by a negative otherness. Bersani refers to this connectedness as the oneness or 'homo-ness' of being. And this mode calls for correspondences – an exploration of those correspondences – as well as the establishment of connections with the similitudes one finds in the external world.

Why is Bersani critical of the former mode – call it acknowledgment – in which humans are separated from themselves and the world? He is critical of it because the only way to reconcile self and other, he claims, is by way of thought; that is, as a mode of knowledge. And, in Bersani's terms, the quest for knowledge is also a quest for domination and control: the only way I can know the other is by dominating them – that's what 'knowledge' is for Bersani. In *The Man Who Loved Women*, this would be one way of accounting for Bertrand's behaviour: his collecting of women is a way of dominating them, all accounted for by the 'split' between himself and the world – and the separation from his mother – and the search for a true self (by writing his memoir/novel). By contrast, Bersani favours an aesthetic relation to the world, a 'new mode of relation' not based on knowledge and mastery. And such would be an alternative way to account for Bertrand's actions. As Insdorf puts it, Bertrand is interested only in women who remain 'unknown' to him. His quest is therefore not one of knowledge, and is therefore not a quest for mastery. Rather, he seeks connections: a non-judgmental, non-possessive mode of relation.

Contemporary sensibilities will surely find it difficult to defend Bertrand's actions in such ways; i.e., that he is pursuing some sort of non-possessive connectedness. Diana Holmes and Robert Ingram, in their 1998 book on Truffaut, argue that the film is to some extent 'about the problematic nature of conventionally androcentric sexual relations', so that a quest for a critique of gender norms might be apparent in the film. But they add that none of that can negate the film's 'phallocentric tone' (Holmes and Ingram 1998, 132). And Geneviève Sellier rather emphatically criticises Truffaut's penchant for the masochistic male figure and an obsession with 'suffering masculinity' (see Sellier 2008, 106–8). Antoine Doinel, Charlie Kohler (Charles Aznavour) in *Shoot the Piano Player* (1962), Louis Mahé in *Mississippi Mermaid*, Claude Roc (Jean-Pierre Léaud) in *Two English Girls* (1973), Julien Davenne (played by Truffaut) in *The Green Room* and, of course, Bertrand Morane: they are all 'suffering' males. Charles Denner claimed that his character, Bertrand, refrained from getting to know the women he 'loved' out of a fear of being hurt by them, hinting that we are supposed to feel sorry for this character (see Insdorf 1994, 206). But surely today most viewers will see Bertrand's conquests as morally questionable. To some degree, the film itself delivers a negative verdict on its own misogyny. Near its end, when Bertrand has slept with the editor of his book, Geneviève Bigey (Brigitte Fossey), she turns to him and declares that his actions and lifestyle belong to a past age; that such lascivious activities are no longer acceptable. She is driving him in her car, and they are diverted by what appears to be a serious car accident. She takes a deep breath and says to him, 'You know how I see your book? As a testimony to man–woman relationships in the twentieth century.' She turns to him and declares, 'You're well aware that it's all changing.' Bertrand responds, grudgingly, 'Yes, yes, perhaps,' and he goes on to say, in an attempt to deny that things are changing, that he enjoys the chase and the conquest. Geneviève then adds that yes, there will always be a 'game', 'it's just that the rules are being changed. The first thing that has to go,' she adds, 'is the play for power. We'll still play, but on an equal footing.'

Geneviève delivers a range of conclusions here: there were problems with man–woman relationships in the twentieth century and those problems need to be addressed. She identifies the main problem as a 'play for power' – the power men exercise over women – so that overcoming that power division and establishing relationships on an equal footing must be the goal.

We should see such ideas as belonging to the realm that Cavell calls acknowledgment, a conception of knowledge based on agreement and sharing – the sharing of ideas – and not on domination or control. In human relationships, a mode of acknowledgment is one in which the shared knowledge between the members of a couple is based on equality and mutual understanding, a way of knowing the world together, as two rather than one. Cavell argues that these aspects of acknowledgment gained traction in the US in the early twentieth century and had their most evocative expression in a cycle of Hollywood films from the 1930s and 1940s which he called 'comedies of remarriage'. By the time we get to France in 1977, we might contend that we are a long way from 1930s Hollywood! And yet, we see these themes being addressed by Geneviève Bigey in Truffaut's film in ways that are perhaps not too distant from those addressed by Lucy Warriner in *The Awful Truth*, a woman married to a man who tries to pass himself off as a lover of women. Geneviève, in *The Man Who Loved Women*, tells Bertrand that the rules of the game are changing. No doubt Truffaut's reference to Renoir's film from the 1930s is intended, and we ought to see Bertrand as a descendent of Robert de la Chesnaye.

Fellini

I have spent a long time discussing *The Man Who Loved Women* because I figure its themes are related in important ways to several films directed by Federico Fellini. Several of Fellini's films could easily be seen as ones in which a man attempts to collect women: *I vitelloni* (1953), *La dolce vita*, *8½*, *Casanova*, *City of Women* (1980) ... Even in the films in which women can be said to be central – *La strada*, *Nights of Cabiria* (1957) and *Juliet of the Spirits* – women are used and abused by men in demeaning and hurtful ways. In all of this, Fellini admits that questions of love are central concerns for him. He claimed, for example, that any human must aim to have 'a real authentic relationship with another person'. 'All our anguish and mistakes occur', he added, 'when there is no love' (quoted in Murray 1976, 60, 61). There is no doubt that questions of love and marriage are central to Fellini's films, even from his earliest efforts – *The White Sheik* (1952) and the short *A Matrimonial Agency* (1953). Thus, if something called 'love' defines the stakes for a range of Fellini's films, then it seems clear that those stakes come to hinge on the ways that men betray the women they love. In Fellini's films, what is then necessary for love to emerge or re-emerge is that the betrayed women forgive the betrayals of their men. Those films come close to Antonioni's in their condemnation of men's betrayals in love, but they also replay Renoir's condemnation of Robert in *The Rules of the Game*, or Varda's questioning of François's extramarital affair in *Le Bonheur*.

We can see all of this in *8½*. This is a film about 'man's sickness', about the inability of men to truly or properly love. The particular man at the centre of this film is Guido Anselmi (Marcello Mastroianni), himself a filmmaker. He has a tendency to engage in affairs. He collects women much in the manner of Bertrand in Truffaut's *The Man Who Loved Women*. He is married to Luisa (Anouk Aimée). At various points during the film she wants to leave Guido and have nothing more to do with him. And yet, certainly as I see it, Guido and Luisa are reconciled at the end of the film. Guido to some degree is determined to change his ways, and the film ends with the hope that this couple will be reconciled, that the marriage will be saved. Immediately, parallels with the ending of Antonioni's *La notte* become apparent. Where the ending of *La notte* plants the seeds by means of which the married couple might find ways to be remarried (as Cavell would say), the seeds of hope are far more evident in *8½*. I am satisfied to accept Fellini's own summation of the ending. He stated that, 'at the end of *8½*, the protagonist realizes that his fear, complexes and anxiety are in fact a kind of wealth' (Fellini 1995, 59).

I will begin by emphasising the theme of adultery in Fellini's works, especially in that pair of films in which adultery is foregrounded: *8½* from the husband's point of view, and *Juliet of the Spirits* from the wife's. From the theoretical perspective of Cavell, the thematisation of the 'comedies of remarriage' is not supposed to concern issues of adultery (see Cavell 1981, 245). And yet, questions of adultery are clearly central for Fellini in this pair of films, as they are for Renoir's *Rules of the Game*, for Antonioni, for Truffaut (in *Jules and Jim*, *Bed and Board*, *The Woman Next Door* and others) and emphatically for Varda in *Le Bonheur*. The issue of adultery needs to be confronted in these films. One trend becomes clear: if there is such a thing as 'new marriage' to be explored in these films, then such a marriage can be defined only as one that does not include adultery. In *8½*, if Guido is to remain with Luisa, then he must renounce all other attachments. Such will be the case for Giovanni in Antonioni's *La notte* as well. The aspiration in *The Rules of the Game* is for Robert to remain faithful to his wife, Christine. However, in that film, as I have argued, the stakes of 'old marriage' reassert themselves against those of new marriage. I argued in Chapter 2 that old marriage was often based on a 'couple + 1' formation such that a marriage was more often than not based on convenience or power or financial alliances, while love and sexual gratification were to be sought outside the marriage coupling. In *The Rules of the Game*, Robert, therefore, seems content to pursue his affair with Geneviève, and my presumption is that their affair would continue after the film's ending.

Both Varda and Truffaut complicate the issue of adultery. On the one hand, Varda might be seen to praise the virtues and pleasures – the happiness – of an adulterous relationship in *Le Bonheur*. But at one and the same time, it is not at all clear that anything is being championed here: the death of a wife is surely no cause for celebration. Truffaut's films, as we have seen, cannot come to terms with marriage at all, and I take the conclusion of the Antoine Doinel cycle, in *Love on the Run*, as something of a celebration of divorce rather than marriage (here Truffaut might be said to echo Bergman's *Scenes from a Marriage*). Fellini, by contrast, holds firm to a conception of marriage.[3] That conception of marriage also seems to be dedicated to a notion of new marriage as a solution to the limitations of old marriage.

For Fellini, the problems of old marriage are spelled out clearly enough in *I vitelloni*, where the key character, Fausto Moretti (Franco Fabrizi), is forced into marriage when one of his lovers, Sandra (Leonora Ruffo), falls pregnant. After marriage, Fausto continues to indulge in adulterous affairs, though it is assumed at the film's end that he will attempt, as best as he can, to amend his ways. A similar sort of libertine can be found in *La dolce vita*'s Marcello Rubini (Marcello Mastroianni), though this character remains unmarried. *La dolce vita* may well be seen as a kind of prelude to *8½*, for in the earlier film we witness the hedonistic revels of Mastroianni's character, a man content with pursuing the pleasures of the flesh – material pleasures – rather than seeking spiritual fulfilment. Such are the typical interpretations of *La dolce vita*. One commentator claims, for example, that Marcello's decline by the end of the film makes it 'impossible for him to believe in any possibility of a spiritual renewal for himself' (Bondanella 1992, 148).

Narcissism

I want to argue here that what is at stake for this series of Fellini's films, especially *8½* and *Juliet of the Spirits*, is the issue of narcissism. I have already tried at one or two points to raise the issue of narcissism in relation to some of the films approached in this book, most markedly in Bergman's *The Passion of Anna*. In that film, narcissism equals isolation. For Andreas Winkelman, the expression of narcissism is a kind of fear lest he might lose part of himself. Because this is the case, he is unable to 'give' himself to Anna, a woman he has tried to love. He remains 'walled in': he cannot break out of the narcissistic prison he has built for himself. He cannot break free from his narcissism in ways that would enable him to form a genuine relationship with Anna. We saw in at the end of Chapter 3 that what Cavell calls acknowledgment presents no easy task for human subjectivity. It requires 'absolute passiveness' (Cavell 2003, 35). Acknowledgment is not something I can *cause* or *determine*. It instead requires something like complete openness to the other person, a fragility that can only respond to the other person with absolute passiveness – that is, a refraining from all possession and control. To refrain from all control: this is what Andreas fears in *The Passion of Anna*. And we can also assume that his fear is well grounded: he had opened himself to his first wife and she had rejected him. Acknowledgment carries great risks with it, and the consequences of those risks can be devastating.

Guido, in *8½*, shows a very different kind of narcissism. His relationships with other people are not grounded in anything like acknowledgment, mutual understanding or intersubjectivity per se. Rather, his world is filled with so many objects which he tries to collect (hence the similarity to *The Man Who Loved Women*). Those objects may well be the things of the world: a film – Guido is a film director, after all – a landscape, a pair of sunglasses (by this point a Fellini signature), a health spa retreat, a casting session, a press conference, a spaceship, a beach, a circus … But for Guido that range of objects also contains people, especially women: Carla, Claudia, his wife, Luisa, La Saraghina and many others. In short, Guido tries to collect the world into himself, to master and control it. He demonstrates the capacities that Leo Bersani criticises as modes of trying to control the world by way of knowledge. Bersani argues that (and we have seen it already) 'The desire to know the other is inseparable from the need to master the other' (Bersani 2015, 3). If nothing else, Guido's search in *8½* is a search for knowledge – why am I like I am? Why is this happening to me? – and the film he makes is something of an autobiography (hence again the similarity to *The Man Who Loved Women*).

To some degree I am calling this narcissism. But what is narcissism? First and foremost, narcissism means love of oneself, or, as in the Narcissus myth, the love of one's own image. A first point to raise, therefore, is to suggest that narcissism is a *withdrawal from the world* rather than a *desire to master the world*. Because satisfaction cannot be found in the external world, there is a turn inwards and away from the world, towards the self, in the search for satisfaction. Psychoanalysis complicates these issues somewhat. Yes, narcissism amounts to a withdrawal of libido from the external world so that the portion of libido which would have been invested in the external world is now invested in the self – it is a transformation of *object-libido* into *ego-libido*. One way to interpret this transformation is to see it as a defence against the potential dangers of the external world. Therefore, narcissism is a way of bolstering the self – the ego – in order that the individuality and identity of the self are maintained. To this degree it is a way of overriding the demands of the external world in order to try to ensure that the external world conforms to the demands and interests of the self (see Freud 1984a, 75–6).

If that is not complicated enough, then we must consider that narcissism gets rather more complicated. Narcissism does its best to override external reality. Strictly speaking, narcissism and external reality are incompatible. Thus, fantasy will intervene to shore up one's narcissism: fantasy will overlay reality with constructions that will satisfy the ego. Fantasy distorts external reality so as to bring it into line with one's internal fantasies. We see all of this clearly at play in Bergman's *The Passion of Anna*: Andreas, frustrated by his relationship with Anna, late in the film fantasises a sexual encounter with the wife from whom he has separated. Thus, when confronted with objects in the external world that constitute a danger or which might threaten the integrity of one's ego – in Andreas's case, Anna, and a range of other anxieties to do with his separation, his financial woes and so on – then fantasy intervenes, covers over reality and shores up the ego. That is narcissism.

We can see this process in play in an expanded form in Fellini's *8½*. Guido's anxieties, whether over the production of his film, his health, his marriage and so on, are dealt with by way of a range of fantasies. These fantasies override reality. We see a simple example of this in the figure of Claudia (Claudia Cardinale), the fantasy figure of Guido's ideal woman. Guido imposes this fantasy figure on external reality, and we see this in a very early scene in which she hands him, with lightness and glory, a glass of the spa's healing water, only for the fantasy to quickly dissipate and reveal a rather plain and exhausted-looking woman, the 'real' woman who is in fact handing him the glass. As the film progresses, Claudia emerges at various points to assuage and clarify the difficulties Guido has with the other women in his life.

Claudia is only one figure, and other fantasy constructions continue throughout the film, probably most famously in the 'harem' sequence. Marilyn Fabe describes this sequence well. Guido's fantasies and daydreams, she writes,

> enable him to live and revise youthful experiences which have laid the foundations for his present conflicts, and his daydreams explore resolutions to his deepest and most guilty desires. As an example of the latter, he imagines his wife and mistress amiably meeting, complimenting one another, and dancing off together in perfect harmony. The daydream becomes a full-blown fantasy production in which he imagines himself the head of a harem comprising all the women he has ever desired – living happily and communally together, dedicated in their service to him, with every woman over age twenty-six banished upstairs. (Fabe 2004, 155)

Fabe fails to mention here that, partway through this fantasy scene, the women begin to stage a revolt. However, the revolt is averted and the pleasures of Guido's fantasy return.

All of this alerts us to another element of narcissism, certainly insofar as it involves sexual satisfaction. One writer characterises narcissistic pleasure as one in which sexual enjoyment is obtained without guilt or shame: a *taking* of pleasure rather than a *giving* or *sharing* of it (see Green 2001, 13–14). Generally speaking, this is precisely what narcissism and narcissistic pleasure amount to: the removal of libido that is invested in the objects and subjects of the external world so that this quantity of libido is turned around upon the self. One way to put this would be to say that the *giving of pleasure to others* instead becomes a way of solely *giving pleasure to the self*. We can call this a matter of mastery, of taking power over others in order to take their pleasure from them in ways that ensure that those other people and objects will instead give their pleasure to the narcissist. Narcissism, therefore, is a way of trying to ensure that the external world is brought into line with one's own ego, a world made to measure for the self, even if this can be achieved only in fantasy. It is narcissism that chiefly characterises Guido's behaviour, as well as that of several other Fellini characters: Fausto in *I vitelloni*, Marcello in *La dolce vita*, the husband (Mario Pisu) in *Juliet*, Casanova (Donald Sutherland) in *Casanova*. *City of Women* (1980) constitutes a special case to which I return at the end of this chapter.

Feminism

If that is one leap, then I wish to make another theoretical jump. If narcissism is what is at stake for the characters and plots of these films, and if Fellini, generally speaking, is offering a critique of narcissism (I believe he is), then that critique can also be taken as one directed towards notions of human subjectivity as reducible to an 'individual identity'. Fellini offers none other than a critique of the subject. We are here back on the territory defined by Sellier's claim that 'each person is constructed through the encounter with another' (Sellier 2008, 219). What the male characters in these films do is reduce the world to the narcissistic contours of the self. Any encounter with another person is merely a pretext for the bolstering of the self. And this is precisely what Fellini is critical of. We have already encountered Fellini's claim that humans must aim to have 'a real authentic relationship with another person' (see Murray 1976, 60). An additional claim I want to make here is that these arguments can be taken in a feminist direction. I would hardly dare to call Fellini a director of feminist films, though *Juliet of the Spirits* or *City of Women* may try to move in that direction. Against any claim to feminism, however, strong arguments could be made for Fellini's status as a 'masculine singular' director who merely uses women as a pretext for feeding his own creative 'genius'.

Fellini as a feminist? Surely not. Fellini nevertheless proposed something of such a perspective. (It is worth noting that Andrea Minuz has written a brilliant work on Fellini and feminism; Minuz 2015, 111–35) Feminism is explicitly a theme in *City of Women* though the approach there is highly problematic. When speaking of *Casanova*, Fellini pointed to his disappointment that feminists had not responded more favourably to his film. 'I'm sorry that feminism didn't pick up on the relevance of the film,' he claimed.

> How can one not see that sex, *eros* and *agape*, understood and practised in a certain manner – namely, as narcissism, without tenderness and any real sense of intimacy, any real emotional and imaginative content, without reciprocity; as mere repetition, physical activity, gymnastic display, a fleeting, frustrating, neurotic contact – leads to nothing but death? How can one not see that a man like that can see a woman only as an object? (Fellini 1995, 94–5)

I take Fellini's claims here as genuine ones. He repeats many of the claims I have made above on the narcissistic traits of his male characters – here, Casanova – and their tendency to treat other people, especially women, as objects.

On the back of this I want to claim that feminist arguments are relevant here, especially some claims made by Luce Irigaray. One writer suggests that Irigaray's work is explicitly invoked in *City of Women*. 'The theorizing', this writer argues, 'of French feminist Luce Irigaray (1980), author of "When Our Lips Speak Together," echoes in the commentary of a slide show on female genitalia at the feminist convention Snàporaz finds himself in the midst of' (Waller 2020, 323). The arguments I want to stress here are those concerning the ways that men tend to prioritise relations with objects rather than relations with people. Irigaray famously defends the differences between men and women by arguing that, if women are to make gains that will counter their subordination to men, then the ways in which they differ from men must be defined, emphasised and celebrated. A key difference, Irigaray contends, is that men tend to prioritise relationships to the world defined by way of objects – of goods, property, possessions. Women, by contrast, prioritise subjective relationships; that is, relationships, conversations, communication with other people (see Irigaray 1996, 130). These differences certainly create conflicts between men and women, and to a large degree explain why men, even today (Irigaray was writing in the 1990s), find ways of reducing women to predefined roles – mother, whore, housewife and so on. Indeed *8½* gives us a kind of catalogue of the negative ways in which Guido treats the women he knows: his wife, mistress, past lovers such as Jacqueline Bon Bon (Yvonna Casadei). Other men in the film are just as guilty of such objectifications, none more than Mario Mezzabotta (Mario Pisu), Guido's old friend who is intending to marry a woman, Gloria (Barbara Steele), much younger than he, as soon as he can finalise a divorce from his wife of many years. It is clear that, for a future in which a relationship between men and women can proceed in a positive way, it is men who need to change. This was certainly the case in 1963, but remains an urgent theme today.

Irigaray is convinced that such changes in men are possible and desirable. 'The couple forms the elementary human community,' she writes (Irigaray 1996, 28) 'We still know nothing of the salvation love brings, individual and collective salvation' (Irigaray 1996, 29). I tend to believe these are precisely the kinds of claims that Fellini, too, could have made. Out of all this Irigaray will make the strikingly simple claim that 'The man and the woman can thus form a human couple' (Irigaray 1996, 28–9). This coupling is something that can be achieved both *singularly* – each as an individual – and *together* – as that which transcends the individual. In other words, the couple, the elementary human community, offers a way out of narcissism, beyond the identity of the individual and into a twoness rather than a oneness of being. Readers should sense that these claims come close to the kinds of claims made by Cavell; that is, for the couple in remarriage to forge a world 'alone together' as an ur-community in which separate individuals construct a shared world. Strikingly, this is also how Cavell tends to interpret Emerson's notion of self-reliance: not as self-containment or narcissism but, rather, as a sense of selfhood that can be achieved only in concert with another person, or other people. A narcissist is not self-reliant. For Irigaray, marriage can play a role here too. She writes that 'It [marriage] is the engagement of two intentionalities to realize the finality of their gender' (Irigaray 1996, 147). Marriage is a project or challenge for each member of the couple to realise themselves in ways that they cannot if they remain separate and separated. 'The wedding between man and woman realizes the reign of spirit. Without it, there is no spirit' (Irigaray 1996, 147). The notion of marriage, or what Cavell calls remarriage, offers one way out of the trap of narcissism.

Bersani and impersonal narcissism

To throw another theoretical spanner into the mix, Bersani too offers a compelling critique of narcissism. For Bersani, narcissistic enjoyment is fundamentally aggressive. But narcissism, he argues, is also an integral part of the human psyche. Bersani characterises it as a human desire to eject all badness into the external world – to fight against the external world – in order to assuage one's guilt: to rid the self of evil by declaring instead that all evil resides in the external world. To 'love thy neighbour' is not at all a natural or easy thing to do (see Bersani and Phillips 2008, 60). Bersani praises Freud on such issues. This is how Bersani characterises the narcissistic ego, an ego conditioned by aggressiveness towards the external world which is, at one and the same time, a way of coping with one's guilt and one's 'inner evil'. In short, narcissism is a way of responding to and coping with one's sense of self-destruction, one's capacity for evil.

Bersani wants to resist such aggressiveness and destructiveness. He asks: might there be another kind of narcissism, a narcissism that fosters and nurtures love rather than protecting and cocooning the evil within us? What Bersani proposes is a concept of love based on sameness; no longer a kind of love based on conquering the other, or mastering or possessing the other, as he sees it. Rather, working from Plato's *Phaedrus*, he argues that, in the love relationships Plato describes, what is seen and desired in the other is part of oneself. As Bersani puts it, on this model, what one loves in the other is *the otherness that is one's own* (see Bersani and Phillips 2008, 84). Thus, love *is* self-love, but the 'self' one loves is located in the other person (Bersani and Phillips 2008, 84–5). We are very close to Lacan's conception of the *ágalma* (which Lacan also gets from Plato, though from the *Symposium*), and more or less on the terrain of 'man's desire is the desire of the other' (as derived both from Hegel or Lacan). But what is very interesting about Bersani's conception of narcissism is this: parts of the self are no longer located in the self, they are located in the other. Bersani calls this *impersonal narcissism*: a narcissism that is not cocooned within the self, but that is external to the subject; a narcissism that is not necessarily 'mine'. We could say that Bersani is building on his earlier work, writing with Dutoit, in which he sought a reoccurrence of all subjects elsewhere (Bersani and Dutoit 2004, 120). The subject does not exist as a narcissistic self. Rather, its narcissism is external, impersonal.

Bersani works hard to make a clear distinction. What he calls 'the hyperbolizing of the ego' – that which is traditionally meant by narcissism – 'is a self-identifying exercise in which the ego can experience itself as a militant identity' (Bersani 2015, 85). Impersonal narcissism, by contrast, promises a very different self, 'a kind of reciprocal recognition in which the very opposition between sameness and difference becomes irrelevant as a structuring category of being' (Bersani 2015, 86). And we would have to say that what occurs here is no longer a self as such. Bersani will favour what he calls 'an ego-free individuality'; an individual who no longer says 'I' (Bersani 2018, 26).

A new conception of love, not based on mastery or possession, as Bersani conceives it, is a non-relation or new mode of relation in which individual selves cease to be defining categories. This depends on accepting a conception of sameness, a oneness or homo-ness of being. Sameness, and not difference, is crucial. Bersani points out that we respond to aspects of the world that correspond to us and which therefore connect us to the world. Such connections are made by way of sameness, not difference, and sameness, in this way, is more fundamental. I eat an apple because I like the taste of it; because it corresponds to me, as it were. '[T]he *object of human desire must*', Bersani writes, '*to a certain extent, correspond to the being of the desiring subject*' (Bersani 2018, 69; italics in original).

There are so many points to raise here that I cannot possibly respond to all of them. What I want to focus on is Bersani's insistence that such modes of selfless love or impersonal narcissism can never be reduced to notions of the couple (see, for example, Bersani 2010b). Rather, the logic at play is one of multiple connections, on the one hand – meaning that no person should be content with having merely one lover – while, on the other hand, any love relation must resist permanence; that is, two loves would never form themselves into a couple, and certainly never a marriage. Bersani is especially scathing when it comes to marriage. It is a negative institution, he argues, it is heterosexual at its core, and therefore limiting. Bersani rejects, for example, calls for 'gay marriage'. And he asks some excellent questions coming out of this: 'What is the limit at which marriage would lose so many of its recognized attributes that it would no longer make any sense to get married?' (Bersani 2015, 22). I guess these are the types of question the current book is trying to ask, and which it has occasionally attempted to answer.

Same and different

Let us get to the bottom of Bersani's distinctions here: he is critical of narcissism insofar as it amounts to a withdrawal from external reality of all elements of the self. He calls this a 'narcissism of mastery' insofar as external reality is made to conform with the desires of the narcissistic ego. Against that conception, Bersani proposes a concept of impersonal narcissism composed of a love of the other based on sameness – one's correspondences with the other – rather than on difference. Bersani offers a conception markedly different from that of Irigaray or Alain Badiou, for example, with the latter claiming that love 'embraces this experience of the world from the perspective of difference' (Badiou 2012, 39).

How can these distinctions between sameness and difference be squared? Stanley Cavell's chapter on Leo McCarey's *The Awful Truth* in his book on the *Pursuits of Happiness* is called 'The Same and Different' (Cavell 1981, 229–63). If, in that film, Jerry finally chooses to choose Lucy, then it is because she is *not* him, or, more forcefully, it is because he discovers something in her *that does not correspond to him*. Call this an embrace of the other that is not the self, an other who does not mirror the self or conform to the self's desires. In short, it is an embrace of difference that does not reduce the other to the conditions of narcissistic sameness, impersonal or otherwise. Thus, for example, Jerry is himself no singer, yet he admires in Lucy that she is a singer: he admires her difference from him. She is a classically trained singer of Italian arias, as it were – thanks to her being taught by the Continental Armand. So when she is toying with a potential lover, Dan Leeson (Ralph Bellamy), he encourages her to sing a folksy (as Cavell calls it) American song, 'Home on the Range'. This is not her kind of song – which is to say it is different from Lucy; it does not correspond to her. And relations between the same and the different get complicated here, such that Cavell then argues from this that Dan *does not know* Lucy, and thus cannot acknowledge her; he does not appreciate or understand her voice, nor does he know what that voice is capable of. He wants sameness – the same as he is: home on the range; no difference.

The climax of *The Awful Truth* begins with Lucy's impersonation of a somewhat non-classical tune, 'My Dreams are Gone with the Wind'. We would have to declare that, like 'Home on the Range', this song is not one that corresponds to Lucy. Where Lucy was *not* prepared to make herself different for Dan Leeson, she *is* prepared to change herself for Jerry. She makes herself different in order to appeal to what she believes are Jerry's sentiments, for he had shown himself to be attracted to this song, and to the performance of it by a woman named Dixie Belle, a woman to whom, it seems, he had been romantically attracted (though it also seems that his appreciation and romantic interest were feigned). But it is Lucy who now sings this song. In doing this, Lucy demonstrates that *she can be different from who she is*, and that she is willing to be different in ways that will accommodate Jerry's desires. And that is not to say that she *will* bend to Jerry's desires or conform to his tastes. Rather, Lucy is demonstrating that she could if she wished. Her rendition of 'Gone with the Wind' is a performance of her willingness and desire to be different from herself, and thus to accommodate the other person, in order to construct, together with that other person, what a marriage can be. Lucy's demonstration of 'self-otherness' is a renunciation of narcissism, a denial of the world's being reduced to the self, a refusal of a world based on 'self-sameness', an embrace of difference. It shows us one side of the ways that love can be considered an experience of the world from the perspective of difference, as Badiou puts it (Badiou 2012, 39). Or, as Cavell writes of the 'Gone with the Wind' number, 'it requires her [Lucy's] respect for the doubleness (at the least) of human consciousness' (Cavell 1981, 252).

The other side is this: for the marriage to work – for it to be a remarriage – Lucy also requires that Jerry adopt a mode of self-otherness. He must refuse narcissism and self-sameness. On this point I am very much in agreement with Glitre's criticisms of Cavell (as noted in my opening chapters). Catherine Constable (2011) agrees: it is Lucy who teaches Jerry to change. She educates him. It is not the man who educates the woman here (see Wheatley 2019, 127–9). Deftly summarising these arguments, Catherine Wheatley proposes the following:

> It is the shock of discovering her [Lucy's] autonomy that proves too hard [for Jerry] to bear. The task for Lucy is then to teach Jerry to acknowledge that autonomy and live with it ... Constable and Glitre point out that in constructing female desirability as conformity to a male defined image, Cavell overlooks the ways in which Lucy teaches Jerry to see her *as she wants to be seen*. (Wheatley 2019, 129)

Such are the strains of what can be called acknowledgment, even beyond the bounds of what Cavell might wish to ascribe to that term: love is a matter of *making oneself other in order to accommodate an other*. Such points place love and acknowledgment, surely, on these terms, well away from anything that might be called narcissism.

Here, then, we reach some real crisis points in Bersani's accounts of love and connectedness; that is, of a love based on correspondences and sameness. The challenge posed by a film like *The Awful Truth* – and readers should be aware that this point is one I will make for Fellini's films too – is that love and remarriage must be based on an acknowledgment of difference as well as sameness. But it is difference that is crucial. Jerry must acknowledge Lucy's autonomy: she is separate from him, different from him, not connected to him, not the same as him, other than him.

Again I will stress the crucial point here: acknowledgment requires a reciprocal relation whereby one becomes two. It cannot be based on a notion of two becoming one, or on a notion of the multiple correspondences of all subjects, to adopt Bersani's language. Bersani's arguments cannot accommodate a logic in which one becomes two. Rather, adopting something akin to a universal oneness or homo-ness, all Bersani can point to are the resonances or correspondences of sameness (of similitude), albeit a multiple sameness as a mode of subjectivity that is dispersed in the external world, a subjectivity incapable of declaring 'I'. How can this distinction between Bersani's and Cavell's conceptions be measured other than by pointing to Cavell's overwhelming defence of the subject's ability to declare 'I am'? Echoing Emerson, Cavell makes this a matter of a journey from conformity to self-reliance, but we could also call it a journey from oneness to an acknowledgment of difference, from oneness to twoness – that is, the ability to declare 'I am', in this way, is a renunciation of narcissism. Yes, Bersani posits a way out of narcissism based on the multiple correspondences of the subject in the external world, but I will simply declare that the mode of impersonal narcissism is not one our current mode of human subjectivity can bear. (Is Bersani's conception therefore utopian? Yes, and I see no problem in that. But that is not our world, not yet.)

Back to Fellini

As ever, we can see a Hollywood comedy finding its way to a happy ending. Cavell charts the remarkable exchanges of the final scenes of *The Awful Truth* that hinge on the same and the different. I won't plunge into details here other than to briefly state that the getting back together of Jerry and Lucy requires that each of them be both the same and different from what they had been before, and also that their marriage be both the same and different from what it had been. I want to bring the discussion back to the films of Fellini – especially *8½* – by way of two claims made by Cavell. The first offers a summation of the conclusion of *The Awful Truth*. He writes, 'We are asked by this ending to imagine specifically how what we are shown adds up to the state of forgiveness the pair have achieved' (Cavell 1981, 261). We shall see to what extent such a claim might apply for *8½*, what the stakes of forgiveness are, who has to forgive whom and why forgiveness might be an issue.

I want to focus also on a second claim made by Cavell. In it he argues that the comedies of remarriage do not revolve around issues of adultery and that the kinds of marriages demonstrated by these comedies are not ones that can exist on the basis of a 'couple + 1' logic, as I have tried to put it at various points throughout this book. Cavell writes, 'Freedom in marriage is not to be discovered in the possibility of adultery, which thus becomes unusable as comedy; it becomes either irrelevant or else the stuff of melodrama' (Cavell 1981, 245). The comedies of remarriage on which Cavell focuses avoid issues of adultery. (Will I say here that Cavell is making things too easy for himself here? Surely a film like *The Awful Truth* has adultery as a theme?) Adultery is central for *8½*, as much as it has been central for many of the films approached in this book (in *The Rules of the Game*, *Contempt*, *La notte*, *Le Bonheur*, *Bed and Board* and many others). I have tried to indicate in this chapter that, typically in these European films, adultery is a matter of a husband's betraying his wife, and that those betrayals figure a narcissism that the man is unwilling to forego. I have also argued that Leo Bersani's conception of connectedness – a search for correspondences in the external world, a search for sense of sameness rather than difference – provides a logic that is very different from that required by marriage or remarriage. What the latter requires is a logic of acknowledgment, on Cavell terms, and a logic of difference whereby 'one becomes two' (perhaps Alain Badiou expresses this with most clarity: 'all love suggests a new experience of truth about what it is to be two and not one'; Badiou 2012, 39). I have thus tried to argue that all of this – love, remarriage, acknowledgment, one-becoming-two – is a matter of *making oneself other in order to accommodate an other*; that is, of changing oneself in order to accept or embrace what is different in the other person. I have thus tried to declare that this is what is at stake for the ending of *The Awful Truth*, a comedy of remarriage according to Cavell.

My question, therefore, is whether Fellini manages to achieve this in some of his films, whether these films show us the terms of 'making oneself other in order to accommodate an other'. The key film in this regard is *8½*, while other of Fellini's films – *I vitelloni*, *La dolce vita*, *Juliet of the Spirits*, *Casanova* – offer discourses on the ways that this achievement fails. It fails, typically, because a man is unwilling or unable to make himself other so that he can acknowledge a woman. On these grounds, a woman will remain unknown to a man, but that unknownness is nothing less than a strategy of the man; it is the man's refusal to accommodate the difference expressed by the woman.

8½ shows us something like a positive version of this expression of love. The man, it seems, at the film's end, is determined to amend his ways, to accept that he cannot control the world that surrounds him and that the people with whom he is engaged in this world cannot simply be made to conform to his desires. From this perspective the ending of 8½ may feel unbearably trite: Guido and Luisa effectively 'kiss and make up', so that all of Guido's sins and betrayals are somehow swept away in a few words. Some commentators will simply declare that Guido has been rotten and treated Luisa in awful ways, only for all of that to be forgiven, for the woman to bear the brunt of the pains of the man's behaviour and, effectively, that he has gotten away with it all. (The sense of 'getting away with it all' seems all-pervading in *City of Women*, for example, where the gallivanting of 'Ole Snàporaz' (played by Marcello Mastroianni, noting that 'Snàporaz' was Fellini's nickname for Mastroianni) is dismissed, in the end, as a dream, and therefore as somehow excusable.) We could add that Guido's promises to change may well be empty promises. It seems he has made such promises before, and that Luisa has offered her forgiveness before too, only for that forgiveness to fade amid Guido's renewed betrayals.

But I do not see things that way. Fellini is charting such issues because he feels they need to be charted. He knows that men are very good at treating women badly – Italian men, perhaps; and certainly himself, for Fellini is not merely replicated in Guido as a filmmaker; he is also replicated in Guido as a womaniser. So I cannot see a film like 8½ as anything less than a plea to men to change their ways (and so too for *I vitelloni*, *La strada* (1954), *La dolce vita* and so on). If such attempts are dismissed as empty gestures or futile promises, then we may was well all give up on love.

The key scenes feature conversations between Guido and Luisa. There are two such scenes. The first occurs quite a way into the film – we are already nearly one and half hours in. Luisa has come to visit Guido at the spa resort where he is both recuperating and trying to save the film he is making. Of course, he is also managing an affair with Carla (Sandra Milo) at this resort, though it is also true that Guido himself has invited Luisa. She has arrived and spent much of her first day there, before dancing in the evening. She has been dancing with another man, Enrico (Mark Herron), who has clearly taken an interest in her. Late at night, she returns to the hotel room she is sharing with Guido, a room to which he has returned some time earlier. He is in bed, feigning sleep. Luisa's first act is to go to the telephone in the room and try to call Enrico, who is also staying at the hotel. The response she receives is that Enrico has not yet returned to his room. Luisa then climbs into bed. For whatever reason, this room has twin beds rather than a double.

Luisa and Guido then talk. She tells him that she doesn't think she could ever cheat on him. And we know that she knows Guido has betrayed her more than once, so why does Luisa feel she cannot betray him? She states here that she could not do such a thing because she would not be able to cope with having to hide and lie, that such is no way to live. We are worlds away, it seems, from *Contempt*, which we saw in the opening chapters of this book, and which featured a woman's cheating on her husband, and so too are we distant from the openness of *Jules and Jim* (and we shall once again see a woman's affairs in Godard's *A Married Woman* in the following chapter). But we are also well away from the flirtings of Lisette in *The Rules of the Game*, where dalliances with the opposite sex outside marriage were more or less entirely necessary. We are very close to *La notte*, where we saw that a wife was also unable to betray her husband even as she seemed to want to do such a thing. And so it seems we are far closer to the world of 'old marriage', perhaps even to *The Rules of the Game*, which rules declare that the upper-class husband, Robert, can entertain a 'couple + 1' existence, while the wife must renounce such things. In *8½* we have a situation here – in this room, in this conversation – whereby the husband seems to believe he should be able to do as he pleases, and that the wife should not poke her nose into situations that needn't concern her. Surely we are not all that far away from Jerry's deceptions of Lucy in *The Awful Truth*: he feigns a vacation in Florida when Lucy discovers he most certainly has not been in Florida (if nothing else, the California oranges give it away). All I can say is that stakes opened in *8½* do not fall at all far from those initiated by a film like *The Awful Truth*. Luisa gets rightly angry at Guido. 'Why did you ask me to come?' she asks. And she goes on to ask, with great anger, 'What good am I to you? What do you expect from me? What is it you want?' And these are the final lines of this scene. Communication fails. There is accusation and bitterness. We are a long way away from any sort of conversation, remorse or forgiveness.

The film wends its way to its remarkable conclusion. We can begin with the famous suicide. Guido is on the exterior spaceship set of his film, and he is facing a barrage of questions from reporters at a press conference. It seems the film is off: he cannot complete it. Unable to cope with the chaos, Guido crawls beneath the table that has been set up for the press conference, pulls out a pistol and shoots himself: he has committed suicide. No sooner has this happened than we see him sitting in a small car, with his scriptwriter Daumier (Jean Rougeul) babbling on about art and life. We realise – at least, this is how I take the film's ending – that Guido has not committed suicide: the suicide was mere fantasy. We then begin to see elements of the parade with which the film concludes. The cast of characters from this film – Carla, Claudia, La Saraghina, Guido's parents and so on; everyone we have seen in the film, it seems – all dressed in white, slowly make their way across the fields near where the external set has been built, gliding as if in slow motion (perhaps they are), while the camera typically tracks their movements gently, as though floating or gliding. We have entered Heaven perhaps, which would go some way towards explaining that Guido's suicide was indeed real, so that what we see here is the afterlife.

Seemingly out of the blue, and even while Daumier continues to babble, Guido asks himself, 'What is this sudden happiness that makes me tremble?' We might claim that his happiness is heavenly: he has been freed from all earthly woes. But what seems to ensue is another conversation with Luisa. Yes, it seems to be a conversation, and yet, Guido is seated at a vast distance from her: Luisa, with her close friend, Rossella (Rossella Falk), is standing in the circus ring where the film will soon come to its conclusion. As with all the other cast members here, Luisa is dressed in white and, as this conversation progresses, Rossella moves away from her, while the camera slowly tracks in towards Luisa. Guido continues to speak: he asks for forgiveness, not just from Luisa, but from everyone. He claims he did not understand; that he was confused. He declares his love for Luisa and then also claims that he feels as though he has been set free.

Is this, then, what Guido has learned, that 'Freedom in marriage is not to be discovered in the possibility of adultery' (and we have seen above that this is Cavell's claim for the remarriage comedies)? We might find this convincing enough, that Guido has learned the errors of his adulterous ways, that he has had his eyes opened, that he can see clearly now. We have seen that he has admitted that he has not understood, that he has been enveloped by confusion. And Guido now accepts this confusion. 'But this confusion is me,' he states. It is 'as I am', he adds, 'not as I want to be'. We could go so far as to state that this is where Guido truly learns to declare 'I am' in the ways, as I have argued above, that enable him to escape from narcissism. He comes to the realisation that the chaos and confusion that surround him are not things he can control.

Endings

In many ways one has to be generous to Fellini to claim this as a triumphant ending. What is required here is forgiveness. Yet the forgiveness is one-sided. Luisa must forgive Guido. The woman must forgive the man. And those acts of forgiveness in which a woman must forgive a man are repeated in several of Fellini's films: in *I vitelloni*, in *Juliet of the Spirits*, where it is granted but not received: Juliet wishes to forgive her husband but he is beyond that, it seems; he decides to leave her. (Compare all this, of course, with Anna's request to be forgiven in *The Passion of Anna*, a request that is refused by Andreas.)

Is that, therefore, the lesson of Fellini's 'feminist' films? That for a marriage to be successful, for it to be a remarriage, a wife must forgive a man for his excesses? I can easily contend that such forgiveness will be too much to ask for many women, and that such forgiveness may do little to amend the narcissism of men. One is tempted to conclude that little has changed since *The Rules of the Game*: the man will rule the roost, and the woman will comply.

Fellini's *City of Women*, released in 1980, is surely a case in point. I find this film almost impossible to watch. If there is humour here, then it is both crude and cruel, an attempt at mastery and an expression of the worst excesses of narcissism, all directed, it seems to me, at the objectification of women. Fellini criticises the film's hero by claiming that 'he knows nothing about women.' '[H]e isn't able', he adds, 'to create in his imagination a single real person' (see Alpert 1987, 248). If Fellini somehow considered this film an attempt to sympathise with the rise of feminism, then his sympathies are worn very lightly.[4]

And yet, I would claim that there is true greatness in the ending of *8½*. The film's exquisite blend of the real and the fantastic, exemplified here by the conversation between Guido and Luisa that appears to be happening in the here and now, provides us with a conversation in which Luisa does seem to forgive Guido, even as Guido himself has also signalled his willingness to change. And that is where we get to: men will stray, and they need to change. In Fellini's films, the inability of men to open themselves passively rather than aggressively to the embrace of an other is a consequence of narcissism, as I have argued. It is a fear of love, if one defines love as a matter of making oneself other in order to accommodate an other. (To reiterate, this can be seen as a version of Sellier's 'each person is constructed through the encounter with another'; Sellier 2008, 219.) And Fellini's male characters are almost universally incapable of taking that step towards otherness. Instead, and we see it clearly in *La dolce vita*, *Juliet of the Spirits*, *Casanova* and *City of Women*, they remain trapped within themselves, incapable of forming what Fellini himself calls 'a genuine relationship with another person'.

I have also reckoned that Bersani's notions of connectedness or correspondences, as well as his conception of 'impersonal narcissism', all fail to offer a clear remedy for the excesses typical of narcissism. I am convinced that the worst of Fellini's male philanderers could claim their sexual conquests as so many connections and thus as expressions of impersonal narcissism.

And I thus see many of those characters as closely related to Bertrand in Truffaut's *The Man Who Loved Women*, with which I began this chapter.

Finally, I do not see the escapades of Fellini's male characters as falling all that far from those of Jerry Warriner in *The Awful Truth* (released, we know, in 1937), noting that Jerry was praised in that film for his having a 'Continental mind'. In *The Awful Truth*, the male character is brought back down to earth: he is *educated* by his wife, Lucy, and he is forced to change. If we take that comedy seriously, then Jerry does change. He changes in ways that seem to be unavailable for Fellini's male characters, with perhaps the only exception being Guido in 8½. Even then we have to be very generous to his character to believe he has changed in any substantial way. For Fellini, a true marriage or conception of remarriage seems always to be an aspiration, but one which cannot be realised.

Notes

1 This statement is made on the book's dust jacket, and is more or less repeated on p. viii by one of the book's editors, Frank Burke (Burke and Waller 2002).
2 Bersani writes: 'The attempt to penetrate the world – more particularly in Proust, to know the secrets of others – continues even after it has been recognized as the displaced repetition of a hopeless attempt to penetrate the self' (Bersani 2015, 44).
3 Fellini remained married to his wife of many years, Giulietta Masina, until his death in 1993. Masina died in 1994.
4 On this point see Missero 2022, 97–106.

Chapter 10

Jean-Luc Godard: in praise of two

10.1 Robert and Charlotte (Bernard Noël and Macha Méril) in *A Married Woman*

Godard: a first approach

We have left the previous chapter on Fellini on what seems like a sour note. A film as great as *8½* promises some sort of reward for women on the basis that men must be determined to alter their ways of thinking and being. That may well be a desirable thing for men to do. But even then, for men to make such gains along the road to transformation requires, as its starting point, an enormous amount of forgiveness on the part of women, if we are to believe Fellini. I gather there might not be so many women willing to be so forgiving.

And so to Godard. During the 1960s and beyond, Godard's exploitations of female characters and actresses are certainly marked. One critic goes so far as to state that 'the misogynistic tendency of the films, and particularly the first ones, cannot be avoided' (Loshitzky 1995, 136).[1] Geneviève Sellier offers an account of the ways in which Godard subordinates women in his New Wave films – between 1960 and 1963 – especially by way of his uses of his key actress during this period, Anna Karina, who was also, of course, his wife at the time (they married in 1961 and divorced in 1965). Typically, Sellier argues, the main male character in a Godard film is a stand-in for Godard himself, and the male's heroism or creativity will be achieved via the use or abuse of a woman in one way or another. For proof of Sellier's claims, we can take the films one at a time, more or less.

- In *Le Petit soldat* (1963) the film's hero, Bruno (Michel Subor), is a photographer and thus a stand-in for Godard. He takes photographs of Anna Karina's character, Véronika, and that is all we need to declare: the man manipulates the woman and her image in order to ensure his artistic success (see Sellier 2008, 154).
- In *A Woman Is a Woman* (1961), particular praise in the French press was reserved for Godard as an auteur as well as for Karina as an actress. But Sellier argues that Karina is merely played for a child. Her character, Angéla, is not intelligent, well rounded, sophisticated or serious. Her desire to have a child is presented as natural – it is what any woman should want – and when her character is not doing her job as a striptease artist (and yes, that role is supposed to be mocking the stereotypical roles of women in 1950s French cinema; but how convenient …), then she is reduced to doing the cooking, cleaning and other domestic chores. This is not a positive depiction of woman (Sellier 2008, 161).
- For *Vivre sa vie* (1962), Sellier points out that in the penultimate sequence, in part a reading out loud of Edgar Allan Poe's 'The Oval Portrait', the active voice is given to none other than Godard himself – it is his voice that read's Poe's lines – while the reading is accompanied at various points by fetishistic close-ups of Anna Karina's character, Nana. Her character will then be shot dead in the film's final scene. The woman is sacrificed for the artistic glory of the man (Sellier 2008, 163).
- For *Contempt* (1963), the stakes are slightly more complicated, for this film produces a female character – Camille, played by Brigitte Bardot – who seems capable of speaking her mind and standing up for herself. Nevertheless, Sellier argues that Camille is associated with consumer culture and low art – hence her decision to flee with the crass, American film producer, Prokosch (Jack Palance) – while Godard himself is associated with Paul (Michel Piccoli) and Fritz Lang, the men who favour 'true' art over consumerist low culture. Thus is maintained a distinction between masculine elite art and feminine mass art (Sellier 2008, 206–9).
- The stakes of *Breathless* (1960) are rather more complicated again. Patricia (Jean Seberg) is associated with high culture, freedom and self-determination. Her boyish look also gives her shades of what could be called a 'new woman'. And yet, at all times, the spectator is made to sympathise with Michel (Jean-Paul Belmondo) and to regard his actions

as heroic. Patricia, by contrast, is associated with indecisiveness and unknowingness, traits central to most Godardian women. 'Patricia is not portrayed as a flirt', writes Sellier, 'but as a young woman who has contradictory projects and desires and who doesn't manage to resolve them ... And the film's conclusion gathers her up into the male fantasy of the fatal woman' (Sellier 2008, 115).[2]

A second approach

Let us call this an active–passive split: the male heroes of these films – substitutes for Godard – are active, while the females are passive. We are told that such an active–passive split is somewhat routine for classical cinema, and that Godard himself has difficulty negotiating that terrain, even if he does so in ways that are ambiguous (see MacCabe and Mulvey 1980). These are all themes pursued by Sellier, and I will return to them. Before doing that, however, I wish to point to another perspective. If there is an active-male/passive-female split in Godard's films, as Sellier suggests, then some of the theoretical terrain charted by Leo Bersani will complicate such issues. Bersani's arguments have, of course, been central for this book. His approach here can be couched in terms of a single question: *What's so good about being active?* And his answer to this question will involve, as a starting point, the contention that various quests of human subjects in terms of action, mastery, possession and control, as well as in terms of the quest for 'knowledge' as such, have all stemmed from an active will's suppression of the passive. With slightly more drama, Bersani also claims that, anatomically, certainly if one conceives of sexual acts, males will invariably be active and females passive insofar as typically it is the penis which penetrates the vagina (Bersani 2010a, 22–3). In making such a claim Bersani is certainly not endorsing its effects. To the contrary, he is asking, if the male is active here, then what's so good about being active? All being active can do is imply control, mastery and perhaps sadism and violence.

From Bersani's perspective, therefore – and we have seen some of this in Chapter 1 – one way to interpret the events of *Contempt* would be to read Camille's responses as passive, to say that she allows herself to go along with events rather than actively guiding them: she goes back to Prokosch's villa; she has an affair with him; she does these things in order to 'try things out', as Bersani and Dutoit put it, rather than as part of an active attempt to control her destiny. Her passive subjectivity here is positive, and all of this can be seen as part of Bersani's quest to define human subjectivity in fragmented ways. Thus, for example, Bersani and Dutoit, as a consequence of a brief discussion of Godard's *Hélas pour moi* (1992), argue that 'the multiplication of the individual's positionality in the universe is, necessarily, a lessening or even a loss of individuality. We *are* not as distinctive subjectivities but rather as that which gives *appearances* to different modes or functions of being' (Bersani and Dutoit 2004, 5). Individual subjects are mistaken to believe they actively do things. Rather, they are mere passive vehicles that express being. What humans do, feel and say are 'appearances' of being. If humans actively impose themselves on the world, then typically they are committing acts that are destructive. Humans should therefore, by contrast, embrace passivity. Rather than striving to control and master the world, humans should simply let the world be. Thus, we might see Camille as an 'appearance' that gives rise to various modes of being. She is not an individual subject who is manipulating Paul, or jumping into bed with Prokosch, or who is sad or happy or in some way seeking fulfilment. She is, in other words, passive, an appearance. Bersani and Dutoit emphasise that this notion of subjectivity is 'not a monumentalizing of the self, but rather should be thought of as a renewable retreat from the seriousness of stable identities' (Bersani and Dutoit 2004, 9). They call this an 'aesthetic' subject rather than a psychological or psychoanalytic subject (also see Bersani 2010c).

There is another side of this coin. Camille is, in fact, active insofar as she makes herself desirable to Paul. As Bersani and Dutoit put it, she inspires contempt in him, and it is this contempt which makes her desirable to Paul – such is Bersani and Dutoit's logic, what they call the 'law of desire' (see Bersani and Dutoit 2004, 74–123). Correspondingly, by way of his gestures, Paul also inspires contempt in Camille: this is their way – the typical way of romantic love (so Bersani and Dutoit claim) – of forming a couple. Thus, the traditional couple is formed by way of mutual contempt, and it is contempt which gives rise to desire and its logic. Bersani's quest, along with Dutoit, is to find a different kind of coupling, and they also believe this is what Godard pursues in a number of his films.

The stakes are fairly clear: when Camille is active, the outcomes are treachery, possessiveness, jealousy and contempt, with all of these forming the foundation of traditional love, according to Bersani and Dutoit. By contrast, when Camille accepts a mode of passivity, then we have the potential for a 'new mode of relation', a new series of couplings that can be tried out, such as is attempted with the Camille–Prokosch couple. Active subjects can inspire only destructiveness, mastery, possessiveness. Passivity opens the way to new modes of relation, new types of love and coupling.

A third approach

If that is part of Bersani's (and Dutoit's) approach to Godard – and we shall see more of Bersani's approach below – then Cavell provides a very different perspective. Writing first of all in 1971 in *The World Viewed*, Cavell strikingly claims that what is distinctive about Godard's characters is their 'inability to feel' (Cavell 1979a, 97). This is probably a way of saying that Godard's characters are not human beings or 'human somethings' (see Cavell 1979a, 26). Because of this, an audience member can have little investment in the plights of those characters. We do not care for them. Cavell's criticisms intensify. He chides Godard's representations as 'arbitrary', then accuses him of failing to take responsibility for what he depicts (Cavell 1979a, 97). Ultimately this adds up to one thing: all Godard can do is to call into question what film is, and assert that what films do is not something he agrees with. As a consequence, all Godard can offer is critique: he has foregone all attempts to seek the truth and does not wish to depict the truth.

That's all Godard can do, Cavell argues: offer critique without redemption. And even then Cavell will add that whatever it is that Godard does cannot even be given the title of 'critique' – it is even less than that. From Godard's perspective, Cavell contends, the world is corrupted by capitalism and so too is cinema, and that's that. 'If you believe', writes Cavell, 'that people speak in slogans to one another, or that women are turned by bourgeois society into marketable objects, or that human pleasures are now figments and products of advertising accounts and that these are directions of dehumanization ...' – well, if you believe such things, Cavell seems to imply, then this really is nothing more than a kind of moral censorship. It is disapproval, not critique. It is not even an argument (Cavell 1979a, 99). And that's all Godard is capable of.

For Cavell, the avoidance of critique in Godard's films is a consequence of his inability to depict real humans. Godard does not put human characters on screen, certainly not humans who exhibit any sort of knowingness about themselves or the world. Humanness and personhood are removed from these characters so that all we are left with, states Cavell, are 'subject[s] incapable of accepting or rejecting anything'. And that, he adds, 'is the condition of prostitution, and of advertisement' (Cavell 1979a, 99). Cavell's statements here can be seen as building on the conclusions he makes in a brief discussion of *Contempt*, mostly referring to the famous 'naked' Bardot scene that follows the credit sequence. He concludes that the scene offers a demonstration that 'our tastes and convictions in love have been pornographized, which above all means publicized, externalized – letting society tell us what to love, and needing it to tell us whether we do' (Cavell 1979a, 95). And perhaps here we are on that terrain of Lacan's dictum that 'Man's desire is the desire of the Other': desire is everywhere and always defined by the social order. From a negative direction, Godard's films demonstrate the externalisation of desire.

Cavell's claims take us back to his arguments on *The Rules of the Game* visited in Chapter 2, which is to say that the conditions of modern marriage that are portrayed in Godard's films do little other than replicate the conditions of old marriage as depicted in Renoir's film. How so? Despite his criticisms of Godard (he will later refer to them as 'stuffy'; Cavell 2005b, 178), Cavell may well have hit upon something here. Godard's discourses may offer a new and significant chapter on the restrictions of love and marriage. Godard's films – certainly in the 1960s – show us the ways in which love and marriage continue to be externally determined, that they are to a large extent matters of social and financial standing rather than being matters of mutual understanding, acknowledgment or a quest for equality between members of the romantic couple. Once again I find myself thinking of Emerson's essay on 'Friendship': 'Two may talk and one may hear', he writes, 'but three cannot take part in a conversation of the most sincere and searching sort' (Emerson 1898, 54). Once a third – the 'social' – enters the scene, conversation becomes performance. What could be key to Godard's films – and readers are correct to sense that this claim will be a central one in my discussion of Godard – is a critique of the modern couple as externally determined, as defined by 'the falsity of social worlds' (the latter being Cavell's chief point on *The Rules of the Game*). Modern society, call it 'consumer society', ushers in a mode of coupling that is entirely theatrical. It is not designed to satisfy either member of the couple. Rather, it is framed and performed such that it will appeal to an audience. It is a matter of how a coupling will define the couple's relationship to the standards and hopes of the societies in which they exist. For old marriage this was mostly a matter of aristocratic social standing, of uniting fortunes and dynasties and providing heirs to those fortunes. For modern marriage – this is Godard's take – it is a matter of social standing as regulated by capitalism: by wealth, by consumption, by making ends meet (think of Nana in *Vivre sa vie* or Isabelle in *Passion*, and others) or by advertising (*A Woman Is a Woman*, *Made in USA* (1966), *Tout va bien* (1972), *Numéro deux* (1975) and others). All of this is played out in the extended apartment scene between Paul and Camille in *Contempt*. Their conversation during the scene is in no way an attempt by either member of the couple to develop their knowledge and understanding of each other – it is not 'a conversation of the most sincere and searching sort' (Emerson, 1898, 54). Their talk is instead suffused with suspicion, allegation, bitterness and anger, as though each of them is weighing up how their coupling is displayed for the eyes of the world, for Camille's mother, to those who need to live in chic apartments, or those who need to sell themselves in order to live up to the wishes of social standing.

These are three approaches to the films of Godard. Sellier approaches the films from a feminist perspective, arguing that Godard's New Wave films of the early 1960s exalt male creativity and heroism while, at the same time, belittling their female characters, especially by associating them with low culture and mass consumption. Bersani and Dutoit, by contrast, observe in Godard's films the potential for revealing a new kind of relationship between human beings and the world, a relationship not based on possessiveness and mastery but which responds to the correspondences between humans and other humans, as well as between humans and the world. I have suggested that this kind of relationship is one that endorses human passivity and which potentially disrupts calls for 'active subjects'. Cavell, like Sellier, is critical of Godard's films, especially of what Cavell perceives as being the non-humanness of his characters. Godard's characters, Cavell argues, lack the capacity for human feeling and, as a result, we as viewers cannot care for them. And yet, Cavell's arguments can be taken in a positive direction. He suggests that Godard's films present to us the falsity of social worlds, particularly when it comes to the clichés of romantic love and marriage.

These three approaches to Godard are varied, to say the least – choosing a 'correct' approach between them would be impossible. And discovering any kind of synthesis between these positions would also be unlikely – and the list of 'possible approaches' to Godard would be a long one (I haven't even mentioned Brecht). For the remainder of this chapter I will navigate my way through these readings.

I will begin with Bersani, undoubtedly the most complicated of the approaches. In my comments above I have stressed Bersani's articulation of human passivity. He couches his claims in terms of a critique of the 'will to knowledge' in ways we have seen a number of times already in this book. Knowledge and the 'will to know' are activities associated with mastery, control and possession, and Bersani traces the will to know back to Descartes and the *Cogito*. In brief, Bersani describes the will to know in terms of a 'Cartesian dualism between a knowing subject and a vast domain of objects principally conceived in terms of their knowability or nonknowability' (Bersani 2010d, 162). Bersani then sketches a series of specific elements which he opposes to the 'will to know'. He lists these as 'potentiality, the transindividual, impersonal correspondences, and a general typology of being beyond, or perhaps before, psychological individuality' (Bersani 2010d, 163). The latter are key concerns, for a psychological individual is one who controls his or her thoughts, is responsible for them and is the origin of them. I 'make' those thoughts, and in doing so I 'make' knowledge. The psychological individual believes it knows what it thinks: it is compelled by a will to know. Bersani, against psychology, wants something far more anonymous and passive. The kind of passivity he seeks is expressed by Godard in a film called *Passion* (1982). Godard's film becomes something of a canonical text for Bersani in his essay on

'The Will to Know' and in later writings (see, for example, Bersani 2015, 64–5).

There are two main axes to Bersani's discussion of *Passion* – noting that he is once again writing here with Dutoit. First of all, the film openly posits itself as being against 'story'. What *Passion* opposes to story is fragmentation and decomposition, a withdrawal 'from any kind of finished statement whatsoever', as Bersani and Dutoit put it (Bersani and Dutoit 2010, 163). If *Passion* declares anything at all, then what it declares will only ever be provisional, temporary and unfinished. That, then, is a first point. The second guiding thread of Bersani and Dutoit's analysis of *Passion* is 'coupling'. Godard's film works by way of pairs, most overtly insofar as it is a film called *Passion* that is about a filmmaker, Jerzy (Jerzy Radziwilowicz), who is also making a film called *Passion*. Thus, the film *Passion*, and the film-within-a-film called *Passion*, form a couple. But this coupling has nothing to do with complementarity or unification. In fact, we are not really sure how these films fit together. Scenes from the one film also seem to be scenes from the other (we are not far from Fellini's *8½* here). Bersani argues that what is particular to the mode of coupling here is a notion of likeness or resemblance. Godard's *Passion* resembles Jerzy's *Passion*, and vice versa. Neither is a copy of the other; neither is the original of the other, which is to say this notion of likeness is not mimetic. They are both similar to and different from one another. They are *similar*, which means they are not identical, but they are also different, and yet also not so different that they might be considered opposites or even 'others'. In other words, Jerzy's *Passion* is not a metaphor for Godard's *Passion*, or vice versa; the one does not teach us what is right (or wrong) about the other. I should add that there is a third element in this coupling: Godard's own doubling of his film in *Scénario du Passion*. I won't comment on this, other than to say that this is how Bersani's logic of coupling works: a series of resemblances that does not stop at a single pairing, but which can expand to more and more pairings.

What is at play between Godard's *Passion* and Jerzy's *Passion* is a series of correspondences. For Bersani and Dutoit, this is what is at stake in Godard's film: an opposition to the will to know by way of a notion of correspondences. If the will to know signifies the individual subject's active attempts to master the world by way of knowledge, then a logic of correspondences presents a passive mode of relation to the world in terms of couplings and correspondences. Bersani and Dutoit put it this way:

> In story telling, elements are added to one another in order to make a sum of completed meaning; the sense we get from narratively coherent stories is, Godard suggests, determined by their epistemologically additive bias. This does not mean, however, that Godard's film – perhaps unlike Jerzy's film – is

structurally incoherent. There are, most notably, couplings that give to Godard's work a certain structural connectedness: the relation of Godard's *Passion* to Jerzy's *Passion*; the aesthetic couples of film and painting, as well as of music and the visual arts; the two types of love – open and closed, Jerzy says – embodied in Isabelle and Han[n]a; the mingling as well as the opposition of home and foreignness (and of the irreconcilable destinations of Hollywood and Poland); and of course the thematic coupling of work and love (Bersani and Dutoit 2010, 165).

Bersani and Dutoit thus make their way through a range of couples and correspondences in *Passion*, from the correspondence–couple of painting–cinema to that of work–love and to the two types of loves, the Hanna–Isabelle couple.

And yet, what does all of this add up to? Part of Bersani and Dutoit's point is that such things simply do not add up, for adding up is a matter of storytelling, and Godard, according to Bersani and Dutoit, is against storytelling. All the same, I have difficulty being convinced by such arguments. Yes, we have couplings and correspondences, but why do we have them? What is their significance? I think we need to ask ourselves what is at stake in these couplings and correspondences. What is at stake, for example, in Jerzy's fascination with Hanna (Hanna Schygulla) and Isabelle (Isabelle Huppert)? Hanna is older and wiser, and is clearly bourgeois: she owns the motel where most of Jerzy's crew is staying during the film shoot, while her husband, Michel (Michel Piccoli), owns the nearby factory where Isabelle works. Isabelle, by contrast, is very much working class: she has recently been fired from Michel's factory for trying to unionise its workers. At any rate, Jerzy finds that he cannot choose between the two women. Near the end of the film, Isabelle confronts him and asks him to decide what he is going to do. Jerzy has come to the decision that he is going to abandon his film, for, much like Paul in *Contempt*, he does not see eye to eye with his producer, László (László Szabó), who has now decided to take the film to Hollywood. Jerzy abandons the film and decides to return to his homeland of Poland. (Additionally, we know he is returning to a Poland that is in the grip of the Solidarność revolution and the emergence of democracy.)

With all of this circulating, Isabelle outlines Jerzy's options in relation to herself and Hanna. There are two options. For option one, Jerzy wants to take Hanna to Poland, but she wants to stay here in Switzerland. For option two, Isabelle wants to go to Poland with Jerzy, but he wants to be with her only if they remain in Switzerland. Both options are deadlocks. Above all else, these are ways in which Jerzy avoids the problem of having to choose (and we can see once again how Jerzy's role is similar to that of Guido Anselmi in Fellini's *8½*; see Bondanella 1992, 166). He invents impediments for himself. By doing so, he avoids having to commit to Hanna or Isabelle (or both, or neither). When Isabelle presents all of this to him, Jerzy's response is to declare 'It's true'. And this, therefore, is a way of saying – and I think this is really what Godard intends – that Jerzy is very good at making excuses for himself. Jerzy is very good at lying to himself, and the consequences of his lying are a range of unfinished projects: his film, his love life, his homeland. And what does Isabelle say to all this? She tells Jerzy that this is the first time he has told the truth. The truth is that he is full of lies.

There is more. *Passion* ends with continuing ambiguity. Hanna looks everywhere for Jerzy, fearing that he has left the small town in Switzerland where the filming has been taking place. She cannot find him, so she determines to leave. As she leaves in her car, she spots Isabelle at the side of the road. Hanna picks her up and states that she is going to Poland. Presumably she is going there in order to seek out Jerzy, even though she also declares that 'It's over'. As they drive off together, they pass one of the other young women who had been working at the motel (she specialised in the acrobatic pouring of coffee). They offer her a lift but she tells them she doesn't like cars. She does not go with them.

Shortly after these events, we see Jerzy, now driving past the same young woman. He offers her a lift. When she says that she does not like cars he replies that this is not a car, it's a flying carpet! She then gets into his car and they drive off. The film ends here.[3]

I suppose I have to declare that this is typical of Godard of this period (the early 1980s): extremely fragmented stories combined with low, slapstick humour, with added doses of nonsense and open endings. Elements of Sellier's arguments tend to emerge, for me, even though this is a film from the 1980s rather than the 1960s. As in this 1960s film we have a stand-in for Godard, the creative 'genius', Jerzy. And this genius then aggrandises himself with a range of female inspirations: Hanna, Isabelle, as well as the woman who jumps into his 'flying carpet'. And much of Jerzy's film-within-a-film appears to be arranged on the basis of *tableaux vivants* of various, mostly naked, attractive women – a thinned-down *Odalisque* after Ingres being a standout. One particular scene raises questions: How do we make sense of Jerzy's use of a young, deaf, mute woman (played by Myriem Roussel), naked, in a pool constructed on a film sound stage, who spreads her legs for him so that he then remarks that he is looking at 'the universal wound'? Are we to suppose that this is some sort of play on Courbet's *Origin of the World* (1866), or perhaps Duchamp's *Étant donnés* (1946–66)? Or should one merely believe that Godard is still engaging in schoolboy-type gags? Or what? Perhaps we will simply have to declare that, in the 1980s as for the 1960s, male creative geniuses continue to exploit women, and also to mock them. Bersani and Dutoit do not mention any of these issues.

I find Isabelle's confrontation of Jerzy central to the film. He lies to himself and other people, and his ability to lie is what is most true about him. That seems to be the point Isabelle – and perhaps Godard too – wishes to make. Of course, there are clear echoes of Fellini's 8½ here, and reference to Truffaut's *Day for Night* is also marked. But I want to take these issues in (at least) two directions. I want to suggest that what is at stake for Jerzy here is what Cavell once referred to, in an essay on *King Lear*, as the 'avoidance of love' (Cavell 2003, 39–123). This is not to say that Jerzy's position mirrors that of Lear (noting that Godard will go on to make a rather enigmatic adaptation of *King Lear* in 1985). It is instead to suggest that Jerzy refrains from any commitment in love because he fears the risks that come with that commitment. It is easier to flee from love, or to keep jumping from one love to another, than to commit to the process of being two. If there are couplings in *Passion*, then the sort of coupling that is most avoided is that which pertains to romantic love: Hanna has left her husband, Michel; Jerzy is coupled both with Isabelle and Hanna, which also means he is coupled with neither of them. Of course, this may well be Godard's point – and Bersani and Dutoit's point too: *Passion* may be precisely about the need to get away from the traditional couplings of romantic love, and so its avoidances of love may be marked in that way.

That is one direction. The other direction to take these issues – Jerzy's lying to himself – is to see *Passion* as a sort of remake of *Contempt*. In *Passion*, Jerzy is the equivalent of the Paul character from *Contempt*, and, like Paul, once again some sort of creative greatness is accorded Jerzy over and above the film's key women. The key women in *Passion*, Hanna and Isabelle, are not associated with artistic creativity, but with the worlds of business and work. We can see Jerzy's position as one that is positively coded as wishing to push beyond the worlds of business and factory work – he wants to establish an artistic world beyond the confines of capitalism – so that, for example, a central theme in the film involves his frictions with his producer, László, and rather clear connections between the brash Prokosch of *Contempt* come to the fore here. Hanna, to some degree, can be seen as a distant cousin of *Contempt*'s Camille: she leaves her husband, Michel, in ways that could be said to mirror Camille's departure from her husband, Paul, in *Contempt*, noting of course that these husbands are played by the same actor, Michel Piccoli. I do not want to make too much of all this. I merely want to suggest that Godard's themes and strategies do not change all that much from the 1960s to the 1980s: he continues to foreground a male creative genius who gains much of his genius from female muses of one sort or another. Sellier's points hold true to a remarkable degree.

Prénom Carmen and *Hail Mary*

The avoidance of love? The exploitation of women? Is that where we end with Godard? Surely not. This is, after all, a filmmaker who would go on to make a film called *In Praise of Love* – an inspiration, no less, for Alain Badiou's short book of the same name – and whose films tackle myriad issues relating to love and marriage. One finds elements of *Passion* linked to just about every other film Godard made – to *Breathless*, *A Married Woman*, *Tout va bien*, *Numéro deux*, with this latter being especially pertinent in its exploration of the relationship between love and work, and many more besides. If all of this is the case, then it is hardly likely that Godard or his characters are avoiding love at all. On the contrary, they are searching for it, and they are doing so in earnest ways. And yes, there is no doubt that women often come off badly in Godard's films. But I am all for compassion and understanding here, for what is it that Godard is exploring? He is surely trying to understand gender roles. What is it that men want? What do women want? How is it possible to reconcile these differing and often incompatible wants? More specifically, why does Jerzy, in *Passion*, avoid love? And thus, why do men constantly avoid love, as Michel does in *Breathless*, or Raoul (Sady Rebbot) in *Vivre sa vie*, Paul in *Contempt* and so on?

These are issues in which Godard's films of this period are deeply embroiled. In Godard's next film after *Passion*, *Prénom Carmen* (1983), it is difficult to discern whether Carmen (Marushcka Detmers) should be admired for her sexual strength, or whether her sexuality is yet more evidence of Godard's desire to exploit his female actors. At the same time, sympathy in this film is surely focused on the character of Carmen, and there are no men at all in *Prénom Carmen* who are the least bit likeable. Thus, like so many other auteurs in this book – Antonioni, Fellini, Bergman, Varda ... – might it be suggested that Godard is investigating the cruelty of men towards women, that he is trying to fathom the continuing sexual exploitation and abuse of women that is perpetrated by men? Perhaps. But I also find it difficult to go beyond the sense that Godard might all too easily be enjoying that cruelty and exploitation (and all of that has been in play since his 1960s films: *Vivre sa vie*, *Masculin Féminin* (1966), *Two or Three Things I Know about Her* (1967) and so on).

I want to suggest that there is a major transition between *Prénom Carmen* (1983) and *Hail Mary* (1985). The transition can be summarised by statements from each of the films, which seem to mark a leap from Godard's scepticism about love to an acceptance of the grand possibilities of love. The motto of *Prénom Carmen*, lifted from Otto Preminger's *Carmen Jones* (1954) and uttered here by Carmen, is 'If I love you, that's the end of you'. By contrast,

I will take the motto of *Hail Mary* as one revealed midway through the film, when Mary states to Joseph, 'One's better as a pair'. If *Prénom* gives us the avoidance of love, then *Hail Mary* embraces love as a matter of one becoming two.

Prénom Carmen features many of the scattered elements that are endemic to Godard's 1980s films. A central plot focuses on the relationship between Carmen and Joseph (Jacques Bonnaffé), so that early on in the film Joseph asks Carmen, 'Why do women exist?' Notably, this occurs during a somewhat violent prelude to sex in which Joseph rips off Carmen's top. Carmen's response is to plead with him to be gentle. Later in the film, Carmen will then ask Joseph, 'Why do men exist?' Even more notably, her question emerges following a shower scene in which, it seems, Joseph masturbates on her. Unsurprisingly, they soon declare that they revolt each other. I don't really know what to make of any of this except to point to the fact that that Godard's characters ask these questions – 'Why do women exist?' 'Why do men exist?' – and that neither Godard nor his characters know how to answer such questions. A way to an answer is possibly suggested by way of Bergman's *Smiles of a Summer Night*. Readers will remember that there is a moment in Bergman's film in which the male protagonist, Fredrik, appears in pyjamas in front of the main female character, Desirée, and asks her, with a great deal of humility, 'How can a woman ever love a man?' I am suggesting that, at this stage of his career, Godard may well be asking a similar question. And I don't know how any woman might come to love any of the men who appear in *Prénom Carmen*. To add another element to the discussion here, Godard himself plays a character in this film. He plays Carmen's duped uncle, a washed-up filmmaker whom Carmen and her associates use as a front for their criminal activities. Godard's character is mocked rather than being honoured as some sort of creative genius. The other cloud that hovers over his character pertains to his clear sexual interest in Carmen when she was younger. This provides yet another reason to see Godard casting a critical eye over the potential for men to exploit women – is he being critical of his own character here? – while at the same time taking some degree of perverse enjoyment from the prospect of a sexual liaison with a young girl. I don't want to sound moralising here: I am not passing judgment on Godard. Rather, I'm pointing to these as issues that Godard is intentionally and openly exploring. Let us praise him for openly depicting such issues of sexual life. He certainly cannot be accused of hiding from them, and the sexually open discourses of his films, especially *Numéro deux*, deserve praise for their audacity.

The discourse on sex continues with *Hail Mary*. But there is a quite extraordinary turnaround with this film. While for *Prénom Carmen* or *Passion* Godard's characters are entirely unable to find ways out of their dilemmas and deadlocks – 'If I love you, that's the end of you' – in *Hail Mary* a miraculous salvation occurs. The film's main characters, Mary and Joseph, via a series of twists and turns, eventually come to express their love for each other. How do they do this? Effectively, Joseph must declare his love for Mary against the greatest odds. She is pregnant, but Joseph has not slept with her. He thus presumes she must have slept with someone else. *Hail Mary*'s allusions are, of course, to the story of Christ's birth, so it is concluded, and a medical doctor confirms it, that Mary is indeed both pregnant and a virgin. Joseph accepts this – he accepts it (almost) as a miracle – and the love between them is sealed only on the basis of faith and trust. For Joseph to declare to Mary, 'I love you', might be enough, but it is as though Mary needs much more than a mere declaration. In one of the film's climactic scenes, Mary allows Joseph to see her naked, and she has not allowed him such a thing before. She says to him, 'Tell me you love me,' and he responds by telling her he loves her a number of times. Mary retorts with an emphatic 'No!', eventually repudiating Joseph entirely with a vehement 'No! No! No!' The Angel Gabriel then intervenes to tell Joseph that he must accept things as they are: Mary is pregnant and a virgin. (He tells Joseph that he must 'sacrifice' himself.) Subsequently, Mary says to Joseph, 'I love you.' He learns that he need not touch her in a violent manner, so that when he gently caresses her belly, she responds positively with a 'Yes'. These actions are repeated: she accepts his appeal, 'I love you.' (Some commentators suggest in all of this allusion to Molly Bloom's emphatic 'Yes ... yes' at the end of James Joyce's *Ulysses*; see Sterritt 1999, 200.)

We will perhaps know exchanges of this type from Antonioni's *L'avventura*, in which Claudia asks Sandro at certain points to tell her he loves her. At one point he says that he shouldn't have to say it because Claudia should know that he loves her. What I argued in Chapter 6 on Antonioni is that Claudia wants to be known or acknowledged by Sandro, and something similar is clearly at stake for Mary in this scene from *Hail Mary*. Joseph can tell her loves her, but Mary demands that he also mean what he says. And that is that: Mary wants to know that Joseph acknowledges her, that their relationship can be based on faith and trust, rather than lust.

Mary is a virgin, so we can also point to a connection between *Hail Mary* and the tradition Cavell calls 'comedies of remarriage'. It is Cavell's own link, as he argues in a short paper he wrote on *Hail Mary* (Cavell 2005b). Cavell contends that one of the features of that cycle of films is that the woman who will discover herself as a member of a remarried couple will do so on the basis of a sense of virginity. It is virginity that symbolically shows to us the conditions of a woman's being reborn or recreated by virtue of entering into a relationship of remarriage with a man on the basis of mutual acknowledgment. In those comedies there is little sense in which the women actually are virgins, but such is the case in *Smiles of a Summer Night*, which I discussed in Chapter 3. Fredrik and Anne have been married for two years and they have not had sex. It is much the same for Mary and Joseph in *Hail Mary*: they have been together for two years and have not yet slept together.

Why does Godard do this? Apart from alluding to the Gospels, Godard is surely drawing *Hail Mary* very close to the conditions of the remarriage comedies insofar as his film is built around a test of faith. In fact, we can see the conflict between Mary and Joseph as being of much the same substance as the conflict between Lucy and Jerry Warriner in *The Awful Truth*, a film that has emerged again and again as a key intertext – even if unintentional – for the films in this book. When Lucy returns home after spending a night 'at an inn' with Armand Duvalle, her husband assumes she has been unfaithful. As Lucy declares here (and Jerry will later repeat her words), 'Marriage is based on faith. When that's gone, everything's gone.' And thus are set in train the conflicts of that film. So too in *Hail Mary*, when Mary declares she is pregnant, Joseph assumes she has been unfaithful. Over the course of the film, Joseph discovers ways to trust and have faith in Mary. Godard makes his obsessions quite explicit here: Mary's virgin pregnancy enables him to emphasise the 'mystery of woman' in ways that expand on the questions posed by *Prénom: Carmen* – 'Why do women exist?' 'Why do men exist?' Most pertinently this occurs when Mary is examined by the doctor. The doctor, a man, asks what it is that a man can know of a woman, and he can only conclude that 'There is a mystery there'.

Godard's intentions are clear. Love cannot be based on knowledge, and a man's (Godard's) knowledge of a woman will never be complete or certain: there are no clear answers to those questions, 'What is a woman?' or 'Why do women exist?' Rather, any knowledge of a woman, certainly in matters of love, can only ever be a matter of acknowledgment. Mary and Joseph's being together is a matter of finding a way towards some sort of mutual understanding, but such an understanding can be based only on faith and mystery. There can be no 'proofs' or certainties of love; no *knowledge* of love as such. I have tried at one or two points in this book to say that this means love is a matter of 'deception'. Love cannot be explained in a rational manner (just as, in *Hail Mary*'s companion plot, the origins of life and the universe, as expounded by the Professor (Johan Leysen), are both mysterious and inexplicable). Love can be experienced only as a series of communicative exchanges that occur over time.

The short video essay compiled as a precursor to *Hail Mary* (available on the UK release of the DVD) bears this out. Emphasis there is accorded to the 'mystery' of love and to the question, 'Where does love come from?' In expanding on these queries, Godard explains that he has always made films about couples and, furthermore, that Mary and Joseph may be considered something of an 'ideal couple'.

All of this also bears on the Shakespearian tradition – and allusions to Shakespeare recur throughout Godard's films of the 1980s (the most explicit links in *Hail Mary* are with *Hamlet*; see Sterritt 1999, 187–8). The dilemmas of *Othello* and *The Winter's Tale*, for example, are those of a husband's suspicion of a wife's infidelity. In *The Winter's Tale* there is the added suspicion that the husband may not be the true father of his child – that Leontes' wife, Hermione, has given birth to a child fathered by another man. (Of course, the theme of infidelity in marriage is also central for *Hamlet*.) *Othello*'s denouement is tragic, while Leontes in *The Winter's Tale* finds his way back to faith as a consequence of an extraordinary miracle, that of Hermione's 'rebirth'. I find the trajectory of Godard's *Hail Mary* to fall not far from *The Winter's Tale*, and thus not far from the overall spirit of remarriage comedy.[4] In his short essay on *Hail Mary*, Cavell also makes connections of this type, though his more explicit reference is to Ibsen's *A Doll's House*, which, he states, calls marriage a 'miracle of miracles' (Cavell 2005b, 180). Mary's statement, 'one's better as a pair', can thus be taken as an affirmation of 'new marriage' or remarriage. Joseph, as well as Mary, come to understand the condition of being two rather than one.

In Praise of Love

The mystery of love takes on its full force in what is often referred to as Godard's third first film (the other two being *Breathless* (1960) and *Slow Motion* (1980)), *In Praise of Love* (2000). I don't want to dwell on this film in too much detail for, like all of Godard's films, it is dense and multilayered, and I simply do not have the space here to dwell on its complexities. I want to focus on one especially enlightening reading of the film, that offered by Douglas Morrey.

Morrey asks what love is in this film. It is a love between Edgar and Berthe (and between Perceval and Eglantine, and perhaps between Tristan and Isolde too).[5] It is certainly no ordinary love. This is how Morrey puts it:

> What Godard seems to stress is not the external contact with the other, but the *internalization* of the other, the way contact with the other can operate a change in the structure of the self. And what this ultimately implies is that the self can only ever be a collection of impressions and inspirations absorbed through other people. (Morrey 2003, 126)

Morrey then backs this up by contrasting it with what he sees as being Hollywood's approaches to love. 'It is not the fixed couple that is important, but the transformation operated in the individual by the other. There is no sense in which this conception of love could tip over into a relationship of possession of one partner by the other' (Morrey 2003, 126). Hollywood romances (noting that Morrey's claim here is a very generalising one) are 'fixed', whereas Godard here places emphasis on a notion of love as a process of continuous transformation.[6] In contrast to Hollywood romances, Morrey claims, Berthe is never objectified or sexualised. (We might have to confess that this is a rare thing for Godard.) As his argument progresses, Morrey makes some other interesting points, especially in relation to the ways that *In Praise of Love* links memory and love. He writes, 'love can only ever be known as a kind of grieving memory for a promise never fulfilled, whose trace remains in those indefinable alterations we notice in ourselves' (Morrey 2003, 128).

These are complicated claims. First of all, love brings about a change in the structure of the self. And the changes in the self are ultimately what the self *is*: a collection of transformations that occur by virtue of contact with other people. One must assume that Morrey is implying that love is an especially important example of contact with another person. I would add here that we have seen claims like this throughout this book, particularly by way of Sellier's claim that 'each person is constructed through the encounter with another' (Sellier 2008, 219). Second, the love presented in *In Praise of Love* is not fixed. It resists all claims of possession of one person by another. Again, this sort of claim has been a common one throughout this book, both in the Hollywood comedies of remarriage and in the European films on which I have focused.

It is Morrey's final point here that is the most intriguing. He states that the kind of love foregrounded by Godard's film is akin to *a grieving memory for a promise never fulfilled*. I cannot clearly understand what Morrey means here. A psychoanalytic take on his statement (I should say Morrey's take is *not* psychoanalytic) would place it in terms of a lost object and the always impossible attempt to refind that lost object – that this version of love is akin to that inspired by the *objet a* or *ágalma*, or a lost, ideal relationship with the mother. That logic is typically one Freud referred to in terms of *Nachträglichkeit*, translated in the Standard Edition as 'deferred action', though Jean Laplanche's French *aprés coup* – 'afterwardsness' – is perhaps a better rendering (see Laplanche 1999). It is this kind of logic that one finds in Hamlet's love for Ophelia, a love that gains its full force only when it becomes impossible, as 'afterwards', as a process of looking back – that is, after Ophelia's death. A love of this type seems to be what happens to Edgar. Certainly he never appears to have any lasting relationship with Berthe, and he also mentions another relationship that he has just left behind, a relationship, he tells us, that had lasted for ten years. It is only now, when the relationship has come to an end, that he realises its significance. He remarks that it is strange that things only really seem to take on meaning once 'the story ends', as he puts it.

Immediately after this admission – and we are now very close to the end of the film, even though the film's second part (in colour) takes place two years earlier than the first part (in black and white) – Edgar repeats a formation initially expressed in the first part of the film. He states that *'thinking always requires thinking of something else'*. And he offers an example of how this works. He says that when you see a new landscape, you know it is new only by comparing it with other landscapes you have known before. Therefore, thinking one thought requires thinking another thought; thinking *this* landscape requires thinking of *other* landscapes. Broadly speaking, I would call this logic Hegelian.[7] On those terms, A can be identified as A only insofar as it is different from B. Or to put it in terms of Hegelian negation, A is A because it is not *not A* (or $A \neq -A$).[8]

I do not wish to go into any detail on these issues other than to point to this: for this logic, any claim to *one* already requires *two*. In other words, to say that this object is what it 'is' also requires differentiating that object from what it 'is not': defining the identity of a thing also requires that its difference from other objects is carried within it. I want to see this logic, therefore, as something like a logic of *two*: of seeing and experiencing the world as *two* rather than *one*.[9] It is none other than a logic of love, a logic of what Cavell, in a Hegelian way, calls acknowledgment.[10] This twoness, it seems to me, is what Godard works towards in *In Praise of Love* and also in *Hail Mary*. Often this twoness will fail, as it does in *Passion* or *Prénom Carmen*, as well as in many films from the 1960s such as *Breathless*, *Vivre sa vie* or *Contempt*. We might begin to think we have a logic that satisfies both Cavell (and Badiou) and Bersani here: *two* rather than *one*; a logic of coupling. And yet, Bersani's logic works by way of correspondences and resemblance – *sameness*: $A \approx A$. Cavell, by contrast (as well as Badiou and Hegel), clearly foregrounds a logic of *difference*: $A \neq -A$.

A Married Woman and some conclusions

Here we have two types of logic, one based on *resemblance, correspondence* and *connectedness* – that is, Bersani's position. Another is based on *identity* and *difference* – broadly speaking, I am placing Cavell's conception of acknowledgment here. Godard works with both logics. Indeed, one might say that his films offer a dramatisation of the conflict between the two approaches, along with some possible resolutions of that conflict.

To try to fathom more clearly how these types of logic work, I want to focus on Godard's 1964 film, *A Married Woman*. The film was a critical success upon release. It was shown for the first time under the slightly different title of *The Married Woman* at the Venice Film Festival of 1964, the year when Antonioni's *Red Desert* was awarded the Golden Lion. (Richard Brody's chapter on the film gives an exceptionally detailed account of its production and release; see Brody 2008, 107–27.) In general terms, the logic is quite straightforward. In *A Married Woman*, Charlotte is married to Pierre, and having an affair with Robert (the actors are Macha Méril, Philippe LeRoy and Bernard Noël). And we should note that she appears to have had at least one other affair in the past. We can call this something like a series of lovers, a husband + a lover + another lover and so on. The logic is one of addition: ... *and* ... *and* .... We can also call this a logic of connectedness: Charlotte wants to be connected with any number of lovers, a project that Bersani would endorse as a process of 'self-expansion'. And all of these connections would be modes of experimentation, of 'trying things out', in much the same way as Camille could be said to be 'trying out' Prokosch in *Contempt*. All of this adds up to a notion of selfhood – a subject – that is composed of these encounters and connections. The more lovers, the more correspondences, the better. (To some degree a similar logic is at work for Jerzy in *Passion*: Hanna + Isabelle + the woman who jumps into his 'flying carpet' at the end of the film.) Overall, we see here a series of equivalences: A≈A≈A ... That is one logic.[11]

There is another logic at play in *A Married Woman*. Yes, Charlotte has a husband and a lover, but most of the film is built around the dilemma of whom Charlotte will choose. For much of the film it appears she will choose her lover, Robert. But then, right at the end of the film, she decides to leave Robert and go back to her husband. Her last words are 'It's over' – exactly the same words used by Hanna at the end of *Passion*. So this is a logic of choosing: not a matter of ... *and* ... *and*, but a matter of *either/or*. We see other 'choices' of Godard's women during this period: Patricia chooses to betray Michel in *Breathless*; Camille ultimately chooses Prokosch in *Contempt*. By contrast, Anna Karina in *A Woman Is a Woman* chooses not to choose: she ends up both with Émile and Alfred. To some degree, therefore, we can see the two logics at play in Godard's films. Charlotte's choice to return to her husband at the end of the film is not a logic of addition, but is instead a logic of choosing. She chooses Pierre, who is not Robert (which is to say: Pierre is not *not* Pierre).

I cannot find a convincing reason why Charlotte decides to return to her husband.[12] We can speculate that it is as a result of the discussion she has with Robert after they have met for an afternoon rendezvous at Orly airport, including retiring to a hotel room there in order to have sex. The extended discussion they have concerns the difference between acting and real life, for Robert is a stage actor, and he is about to perform in Racine's *Bérenice* (he is at the airport so as to fly to Marseille in order to perform there). Robert tries to tell Charlotte that he is very good at knowing when he is acting and when he is in real life. Acting is a matter of reading someone else's lines, whereas in real life, he claims, he is free to say what goes through his mind. 'The script is mine,' he says, 'the thoughts are my own.' I think that what we are supposed to conclude from all of this is not so much that Charlotte believes Robert is only acting – that he is faking it so as to get her into bed. Rather, I think we are supposed to conclude that Charlotte herself comes to the conclusion that, by pursuing her affair with Robert, she has, in fact, been acting, 'playing a role'. She has been living a life that is a performance, one that is not real. It is not Robert who is acting; it is she who is acting. She comes to realise this, and in doing so realises that her relationship with Robert is not genuine: she is merely 'playing a role'. It is her relationship with her husband that is real. She decides that her love for her husband is real.

What evidence is there for such an interpretation? We have the conversation between Charlotte and Robert, but that hardly seems definitive. It seems to me that the only evidence in *A Married Woman* is provided by media advertising and consumerism. The bottom line is something like this: Charlotte is pursuing her affair with Robert because the magazines she reads, the popular songs she listens to and the products she buys – sex tonics and bust improvers – all tell her she should be having affairs. She should be pursuing the instant pleasure and gratification that are provided by promiscuous sexual encounters. 'Consumer society' tells her this, so it is pleasure she seeks, a pleasure associated with being-in-the-present and 'not thinking', she tells us at one point. If this is the case, then we would have to declare that Cavell's summation is correct: Godard shows us 'the falsity of social worlds' and that 'human pleasures are now figments and products of advertising accounts', as Cavell puts it (Cavell 1979a, 99). That is the 'role' Charlotte is playing: that of the duped, mass-consuming female. This is the pleasure of instant-gratification-in-the-present; a pleasure seeking that eschews the past. By contrast, the men in Charlotte's world, especially her husband, Pierre, do not obsess about the present but instead focus on the past and memory. And then – *voila!* – it is at the end of the film that Charlotte realises the error of her ways: Pierre and memory and the past win out over the instant gratification of the present. She returns to her husband. If nothing else, her return to her husband places *A Married Woman* in the thematic region occupied by 'remarriage'.

A remarriage comedy, perhaps. But what *A Married Woman* also delivers is what Cavell would call a discourse on 'the falsity of social worlds'. Here that discourse is dressed up as a critique of consumer society and advertising.

I am satisfied to call this a moral judgment rather than a critique: Godard disapproves of adultery – and we know that the film is in part his response to Anna Karina's infidelities – so the film's conclusion is merely a moral gesture. (And a personal one at that: Godard disapproves of his wife's betrayals.) We are, I would suggest, a long way away from Agnès Varda's lack of moral reprimand in *Le Bonheur* (and that is what makes Varda's film so stunning, certainly as I see it: François, in that film, really does follow a logic of *and ... and ...*). And haven't we also therefore landed back on the terrain charted by Sellier in relation to Godard's New Wave films? The Godardian woman is once again associated with the fripperies of consumption and popular culture, while men are endowed with the seriousness of history, the Frankfurt trials,[13] Beethoven, Racine and Resnais's *Night and Fog*? Male high culture wins out over female mass consumption. Might I add that, midway through the film Pierre jokes about raping Charlotte? Male sexual violence towards women is passed off here as though it is not at all serious. I do not find any of this positive at all.

There is another way to take the ending of *A Married Woman*. We could speculate that Charlotte's decision to return to her husband will be only temporary. It is, in fact, in precisely this way that a logic of difference can be reconciled with a logic of resemblance. What ultimately drives Charlotte's romances is the conviction that love will always be *elsewhere*. When she is with her husband, then she dearly wishes to be with her lover. Then, when she is with her lover, she wants to return to her husband. Love, true love, will always be elsewhere, over there. The seeming conclusion of *A Married Woman* – that Charlotte returns to Pierre – may well be just another metonymy of desire, another quest to find the real (or 'Real') lost object, that object which will always be elsewhere, just out of reach.

And ultimately this may be what the theory of love expounded in *In Praise of Love* comes down to. We have seen that Morrey calls this version of love 'a grieving memory for a promise never fulfilled'. What is key here is that the promise is never fulfilled. It is always over there, elsewhere, just beyond my grasp. For Godard, that is what love is. (As an aside, the connections between *In Praise of Love* and *A Married Woman* abound. On the one hand, an intense discourse on marriage and love, and on the other, a deep investigation into the Holocaust and the sins of the past. All along the way, popular culture is derided. In *In Praise of Love* this derision is reserved for Hollywood cinema, especially Steven Spielberg and Julia Roberts.)

How do I wrap this up? I fear I have overcomplicated Godard's work, on the one hand, and adopted a perspective that is far too critical of his films, on the other. I partly want to argue that Godard deeply believes in love, but also that he cannot quite fathom how such a thing ever comes about.

In part this also seems to be a response to the 'mystery' of woman. His view of woman is not exalted. Godard's portrayals of women are often crude, belittling and verging on the pornographic (see Sterritt 1999, 185–7). As for marriage, Godard's films paint a bleak picture, to say the least. Just look at *Contempt*, *A Married Woman*, *Weekend*, *Tout va bien*, *Numéro deux*. We have seen that *Hail Mary* is just about the only of his films that provides a positive depiction of the stakes of marriage, and that comes only as a miraculous and mysterious achievement. (And how does *Hail Mary* end? Mary famously applies some bright red lipstick to her lips as she sits in her car. Such an ending is ambiguous and open.) Perhaps all I can say is that, for Godard, love and marriage are topics that are difficult for humans and the world to contain: they are topics that rightly belong in the heavens.

Notes

1 Also see Sellier's (2008, 153–4) discussion of Loshitsky's arguments.
2 Many thanks to an undergraduate student of mine, Leah Parker, who opened my eyes to Godard's portrayals of women.
3 Richard Brody (2008, 440) notes that the ending is a reference to the end of Truffaut's *Day for Night*.
4 Another discourse could be on that of the Professor and his lover, Eva, whose name he constantly mistakes as 'Eve'. That the Professor eventually leaves Eva in order to go back to his wife might provide a counter-story to that of Mary and Joseph, but both stories can be said to be, in their own ways, remarriage tales.
5 Edgar is played by Bruno Putzulu; Berthe by Cécile Camp.
6 Readers should know by now that I have resisted such easy contrasts. Certainly for the comedies of remarriage theorised by Cavell, Hollywood romance has the ability to emerge as an ongoing process of transformation and rebirth.
7 Fredric Jameson (2010, 48) points out that, in this regard, Hegel is very much a structuralist.
8 I am simplifying. For a thorough excursion through these concepts, see Robert B. Pippin, 'Logic and negation' (Pippin 2019, 139–80).
9 Daniel Morgan's *Late Godard* (2013) is exceptional in this respect. Morgan argues that one of the guiding aims of Godard's late work (from the 1980s onwards) is to propose, by way of a combination of montage and history, as exemplified by the *Histoire(s) du cinéma* project, a way of being two. Morgan describes this as a process of 'bringing two things together, holding them up against one another, and then judging them' (Morgan 2013, 261).
10 Cavell puts it this way: 'Our films may be understood as parables of a phase of the development of consciousness between a woman and a man, a study of the conditions under which this fight for recognition (as Hegel put it) or demand for acknowledgment (as I have put it) is a struggle for mutual freedom' (Cavell, 1981, 18).

11 Notably, Gilles Deleuze (1989, 180) attributes such a logic to Godard.
12 It is not entirely evident that Charlotte will return to her husband, but that seems to be the critical consensus (see, for example, Brody 2008, 196).
13 Richard Brody gives the following account: 'On December 20, 1963, twenty-two officials and guards of the Auschwitz concentration camp went on trial in Frankfurt. The trial, which lasted until August 1965 and ended with eighteen convictions and four acquittals, featured a factually and emotionally overwhelming weight of evidence, provided by 359 witnesses, 211 of whom were survivors of Auschwitz. Despite the sharply detailed recollections of the witnesses, none of the accused admitted their crimes, and their defense attorneys attempted to shake the survivors' testimony on cross-examination' (Brody 2008, 196). Pierre, at the beginning of *A Married Woman*, has just returned from Frankfurt and an involvement in the trials.

Chapter 11

Éric Rohmer: the ordinary miracle of love

11.1 Pauline and Sylvain (Amanda Langlet and Simon de la Brosse) in *Pauline at the Beach* (Éric Rohmer, 1983)

A note on queer sexualities

This is the final chapter of this book, so I feel that a number of unresolved issues need to be addressed. The first of these concerns queer sexuality, or, more generally, non-heterosexual modes of love. All of the relationships I approach in this book are heterosexual ones, with the exception, perhaps, of the friendship between Suzanne and Pomme in Varda's *One Sings, the Other Doesn't*. All of the films in this book deal with issues that pertain to a man's love for a woman, and vice versa. To some degree, the reason for this is defined by the films themselves: they are about heterosexual relationships. Notably, the one overtly queer relationship that emerged across these films, that involving M. Albany in Truffaut's *Stolen Kisses*, offers only an appalling set of negative stereotypes of homosexuality in ways that are completely at odds with today's sensibilities, including my own.

Stanley Cavell's work on Hollywood's 'comedies of remarriage' and 'melodramas of the unknown woman' – these have been central to my discussions in this book – are resolutely heterosexual. A brief aside on homosexuality emerges in Cavell's analysis of *Now, Voyager*, especially in relation to Henry James's 'The Beast in the Jungle' and Eve Kosofsky Sedgwick's famously queer interpretation of that short story (Sedgwick 1994). But to my mind Cavell's remarks there are clumsy and of little consequence (Cavell 1996, 186–7). Leo Bersani, by contrast, is proudly queer, and a good deal of his writings are devoted to theorising and defending queer lifestyles and practices. My approach here has pitted Bersani's theories against those of Cavell, to a large degree, so might it be the case that I am rising to the defence of heterosexuality against those sexualities defined as queer (or any other non-heterosexual way of being)? And furthermore, wouldn't my approach therefore be one that is defending entrenched, ideological, normative and normalising practices of love, marriage and sexuality? Isn't it clear that this whole book is a conservative defence of normative, heterosexual ways of life over and against any deviant or subversive ways of life?

I can only say that such is not my intention. If I have pitted Cavell's conception of acknowledgment against Bersani's notion of connectedness, then I see no reason why acknowledgment cannot be applicable to non-heterosexual relationships. Bersani certainly does not make 'connectedness' a matter of queer relationships. Rather, as we have seen via his discussions of Godard – in *Contempt* and *Passion* – he applies that notion to heterosexual relationships. We shall see his doing the same in relation to the films of Éric Rohmer too in this chapter. Indeed, Bersani very rightly dismisses any simple distinction between heterosexual and queer sexuality. 'An intentionally oppositional gay identity', he writes, 'by its very coherence, only repeats the restrictive and immobilizing analyses it sets out to resist' (Bersani 1995, 3). In other words, to make heterosexuality 'normal' and gay or queer 'abnormal' is merely to reproduce a binary opposition that a restrictive version of heterosexuality has already put in place. Bersani, rather, argues that there are many ways of being queer, and so we must also believe there are also many ways of being heterosexual, and many ways of being sexual as such.

At the same time, Bersani goes on to argue in *Homos* that calling someone 'gay' can serve important political ends, and the same can surely be argued of the term 'queer'. The signifier 'gay' can elicit and inspire forms of opposition to oppressive forms of heterosexual normalisation – to what Bersani calls 'hegemonic regimes of the normal' (Bersani 1995, 4). One of Bersani's key theoretical aims is to critique existing structures of the social, and that existing structure typically has as its foundation the nuclear family, with a married mommy and daddy at the helm. Heterosexuality has created, certainly in modern times, the structures of a repressive and persecutory normalisation. For Bersani, everything to do with such structures needs to be reinvented. '[T]he homo-ness I will be exploring in gay desire', Bersani writes – and homo-ness does not necessarily mean homosexuality, but a *homo-ness of being*, a homo-ness of the ways we are all connected to each other and the world – 'is a redefinition of sociality so radical that it may appear to require a provisional withdrawal from relationality itself' (Bersani 1995, 7). To backtrack over some of Bersani's arguments that we have seen throughout this book, his approach to gay sexuality offers a way of breaking apart traditional modes of heterosexual, romantic love. If romantic love and monogamy offer a traditional version of relationality – one based on contempt, mastery and possessiveness, as we have seen – then Bersani's theories want to withdraw from that kind of relationality so as to define new forms of relation. And we have seen how the stakes of many of Bersani's arguments for new modes of relation have emerged throughout this book, primarily by way of his calls for connectedness and correspondences. Such relations define, for Bersani, new modes of relation.

And yet, I would want to believe that new forms of relation are at stake for Cavell's arguments. Relations of acknowledgment are forged on the basis of freedom and equality, as well as mutual recognition, between members of a loving, 'remarried' couple. Cavell certainly argues, as much as I do, that relations between humans made on such a basis have the ability to resist forms of oppression, possessiveness and the power of one human being over another. The stakes of those arguments are humble enough to declare that such relationships need to be forged one at a time: the social begins when one human being comes into agreement with another human being. The social begins with two, and then must expand, one person at a time. It does not commence, for Cavell, when one human being exercises power over another, or when a predetermined social realm exerts its power over one or two. (Such is the logic of Emerson's essay on 'Friendship' that I have referred to a number of times in this book; Emerson 1898.) If we take 'normal' social relations as ones denoted by power relations – whether this be the power of heterosexuals over homosexuals, of men over women, of rich over poor and so on – then Cavell's formulations resist those 'normal' social relations. Yes, Cavell's new mode of relation is very different from Bersani's, but both theorists are trying to imagine how to get beyond and dismantle 'old' social relations.

Self-reliance

A clear example of the ways that Cavell's arguments resist 'normalisation' can be found in his advocacy of Emerson's distinction between self-reliance and conformity. If conformity defines the ways in which a society's power relations are accepted without contestation – 'I do this because that's what my society does, or because that's what my society tells me to do' – then self-reliance is precisely what contests that conformity. Self-reliance is what contests that which society deems 'normal'. Self-reliance is a way of ensuring that my world is defined and expressed in ways that I have defined, or, at the very least, that I have approved. Granted, one may well accept what society decrees: self-reliance is not a simple refusal of society. But if one decides to conform to a society's norms, then one must accept those norms *on one's own terms* if one is to be self-reliant; one must make that acceptance as though it were one's own invention. In my own society, I must confess that such acceptance is all too often impossible to do.

What would Bersani think? To my knowledge, Bersani has not commented on Cavell's work, nor on Emerson's. But I suspect he would have great difficulty with a term like self-reliance, for such a term reeks of psychology and the individual subject. We have seen time and again in this book Bersani's antipathy towards psychological subjectivity. He traces the conception back to Descartes's *Cogito* (at the very least). Everything about Emerson's defence of self-reliance, including Cavell's advocacy of it and his tracing of the concept back to Descartes's 'I think, therefore I am', a tracing itself made explicit by Emerson himself ... well, it seems that self-reliance could easily define everything Bersani wishes to critique.[1] I would also want to stress that Cavell makes Descartes central to his definition of cinema (call it an ontology). The cinema's operations of recording and projection are a figure of the ways that humans themselves are disconnected from the world. By way of the cinema camera, we *look out at* the world from behind a screen. We do not *directly encounter* that world. Rather, it is screened from us and for us, *over there*, on the cinema screen. And that is a demonstration of the ways in which humans are, by way of being in trapped in their subjectivity, separated from the world; disconnected from it. Cinema, by virtue of its very mechanism or apparatus, shows us this. And that is why cinema feels so natural to us: it shows us the disconnected conditions of our existence, an existence – 'modern subjectivity' – elaborated by Descartes in the seventeenth century (see Cavell's argument, 1979a, 24, 186).

But that is not all we get from Cavell's appeal to modern subjectivity. If humans feel disconnected from the world, then that is no occasion for celebration. Humans want to be connected or reconnected with the world. To do this they must find a way to overcome their state of disconnection; they must overcome the state of being 'trapped in subjectivity'. This takes effort, an effort that could be called self-reliance. That is, the effort to define a world that I can be connected to; to have the confidence in my experience of the world so as to not feel disconnected from it. One way to conceive of such a thing is to declare that I can be 'married' to the world: to overcome the state of being trapped in my subjectivity and thus of disconnection from the world would be to find a way to agree with the world, to be married to it. This is an achievement; or a potential achievement. Cinema, which has the capacity to show humans the ways that they are trapped in subjectivity, also has the ability to show us how to overcome that entrapment.[2]

For Cavell, then, connection to the world is desirable. For Bersani, too, a connection to the world is desirable. Where Cavell sees such a connection as an achievement and an overcoming of our prior estrangement from the world, Bersani sees things the other way around. Our prior condition – an ontological condition – is one in which we, as human beings, are always already connected to the world. That is both what and how we *are*: we are connected. That is a given for Bersani. What has gone wrong – the reason we no longer feel connected to the world – is that specific modes of thought, originating more or less with Descartes's *Cogito* and its consequent mind–body split, have created a distorted world in which humans are brought up to believe that everything external to the self – the objects of the world as well as other human beings; the external world per se – is different from and antagonistic to the self. The world out there is hostile and I am disconnected from it. Against that Cartesian trajectory, Bersani argues that things do not have to be like that. If humans put away their Cartesian prejudices, especially that prejudice which places the mind and thought above the body and its ability to touch and connect with other humans and the world; if we can dismantle those prejudices, then humans will be free to connect with the world. I have already suggested that this is a rather utopian vision (and I admire that vision). It will be less an achievement than something that simply happens, for it is a process of *letting things be* rather than dominating or mastering those things. If the shackles of Cartesian mastery are withdrawn, then, as Bersani and Dutoit put it, 'everything is illuminated' (Bersani and Dutoit 2004, 70). Our natural, cosmic relation to the world will be restored.

On Rohmer

Bersani's thoughts are brought into contact with the films of Éric Rohmer in a short essay written with Ulysse Dutoit published in 2009. There is a central premise of their argument, and it goes something like this. Rohmer's films, as is well known, are full of conversations. Many of those conversations concern matters pertaining to love. So shouldn't this be a way into Rohmer's films; that they offer discourses on romantic love? Bersani and Dutoit hesitate. Yes, there is a lot of talk, but it is talk that is *around* love. It never or rarely comes straight out to declare what love is; it never seems to speak directly of love. Therefore, in fact, Bersani and Dutoit suggest, the films are less about love than they are about the spaces between the conversations. They concern themselves with what intervenes once talk has been exhausted or silenced. And what is that? It primarily concerns moments of contact and touching; that is, relations defined not by conversation and 'rational' discourse, but by the intimacy of human contact. Perhaps this is nowhere more evident than in *Claire's Knee*. When, near the end of the film, Jérôme (Jean-Claude Brialy) is taking Claire (Laurence de Monaghan) to Annecy in his boat, they pull in to the shore to shelter from heavy rain. Here, they talk. Their talk makes Claire upset, for Jérôme tells her that he saw her boyfriend, Gilles (Gérard Falconetti), kissing another girl. She begins to cry. But their conversation comes to an end, and Jérôme gently caresses Claire's knee. He does so in order to satisfy his desire – let us say he has felt himself to be 'connected' to Claire's knee – and Claire accepts his touch on the basis that he is comforting her in her sadness. The touch, the correspondence, the connection is all. None of their conversation now matters. What matters is the demonstration that these humans are connected. That is what is at stake in Rohmer's films. Not conversation, and not the endless digressions around love. Rather, what are key are these moments of contact. Bersani and Dutoit call them 'other forms of contact' (Bersani and Dutoit 2009, 33), forms of contact that are not reducible to love.

A second major example of connectedness comes from *Girlfriends and Boyfriends* (1987), the last of the 'Comedies and Proverbs' series. As ever with Rohmer's films, there is a lot of talk. But there is a remarkable sequence where two of the main characters are reduced to silence. One day, two friends, Blanche (Emmanuelle Chaulet) and Fabien (Éric Viellard), decide to explore the towpath that runs along the edge of the River Oise. They do so, and end up entering a forested area. They walk here, and any chat between them fades out. They enter a small glade in the forest and Blanche is overwhelmed. Overwhelmed with the beauty of nature? Overwhelmed because of the deep connection she feels with Fabien? Overwhelmed because of the ways in which the experience of the forest has intensified her feelings for Fabien? Or even overwhelmed because she knows she is transgressing, for Fabien is the boyfriend of her good friend, Léa (Sophie Renoir)? Blanche is therefore aware that she is doing something that, morally, she should not be doing: moving in on another's boyfriend. Earlier in the film, while talking with Léa, Blanche had thought the idea of moving in on someone else's boyfriend to be very much off limits, so her falling for Fabien here is distinctly contrary to her own moral codes. However we take this scene, for Bersani and Dutoit, it offers a clear example of 'human contacts with the nonhuman world' (Bersani and Dutoit 2009, 33), for it is the forest glade that brings all conversation to a halt and energises the scene. I agree with their claims. The scene is a remarkable one and it has been the focus of many commentaries (see Leigh 2012, 148–9). I am convinced that the scene is a crucial one in the context of the film as a whole. In short, there may well be good grounds for Bersani and Dutoit's argument. Rohmer's film might on the surface appear to be full of words, but, deeper down, the key moments occur when words stop and the world reveals itself in all its majesty.

And yet. Blanche and Fabien caress and kiss in the idyllic forest glade. But then Fabien speaks. He suggests that he feels as though they are on a desert island, which I take to mean that they have separated themselves from the everyday world of jobs and work and social concerns. They have discovered a world in which only they exist. Then Fabien suggests something else. 'I used to dream', he says 'of seeing a girl in a forest. We'd meet in a clearing,' he continues, 'spellbound, then drift apart again, still nameless.' He tells Blanche that he thinks it's a boy's dream, but Blanche replies that it could just as easily be her dream. It is a reverie they could share. We might be tempted to call it a statement of love. But is this love, for Fabien states that the dream features a couple who are only temporarily spellbound? They soon drift apart. They do not even share their names. Nevertheless, we are very close here to the reveries that emerge in two significant comedies of remarriage as theorised by Cavell: Peter's dream of a south sea island in *It Happened One Night* and Charles's fantasy that his knowledge of Jean/Eve goes 'way, way back', as he puts it, in *The Lady Eve* (I discuss these scenes in Chapters 3 and 4). These reveries single out just *this* couple as a couple who are made for this world in ways that place them alone together. That is what Blanche and Fabien discover here.

It is worth pushing further with these thoughts. Charles, in *The Lady Eve*, remarks, as he tries to pinpoint his love for Jean/Eve, that 'What I see inside I'll never be able to put into words.' That is, what he sees inside Jean (or Eve) is something he feels or senses, or even something he knows, but he cannot put that something into words – it is beyond expressing. I wrote in Chapter 4 that Julia Kristeva, in *Tales of Love*, had sensed much of this in relation to theories of love. That is to say, love happens at a point 'infinitely remote', Kristeva writes, to the degree that whatever love *is* is not something that can be put into words. At the same time, Kristeva also declares that, even if we cannot put our love into words, we are nevertheless condemned to try to express our love in words. What love *is* is the exchange of words between people: that is how love comes into being. Without words – without discourse – it cannot come into being. I tried to call this a paradox of love: that it cannot be expressed in words, but also that it can only be expressed in words.

To define love as 'infinitely remote' seems to be the point Godard wishes to make, as I tried to fathom in Chapter 10; in effect, that love is otherworldly, heavenly, always something that is elsewhere; certainly it is beyond words. This may be a reason why Bersani and Dutoit push the discourses of Godard – and Rohmer too – beyond words so that it is cosmic correspondences, silences and heavenly auras that inspire those characters, rather than 'rational discourse', those ordinary, messy, bickerings about love. They emphasise these points in relation to Rohmer; that love is a matter of correspondences and not words, whether this be via Blanche and Fabien's walk in the forest, Delphine's (Marie Rivière) wondrous experience of the green ray produced by the sunset in *The Green Ray*, or – miracle of miracles – Félicie's (Charlotte Véry) remeeting of Charles (Frédéric Van Den Driessche) in *A Tale of Winter* (there are other examples I will come to). I find some of this theorising compelling: that, at the origin of love, there is a spark or treasure which is beyond rational discourse – we are on the terrain of Lacan's *ágalma* once again. I will simply call it a 'fantasy' (a positive fantasy). We have seen Bersani and Dutoit call such things 'human contacts with the nonhuman world' (Bersani and Dutoit 2009, 33).

This heavenly love, however, finds ways to come back down to earth. And it typically does so by way of rational discourse. Certainly that is the case in Rohmer's films. Blanche and Fabien each go through ups and downs in *Girlfriends and Boyfriends*, they suffer from suspicions and misunderstandings and tests of faith, but in the end, when they each finally meet with Léa and Alexandre (François-Éric Gendron) – each of whom has, in one way or another, been a competing lover – rational discourse wins the day. These couples discover they are in love, however permanent or temporary that love may be. Correspondences occur, yes, but these characters find their way to love by way of conversation. That is what Rohmer's films do.

A Tale of Winter

Rohmer's *A Tale of Winter* (the title *Conte d'hiver* is essentially a translation of the title of Shakespeare's *The Winter's Tale*, which itself is the inspiration for Rohmer's film and the films that comprise the 'Tales of the Four Seasons') provides, for Bersani and Dutoit, a unique example in Rohmer's oeuvre of a film that ends with a united couple; a 'uniquely happy couple', they say (Bersani and Dutoit 2009, 35).[3] The authors then link *A Tale of Winter* to the theory of love proposed by Plato in the *Phaedrus*, whereby love is implanted in us, transcendently, by the gods. Love is heavenly.[4] 'Rohmer teases us', Bersani and Dutoit argue, 'in *A Tale of Winter*, with the suggestion that this exceptional experience of a happy, unqualified romantic love is in fact one of transcendent love, a love outside of or beyond all earthly experience' (Bersani and Dutoit 2009, 35). In the film itself, Loïc (Hervé Furic) also invokes Plato's *Phaedrus* when he and Félicie discuss the production of *The Winter's Tale* they have just seen.

Cavell also defends this film's sense of transcendence on the two occasions when he wrote extensively on *A Tale of Winter*. He argues that it is a typical feature of a Rohmer film for a main female character to undergo an experience of 'transcendence'.[5] The way Cavell figures the workings of transcendence in *A Tale of Winter* is somewhat complicated. Yes, the clear miracle is that of Félicie's remeeting Charles on a bus five years after they had parted. This conclusion brings the film close to the conditions of remarriage comedy: Félicie and Charles get back together again. And yes, this miracle is Rohmer's version of the miraculous resurrection of Hermione in Shakespeare's play. And yes, to add, Rohmer is very much aware that he is dallying in issues of plausibility and fiction and fantasy in ways that may have us believing in magic or religion or some such power of the heavens.

Cavell argues, however, that this is not a heaven located in the heavens. Rather, it is a heaven located in the everyday and the ordinary. If *A Tale of Winter* is in some way an adaptation of *The Winter's Tale*, then the film takes Shakespeare's tale out of the realm of kings and princesses and the other-worldly locations of Bohemia and Sicily and places its events in the streets, cafes, trains, buses and apartments of this world. Much of this has to do with exploring something like Heaven on Earth (Rohmer's Catholicism is well known). Cavell puts the matter this way: it is a matter of 'recognizing the extraordinary in what we find ordinary and the ordinary in what we find extraordinary' (Cavell 2004, 422; also see 2005d, 290–1). Later he will write that 'Rohmer's great subject is the miraculousness of the everyday, the possibility and necessity of our awakening to it every day, call it the secularization of the transcendental' (Cavell 2004, 427).

In terms of plotting, Cavell notes a puzzle in Rohmer's adaptation. Key to Shakespeare's play is the sheer venom and cruelty that emerges from Leontes' jealousy. When he suspects Hermione of infidelity and of giving birth to children that are not his, the viciousness he unleashes upon her is as chilling as anything in Shakespeare. But there is none of this in Rohmer's film. There is bliss and magic in the love affair between Félicie and Charles at the start of the film. (I cannot help but make connections here with Bergman's *Summer with Monika* and *Summer Interlude* as depictions of 'summer love'. With some cheer, Rohmer's tale ends more positively than do Bergman's.) It then comes to pass that, when they part at the end of their summer of love, Félicie gives Charles an incorrect address. Because she has done this, after they part, Charles can no longer find her.

Cavell quite rightly makes a lot of this issue. Why does Félicie give Charles the wrong address? Cavell suggests there might be Freudian answers. A Freudian slip has occurred, as it were, so that Félicie's mistake may well be concealing a deeper, hidden issue. Cavell links Félicie's slip with another issue. Near the end of their summer the couple engage in unprotected sex, with the possibility that Félicie will fall pregnant. 'You are taking a risk,' Charles says to her and her response is to laugh. Why does she laugh? And indeed she does fall pregnant. The consequences of her 'risk' turn out to be have been very significant.

These questions turn out to be crucial. Why does Félicie take the risk of falling pregnant? And why does she give Charles the wrong address? Cavell takes these as the events that more or less substitute for Leontes' rage in Shakespeare's plot. For Leontes, those events figure his verging on madness – such is Cavell's argument – and Cavell is keen to discover a parallel between this madness and Félicie's actions. Leontes' rage is linked with scepticism insofar as 'madness' is itself a species of scepticism – that is, Leontes' sense that he doubts his own existence and doubts the faith he has placed in his wife and in the world as such. In *A Tale of Winter*, Félicie exhibits similar doubts about her own world and her existence in ways that verge on madness (Cavell 2004, 426). Indeed, when recounting to Maxence (Michel Voletti) her experience of giving Charles the wrong address, Félicie says that she must have been 'stark raving dumb (*sotte à lier*)'. Maxence corrects her by saying that she must mean 'stark raving mad (*folle à lier*)'.[6] Later in the film, when she has decided to break up with Maxence, she tells him she could live only with someone she is madly in love with. His response is to call her 'insane'. *A Tale of Winter* thus foregrounds Félicie's relationship with madness. Somewhat philosophically, Cavell argues that the kind of scepticism exhibited by Félicie is typical of an everyday scepticism that will often emerge in our own lives when things happen that we have difficulty making sense of. 'Why did this happen?' or 'Why did I do that?' might be the kinds of questions we ask, and these are very common questions, ordinary ones. They offer the sense, as Cavell puts it, 'that the world and I and others are radically unknown to me' (Cavell 2004, 426).

Why, then, does Félicie take the risk of falling pregnant? Cavell's answer strikes me as being a little strange. He tries to argue that Félicie's response is to laugh when Charles tells her she is taking a risk *because she is already pregnant with his child*. Their romance has been ongoing for some three months, and the deed has already been done. In short, Félicie is taking no risk, and that is why she laughs. To me, Cavell has to work a little too hard to read this into the film. (Leigh declares that 'there is no evidence to confirm or contradict Cavell's interpretation'; Leigh 2012, 313 n. 45). My own answer is this: Félicie knows she loves this man, and she also knows Charles loves her. To that degree there is no risk. On the contrary, this is what Félicie wants: to be with Charles and to have a child with him. With this man, she overcomes scepticism: the world, other people, her own existence and her own desire become known to her.

I offer this as an answer to one of the questions posed here – that is why Félicie laughs at the risk of unprotected sex. Surely, we might think, if Félicie is so happy with Charles, then why would she be so careless as to give him the wrong address? We might think this error puts paid to the truth of Félicie's happiness. A Freudian might say that she gives Charles the wrong address because, deep down, she does not really love him. Cavell's short answer as to why she gives him the wrong address is that she wants him to find her (to find her again). In other words, she tests him to see if he is worthy of her love. Wheatley interprets Cavell's moves thusly: 'Félicie doubts. She throws down a challenge to the father of her child to overcome this doubt. And as she waits for him, she herself, by herself, learns to overcome her suspicions' (Wheatley 2019, 203).

Let's try to put these pieces together. I think the reason – call it accidental or unconscious – Félicie gives Charles the wrong address is not because she wants to test Charles, but because she wants to test herself. Yes, she declares to herself, this really is the right man for me. And yet, how can she really be sure? In a sense, what she needs to do is to test what her life might be like without this man. Might she find that, in fact, her life really is fine without this man, that Charles is not the 'right man' for her after all? Such a mode of questioning brings *A Tale of Winter* very close to the comedies of remarriage so prized by Cavell. Early in this book I emphasised the ways in which Cavell figured that the American invention of 'remarriage' counted on the fact of one's not feeling 'trapped' in a marriage. It is a matter of choosing to be married. 'This would be creating within marriage', Cavell writes, 'a logical space in which to choose to be married, a way in which not to feel trapped in it' (Cavell 1981, 245). I have also characterised Cavell's account of modern subjectivity as a matter of any one person's feeling as though they are 'trapped' in subjectivity. To find one's way out of that entrapment is, for Cavell, a way of finding one's self, of finding one's true self, of affirming one's existence.

These dramas, it seems to me, are at play in *A Tale of Winter*. Félicie's mistake in giving Charles an incorrect address opens the way for her both to prove her love for Charles – her faith in him – as well as to prove her own existence to herself, as it were (as Wheatley puts it, she 'learns to overcome her suspicions'). The bulk of the film is in fact taken up with Félicie's relationships with two other men, Loïc and Maxence. Both of these men love her, but Félicie realises that neither of them is right for her. Indeed, her experiences with these men convince her that Charles really is the right man for her, even though he is currently lost to her. She proves this to herself. And it is only by first losing him that she can prove it to herself. When she proves it, she is happy. The key scene occurs just after she has seen a production of Shakespeare's *The Winter's Tale*. Loïc, who had also seen the play, asks her the standard question: did Hermione really die and come back to life, or was she alive all along? Félicie replies to him, 'You don't get it. Faith brought her back to life.' And so we take this as an affirmation of her continuing faith in Charles (see Cavell 2005d, 291). Félicie is happy to still be in love with Charles even before she miraculously refinds him. To this degree, her giving Charles the wrong address was less a test of him than a test of herself. She proves to herself that her love for Charles was not one in which she had been trapped. She proves to herself that she loves him and that her choosing to love him was, and is, a choice freely made.

Félicie is a positive version of a female character from an earlier Rohmer film, *Full Moon in Paris* (1984). The stakes of that film are somewhat similar to those of *A Tale of Winter*. In the earlier film, Louise (Pascale Ogier) is in love with Rémi (Tchéky Karyo), and has been living with him for some time. It appears they are set for marriage. Louise is, however, uncertain of her commitment. She is courted by Octave (Fabrice Luchini), himself a married man, and also sleeps with the dashing young Bastien (Christian Vadim). In doing this, she is testing her love for Rémi. At the end of the film, having slept with Bastien, she realises that she does love Rémi after all, and that her flirtations have been shallow. She returns to Rémi only to find that he has fallen in love with another woman. He calls it true love. He has no desire to restart his relationship with Louise. It's over.

Full Moon in Paris delivers an uncharacteristically cruel ending for a Rohmer film. Louise has tested her love with two other men, and her love for Rémi is affirmed, only for her to discover that her love is no longer reciprocated. The contrast with *A Tale of Winter*'s miraculous happy ending could hardly be more stark. There, Félicie too tests her love for one man via relationships with two other men. When she is then reunited with Charles, their love is mutual. They get back together again in ways that more or less satisfy the tropes of what Cavell calls comedies of remarriage. Above all, Félicie tests her love, and the test of that love turns out to be successful.

Self-reliance and rational discourse: 'consciousness goes out'

I think we have to say that 'discourse' wins the day here. Yes, the 'transcendence' that characterises the love between Félicie and Charles is marked, and it is miraculous that they remeet each other five years after their separation. All the same, Rohmer works hard to try to figure their transcendent love as one that is also grounded in the everyday – they remeet, after all, on a bus, an everyday mode of transport in a movie whose modes of transport are characteristically mundane. It is also clear that Félicie rationally tests out her prospects: she tests her love for Charles by way of her relationships with Maxence and Loïc. Yes, the talk in Rohmer's films is 'around' love, as Bersani and Dutoit suggest, but that is all we can do with love: we cannot speak it; we can only ever speak around it. And that is what Félicie does. (It is what pretty much all of Rohmer's characters do.)

Félicie comes to her conclusions by way of rational discourse and subjective reflection. If there is a 'connectedness' – a connection or correspondence between Félicie and Charles – then this connection is eventually won as an achievement. It is not, as Bersani would think, an ontological given. I think we must call this achievement Cartesian, and that is certainly the argument Cavell makes for *A Tale of Winter*. He foregrounds Félicie's call to self-reliance. She learns to affirm her own experience of herself, and Cavell calls this 'an independence from the dictations of the world' (Cavell 2005d, 291). It therefore does not matter if the world is against her; and it certainly is not a matter of her connectedness to the world. On the contrary: Félicie is disconnected from the world. The world is against her, whether this is by way of Loïc's or Maxence's protests, or that the world or the cosmos seems to prevent the return of Charles. The simple fact of Félicie's finding *what it is that she wants* is enough. She contents herself with knowing that she wants Charles, and it is enough to know this, even if Charles is not physically present with her. In this context, Cavell then goes on to invoke Descartes.

> This negates Descartes's negation of my dependence on the world: thinking my existence secures my existence by preserving me in the absence of the world; finding my desire exposes me to the world, but whether the world goes on to provide the satisfaction of my desire is a measure not of my existence but of the world's worth. (Cavell 2005d, 292)

These are strong remarks. Could we be further from Bersani's sense that all humans are connected with and correspond to the world and other people? Cavell is effectively saying here that my worth, my existence, cannot rely on the world for affirmation. That affirmation can come only from me. All of this sounds to me like an extreme subjectivism, a form of self-reliance that shuns the world.

In an essay published in 1978, Cavell made a series of connections between the conventions of romance and Descartes's procedures in the *Meditations*. He argued that

> romance ... shares with skepticism the realization, in the terms of Descartes's *First Meditation*, that 'there are no conclusive indications by which waking life can be distinguished from sleep'. The consequence of this realization, Descartes goes on to say, is that 'I am quite astonished, and my bewilderment is such that it is almost able to convince me that I am sleeping'. In both skepticism and romance, knowledge, call it consciousness as a whole, must go out in order that a better consciousness can come to light. (Cavell 2005a, 7)

We know that Descartes proposes procedures that shun the world. That is one thing: self-consciousness entails a withdrawal into the self. But there is another thing to consider. Cavell here claims that the procedure Descartes follows is one in which *consciousness goes out*. Consciousness must first go outside of itself before being able to then return. And it does not return as a self-same consciousness. Rather, it returns as a 'better' consciousness, argues Cavell.

What does Cavell mean here? First and foremost he means that what might be called self-consciousness is not a mere reduction to the self over and against the world. It is not a retreat from the world. Rather, what is necessary for the achievement of self-consciousness is first of all to go out of self-consciousness: to lose one's self. We have known throughout this book that Cavell calls this process 'acknowledgment'. His own tale of how this comes to pass, recounted in *The Claim of Reason*, unfolds in the following way. An account of what it is to be a human being will require a history of what human beings have imagined themselves to have been. Central to that history will be an instance in which the human mind imagined itself as severed from others and from the world – this is the issue of scepticism – and then of how such a severance can be overcome. We are disconnected from the world. If we are to be connected to the world, we must build those connections ourselves (see Cavell 1979b, 470).

It is such a journey that Félicie takes in *A Tale of Winter*. By testing herself against the world, by testing her relationships with Maxence and Loïc, Félicie is undertaking a journey of self-consciousness. First of all her consciousness goes out, as though she is verging on madness. Eventually that consciousness returns to her. Its return can be placed at the point where she realises she can no longer live with Maxence. It may be that this comes as a revelation when she visits the cathedral in Nevers. Surely Rohmer wants us to believe something along such lines. But we know, and Félicie knows, and Cavell knows, that self-consciousness today must be without God. Cavell will write in *The Claim of Reason* that 'As long as God exists, I am not alone' (Cavell 1979b, 470). But we know now that God does not exist and my confirmation of my existence must come from elsewhere. In writing on *A Tale of Winter* Cavell will therefore state that Félicie 'has placed her infinite stake in her life not on God's existence but on the reality of her own desire' (Cavell 2005d, 291.)

All of this can be related to Cavell's reflections on Shakespeare's *Antony and Cleopatra*. I have referred to these reflections above (see Chapter 3), but will take them here as ones that bear particularly on Rohmer's film. Cavell posits the question: in what ways can a woman ever be satisfied? And we know he is asking this from the perspective of being a man, as do Antony or Leontes or Othello, and along with them a certain Jean-Luc Godard who provoked similar questions in my previous chapter; and so too might we think this is a question for Éric Rohmer across a range of films. Cavell tries to answer.

The answer I have depends on taking the existence of the woman's satisfaction as the essential object or event of the skeptical question: Is she satisfied and is the satisfaction directed to me? There is no satisfaction for me (masculine side) apart from a favorable conclusion here; it is a conclusion that must be conferred, given, not one that I can cause or determine on the basis of my senses. My senses go out; satisfaction happens in my absence, only in it, by it. (Cavell 2003, 34–5)

Do we call this faith? That my connection to the world requires my faith in it? And that my connection to other people requires my faith in them, and their faith in me? The stakes of acknowledgment are risky. They require my exposure to the other in ways that can lead to acceptance and satisfaction, but which can also lead to rejection and deep misery.

Cavell's formulations here have little to do with possession or mastery. On the contrary, he stresses an extreme lack of control in matters of acknowledgment: 'my senses go out' in ways that demand 'absolute passivity'. I will simply contend here that Cavell is correct and Bersani is wrong. Cavell's take on Descartes is appropriately creative and generous, while Bersani's reading is restrictive and reductive. The exercises of doubt, scepticism and exposure – 'consciousness goes out' – are central to Descartes's and Cavell's strategies, as much as I also believe they are strategies that every human being engages in. We are not automatically connected to the world. Rather, we have to build those connections ourselves. Those connections are achievements and they can be successful, but they can also fail.

Passivity

Bersani has always opposed theories based on sadism and control, so he instead advocates modes of passive receptivity (Bersani 2018, 20–5). And we have also seen that Cavell's notion of acknowledgment necessitates human subjects who place themselves in positions of 'absolute passivity' (Cavell 2003, 35). Why, then, have I been claiming such a stark contrast between Bersani's 'connected' approach and Cavell's defence of acknowledgment? Might they, in fact, be saying similar things? Well, perhaps not. We have seen that Cavell's perspective is indebted to Descartes, while Bersani flatly rejects Descartes's dualism, his subject–object split. Overall, Bersani criticises Descartes on the basis that his philosophy is based on the subject's ability to master the world by way of knowledge. At one point in *Thoughts and Things*, Bersani articulates this objection in terms of fantasy. He puts it this way: 'In fantasy, as in Cartesian introspection, the world is set aside in order that the elements of its presence within the subject may be reassembled in view of mastering the world' (Bersani 2015, 54). We have seen

Cavell make a similar claim: that Descartes or Félicie cling to the value and worth of a singular subjective existence over and against the world. '[T]hinking my existence', writes Cavell, 'secures my existence by preserving me in the absence of the world' (Cavell 2005d, 292). Where this introspection amounts, for Bersani, to a mastery of the world, for Cavell it is no such thing. How can this be so? And then, additionally, why does Bersani invoke the term *fantasy* to explain the stakes of this issue?

Pauline at the Beach

We can get a clear sense of the stakes of fantasy by virtue of the contrast between the two main female characters in Rohmer's *Pauline at the Beach* (1983). In a clear homage to Marivaux's *Game of Love and Chance* (and perhaps further to Renoir's *Rules of the Game* or Bergman's *Smiles of a Summer Night*), *Pauline at the Beach* features criss-crossed romances between a number of characters. All of these characters are enjoying their summer holidays in northern France, though one of them, Louisette (Rosette), is also working. Fifteen-year-old Pauline (Amanda Langlet) and her older cousin, Marion (Arielle Dombasle), embark on holiday love affairs. Notably, Marion has been married before – she is awaiting the finalisation of her divorce, so elements of Cavellian remarriage comedy can be said to be in play. The 'green world' away from the hustle and bustle of the city adds another element of the remarriage genre. Finally too, Marion falls for Henri (Féodor Atkine), an adventurous ethnographer, who has also been married and is now divorced. I make these points in order to show that the cinematic world Rohmer creates in the 1980s is markedly different from Renoir's visions of the 1930s, or Resnais's or Varda's or Antonioni's – or even Rohmer's own visions – of the 1960s.[7]

In contrast to Marion, Pauline is young and inexperienced in love. She enters into a holiday romance with a young man named Sylvain (Simon de la Brosse). As the plot progresses, there are claims of infidelity. Another character, Pierre (Pascal Greggory), thinks one day that he has seen Henri sleeping with another woman, Louisette, for he happened to see, through a window, Louisette naked in Henri's bedroom, and clearly she was engaging in some sort of sexual activity there. Henri, fearing he will hurt Marion's feelings if she finds out about his infidelity, manages to convince Marion, as well as Pierre and Pauline, that Louisette wasn't having sex with him, but was sleeping with Sylvain. This revelation, which the film's viewers know is a convenient lie told by Henri to cover up his sexual promiscuity, results in accusations all round. It is especially damaging for Pauline's relationship with Sylvain.

By the time we reach the end of the film, Pauline has clearly come to know that it was Henri, and not Sylvain, who was sleeping with Louisette. Henri has been quite frank with her and revealed to Pauline that he does not much care for Marion, even if he has enjoyed having sex with her. And yet, by the end of the film, Marion has refused to accept that Henri has betrayed her. She retains the hope that their romance will turn into something more permanent. In the final scene of the film, as they sit in a car ready to depart from their holiday home, Marion says to Pauline that they can both be happy with their romances. Marion can believe that Sylvain slept with Louisette, while Pauline can believe it was Henri. That way, both Marion and Pauline can believe they have been spared from infidelity.

Of course, we know, and Pauline knows, that it is only Marion who will have to believe such a thing. All of the other characters know that it was Henri who slept with Louisette. By continuing to believe that Henri has remained faithful to her, Marion is deceiving herself. What she believes satisfies her desire, but it does not correspond to the world – it does not correspond with what has really happened. Can we therefore say that Marion's deceptive version of events satisfies, in some way, a certain fantasy she has of the world? As Bersani puts it, couldn't we say that, here, in fantasy, 'the world is set aside in order that the elements of its presence within the subject may be reassembled in view of mastering the world' (Bersani 2015, 54). But then, also, does not Cavell suggest this kind of route towards fantasy: 'thinking my existence secures my existence by preserving me in the absence of the world' (Cavell 2005d, 292). In short, might there be an argument to say that a Cartesian account of subjective experience cannot find a way to free itself from delusion? That it cannot ever know that it has broken away from dreaming, and that its worlds might be nothing other than fantasies?

Conclusions

Much earlier in this book I proposed that love is based on deception. Such is one of the tropes of Cavellian remarriage comedies: that love is a con or trick. I also claimed that psychoanalysis provides a theory of 'transference love' in which a pretend version of love is more or less identical to what true love is. Another way of putting this was to say that love is a fantasy; a fantasy I have about the person I love. From these angles, love is always a matter of deception: true love, as much as false love, is based on deception.

The only marker of the truth of a love will be if more than one person comes to agree on a deception. What I mean to say is that love is a shared deception – call it a shared fantasy. One person may well be deceived, to the point of verging on madness, but if a couple (or more than a couple, for that matter) decide to pursue their deceptive madness together, then they are following a path towards love. Little wonder Cavell will call such a thing, with reference to Bergman's *Smiles of a Summer Night*, a 'reckless dash into the unknown' (Cavell 2005c, 201). Love cannot be known, and to that degree will never be true in the sense of something that can be proven. On the contrary, love is something that is made up, built, created, by two (or more) people who come to agree upon a world together.

I cannot help but feel that all of this sounds either too vague or too simplistic (or both). I have said that Félicie, in *A Tale of Winter*, retreats into herself. This means that she accepts the truth of her own desire, whether or not the external world can respond to that desire. This means that she fully accepts her desire in the knowledge that the world might remain absent to her (by which I mean Charles will remain absent to her). She accepts this. In *Pauline at the Beach*, Marion retreats into herself. She clings to the fantasy that Henri loves her. Even more than this, she clings to the belief that she can change him. She believes she can change him in such a way that he will be solely devoted to her. He will, she hopes, abandon his philandering ways and live with her, in love, happily ever after. This is her fantasy.

We are well aware that Henri's approach to love is very much at odds with Marion's. Near the beginning of the film Marion confesses that she is looking for a deep and lasting love, while Henri, by contrast, is happy to have fleeting affairs: he does not want to be tied down. As the film unfolds, it transpires that Marion's vision of love is incompatible with Henri's. Her only hope is to change him. I think the best way to characterise this is to declare that Marion is trying to force her fantasies on Henri. She wants to change the world so that it will conform to her fantasy. And this is pretty much how Bersani sums up a 'Cartesian' perspective: in fantasy, 'the world is set aside in order that the elements of its presence within the subject may be reassembled in view of mastering the world' (Bersani 2015, 54).

Do we therefore declare that Marion is Cartesian in this way? That she sets herself in such a way as to be determined to master the world? And cannot this same tendency be found in other of Rohmer's heroines of this period, so that Louise in *Full Moon in Paris* is determined to assemble men around her in ways that conform to her wishes; or Magali's (Béatrice Romand) friends in *An Autumn Tale* (1998) are determined to find the right man for her in ways that verge on forcing the men on her; or that Sabine (Béatrice Romand) in *A Good Marriage* (1982) is determined to force Edmond (André Dussollier) to love her? Or indeed that Loïc or Maxence – the latter especially – try their best to force Félicie into relationships with them? The sense of forced choices here seems somewhat different from the dilemmas of the earlier cycle of Rohmer's, the 'Moral Tales'. There, male protagonists are presented with dilemmas of choice and temptation, especially in *Love in the Afternoon* (1972) and *My Night with Maud* (1969). Their dilemmas are ones that hinge on making the correct moral choice (these films are perhaps rather too indebted to an existentialist viewpoint). And so too, to some extent, with *Claire's Knee*: Jérôme makes a 'correct' moral choice by merely touching Claire's knee, so that he finds a way in which the world will correspond to his desire. Significantly, via their choices, Frédéric (Bernard Verley) in *Love in the Afternoon* and Jean-Louis (Jean-Louis Trintignant) in *My Night with Maud* also find ways in which their choices correspond to the world; the former by returning to his wife, and the latter by choosing Françoise (Marie-Christine Barrault) over Maud (Françoise Fabian).

We find similar concessions to the world in the later films too. Sabine in *A Good Marriage* remeets the man on the train who had glanced at her in the film's opening scene: in this way, the world, in the form of this man, responds to her. When actively forcing her desire on the world, the world resists – the world 'absents itself', as it were. When Sabine instead takes a passive stance – Rohmer and many critics will call this chance or coincidence – the world responds to her in the form of this man on the train. And so too with Magali in *An Autumn Tale* – with Gérald (Alain Libolt) at the end of that film – or with Delphine in *The Green Ray*: when she least expects it, the world responds to her when she meets a man – quite by chance – at Biarritz train station. And so too, therefore, with Pauline in *Pauline at the Beach*. If Marion is the character who actively tries to force her fantasy on the world, then Pauline is the character who steps back and is passive. And she ends the film with wisdom, in stark contrast to Marion's delusion.

It is significant that, near the end of *Pauline at the Beach*, while Pauline is having dinner with Pierre, she declares that 'No one tolerates other people's choices.' Pierre disapproves of Marion's relationship with Henri; Marion disapproves of Pauline's relationship with Sylvain; and she also cannot bear the thought of a relationship between Henri and Louisette. We might put it this way: Pauline observes these things; she waits for the world to respond. In doing this, she establishes a much closer correspondence to the world than does Marion (or Pierre, or Henri). I think this is a clear moral lesson of *Pauline at the Beach*: do not force your choices onto other people. Rather, wait for the world to respond. Of course, we can see similar themes at play in *Girlfriends and Boyfriends*. Blanche is a very passive character (Rohmer remarks that much of the formation of Emmanuelle Chaulet's acting for the part concerned her capturing this sense of passivity or shyness; a lack of confidence that contrasts with Léa's bold assertiveness).[8] She waits for the world to respond. And so it does in the shape of Fabien. And so too, of course, for Félicie in *A Tale of Winter*. In a most miraculously everyday way, the world eventually corresponds to her when she is reunited with Charles.

How do we conclude here? Am I saying that Bersani is right after all? That a Cartesian subject is one who forces their fantasy on the world in order that the world be made to conform to that fantasy? Thus, to counter the Cartesian subject one must adopt a passive mode of 'correspondence'. One must refuse the temptation to force one's own fantasies on the world and instead wait for the world to exhibit its correspondences. To some extent, that *is* what I mean. And yet, as I have tried to argue throughout this chapter, any correspondence I have with the world will only ever be an *achievement*. My correspondence with the world cannot come automatically. It will not be an ontological given, as Bersani seems to think. Rather, it is something I must create. For Cavell, that creation must open itself to the world in a mode of absolute passivity. *My senses go out*, or *my consciousness goes out* – or both. And that is the only way to avoid imposing my fantasy on the world. If my fantasy is to transcend the inwardness of my own consciousness, then such fantasies must be married to the world.

If this is where we leave Rohmer, then how can Rohmer's position in the 1980s and 1990s be compared with the other examples we have come across in this book? For Rohmer, the question of marriage is far less important than it was for Renoir's *Rules of the Game*, or for Antonioni or Fellini or Varda, or for other filmmakers working in the 1960s, Rohmer's own films included. For the later films, it is not entirely important if these men and women are married or not, nor does it matter if they are divorced. These social or cultural taboos are no longer of great relevance. At the same time, a sense of the genuineness and worth of love, of relationships in which one human being can be said to love another: these are themes that Rohmer treats with great seriousness. Mary Harrod sums all of this up very succinctly by stating that these themes 'include a recurrent concern with the (a)synchronization of self and other; the narrative promotion of female subjectivity; a stress on the role of coincidence, wonder, and playfulness in self-realization through love; the staging of romance in a place marked as outside the everyday; and an ostensible championing of commitment to another person, the love object' (Harrod 2014, 102).[9] The themes central to this book are played out in Rohmer's films, whether this be a matter of Sellier's claim that 'each person is constructed through the encounter with another' (Sellier 2008, 219), or by way of Badiou's formulation that 'What is universal is that all love suggests a new experience of truth about what it is to be two and not one' (Badiou 2012, 39).

There are many things I have failed to do in this book, and one of them is to give sufficient space to the question of *conversations between women*. This is an issue that came up first of all in my discussion of *The Rules of the Game* and was furthered by my analysis of *Smiles of a Summer Night* and, to some extent, *La notte*. The key film to feature a friendship between women over the course of this book has been Varda's *One Sings, the Other Doesn't*. And it is Rohmer's late films that feature a wonderful range of friendships between women – the friends in *A Good Marriage*; Blanche and Léa in *Girlfriends and Boyfriends*; Reinette (Joëlle Miquel) and Mirabelle (Jessica Forde) in *The Four Adventures of Reinette and Mirabelle* (1987); Rosine (Alexia Portal) and Isabelle (Marie Rivière), who are good friends to Magali in *An Autumn Tale*; and the sometimes strained friendship between Jeanne (Anne Teyssèdre) and Natacha (Florence Darel) in *A Tale of Springtime* (1990). Bersani and Dutoit foreground such contacts between women in their essay on Rohmer by calling it an '*other* eroticism', the 'nonsexual sexuality', they add with reference to *Pauline at the Beach*, 'of an affectionate, mildly teasing friendship' (Bersani and Dutoit 2009, 29).

If nothing else, Rohmer's ability to depict conversations between women marks a contrast with several of the other male film directors featured in this book. It was with Truffaut, Fellini and Godard that the power of men over women, and the exploitation of women by men, became a significant issue, with Truffaut's *The Man Who Loved Women* and Fellini's *City of Women* presenting the most troubling cases. Rhetorically I have done my best to foreground acknowledgment and connectedness as being of great importance for human happiness. But I have also, I hope, made it clear that these are exceptionally difficult achievements for human beings to manage. Men, it seems to me, if we believe the filmmakers on view in this book, have made these achievements inordinately difficult. As we saw from the research of Luce Irigaray, men tend to favour relationships with objects, while women crave communication and friendship with other subjects. The social or cultural conditioning of men seems almost destined to provoke these outcomes – outcomes that retard acknowledgment. It remains clear to me that substantial transformations in gender relations must still be called for, even twenty or more years on from Rohmer's late films. I believe cinema has a role to play in these transformations.

Seeing the world from the perspective of two rather than one, but also rather than three or four ... Perhaps that is what Rohmer shows us: some connections are positive, while others are negative. Part of the struggle of what it is to be human is to figure out which connections are positive and which are not. At the limit, the positive connections can lead to what Cavell calls a 'best case of acknowledgment', and thus to the sense of a shared world and a shared identity (of two rather than one). Here 'I' is no longer a singular 'I', but it is an I that is split and made up of its connections with another I. That is the experience of being two rather than one. And this mode of connection is one that foregrounds difference: an I that is contrasted by way of a twoness that is beyond the control of the singular I. Such an I must other itself; make itself other than it is ('My senses go out'). And it will be doing this constantly. That is passivity. It is also a way out of narcissism and loneliness.

Bersani does not offer these options whereby some connections are positive and others are not. Rather, he argues that connection is all, as though there can never be any negative connections. I have referred to such claims as being utopian, for it is indeed a wonderful dream to believe that all of our connections will be positive ones. But that is not my world – it is not a human world I know of. The human world is full of the tragedies of misconnection, rejection and horror, as much as it is full of conditions of mastery, control and cruelty. Those negatives cannot be magicked away by an appeal to the grace of connectedness. Perhaps, more than anything else, it is the negatives and tragedies of human disconnectedness that allow us to discern the joys and fulfilments of being positively connected, however rare and precious those connections are.

And what of marriage? In Rohmer's later films, marriage is no longer at stake. And yet couples – being two rather than one – are very much at stake. It may be that a new language is necessary in order to mark this change. If it is a shift which tells us that something like 'marriage' is no longer at stake, then perhaps also the term 'remarriage' needs to be dispensed with. Terms like acknowledgment, mutual recognition (or reciprocal recognition) and equality remain, it seems to me, of significance, but perhaps our present task is to imagine these as ones that are no longer tied to marriage or remarriage. These changes also beg the question of the relationship between love and friendship. I have focused at many points in this book on Emerson's statement on friendship – 'Two may talk and one may hear, but three cannot take part in a conversation of the most sincere and searching sort' (Emerson 1898, 54) – while I have also ignored his essay on 'Love' (I do not know what to make of it). Given the importance in this book of elaborating conversations between women – let us call this friendship – nowhere more evident than in the friendship between Suzanne and Pomme in Varda's *One Sings, the Other Doesn't*, as well as in the crucial roles given to female friendships in Rohmer's films, then there must be some way of charting the terrain that both divides and joins friendship and love. That such distinctions have something to do with sex must surely be beyond question: the joyous sex between Félicie and Charles in *A Tale of Winter* assures me of such, as much as I imagine the sex between X and A in *Last Year in Marienbad* to have been central for that film's concerns – and so too for most of the other films mentioned in this book. But these are questions I cannot answer here.

My conceptualisation of this project has primarily hinged on the philosophical positions of two male thinkers, Stanley Cavell and Leo Bersani. I am therefore keen to end with words from female thinkers who have been utilised in this book, though perhaps not as extensively as they might have been. I do not want so much to comment on these claims but, rather, to leave the final words to these voices.

I have relied at various points on ideas put forward by Julia Kristeva in *Tales of Love* (and, to a lesser extent, her *Black Sun*). Kristeva has also, among her many publications, co-written a book on marriage with her novelist husband, Philippe Sollers, a book called *Marriage as a Fine Art* (*beaux-arts*). The book is a scattered collection of reflections and interviews, but some of its claims strike me as significant. Some examples: 'Love is the full recognition of the other in their otherness' (Kristeva and Sollers 2016, 1). This otherness is not at all straightforward, and Kristeva will go on to claim that 'The deal therefore is to love a contradiction' (Kristeva and Sollers 2016, 1). Kristeva will bolster such ideas by claiming that there is no such thing as romantic 'fusion'. As for marriage, she argues that 'There is no possible meaning to any marriage other than *singular*' (Kristeva and Sollers 2016, xi). In other words, there are no universal rules one can establish for marriage. Rather, each and every marriage has to be constructed for itself, on its own terms, the terms that the couple itself constructs. She will add that 'the *endurance of the couple in time* is a permanent composition, in the musical sense, implying the tact necessary for recognizing the foreignness of the other and the self and allowing that to flourish. Not swallowing up the other in a pseudo fusion that ultimately proves to be dominated by the narcissism of one partner alone, either the man or the woman, but continuing to construct the difference, even the foreignness, of the partner' (Kristeva and Sollers 2016, 82).

For Luce Irigaray – used far too sparingly in this book – what is philosophically at stake from a feminist perspective is the need to define the specificity of gender. Gender means, for the Irigaray of these books (*I Love to You, Democracy Begins with Two*), men and women. Human subjectivity has typically been defined in terms of the male, so Irigaray pursues the hope that a revolution of sorts will occur in which there will be a complete recalibration of the definition of 'woman', and thus also of the human. Men, too, must be part of this revolution, and Irigaray places great stress on the role that love between men and women will play in this revolution. All of this necessitates *mediation* between men and women (Irigaray 1996, 5), an 'alliance between the genders' (Irigaray 1996, 15). To add, 'The couple forms the elementary social community. It is where sensible desire becomes potentially universal culture, where the gender of the man and of the woman may become the model of male human kind or of female human kind while keeping to the singular task of being *this* man or *this* woman' (Irigaray 1996, 28).

And a word for a British philosopher, Mary Midgley, a writer not usually associated with feminism, but whose late writings offer an excellent bird's-eye view of a range of issues, even though I have not used any of her thoughts so far in this book. I offer the claim below as a final repudiation of Bersani's attempts to de-subjectivise subjectivity by way of 'connectedness' or the notion of the 'aesthetic' subject. I might also take it as a final definition of what Cavell means by *acknowledgment*. This is Midgley's claim:

> subjectivity is not just a term of abuse. It is an objective fact about the world. It is true that we each do our thinking separately and subjectively. Our imaginations have to work hard to bring us together sufficiently to believe in a shared world, which we can then see as *intersubjective*, or *objective*. (Midgley 2018, 170)

Finally, a word from Simone de Beauvoir, a writer whose thoughts have been used sparingly in the text of this book, but whose thoughts have shadowed it throughout in ways that I have been unable to incorporate. 'Let both men and women overcome their distrust, and they will find that it is possible to restore, in freedom and equality, the human pair' (de Beauvoir 2015, 79).

Notes

1. Emerson (2001b, 269) states, 'So far as a man thinks, he is free.'
2. See my arguments in Rushton 2011, 106–25.
3. I query such a claim: *A Good Marriage* features its main character, Sabine, remeeting a man on a train whom she had first laid eyes on at the film's beginning. The implication is that a romance may ensue, and I would call that a happy ending. *The Green Ray* ends very similarly, with Delphine meeting a man, Jacques (Vincent Gauthier), while waiting at Biarritz railway station, all measured by the miraculous green flash of the setting sun (see Leigh's description, 2012, 136–7). *An Autumn Tale* ends with the prospect that Magali will pursue a romance with Gérald. There are other examples: *Claire's Knee*, *My Night with Maud*, *The Aviator's Wife* (1981).
4. Bersani makes extensive use of *Phaedrus* in *Intimacies* (Bersani and Phillips 2008, 77–87) to propose a theory of love.
5. To me, Cavell is a little wide of the mark here. Apart from *A Tale of Winter*, his only other example is *The Green Ray*. One might argue, of course, that there are 'small' transcendences by way of chance and coincidence in many of Rohmer's films.
6. Rohmer (2013, 112) has commented on this. 'My characters can be wise or "mad". It's never madness as such, but a sort of exaltation, a spiritual fervour, the refusal of a flat reality, sometimes even a Don Quixotesque madness. I think Félicie has this kind of gentle madness.'

7 Leigh (2012, 51) writes that '*L'amour, l'aprés-midi* [made in 1972] acknowledges the changing roles of women in French society, taking marriage and male responsibility as topics. It is a film about the difficulty of marriage in a society where marriage has lost its status as a social, legal or religious pre-requisite for a sexual relationship.'
8 Rohmer makes these claims in a television interview included in the 2017 Arrow Films Blu-ray release of *My Girlfriend's Boyfriend* (*Girlfriends and Boyfriends*). Also see the account in De Baecque and Herpe 2016, 376–8.
9 Also see Handyside 2010.

References

Alpert, H. (1987) *Fellini: A Life*, London: W. H. Allen.
Althusser, L. (1971) 'Ideology and Ideological State Apparatuses (Notes Towards an Investigation)', in *Lenin and Philosophy and Other Essays*, trans. Ben Brewster, New York: Monthly Review Press, 85–126.
Badiou, A. (2012) *In Praise of Love*, trans. P. Bush, London: Serpent's Tail.
Bergman, I. (1960) *Four Screenplays of Ingmar Bergman*, New York: Simon and Schuster.
Bergman, I. (2007) *Ingmar Bergman: Interviews*, Jackson: University Press of Mississippi.
Bersani, L. (1995) *Homos*, Cambridge, MA: Harvard University Press.
Bersani, L. (2010a) 'Is the Rectum a Grave?' in *Is the Rectum a Grave and Other Essays*, Chicago: University of Chicago Press, 3–30.
Bersani, L. (2010b) 'Against Monogamy', in *Is the Rectum a Grave and Other Essays*, Chicago: University of Chicago Press, 85–101.
Bersani, L. (2010c) 'Psychoanalysis and the Aesthetic Subject', in *Is the Rectum a Grave and Other Essays*, Chicago: University of Chicago Press, 139–53.
Bersani, L. (2010d) 'The Will to Know', in *Is the Rectum a Grave and Other Essays*, Chicago: University of Chicago Press, 154–67 (this essay is partially co-written with U. Dutoit).
Bersani, L. (2015) *Thoughts and Things*, Chicago: University of Chicago Press.
Bersani, L. (2018) *Receptive Bodies*, Chicago: University of Chicago Press.
Bersani, L. and Dutoit, U. (1994) *Arts of Impoverishment: Beckett, Rothko, Resnais*, Cambridge, MA: Harvard University Press.
Bersani, L. and Dutoit, U. (2004) *Forms of Being: Cinema, Aesthetics, Subjectivity*, London: BFI.
Bersani, L. and Dutoit, U. (2009) 'Rohmer's Salon', *Film Quarterly* 63: 1, 23–35.
Bersani, L. and Dutoit, U. (2010) 'The Will to Know', in *Is the Rectum a Grave and Other Essays*, Chicago: University of Chicago Press, 163–7.
Bersani, L. and Phillips, A. (2008) *Intimacies*, Chicago: University of Chicago Press.
Bondanella, P. (1992) *The Cinema of Federico Fellini*, Princeton: Princeton University Press.
Bordwell, D. (1989) *Making Meaning: Inference and Rhetoric in the Interpretation of Cinema*, Cambridge, MA.: Harvard University Press.
Brody, R. (2008) *Everything Is Cinema: The Working Life of Jean-Luc Godard*, New York: Metropolitan Books.

Brunette, P. (1998) *The Films of Michelangelo Antonioni*, Cambridge: Cambridge University Press.

Burke, F. and Waller, W. (eds) (2002) *Federico Fellini: Contemporary Perspectives*, Toronto: University of Toronto Press.

Cavell, S. (1979a) *The World Viewed: Reflections on the Ontology of Film*, enlarged edition, Cambridge, MA and London: Harvard University Press.

Cavell, S. (1979b) *The Claim of Reason: Wittgenstein, Skepticism, Morality, and Tragedy*, New York: Oxford University Press.

Cavell, S. (1981) *Pursuits of Happiness: The Hollywood Comedy of Remarriage*, Cambridge, MA: Harvard University Press.

Cavell, S. (1996) *Contesting Tears: The Hollywood Melodrama of the Unknown Woman*, Chicago: University of Chicago Press.

Cavell, S. (2002) 'Knowing and Acknowledging', in *Must We Mean What We Say? A Book of Essays*, 2nd edn, Cambridge: Cambridge University Press, 2202–45.

Cavell, S. (2003) *Disowning Knowledge in Seven Plays of Shakespeare*, updated edition, New York: Cambridge University Press.

Cavell, S. (2004) *Cities of Words: Pedagogical Letters on a Register of the Moral Life*, Cambridge, MA: Harvard University Press.

Cavell, S. (2005a) 'What Becomes of Things on Film?' in W. Rothman (ed.), *Cavell on Film*, New York: SUNY Press, 1–10.

Cavell, S. (2005b) '*Prénom*: Marie', in W. Rothman (ed.), *Cavell on Film*, New York: SUNY Press, 175–82.

Cavell, S. (2005c) 'Seasons of Love: Bergman's *Smiles of a Summer Night* and *The Winter's Tale*', in W. Rothman (ed.), *Cavell on Film*, New York: SUNY Press, 193–204.

Cavell, S. (2005d) 'On Eric Rohmer's *A Tale of Winter*', in W. Rothman (ed.), *Cavell on Film*, New York: SUNY Press, 287–94.

Cavell, S. (2010a) 'Emerson's Constitutional Amending: Reading "Fate"', in J. Hodge (ed.), *Emerson's Transcendental Études*, Stanford, CA: Stanford University Press, 192–214.

Cavell, S. (2010b) *Little Did I Know: Excerpts from Memory*, Stanford, CA: Stanford University Press.

Chatman, S. (1985) *Antonioni, or The Surface of the World*, Berkeley: University of California Press.

Constable, C. (2011) 'Seeing Lucy's Perspective: Returning to Cavell, Wittgenstein and "The Awful Truth"', *New Review of Film and Television Studies* 9: 3, 358–75.

Conway, K. (2015) *Agnès Varda*, Urbana: University of Illinois Press.

Coontz, S. (2005) *Marriage: A History, From Obedience to Intimacy or How Love Conquered Marriage*, New York: Viking.

Cooper, M. G. (2003) *Love Rules: Silent Hollywood and the Rise of the Managerial Class*, Minneapolis: University of Minnesota Press.

Cowie, P. (1982) *Ingmar Bergman: A Critical Biography*, New York: Secker & Warburg.

De Baecque, A. and Herpe, N. (2016) *Éric Rohmer: A Biography*, New York: Columbia University Press.

References

De Baecque, A. and Toubiana, S. (1999) *Truffaut: A Biography*, New York: Knopf.
de Beauvoir, S. (1976) *The Ethics of Ambiguity*, trans. B. Frechtman, New York: Citadel Press.
de Beauvoir, S. (2009) *The Second Sex*, trans. C. Borde and S. Maloney-Chevallier, London: Jonathan Cape.
de Beauvoir, S. (2015) *Feminist Writings*, ed. M. A. Simons and M. Timmerman, Urbana: University of Illinois Press.
Deleuze, G. (1989) *Cinema 2: The Time-Image*, trans. H. Tomlinson and R. Galeta, London: Athlone, 1989.
De Tocqueville, A. (2003) *Democracy in America and Two Essays on America*, trans. G. E. Bevan, ed. I. Kramnick, London: Penguin.
DeRoo, R. J. (2018) *Agnès Varda: Between Film, Photography, and Art*, Oakland: University of California Press.
DiBattista, M. (2001) *Fast-Talking Dames*, New Haven: Yale University Press.
Due, R. (2013) *Love in Motion: Erotic Relationships in Film*, New York: Columbia University Press.
Durgnat, R. (1975) *Jean Renoir*, London: Studio Vista.
Ecolivet-Herzog, B. (1977) 'The New French Divorce Law', *International Lawyer* 11: 3, 483–99.
Elsaesser, T. (2005) *European Cinema: Face to Face with Hollywood*, Amsterdam: Amsterdam University Press.
Emerson, R. W. (1898) 'Friendship', in *The Complete Prose Works of Ralph Waldo Emerson*, London: Ward, Lock & Co., 50–7.
Emerson, R. W. (2001a) 'Self-Reliance', in *Emerson's Prose and Poetry*, New York: Norton, 120–37.
Emerson, R. W. (2001b) 'Fate', in *Emerson's Prose and Poetry*, New York: Norton, 261–79.
Fabe, M. (2004) *Closely Watched Films: An Introduction to the Art of Narrative Film Technique*, Oakland: University of California Press.
Fellini, F. (1995) *Fellini on Fellini*, ed. C. Constantini, London: Faber.
Flitterman-Lewis, S. (1990) *To Desire Differently: Feminism and the French Cinema*, Urbana: University of Illinois Press.
Foucault, M. (1970) *The Order of Things: An Archaeology of the Human Sciences*, trans. A. Sheridan, London: Tavistock.
Foucault, M. (1985) *The Use of Pleasure: The History of Sexuality Volume 2*, trans. R. Hurley, New York: Random House.
Foucault, M. (1986) *The Care of the Self: The History of Sexuality Volume 3*, trans. R. Hurley, New York: Random House.
Foucault, M. (2005) *The Hermeneutics of the Subject, Lectures at the Collège de France, 1981–2*, trans. G. Burchell, Basingstoke: Palgrave Macmillan
Foucault, M. (2010) *The Government of Self and Others, Lectures at the Collège de France, 1982–3*, trans. G. Burchell, Basingstoke: Palgrave Macmillan.
Freud, S. (1977) 'The Dissolution of the Oedipus Complex', in *On Sexuality: Three Essays on the Theory of Sexuality and Other Works*, London: Penguin, 313–22.

Freud, S. (1984a) 'On Narcissism: An Introduction', in *On Metapsychology: The Theory of Psychoanalysis*, London: Penguin, 59–97.

Freud, S. (1984b) 'Mourning and Melancholia', in *On Metapsychology: The Theory of Psychoanalysis*, London: Penguin, 245–68.

Freud, S. (1990) 'Some Character-types Met with in Psychoanalytic Work', in *Sigmund Freud: Art and Literature*, London: Penguin, 291–319.

Freud, S. (1991) *Civilization and its Discontents*, in *Civilization, Society and Religion*, London: Penguin, 243–340.

Freud, S. (2002) 'Observations on Love in Transference', in *Wild Analysis*, trans. A. Bance, London: Penguin, 65–79.

Fullbrook, E. and Fullbrook, K. (2008) *Sex and Philosophy: Rethinking De Beauvoir and Sartre*, London: Continuum.

Gillain, A. (2013) *François Truffaut: The Lost Secret*, trans. A. Fox, Bloomington: Indiana University Press.

Glitre, K. (2006) *Hollywood Romantic Comedy: States of the Union, 1934–65*, Manchester: Manchester University Press.

Green, A. (2001) *Life Narcissism, Death Narcissism*, trans. A. Weller, London: Free Association.

Handyside, F. (2010) 'Love and Desire in Eric Rohmer's "Comedies and Proverbs" and "Tales of the Four Seasons"', *Senses of Cinema* 54 (online).

Harrod, M. (2014) 'Auteur Meets Genre: Rohmer and Rom-Com', in L. Anderst (ed.), *The Films of Eric Rohmer*, Basingstoke: Palgrave Macmillan.

Hegel, G. W. F. (1977) *Hegel's Phenomenology of Spirit*, trans. A. V. Miller, New York and London: Oxford University Press.

Hegel, G. W. F. (1991) *Elements of the Philosophy of Right*, Cambridge: Cambridge University Press.

Higgins, L. A. (1991) 'Screen/Memory: Rape and Its Alibis in L. A. Higgins and B. R. Silver (eds), *Last Year at Marienbad*', in *Rape and Representation*, New York: Columbia University Press, 303–22.

Holmes, D. and Ingram, R. (1998) *François Truffaut*, Manchester: Manchester University Press.

Ibsen, H. (1958) *Rosmersholm*, in *The Master Builder and Other Plays*, Harmondsworth: Penguin, 27–119.

Insdorf, A. (1994) *François Truffaut*, New York: Cambridge University Press.

Irigaray, L. (1980) 'When Our Lips Speak Together', *Signs* 6: 1, 69–79.

Irigaray, L. (1996) *I Love to You: A Sketch for a Felicity within History*, trans. A. Martin, New York: Routledge.

Irigaray, L. (2000) *Democracy Begins Between Two*, trans. K. Anderson, London: Athlone.

Jameson, F. (2010) *The Hegel Variations*, London: New Left Books.

Jeffers McDonald, T. (2013) *Doris Day Confidential: Hollywood, Sex, and Stardom*, London: I. B. Tauris.

Kirkpatrick, K. (2019) *Becoming Beauvoir: A Life*, London: Bloomsbury.

Klein, M. (1986) 'Notes on Some Schizoid Mechanisms (1946)', in Juliet Mitchell (ed.), *The Selected Melanie Klein*, London: Hogarth Press, 175–200.

Kline, T. J. (1992) 'Rebecca's *Bad* Dream: Speculations on/in Resnais's *Marienbad*', in *Screening the Text: Intertextuality in New Wave Cinema*, Baltimore: Johns Hopkins University Press, 54–86.

Kovács, A. B. (2007) *Screening Modernism: European Art Cinema, 1950–1980*, Chicago: University of Chicago Press.

Kristeva, J. (1987) *Tales of Love*, trans. L. S. Roudiez, New York: Columbia University Press.

Kristeva, J. (1989) *Black Sun: Depression and Melancholia*, trans. L. S. Roudiez, New York: Columbia University Press.

Kristeva, J. and Sollers, P. (2016) *Marriage as a Fine Art*, trans. L. S. Fox, New York: Columbia University Press.

Lacan, J. (1977a) *The Four Fundamental Concepts of Psychoanalysis*, trans. A. Sheridan, London: The Hogarth Press.

Lacan, J. (1977b) 'Desire and the Interpretation of Desire in *Hamlet*', trans. J. Hulbert, *Yale French Studies* 55/56, 13–52.

Lacan, J. (1992) *The Ethics of Psychoanalysis, The Seminar of Jacques Lacan Book VII*, trans. D. Porter, London: Routledge.

Lacan, J. (2006) 'The Function and Field of Speech and Language in Psychoanalysis', in *Écrits: The First Complete Edition in English*, trans. B. Fink, New York: Norton, 197–268.

Lacan, J. (2015) *Transference: The Seminar of Jacques Lacan, Book VIII*, trans. B. Fink, Cambridge, UK: Polity.

Lacan, J. (2019) *Desire and Its Interpretation, The Seminar of Jacques Lacan Book VI*, trans. B. Fink, Cambridge, UK: Polity.

Laplanche, J. (1999) 'A Short Treatise on the Unconscious', in *Essays on Otherness*, London: Routledge, 84–116.

Lapsley, R. and Westlake, M. (1993) 'From *Casablanca* to *Pretty Woman*: The Politics of Romance', in A. Easthope (ed), *Contemporary Film Theory*, London: Longman, 179–202.

Leigh, J. (2012) *The Cinema of Eric Rohmer: Irony, Imagination, and the Social World*, London: Continuum.

Loshitzky, Y. (1995) *The Radical Faces of Godard and Bertolucci*, Detroit, MI: Wayne State University Press.

MacCabe, C. and Mulvey, L. (1980) 'Images of Women, Images of Sexuality', in C. McCabe, M. Eaton and L. Mulvey (eds) *Godard: Images, Sounds, Politics*, London: Macmillan, 79–104.

McDowell, J. (1996) *Mind and World*, 2nd edn, Cambridge, MA: Harvard University Press.

McGowan, T. (2015) *Psychoanalytic Film Theory and the Rules of the Game*, New York: Bloomsbury.

Midgley, M. (2018) *What is Philosophy For?* London: Bloomsbury.

Minuz, A. (2015) *Political Fellini: Journey to the End of Italy*, trans. M. Perriman, London: Berghahn Books.

Missero, D. (2022) *Women, Feminism and Italian Cinema: Archives from a Film Culture*, Edinburgh: Edinburgh University Press.

Moi, T. (2006) *Henrik Ibsen and the Birth of Modernism: Art, Theater, Philosophy*, Oxford: Oxford University Press.

Moi, T. (2008) *Simone de Beauvoir: The Making of an Intellectual Woman*, New York: Oxford University Press.

Moi, T. (2010) 'The Adventure of Reading: Literature and Philosophy, Cavell and Beauvoir', *Literature and Theology* 25: 2, 125–40.

Moi, T. (2017) *Revolution of the Ordinary: Literary Studies after Wittgenstein, Austin, and Cavell*, Chicago: University of Chicago Press.

Morgan, D. (2013) *Late Godard and the Possibilities of Cinema*, Berkeley: University of California Press.

Morrey, D. (2003) 'History of Resistance/Resistance of History: Godard's *Eloge de L'amour* (2001)', *Studies in French Cinema* 3: 2, 121–30.

Mulvey, L. (1989) 'Visual Pleasure and Narrative Cinema', *Visual and Other Pleasures*, London: Macmillan, 14–26.

Mulvey, L. (2019) 'The Decline and Fall of Hollywood According to Jean-Luc Godard's *Le mépris*', in *Afterimages: On Cinema, Women and Changing Times*, London: Reaktion, 72–87.

Murray, E. (1976) *Fellini the Artist*, New York: Ungar.

Neupert, R. (2007) *A History of the French New Wave*, 2nd edn, Madison: University of Wisconsin Press.

Nowell-Smith, G. (2008) *Making Waves: New Cinemas of the 1960s*, New York: Continuum.

Passerini, L., Labyani, J. and Diehl, K. (eds) (2012) *Europe and Love in Cinema*, Bristol: Intellect.

Petrie, G. (1970) *The Cinema of François Truffaut*, New York: A. S. Barnes.

Pippin, R. B. (2019) *Hegel's Realm of Shadows: Logic as Metaphysics in the Science of Logic*, Chicago: Chicago University Press.

Plato (1938) *Symposium, Five Dialogues of Plato*, trans. M. Joyce, London: J. M. Dent, 17–81.

Renoir, J. (1974) *My Life and My Films*, London: Collins.

Resnais, A. (1970) 'Alain Resnais and Richard Roud from an Interview', in *The Rules of the Game, A Film by Jean Renoir*, London: Lorimer, 14–15.

Rohdie, S. (1990) *Antonioni*, London: BFI.

Rohmer, E. (2013) *Eric Rohmer: Interviews*, ed. F. Handyside, Jackson: University Press of Mississippi.

Ross, K. (1995) *Fast Cars, Clean Bodies: Decolonization and the Reordering of French Culture*, London: MIT Press.

Rushton, R. (2011) *The Reality of Film: Theories of Filmic Reality*, Manchester: Manchester University Press.

Rushton, R. (2013) *The Politics of Hollywood Cinema: Popular Film and Contemporary Political Theory*, Basingstoke: Palgrave Macmillan.

Sedgwick, E. K. (1994) 'The Beast in the Closet: Henry James and the Writing of Homosexual Panic', in *Epistemology of the Closet*, Harmondsworth: Penguin, 182–212.

Sellier, G. (2008) *Masculine Singular: French New Wave Cinema*, trans. K. Ross, London: Duke University Press.

Shumway, D. (2003) *Modern Love: Romance, Intimacy, and the Marriage Crisis*, New York: New York University Press.

Smith, A. (1998) *Agnès Varda*, Manchester: Manchester University Press.

Sparrow, T. (2014) *The End of Phenomenology: Metaphysics and the New Realism*, Edinburgh: Edinburgh University Press.

Sterritt, D. (1999) *The Films of Jean-Luc Godard: Seeing the Invisible*, New York: Cambridge University Press.

Thoreau, H. (2008) 'Civil Disobedience', in W. Rossi (ed.), *Walden, Civil Disobedience, and Other Writings*, New York: Norton, 227–46.

Truffaut, F. (2014) *The Films in My Life*, Newburyport: Diversion.

Varda, A. (2014a) 'Agnès Varda: The Hour of Truth (1962)', in T. J. Kline (ed.), *Agnès Varda: Interviews*, Jackson: University Press of Mississippi, 17–22.

Varda, A. (2014b) 'A Secular Grace: Agnès Varda (1965)', in T. J. Kline (ed.), *Agnès Varda: Interviews*, Jackson: University Press of Mississippi, 23–37.

Varda, A. (2014c) 'Interview with Agnès Varda (1967)', in T. J. Kline (ed.), *Agnès Varda: Interviews*, Jackson: University Press of Mississippi, 38–40.

Varda, A. (2014d) 'Agnès Varda Talks about the Cinema (1975)', in T. J. Kline (ed.), *Agnès Varda: Interviews*, Jackson: University Press of Mississippi, 64–77.

Varda, A. (2014e) 'Agnès Varda (1977)', in T. J. Kline (ed.), *Agnès Varda: Interviews*, Jackson: University Press of Mississippi, 89–91.

Varda, A. (2014f) 'Agnès Varda: A Conversation (1986)', in T. J. Kline (ed.), *Agnès Varda: Interviews*, Jackson: University Press of Mississippi, 126–38.

Waller, M. (2020) '"*Il Maestro*" Dismantles the Master's House: Fellini's Undoing of Gender and Sexuality', in F. Burke, M. Waller and M. Gubareva (eds), *A Companion to Federico Fellini*, Hoboken, NJ: Wiley-Blackwell, 311–30.

Wheatley, C. (2019) *Stanley Cavell and Film: Scepticism and Self-Reliance at the Cinema*, London: Bloomsbury.

Wilson, E. (2006) *Alain Resnais*, Manchester: Manchester University Press.

Index

Adam's Rib (Cukor) 55
ágalma (Lacan) 61, 62, 74, 82, 83, 189, 215, 229
Aimée, Anouk 15, 176, 181
Albertazzi, Giorgio 91, 95
Alpert, Hollis 197
Althusser, Louis 4, 108
Amants, Les (Malle) 92–4, 97, 102, 104
Anderson, Judith 50
Andersson, Bibi 17, 80
Andersson, Harriet 8, 53, 76
Antonioni, Michelangelo 1, 3, 6, 7, 8, 14 n.1., 16, 30, 42, 56, 73, 116–136, 138, 139, 140, 143, 161, 176, 181, 182, 210, 212, 217, 237, 241
   Amiche, Le 1, 118–26
   Avventurra L' 8, 14, 117, 119, 126–8, 134, 135 n. 4, 138, 161, 212
   Blow-Up 138
   Eclisse, L' 1, 117, 128–30, 133, 138, 161
   Grido, Il 8, 117, 119
   Lady without Camellias, The 120–2
   Notte, La 1, 8, 14 n. 1, 16, 116, 117, 120, 128, 130–5, 136, 138, 161, 182, 193, 195, 242
   Red Desert 1, 117–19, 120, 135 n. 2, 136, 138, 161, 217
   Story of a Love Affair 1, 120
Ardant, Fanny 166
Arditi, Pierre 112
Arrighi, Nike 163
Atkine Féodor 237

Auffey, Patrick 158
Aumont, Jean-Pierre 171
Austen, Jane 21, 124
Awful Truth, The (McCarey) 9, 13, 15, 18, 21–5, 27, 28, 29, 31 n. 3, 56, 57, 66 n. 3, 69, 140, 181, 190–2, 193, 195, 198, 213
Azéma, Sabine 112
Aznavour, Charles 180

Badiou, Alain 4, 47, 86, 132, 133, 137, 190, 191, 193, 210, 216, 241
Balzac, Honoré de 170
Bardot, Brigitte 5, 25, 30, 200, 203
Barrault, Marie-Christine 240
Bartoleschi, Valerio 119
Baye, Nathalie 163
Beauvoir, Simone de 151, 157 n. 2, n. 3, 245
Beethoven, Ludwig van 219
Bellamy, Ralph 190
Belmondo, Jean-Paul 166, 200
Benedetti, Nelly 165
Berbet, Marcel 168
Bergman, Ingmar 1, 3, 6, 7, 8, 12, 13, 17, 30, 32, 42, 49–89, 90 n.8, 92, 93, 94, 109, 114, 122, 129, 131, 140, 143, 157, 161, 170, 176, 182, 183, 184, 210, 211, 230, 237, 239
   Autumn Sonata 67, 79
   Cries and Whispers 67, 79
   Dreams 79
   Lesson in Love, A 1, 67–8, 79
   Passion of Anna, The 8, 54, 57, 67–76, 80, 81, 84, 86–9, 90 n. 6,

92, 109, 114, 124, 125, 131, 161, 170, 183, 184, 197
Persona 8, 67, 79
Scenes from a Marriage 17, 67, 93–4
Silence, The 79
Smiles of a Summer Night 1, 32, 49–59, 62–9, 72, 73, 79, 80, 82, 83, 85, 87, 89, 91, 93, 122, 124, 135, 150, 161, 211, 213, 237, 239, 241
Summer Interlude 1, 67, 75–7, 79, 82, 83, 230
Summer with Monika 8, 58, 76–7, 83, 230
Through a Glass Darkly 79
To Joy 67, 75, 77, 79, 82, 83
Virgin Spring, The 57
Waiting Women 67
Winter Light 67, 79–80
Bergman, Ingrid 69, 114
Bersani, Leo 11, 12, 13, 14 n. 9, 18, 27–31, 47, 57, 86, 130, 137–8, 144, 150, 152, 154, 155, 158, 160, 161, 164, 165, 167, 169, 174, 175, 177, 178, 179, 184, 188–90, 192, 193, 197, 198 n. 2, 201, 202–9, 216, 217, 223–9, 233, 234, 236–9, 241–3, 245 n. 4
Homos 223–4
Forms of Being 12, 13, 27–8, 137, 150, 164, 177, 189, 202, 226
Thoughts and Things 13, 86, 137, 154, 160–1, 177–8, 184, 189, 190, 198 n. 2, 206, 236, 238, 239
Receptive Bodies 13, 14 n. 9, 138, 154, 165, 189, 236
Birkin, Jane 115
Bisset, Jacqueline 163
Bjelvenstam, Björn 53
Björnstand, Gunnar 49, 52, 79
Bondanella, Peter 183, 207
Bonitzer, Pascal 138
Bonnaffé, Jacques 211
Bonnaire, Sandrine 140
Borgeaud, Nelly 113
Bory, Jean-Marc 92
Bosé, Lucia 120

Boursellier, Antoine 142
Boyer, Charles 69, 114
Boyer, Marie-France 136, 139, 144
Boyle, Marc 163
Brecht, Brechtian 81, 88, 152, 205
Brialy, Jean-Claude 227
Britt-Nilsson, Maj 76, 77
Brody, Richard 217, 220 n. 3, 221 n. 12
Brosse, Simon de la 222, 237
Brunette, Peter 8, 127, 138
Burke, Frank 198 n. 1

Camp, Cécile 220 n. 5
Capra, Frank 31 n. 4
Cardinale, Claudia 15, 185
Carette, Julien 36
Carlquist, Margit 53
Carmen Jones (Preminger) 210
Casadei, Yvonna 187
Cavell, Stanley
Claim of Reason, The 10, 59, 65, 66 n. 2, 77, 137, 235
Cities of Words 12, 60, 90 n. 6, 98, 123, 126, 135 n. 3, 230, 231
Contesting Tears 20, 31 n. 2, 41, 55, 69, 73, 98, 114, 223
Disowning Knowledge 65, 66, 78, 86, 183, 209, 236
'Emerson's Constitutional Amending' 72
'Knowing and Acknowledging' 10
Little Did I Know 117
'On Eric Rohmer's *A Tale of Winter*' 12, 230, 233, 234, 235, 237, 238
Pursuits of Happiness 5, 18, 22, 24, 25, 31 n. 4, 32, 54, 57, 59, 60, 66 n. 1, 84, 90 n. 5, 114, 141, 182, 190–1, 193, 220 n. 10, 232
'*Prénom: Marie*' 12, 204, 212, 214
'Seasons of Love' 12, 51, 53, 54, 59, 66 n. 1, 128, 239
'What Becomes of Things on Film?' 234
The World Viewed 12, 40, 44, 47, 62, 89, 203, 218, 225
Chatman, Seymour 117, 126, 130
Chaulet, Emmanuale 227, 240
Checchi, Andrea 120

Chionetti, Carlo 118
Cochran, Steve 8, 119
Colbert, Claudette 59
communication 8, 55, 58, 71, 84, 91,
    107, 111–14, 128–9, 133, 139,
    142, 153–4, 161, 170, 174, 187,
    195, 213, 242
Compton, Joyce 141
connectedness 1, 11–12, 13, 27, 29,
    31, 47, 57, 130, 137–9, 144,
    149, 150, 152, 154–5, 158,
    160–1, 165, 166–7, 169, 172–5,
    177–9, 189, 192, 193, 197, 207,
    216, 217, 223, 224, 226–7, 234,
    236, 242–2, 245
Constable, Catherine 191
Conway, Kelley 141, 143, 144,
    157 n. 1
Coontz, Stephanie 19
Cooper, Mark Garrett 6, 11
Corbello, Vincenzo 132
Cortese, Valentina 122
Cotten Joseph 114
Courbet, Gustave 208
Cowie, Peter 94
Cukor, George 79, 80, 85
Cuny, Alain 92, 121
Curtis, Tony 16

D'Arcy, Alexander 23
Dadiès, Robert 156
Dahlbeck, Eva 49, 52, 157 n. 4
Dalio, Marcel 34, 40
Dame aux Camélias, La (Dumas)
    31 n. 2, n. 3, 120
Dani 163
Darel, Florence 242
Davis, Bette 114
Day, Doris 58
Deleuze, Gilles 115 n. 2, 221 n. 11
Delon, Alain 128
Demy, Jacques 147–8
Deneuve, Catherine 157 n. 4, 167
Denner, Charles 175, 177, 180
Depardieu, Gérard 17, 113, 166
DeRoo, Rebecca 145–6, 152, 157 n. 2
Desailly, Jean 165
Descartes, René 14, 160, 165, 179,
    205, 225, 226, 234–8, 239,
    241

Design for Living (Lubitsch) 7
Desny, Ivan 120
Detmers, Marushcka 210
DiBattista, Maria 24
Dieu créa la femme, Et (Vadim) 5
divorce 22–5, 36, 94, 140–1, 156–7,
    171, 173, 174, 182, 237, 241
Divorce Italian Style (Germi) 16
Doll's House, A (Ibsen) 69, 93, 124,
    156, 214
Dombasle, Arielle 237
Dorléac, Françoise 165
Drago, Eleanora Rossi 119
Dreissche, Frédéric Van Den 229
Drouot, Claire 139
Drouot, Jean-Claude 136, 139
Dubois, Marie 17, 113
Dubost, Paulette 34
Duchamp, Marcel 208
Due, Reidar 6, 11
Dumas, Alexandre (*fils*) 31 n. 2, n. 3,
    120
Dunne, Irene 15, 22, 140
Durgnat, Raymond 32, 39
Dussollier, André 112, 239
Dutoit, Ulysse 11, 12, 13, 14, 18,
    27–30, 137, 150, 164, 165, 177,
    189, 201, 202, 205–9, 226–9,
    233, 242

Ecolivet-Herzog, B. 171
Ekborg, Lars 76
Elsaesser, Thomas 9
Emerson, Ralph Waldo 14 n. 8, 43,
    45, 52, 70, 72, 90 n. 6, 98, 121,
    123, 124, 129, 135 n. 3, 188,
    192, 204, 224, 225, 243,
    245 n. 1
  'Fate' 45, 90 n. 6, 245 n. 1
  'Friendship' 43, 52, 70, 98, 129,
    204, 224, 243
  'Self-Reliance' 123
Fabe, Marilyn 185
Fabian, Françoise 240
Fabrizi, Franco 125, 183
Falconetti, Gérard 227
Falk, Rossella 196
fantasy 61, 62, 63, 70, 71, 74, 89 n. 2,
    119, 158, 184–6, 228–30,
    236–41

Index

Fassbinder, R. W. 40
Fellini, Federico 1, 3, 7, 15, 16, 30, 42, 73, 175, 176–98, 199, 206, 207, 209, 210, 241, 242
   8½ 15, 176, 181, 182–5, 187, 192–5, 197, 198, 199, 206, 207, 209
   Casanova 177, 181, 186–7, 193, 197
   City of Women 186, 187, 194, 197, 242
   Dolce vita, La 16, 176, 181, 183, 186, 193, 194, 197
   Juliet of the Spirits 16, 176, 181, 182, 183, 186, 193, 196, 197
   Matrimonial Agency, A 181
   Nights of Cabiria 181
   Strada, La 181
   Vitelloni, I 181, 183, 186, 193, 195, 196
   White Sheik, The 181
Ferzetti, Gabriele 119
Fischer, Madeleine 119
Flitterman-Lewis, Sandy 142, 145, 146, 152
Fonda, Henry 56, 95
Forde, Jessica 242
forgiveness 78–80, 88, 118, 127, 150, 162, 176, 181, 193–7, 199
Fossey, Brigitte 180
Foucault, Michel 4, 29, 31 n. 5, 177
Francoeur, Richard 45
Fresson, Bernard 17
Freud, Sigmund 3, 73, 90 n. 7, 107, 108, 131, 133, 159, 160, 184, 188, 215, 230, 232
Fridell, Åke 53
friendship 35, 43, 52, 56, 70, 98, 124, 129, 157, 174, 204, 224, 242, 243
Frye, Northrop 54, 90 n. 5
Fullbrook, Edward and Kate 157 n. 3
Furic, Hervé 229
Furneaux, Yvonne 125

Gable, Clark 59
Gale, Eddra 15
Garcia, Nicole 113
Gaslight (Cukor) 69, 85, 114
Gauthier, Vincent 245 n. 3

Gendron, François-Éric 229
Germany, Pale Mother (Sanders-Brahms) 40
Gillain, Anne 158–9, 162, 164, 165, 166, 167, 168, 174–5, 177, 178
Glitre, Kathrina 20, 23, 31, 56, 58, 66 n. 3, 191
Godard, Jean-Luc 1, 7, 9, 12, 13, 16, 17, 18, 21, 25, 26, 27, 30, 44, 50, 80, 143, 149, 150, 157 n. 1, 164, 195, 199–221, 223, 228, 229, 235, 242
   Contempt 1, 9, 13, 17, 18, 25–30, 31 n. 3, 69, 149, 150, 164, 193, 195, 200–2, 203, 204, 207, 209, 210, 216, 217, 220, 223
   Hail Mary 17, 210–14, 216, 220
   Hélas pour moi 201
   In Praise of Love 17, 210, 214–16, 219
   Married Woman, A 1, 16, 195, 199, 210, 216–20, 221 n. 13
   Masculin Féminin 210
   Passion 13, 204–11, 216, 217, 223
   Petit soldat, Le 200
   Prénom Carmen 210–11, 213, 216
   Scénario du Passion 206
   Slow Motion 214
   Two or Three Things I Know About Her 44, 210
   Vivre sa vie 1, 200, 204, 210, 216
   Woman is a Woman, A 1, 7, 149, 200, 204, 217
Godard, Paulette 50
Grant, Cary 15, 22, 140
green world (Frye, Cavell) 54, 76, 80, 90 n. 5, 97, 144, 237
Green, André 185
Greggory, Pascal 237
Grégor, Nora 32, 34

Handyside, Fiona 246 n. 9
Harmon, Graham 14 n. 7
Harris, Richard 118
Harrod, Mary 241
Hatfield, Hurd 50
Hegel, G. W. F. 3, 4, 153, 189, 216, 220 n. 7
Hell, Erik 84

Hemingway, Ernest 134
Henreid, Paul 114
Hepburn, Katahrine 55, 85
Herron, Mark 194
Higgins, Lynne A. 99, 102, 103, 108
Holmes, Diana 179–80
How to Murder Your Wife (Quine) 16
Huppert, Isabelle 207
hyperbolic love 78, 79, 83, 86, 109, 114, 125
Ibsen, Henrik 93, 107–12, 117, 125, 156, 214
Ingram, Robert 179–80
Ingres, Jean-Auguste-Dominique 208
Insdorf, Annette 177, 178, 179, 180
Irigaray, Luce 4, 14 n. 4, 86, 137, 152–3, 187–8, 190, 242, 244
It Happened One Night (Capra) 31 n. 4, 57, 59, 61, 66 n. 3, 72, 76, 114, 169, 228

Jacobsson, Ulla 52
Jade, Claude 158, 167
James, Henry 69, 223
Jameson, Fredric 220 n. 7
Jeffers MacDonald, Tamar 66 n. 5
Joly, Gaston 163
Josephson, Erland 17, 88, 94
Joyce, Michael 90 n. 4

Kant, Immanuel 14 n. 8, 72, 78
Karina, Anna 30, 200, 217, 219
Karyo, Tchéky 233
Kérien, Jean-Pierre 112
Kirkpatrick, Kate 157 n. 3
Kjellin, Alf 76
Klein, Melanie 160
Kline, T. Jefferson 107–8
Kovács, András Bálint 8, 14 n. 5, 128
Kristeva, Julia 70–5, 80, 83, 86, 90 n. 9, n. 10, 114, 228, 244
Kulle, Jarl 53

Laborit, Henri 113
Lacan, Jacques 46, 61, 62, 74, 76, 78, 86, 89 n. 2, 90 n. 3, 108, 159, 160, 189, 203, 229
Lady Eve, The (Sturges) 9, 56, 57, 59–60, 66 n. 3, 72, 81, 94–5, 228

Lamont, Molly 141
Lang, Fritz 26, 200
Langlet, Amanda 222, 237
Laplanche, Jean 215
Lapsley, Robert 11
Léaud, Jean-Pierre 158, 159, 163, 180
Lederer, Francis 51
Leigh, Jacob 228, 231, 246 n. 7
Lemmon, Jack 16
LeRoy, Philippe 17, 217
Letter from an Unknown Woman (Ophuls) 73
Lévi-Strauss, Claude 26, 41 n. 4
Leysen, Johan 213
Libolt, Alain 240
Liotard, Thérèse 140
Lisi, Virna 16
Lonsdale, Michael 168
Loren Sophia 16
Loshitzky, Yosefa 200
Love Parade, The (Lubitsch) 58
Lover Come Back (Mann) 58
Lubitsch, Ernst 7, 48 n. 1, 58
Luchini, Fabrice 233

Madame Bovary (Flaubert) 69, 124
Mairesse, Valérie 139
Malle, Louis 92–4, 97
Malmsjö, Jan 17
Malmsten, Birger 76
Mamou, Sabine 155
Manni, Ettore 122
Marchand, Corinne 141
Marie Antoinette (Van Dyke) 36
Marivaux, Pierre 50, 237
Markham, David 163
Marriage Circle, The (Lubitsch) 48 n. 1
Marriage Italian Style (De Sica) 16
Marriage of Maria Braun, The (Fassbinder) 40
Masina, Giulietta 16, 198 n. 3
Massari, Lea 119
Mastroianni, Marcello 15, 16, 116, 130, 131, 176, 181, 183, 194
McCarey, Leo 9, 15, 18, 190
McDowell, John 14 n. 7
McGowan, Todd 46, 70
Meillassoux, Quentin 14 n. 7
Ménez, Bernard 163

Meredith, Burgess 51
Méril, Macha 17, 199, 217
Merry Widow, The (Lubitsch) 48 n. 1
Middlemarch (Eliot) 124
Midgley, Mary 245
Millet, Jean-François 161
Milo, Sandra 15, 194
Milton, John 22, 84, 142
Minuz, Andrea 186
Miquel, Joëlle 242
Missero, Dalila 198 n. 4
Modot, Gaston 35, 92
Moi, Toril 107, 109, 110, 111, 117, 117, 157 n. 3
Moll, Giogia 26
Monaghan, Laurence de 227
Monfort, Silvia 139
Morante, Laura 112
Moravia, Alberto 26
Moreau, Jeanne 8, 16, 92, 116, 130, 132, 164
Morgan, Daniel 220 n. 9
Morrey, Douglas 214–15, 219
Mulvey, Laura 29, 131, 201
Murray, Edward 181, 186

narcissism 5, 56, 65–6, 87, 89, 118, 119, 122, 123, 125, 137, 141, 142, 183–93, 196, 197, 243, 244
Nay, Pierre 38
Negro, Giorgio 16, 132
Neupert, Richard 6
Noël, Bernard 17, 199, 217
Noiret, Philippe 139
Not with My Wife, You Don't! (Panama) 16
Now, Voyager (Rapper) 114, 223
Nowell-Smith, Geoffrey 6

O'Neill, Barbara 55
objet a (Lacan) 61, 74, 82, 215
Ogier, Pascale 233
Okada, Eiji 17
One Hour with You (Lubitsch) 58
Ophuls, Max 73
Owen, Reginald 51

Palance, Jack 25, 29, 30, 200
Passerini, Luisa 14 n. 6

Pellegrin, Jean-Pierre 140
Petrie, Graham 173–4
Phillips, Adam 12, 188, 189, 245 n. 4
Piccoli, Michel 25, 157 n. 4, 200, 207, 209
Pierre, Roger 17, 113
Pillow Talk (Gordon) 58
Pippin, Robert B. 14 n. 7, 220 n. 8
Pirély, Mira 34
Pisier, Marie France 168
Pisu, Mario 16, 186, 187
Pitoëff, Sacha 96
Plato 61, 78, 86, 90 n. 4, 188, 189, 229
Poe, Edgar Allan 200
Poliolo, Dorothy de 126
Portal, Alexia 242
Portrait of a Lady (James) 69
Proust, Marcel 179, 198 n. 2
psychoanalysis 3, 46, 61, 73, 74, 78, 79, 82, 90 n. 11, 102, 107, 108, 158–60, 162, 178, 179, 184, 215, 238
Putzulu, Bruno 220 n. 5

Rabal, Francisco 129
Racine, Jean 218, 219
Radziwilowicz, Jerzy 206
Rafie, Ali 139
Rains, Claude 114
Rebbot, Sady 210
remarriage 5, 11, 13, 15, 18–22, 24, 25, 29, 33, 34, 40–8, 49, 52–61, 65, 67, 69, 72, 75, 77–80, 83, 85–9, 91, 93–8, 101, 102, 106, 113, 114, 115 n. 4, 117, 127, 129, 135, 136, 139, 140, 142, 143, 144, 149, 150, 152, 154, 156, 161, 168–70, 172–4, 177, 180, 182, 188, 191–3, 196–8, 212–15, 218, 220 n. 4, n. 6, 223, 224, 228, 230, 232, 233, 237, 238, 243
Renoir, Jean 1, 12, 13, 32, 34, 36, 38, 40, 42, 44, 45, 49, 50, 51, 52, 68, 80, 92, 96, 97, 132, 134, 157 n. 1, 181, 182, 204, 237, 241
Diary of a Chambermaid 50–2
Grande Illusion, La 40

Rules of the Game, The 12, 32–47, 49–51, 52, 54, 56, 64, 68, 69, 70, 80, 91, 92, 94, 96, 97, 102, 113, 123, 124, 132, 134, 145, 157 n. 1, 161, 162, 171, 181, 182, 193, 195, 197, 204, 237, 241
Renoir, Sophie 227
Resnais, Alain 1, 9, 13, 14 n.1, 17, 30, 32, 91–115, 129, 139, 140, 143, 161, 219, 237
  Coeurs/Private Fears in Public Places 112
  Connaît la chanson, On 17, 112, 113
  Hiroshima, mon amour 1, 14 n. 1, 17, 112
  Je t'aime, je t'aime 17, 113
  Last Year in Marienbad 1, 9, 14 n. 1, 91–117, 120, 124, 243
  Love unto Death 113
  Mélo 17, 112, 113
  Mon Oncle d'Amérique 17, 112–13
  Muriel, or the Time of Return 112
  Night and Fog 219
  Providence 112, 113
Riva, Emmanuel 17
Rivière, Marie 229, 242
Robbe-Grillet, Alain 99
Roberts, Julia 219
Rohdie, Sam 128
Rohmer, Éric 1, 7, 12, 13, 30, 56, 73, 222–46
  Autumn Tale, An 239, 240, 242, 245 n. 3
  Claire's Knee 227, 240, 245 n. 3
  Full Moon in Paris 233, 239
  Girlfriends and Boyfriends 227, 229, 240, 242, 246 n. 8
  Green Ray, The 229, 240, 245 n. 3, n. 7
  Love in the Afternoon 239, 240, 246 n. 7
  Pauline at the Beach 222, 237–40, 242
  Tale of Winter, A 229–35, 239, 240, 243, 245 n. 5
Romand, Béatrice 239
Rosette 237
Rosmersholm (Ibsen) 106–12, 114, 125
Ross, Kristin 7
Rossellini, Roberto 157 n. 1
Rossi, Zénaïde 163
Rougeul, Jean 195
Rousseau, Serge 172
Roussel, Myriam 208
Ruffo, Leonora 183
Rushton, Richard 14 n. 2, 89 n. 1, 115 n. 3, 245 n. 2

Sanders-Brahms, Helma 40
Sartre, Jean-Paul 151, 157 n. 3
Schygulla, Hanna 207
Seberg, Jean 200
Sedgwick, Eve Kosofsky 223
Sellier, Geneviève 2–3, 5, 8, 9, 12, 42, 70, 71, 125, 137, 139, 141, 143, 146, 177, 180, 186, 197, 200–1, 204, 208, 209, 215, 219, 220 n. 1, 241
Serre, Henri 164
Seyrig, Delphine 91, 95, 112, 168
Shakespeare, William 51, 54, 58, 66, 72, 85, 86, 90 n. 8, 214, 229, 230, 231, 232, 235
  Antony and Cleopatra 66, 235
  As You Like It 66 n. 4
  Winter's Tale, The 51, 64, 65, 66 n. 4, 72, 79, 85, 214, 229–30, 232
  Hamlet 74, 76, 78, 86, 214, 215
  Romeo and Juliet 86, 90 n. 9
  King Lear 63, 64, 65, 72, 85, 209
  Othello 63, 64, 65, 72, 77, 85, 214, 235
  Midsummer Night's Dream, A 66 n. 4
  As You Like It 66 n. 4
Shearer, Norma 36
Shop Around the Corner, The (Lubitsch) 48 n. 1
Shumway, David 6, 11, 18, 19, 20, 46
Simono, Albert 171
Smith, Alison 148
Sollers, Philippe 244
Sparrow, Timothy 14 n. 7
Spielberg, Steven 219

Stanwyck, Barbara 55, 59, 94
Steele, Barbara 187
Stella Dallas (Vidor) 55, 69, 98, 126
Sterritt, David 212, 214, 220
Stewart, Alexandra 163
Strindberg, August 90 n. 8
Sturges, Preston 9, 56, 59, 94
Subor, Michel 200
Sutherland, Donald 186
Sydow, Max von 8, 67, 80
Szabó, László 207

Terra trema, La (Visconti) 144
Teyssèdre, Anne 242
Thierée, Jean-Baptiste 112
Thomas, Jameson 114
Thoreau, Henry David 90 n. 6
Thulin, Ingrid 79
Tocqueville, Alexis de 19
Toutain, Roland 32, 34
Tracy, Spencer 85
tragedy, tragedies of marriage/
    remarriage 2, 45, 49, 51, 52,
    63, 64, 65, 66, 67, 69, 73, 77,
    78, 79, 80, 84, 86, 89, 91, 97,
    117
Trintignant, Jean-Louis 240
Truffaut, François 1, 3, 7, 13, 29, 30,
    32, 149, 156, 158–82, 198, 209,
    223, 242
    400 Blows, The 158–9, 164, 167,
        174, 175
    Bed and Board 167, 172, 173, 182,
        193
    Bride Wore Black, The 162, 166
    Day for Night 162–3, 167, 209,
        220 n. 3
    Fahrenheit 451 162
    Finally Sunday 162
    Gorgeous Girl Like Me, A 167
    Green Room, The 162
    Jules and Jim 149, 162, 164–5, 166,
        167, 182, 195
    Last Metro, The 162
    Love at Twenty 168, 172, 175
    Love on the Run 162, 164, 167,
        171, 172, 173, 182
    Man Who Loved Women, The 175,
        177–81, 184, 198, 242

Shoot the Piano Player 180
Small Change 167
Soft Skin, The 162, 165, 166, 167,
    171, 174
Stolen Kisses 158, 162, 167–74,
    175, 223
The Story of Adèle H. 162, 167
Two English Girls 180
Woman Next Door, The 162, 166,
    167, 173, 174, 182

Ullmann, Liv 8, 17, 67, 68, 80, 81, 94
Ulysses (Joyce) 212

Vadim, Christian 233
Vadim, Roger 5
Varda, Agnès 1, 2, 13, 29, 30, 42, 56,
    136–57, 158, 161, 162, 171,
    181, 182, 210, 219, 222, 237,
    241, 242, 243
    Beaches of Agnès, The 139, 155,
        161
    Bonheur, Le 136, 139, 140,
        144–52, 155, 156, 162, 181,
        182, 193, 219
    Cléo from 5 to 7 2, 137, 139,
        141–4, 149, 152, 155
    Créatures, Les 157 n. 4
    Documenteur 155
    Faces/Places 139, 155, 161
    Gleaners and I, The 139, 155, 161
    Jacquot de Nantes 147–8, 155, 161
    Kung-Fu Master 155
    Lion's Love 149
    Mur Murs 161
    One Sings, the Other Doesn't 139,
        148, 151–2, 154, 155, 156, 161,
        171, 222, 242, 243
    Pointe Courte, La 139, 140, 143–4,
        149, 155, 157 n. 1, 161
    Vagabond 140, 155, 161
    Varda by Agnès 139, 155, 161
Varda, Rosalie 142
Verley, Bernard 240
Véry, Charlotte 229
Vidor, King 69, 98
Viellard, Éric 227
Villalonga, José 92
Visconti, Luchino 144

Vitti, Monica 8, 118, 119, 128, 132
Voletti, Michel 231
Voyage to Italy (Rossellini) 157 n. 1

Waller, Margaret 187, 198 n. 1
Werner, Oskar 164

Westlake, Michael 11
Wheatley, Catherine 123, 191, 232
Wicki, Bernhard 120
Wilson, Emma 113
Wilson, Lambert 112
Winnicott, D. W. 158

EU authorised representative for GPSR:
Easy Access System Europe, Mustamäe tee 50,
10621 Tallinn, Estonia
gpsr.requests@easproject.com

www.ingramcontent.com/pod-product-compliance
Lightning Source LLC
Chambersburg PA
CBHW051607230426
43668CB00013B/2011